# COLLECTED WORKS *of* DONALD CHARLES LACY

# COLLECTED WORKS

## DONALD CHARLES LACY

PROVIDENCE HOUSE PUBLISHERS
Franklin, Tennessee

05     04     03     02     01          1     2     3     4     5

Library of Congress Catalog Card Number: 2001088222

ISBN: 1-57736-230-6

*Cover design by Gary Bozeman and Elaine Kernea Wilson*
*Cover photo by John P. Cleary,* Herald Bulletin *of Anderson, Indiana*

PROVIDENCE HOUSE PUBLISHERS
238 Seaboard Lane Franklin, Tennessee 37067
800-321-5692
www.providencehouse.com

To the glory of God the Father,
the Son, and the Holy Spirit,
Who taught me to "do justice,
and to love kindness,
and to walk humbly" with Him.

# CONTENTS

# PREFACE

HOW DOES ONE begin to tell about forty years of writing and publishing? I have considered several avenues. Hopefully, you will be pleased with my approach.

I began my professional career as a social studies and English teacher in Jay County, Indiana. My early ambitions were centered around being an attorney and/or professor of American history with an eye on a political career. Well, a corner was turned and I pursued a theological education. While I have been a Methodist (United) under appointment for more than forty years, it became obvious two other fields would run concurrently. They were the literary world and a strong involvement in ecumenical/interreligious concerns. So, these three areas of ministry have been separately distinct at times and then so tightly interwoven one could hardly separate them. My life has been one of ongoing gratitude. I have deeply appreciated the opportunities provided.

As you might guess, every writing that appears in this selection has a story behind it. I have tried to select very carefully, so that the volume would be representative. Actually, what appears is approximately 20 percent of what—in fact—I have published. In terms of who has read what, of course, it is impossible to determine. I have never sought to be a popular writer in the sense of providing something that someone wanted to read. Quite the reverse approach has been my method. In short, whenever convinced I had something that needed to be in print, I have left no stone unturned in seeing it was published. Financial gain has never been a major consideration. Distribution has always been considered above sales. God's Spirit has abided and provided without exception.

You will discover that it has made little difference in terms of known circulation, as to what is included. My work on Mary, the Mother of Jesus has found its way among millions. Some columns and book reviews are lucky to have made it beyond a few thousand. The selections from the nine books of sermons was the most difficult to make. To my knowledge, none of them ever made it to a best-seller. Homiletically, *Called to Be* received high marks. Of course, no author of published sermons ever knows how many ideas he provides for other preachers! Having been a ghostwriter for one service that provided sermons, I have the ambition to hear one of them preached some Sunday morning. Preaching should always be more than speech making. Hopefully, the preacher is a vehicle or channel for the living God.

In my lifetime I have seen the number of published authors among clergy in Indiana go from just a few to many. When my first sermon appeared in "Pulpit Digest" in 1970, it really caused others to take notice. It was entitled "An Attitude of Gratitude" and was the last sermon my father would hear me preach. It was originally preached some three years before that from the pulpit of the First United Methodist church in Hagerstown, Indiana. How we measure our writing, especially sermons, is not easy. So much quality work is not published, primarily because it is seen as not financially profitable. Yet, that situation has improved for which we should give thanks. I have always believed strongly in inspiration as a necessity for quality work.

My first opportunity to be a published writer came from Dr. Ronald E. Osborn, professor of history at Christian Theological Seminary, in Indianapolis. In 1959 he asked me to write an interpretation of a painting of John Wesley for *The Church and the Fine Arts*. The anthology was published in 1960 and my name appeared in a footnote. Little did I know that was the beginning of a ministry now in its fifth decade. Hopefully, there will be more decades! I am continually amazed by the opportunities all of us have. It seems like only yesterday all of this began. There are so many to thank. While we may be confident and skilled, so much depends on the attitudes of others. God has a way of making us humble and teachable. I believe every human being I have known has taught me something.

One of the most amazing experiences involved in being an author is the timing. For example, several pieces of mine have been published years after they were originally written. The message: don't throw any of your work away! You may be exhausted and the pages look like doggerel but don't throw them into the wastebasket. In terms of writing sermons, my most fruitful years were spent at the First United Methodist church of Seymour, Indiana. At least six books were written there and five have been published. A number of features and columns published in recent years were actually written well before. In God's great scheme of things we must get used to His sense of timing. I found this especially true among my friends in the Catholic media.

I sincerely hope you will enjoy reading this somewhat lengthy volume. It is presented to you in an attitude of gratitude. I make no claims of being a professional journalist. My only claim is that in all cases I have sought to be faithful to the inspiration granted to me by Almighty God. The future is bright but remember whatever you say or write has most likely been articulated before by someone . . . someplace . . . sometime. Regardless, always give God the credit.

# COLLECTED WORKS *of* DONALD CHARLES LACY

PART 1

SELECTED SERMONS

DONALD
CHARLES
LACY

# gems
# from James

*1974 and 1982*

Gems from James *was first published in a hardcover edition. It found easy acceptance as general inspiring reading, homiletical helps, and especially as a study book. Perhaps the "North Carolina Christian Advocate" said it best: "This book is an excellent study of the great truths in the Book of James and could be used most profitably by Church groups." It led to my writing "A Pilgrimage Through the Epistle of James" which was published as a curriculum resource by Graded Press of the United Methodist Publishing House. It was used by many as a ready Leader's Guide with* Gems from James. *Two of ten sermons are presented.*

# CHAPTER 1

# Gems from James

## ✦RELIGION WITHOUT BLEMISH✦

*Religion that is pure and undefiled before God and the Father is this: to visit*
*orphans and widows in their affliction,*
*and to keep oneself unstained from the world.*
*—James 1:27—*

"IMMACULATE" IS one of those very special words in the English language. It means "totally clean" or "completely pure." We reserve it for those high moments in our lives. Great compliments are paid by saying it— "Her appearance is immaculate"; "His grooming is immaculate." We are not prone to use it loosely, as we do with so many other descriptive words. When someone does, we readily recognize it. We reserve it for special occasions. When it is spoken, we perk up our ears and listen. It is one of the few aristocrats among the hundreds of thousands of words in our language. Some will vie against others just to have the word applied to themselves. The uneducated may not be able to pronounce it. They may not be able to spell it. But they know its value. You and I appreciate its worth. "To be without blemish" is something!

"What is a blemish to one, is not a blemish to another" is good, acceptable reasoning for our own day. We are reminded of the farmer who tries to give an absolute definition for a weed. Soon his wisdom tells him that it can be anything that grows, if it's in the wrong place at the wrong time— a stock of corn in a soybean field, wheat in a cornfield, potatoes in a tomato field, even a rose in a strawberry patch.

Toleration of diverse points of view is an inspiration to us. So much in life is dependent on who we are, where we are, and what time it is. Our enlightenment has created possibilities for growth and development in human relations which far exceed anything our ancestors knew. Even in matters considered strictly religious, this is still the case. This is neither empty activism nor sinning against God's absolute laws. That's just the way we find things in our day.

We can quickly perceive ideas and ideals in James's lesson which have proven their value. Pure and undefiled religion is both "reaching out" and "keeping out." The Christian pulls the world unto himself and bleeds with and for others. The Christian pushes the world away and keeps himself free from sin. There are two dimensions, but one without the other is null and void. We must understand that the two are parts of the same imperative. James means this in a very personal way. Each precious human being who professes the Christian faith is called to go out into the world in the spirit of brotherly service. Each precious human being who professes the Christian faith is called to stay away from the world and be distinctively "without blemish." Our course is clear.

"To visit orphans and widows in their affliction" is *reaching out.*

We are to move out into the world. Our Lord grew up under the influence of a very wise Jewish heritage. Orphans and widows were especially protected by law. They were a symbol of Jewish compassion. Women whose husbands were dead and children who had lost one or both parents were given care. Our Lord's ancestors treated them better than any other nation of people. Our Lord reaffirmed this position. In our day, the passage speaks to us, because we see in the widows and orphans the image of all needy people. The needy are those who, for the most part, will not come to us. We must go to them. As James says, we are "to visit." The Christian visitor may be a man of the cloth or a layman who takes his religion seriously. To "stay at home" may mean several different things. It is certain that it does not mean the needy of the world are continually to seek the help of professing Christians. We are to go to them. Laymen, generally, are not nearly aggressive enough. In the best sense of the word, Christian aggressiveness simply means bold and energetic pursuit in the cause of Christ.

In our day, this can be and is a dynamic way of life. The live-wire life insurance and automobile salesmen are not the only practitioners of "beating the bushes." Every Christian church member should be beating the bushes for Christ and His Church. I did not use the phrase "institutional recruitment." Sometimes we communicate the idea that we are only interested in someone's name being on the church rolls. This is important, and don't ever underestimate it. Joining a service club or a sorority is not the same as uniting with the Church of Jesus Christ. There are those who like to draw similarities, and some are legitimate. I am sure the spirit of our Lord and Savior works through such organizations. However, I doubt that Saint Peter will be interested in the size and ornamentation of our organization's pins. There is no more exciting and vital activity than the Christian working in the community in the name of Jesus Christ.

How well do you and I measure up? A common reaction is, "Well, I just naturally reach out in helping those in need." There are dedicated people who, in fact, do this very thing. How many do you know? For those of us who rate a more average standing in the Christian life, it takes some planned or systematic work. When we think the job of going to the spiritually and materially needy is going to be done by those who will naturally do it, we are pulling the wool over our own eyes. The word "Methodist" comes from the word "methodical." John and Charles Wesley practiced methodical study and worship. Our Wesleyan heritage is a great and meaningful one. "Plan your Christian work and work your Christian plan" is a timely message for modern followers in the tradition of the Wesleys. God spoke through the founders of Methodism, and He wants to speak through us.

It is what God considers important that matters. An immaculate religion or one without blemish is on God's terms. The religious experiences of men, women, and youth have been bogged down innumerable times by human beings getting in the way. Through the Letter of James come the inspired words that religion which is pure and undefiled before God is "to visit orphans and widows in their affliction, . . ." Broadly speaking, God says, "Go to those in need and minister to them." In our day, because of complicated living, we seem to hang out a shingle here and there which reads: "Professional Christian Problem Solver—Help by Appointment at the Office Only." It is true that the clergy and laity, regardless of their time and talents, have just so much time they can give. It is also true that some will waste our precious time, even under the pretense of needing religious help. Yet, this must never become an alibi which freezes out the reluctant. If the men and women of the church want to serve the needy they say they are concerned about, they must do some visiting—and I don't mean over the telephone. God says a necessary part of religion without blemish is to visit the needy. The church must be taken from the confines of a sanctuary and put in direct contact with those in need.

We have dealt with the first part of the imperative. The second part is no less important. It may appear more or less difficult, depending on our personalities.

"To keep oneself unstained from the world" in *keeping out.*

We are to be separate and apart from secular life and interests. A radical interpretation can cause a serious rupture in our understanding of the faith. On the other hand, let us not explain away the message. Religion without blemish necessarily involves a conservative approach, in terms of our activities. The Christian is deeply and sincerely concerned about everything that goes on in the world, on the moon, and elsewhere. Direct involvement in many questionable areas is not apt to keep one unstained. This is not "the ostrich with his head in the sand" attitude. It is an affirmation of the truth the Apostles knew only too well: Christians are different from others; and even though they do not run from worldly affairs, nevertheless, they do stay clear of some surroundings. The early Christians had to face the fact that emperor worship was expected of them. They evaded situations where it had to be practiced. Premeditated martyrdom was not and is not essential in proving one's faith.

Where many present-day Christians get themselves into trouble is by fulfilling only this part of the condition for an immaculate religion. Only sticking one's head out of the house just long enough to gain a livelihood and attend church regularly is disastrous and, in truth, shows "no guts," in modern terminology. Yet, to go on a binge of poking one's Christian nose into every area of the secular world is also a disastrous approach to life. Perhaps the hardest lesson Woodrow Wilson, a Christian president, had to learn was that the world was wicked when he came into it, and it would be wicked when he left it. This kind of realism is not easy for some to come by.

From another point of view, it is difficult but realistically possible to be possessed by a religion which is pure and undefiled. Some preaching may be so idealistic and theoretical that it becomes a theological labyrinth of little or no value, except for intellectual gymnasts. The Letter of James, specifically our present excerpt, never makes that mistake. The words deal with attainable ideals, provable theories, and practical theology. If what James is talking about is "way out there some place," we have drifted too far from the roots of our faith. The first century and New Testament churches are our spiritual forebears, and we are irrevocable tied to them. There is a gospel song which goes: "It is real, it is real; thank God the doubts are settled, I know it is real."

How well are you and I doing? The dividing line between Christian concern and "crass nibbiness" is sometimes clouded. It is a line each sensitive Christian has to draw for himself or herself. You and I are under pressure today to "get involved" in anything that has some semblance of salvation. Those of us who have committed ourselves unreservedly to Jesus Christ and His Church *do* hear a very personal voice calling us to be unblemished by pushing away those elements of the world that promise only to hinder.

Again, it is what is important to God that matters. He speaks through His servants. The writers of the New Testament were His servants. God says an essential part of religion without blemish is to keep oneself unsoiled by worldly matters not conducive to the strengthening of the faith. Each of us wrestles with this in the inmost recesses of his or her soul. No preacher or priest can draw up exact specifications for you. This is between you and your God.

Shakespeare wrote, "Above all, to thine own self be true." Religion without blemish says to the Christian, "Above everything else, be true to your best self." When you and I are hard pressed by the vicissitudes of life, we are called upon to be faithful. Perhaps we cannot stand without wavering, but we can hold our ground. Be alert to the needs of the world and do something about them. Be not drowned by the strident voices and cleverly disguised undercurrents of an evil world—a world which will be evil when you and I leave it. By apostolic decree and personal integrity, let us "reach out," but also "keep out."

Holiness before God is all that really matters. It is of supreme importance to be spiritually successful within His boundaries. "To visit orphans and widows in their affliction, and to keep oneself unstained from the world" is sound doctrine. The practical fulfillment of it is holiness before God and wholeness of the individual Christian.

# ❉PRECARIOUS PREDICAMENT❉

*For where jealousy and selfish ambition exist,*
*there will be disorder and every vile practice.*
*—James 3:16—*

LIFE ITSELF IS a precarious predicament.

You and I did not ask to come into this world. Had it been left up to us, some might have chosen otherwise. The ups and downs are sometimes like the ride on a roller coaster. There are days when it is quite a ride. There is boredom, too. Life is sometimes the greatest pain. One of the finest Christian spirits I ever met said, "Son, there are more downs than ups in this life." For her, I am certain this was true. At times, our Lord must have thought the same thing, and yet, His life, death, and resurrection were supreme victories. The pessimist can always moan, "I didn't ask for this life, which continually kicks me in the shins and then closes out with a few shovels of dirt to cover my remains." The Christian is an optimist, because he can't help being anything else.

Even though we did not ask to come into this world, we have been given strength to confront it. This should prevent us from becoming fatalistic and distressingly negative. Life is a gift. What we do with it is largely up to us.

We have all been in tight, explosive situations in this life. The Letter of James lends a personal and practical hand in identifying such a situation:

"For where jealousy and selfish ambition exist, there will be disorder and every vile practice." Note, there isn't a wasted word. There is neither varnish nor veneer. He calls a spade a spade. The words have a way of crushing rationalizations that last a lifetime. These rationalizations even find expression beyond the grave, long after the human beings involved have gone to receive whatever reward is due them. The text is speaking of a situation which exists or has existed in every culture. No system, democratic or communistic, has functioned in its absence. The perpetual power struggles in Washington and the Kremlin illustrate it very well. The history books give us examples galore. The battlefields have been drenched with blood and gore. Think of the community or communities in which you live and work. In all of them, corruption and hatred tell their story. This predicament is perhaps the most precarious one in which we can find ourselves. Who can doubt the doctrine of original sin?

If you are like me, numerous questions enter your mind as you read the verse. There is neither the time nor the space to list all of them. We say "jealousy, selfish ambition, disorder, and vile practice" are wrong. But why? We are prone to reply with meager concentration, "It's obvious." Is it?

There is a violation of the law of God which intends all men to be brothers. That's the answer, isn't it? Why is it a violation? There are three excellent reasons. You will discover all of them in every precarious predicament our text speaks about.

The first reason is the *exaltation of oneself.*

No one else really matters. Family, friends, associates, and acquaintances are of little importance. Capital "I" emblazoned on every relationship is of consistent significance. Taking very good care of "Number One" is the stuff out of which life is made. Some are uncanny in the logic with which they apply this. Some make no bones about it. This is what they believe and set out to practice. There is a certain low grade of honesty here, but let us not dignify it by calling it worthy of imitation.

Inborn self-preservation is not nearly enough. Seeking the usual needs and conveniences of life offers no satisfaction. Not only must the "I" be cared for, it must be elevated to august heights. To ward off an enemy and go safely on one's way seems normal. Those filled with jealousy and selfish ambition are not satisfied. The enemy must be made to look bad and exposed as dangerous to others. A plentiful supply of good food, quality clothing, and well-built homes are fine; but they don't do much for the person pictured, except as they serve to build his image and ego.

A godlike status is sought. Who wants to be human? Deification of a perishable *Homo sapien* is an ominously treacherous pathway. The Man of Steel, Joseph Stalin, has been praised or damned, depending upon the brand of communism in power. This is true with anyone who sets out to be a god. Here we witness the terrible twisting of man's creation in God's image, which in reality is our only valid claim to fame. This was meant to be our crown of glory. It was never intended to curse our immortal souls beyond recognition.

The laws of morality are suppressed by egomania. The person afflicted becomes a monster. The monster becomes his own lawgiver. The lawgiver becomes a means to elevate himself. At this stage, mirrors are insufficient, because they only reflect what they are supposed to reflect. Criticism is either unwarranted or the raving of a misguided soul. There is only one ultimate: the self needs to remain at the top of the heap. Morals are seen in the context of "whatever elevates me must be right."

What can the Christian say to all of this? Only God truly exalts anyone. Jesus Christ, His Son, says, "I am the way, the truth, and the life." Will you join me as we survey another reason?

The second reason is the *infatuation with self-seeking influence*.

To dominate institutions and organizations is the continual objective. Some servants of society have been destroyed by those who valued influence above their productive existence. Some bulwarks of brotherhood have been mutilated by those whose chief concern was influence over their beneficial workings. Our institutions may be purely an outgrowth of cultural conditions, but they are needed. Our organizations may likewise be products of a given time, place, and persons, but they too are needed. No one has the right to destroy or mutilate by insanely putting his or her heavy fingerprints upon everything. Some individuals are so in love with their powers of control that they are incapable of understanding *agape*, or brotherly love.

To manipulate people is a must. Do individuals matter to those possessed by jealousy and selfish ambition? The answer is loud and clear. Yes—as instruments to channel one's abnormal attraction to influence strictly for personal gain.

The greatest good for the greatest number is a foreign idea. What may be good for the many gives way to the imprint of "number one." This is done by simply not permitting such an idea into one's frame of reference. If it is not there to receive consideration, it has no possibility of being implemented. The measurement of *a* good or *the* good is uncomplicated.

One merely asks the question, "What will keep my present influence intact?" and, "What can I do to extend it?" Other influences are not weighed on their merits. They are given lip service. Concepts that could possible erode one's overshadowing dominance are predetermined to have no merit. The news has to be managed, so that control will not slip away or diminish. Isn't it interesting how many police states exist or potentially exist in our own nation? "Freedom" may very well be our most misused term.

What can the Christian say to all of this? Only God can and does ultimately influence anyone or anything. Jesus Christ, His Son, says, "But woe to you, scribes, and Pharisees, hypocrites! because you shut the kingdom of heaven against men; for you neither enter yourselves, nor allow those who would enter to go in." We might add: "The only difference between men and little boys is the price of their toys."

Won't you join me for a final reason why the precarious predicament in question is a violation of God's law?

The third reason is the *degradation of everyone else*.

No other person can speak with authority. Every deeply religious person knows with certainty and feels deeply that he or she is inspired from time to time. This gives none of us a corner on the market of inspiration. The personality saturated with jealousy and selfish ambition does not begin to develop at that point. Whether it be the authority of inspiration or some other, he or she is the only one capable of commanding and enforcing. The only technique every other person needs to know is how to obey. Subservience is an expected mode of acting and reacting.

People are pawns. God did not give us life to be subjected to someone's whims, but we are subject to "disorder and every vile practice." I cannot imagine anything much worse. We were created by God and for God.

Respect for human dignity and worth is invariably missing. No one who stands on his self-constructed platform and peers out across the multitudes can see their faces of joy and sorrow, and their just wanting to be somebody. Our Lord walked and talked among the people. To pontificate the message from His Father would have sealed its doom. Instead of ringing with vitality and the promise of eternal life, it would have been given a convenient burial among the works of other religious teachers and prophets. The personality held securely in the clutches of a precarious predicament may have little or no connection to racism. The color of skin is immaterial, as long as everyone stays in his or her secondary position.

The great men and women of the past are labeled usable or nonusable. A careful piece of editing goes on in the mental machinery. The very concept of greatness is ripped apart by those allocating inferior positions to others. The question asked in the dark, demonic recesses of one's soul is, "Will the words of highly respected, even idolized, figures leave me in the limelight?" It is a mania, isn't it? It isn't something we can conscientiously relegate to communism, is it? It is a fact of life wherever we find "jealousy and selfish ambition."

What can the Christian say to all of this? Only the everlasting God measures value and values. Jesus Christ, His Son, says, "You shall love your neighbor as yourself."

By way of conclusion, we need to discern two all-important differences.

Let us recognize the distinction between jealousy and vigilant attitudes. To be critical of another's success is not necessarily jealousy. Success which runs rampant may be the result of scores of people getting hurt in their business and personal lives. As Christians, we are the watchdogs, so to speak, of society. At its deeper levels, the Christian spirit is always a reformation program in operation. People are not the way they should be—including ourselves—and God expects us to be sensitive to this. There is no indication in the Bible of our Lord ever being jealous of the worldly powerful scribes and Pharisees. He did speak often about their religious establishment, which He usually characterized as hypocrisy.

Let us also be quick to recognize the distinction between selfish ambition and healthy competition. It is doubtful if anything of consequence is ever accomplished without some degree of competition. Even though communism has damned the capitalistic competitive spirit, communists have found it indispensably useful! Psychologists tell us that we all need occasional personal victories in competition with others, just to have good mental health. Selfish ambition is eventually always vicious, malicious, and venomous. Recall the text says, "disorder and every vile practice." Yet, we are made to compete. That rugged competitor, the Apostle Paul, points out, "Do you not know that in a race all the runners compete, but only one receives the prize? So run that you may obtain it."

We must not violate God's law that all men are meant to be brothers. It has been pointed out why this particular precarious predicament is a violation of that law. Let us mistake neither jealousy for vigilance nor selfish ambition for wholesome competition.

CALLED TO BE

Donald Charles Lacy

*1978 and 1980*

Called to Be *is a preaching/teaching series emerging from the living
concerns of a congregation and community, plus my own affirmation that
preaching (both verbal and written) is a very special instrument bringing
God's grace in touch with human need. The book is intended for clergy
and laity alike who are preaching and studying from the Sermon on the
Mount. It can be helpful in both personal and group settings. In a real
sense it is a handbook for spiritual growth spoken to, for, and with that
vast number of us who know the grace of our Savior and Lord; yet, we
have only nibbled away at crusts of bread when we should have been
enjoying the riches of the Faith. Four of twenty sermons are presented.*

# CHAPTER 2

*Called to Be*

## ❋CALLED TO BE PURE❋

### 1.

OUR LORD IS primarily interested in the internal man.

Among His contemporaries this was one characteristic that made Him stand out. He knew it was what went on inside a human being that really counted. External behavior, regardless of how upright it was, could be a matter of discipline and little or no noble intent. His insistence on being born again gave to His ministry a glow and a uniqueness. To force a person to be moral doesn't ever really accomplish much. Certainly there were persons who were epitomies of high moral standards. The Greeks, Romans, and Jews all had their examples. Come to think of it, maybe this was an underlying reason why our Lord was crucified. He brought a religion that made those who felt externally right and proper look internally, and they could not tolerate the darkness. They were "living a lie" and the Christ had the only real answer to rectify their split personalities.

Through the ages as mankind has moved away from the central core of His teaching it has had to return to a singular truth: man's heart, mind, and spirit—his entire inner workings—have to undergo change. This is what every legitimate revival is all about. It is what prompted the Reformation. It is the reason for the Wesleyan movement. The various forms of church renewal in and out of the institution have come into being because of this. Every body of Christian people sooner or later finds it necessary to rediscover the imperative of being purified inside. A reputation for goodness and moral standing rests on shaky legs unless it is born and given incentive from within.

More specifically, our Lord points to a dimension of living that is simultaneously magnificent and difficult.

In Matthew 5:21–22, He says, "You have heard that it was said to the men of old, 'You shall not kill; and whoever kills shall be liable to the judgment.' But I say to you that every one who is angry with his brother shall be liable to judgment; whoever insults his brother shall be liable to the council, and whoever says, 'You fool!' shall be liable to the hell of fire." It is not enough to refrain from killing. It is not right even to be angry, insulting, or call your brother a fool. Our blessed Lord shows us the purification necessary to be one of His disciples.

13

So, He steers us away from the fringes and externals that may be mere trappings. As His followers, the call is unmistakable. We are called to be pure.

## 2.

Called to be pure is to let love have its way. Specifically, this is spelled out in five major ways.

## 3.

*The ability to turn the other cheek in love is the first way.*

It is a matter of Christ working through us which makes this happen. He empowers us to do that which He calls us to be. It is not of our own doing. It is the transformation. He works through us. Shout His praises, this can and does happen! Sing songs of joy toward the heavens . . . and to one another for the proof of His promises.

Christians are not doormats, but they are so cleansed inwardly they can and do absorb and redirect hate energies. This has been the case since our Lord walked the earth. It is no different today. There are those who will ignore, undercut, and even attempt to destroy us. The Faith, wherever lived in a vibrant fashion, has invariably confronted such unpleasant harassment and viperous hypocrisy. The real test comes when we are expected to receive the hateful and sometimes horrendous attacks of those professing His Name. In short, how is it possible for one called to be pure to press for the destruction of a brother or sister in Christ likewise called to be pure? Never underestimate the wiles of the devil! As one kindly, elderly district executive once told me: "I never knew the saints could be so mean until I entered the superintendency."

Jesus prods us with grace to be like Him. I suppose it would have been possible for Him to run away and hide or even leave His homeland to avoid turning the other cheek. He didn't. Our purity is found in not running. However, it is found neither in open display of bravery just to prove a point nor in fanatical aggressive movements in an effort to overpower the devil. Our purity is evidenced at the moment under the lordship of the Christ. His presence in us makes all the difference.

*The confidence to speak the truth in love is the second way.*

Christians are often delineated by the world as milquetoasts or well-intended weaklings. Their perceptions tell them we mean well but are not the real movers and shakers in a community. How can those untouched by Christ think any other way? I don't know that you and I should expect anything else. From our perspectives within the Faith, a great many things seem to get moved that don't need moving and shaken when they don't need shaking. We are too apologetic at times. Christ didn't tell His followers to apologize for being Christians. Our confidence to speak the truth in love is discovered simply by being what we are called to be and that means purity in our innermost being.

"The truth never hurt anyone" is a cliche with mixed messages. Christians understand that, in the long run, to speak the truth is not optional but necessary. They also understand their Lord grants to them a confident air which is one of the gifts of being in Christ. Our responsibility is clear. If those who are the recipients of truth disregard, disclaim, and disown it, that's their problem. Hell was created for those who are disobedient to light. This all began with Satan and his crowd.

We must be careful to move in harmony with Christ's Spirit. There is nothing quite so disastrous as a Christian far off base being cut down by a good throw from the catcher. That doesn't mean we are to succumb to the world's definition of success and failure. No one knows better or feels more keenly than the Christian whether or not he or she is in fact confidently speaking the truth in love.

*The honesty to admit mistakes in love is the third way.*
It's so beautifully refreshing and creatively revealing to admit, "Well, I blew it" or some other similar expression. I am drawn to people like that, aren't you? Despite what you and I may at first think, this is a method of witnessing to others. Everyone in the Faith can have a good laugh or cry and move on as growing, maturing Christians. The world—at least some will say—"Those Christians aren't so uptight about their righteousness after all. Maybe their Christ is One who tolerates sinners." Our Lord "blew the cover" of some very pious and meticulously upright people centuries ago. They thought a right relationship to God was primarily dependent on keeping score of morals attained and rules obeyed. Failure may be the only way to draw others to the validity of the Faith.

A word of caution: Don't allow the world to be the final determinant of whether or not you have made a mistake. The devil can lead us astray through our own goodness. Accountability to God through Christ and service to others are always in the pattern. Life becomes the most hectically negative at the time Christians lean on the world's definition of mistakes. No person or institution can take from us that all-important, blessed relationship that is our destiny. There are those in the world who will tell us it was a mistake for us to be born in the first place.

"I love you" are three of the most precious and lofty words you and I will ever hear. It just may be that the only way a brother or sister in the fellowship of believers will ever count you and me as a comrade is as he or she owns up to a mistake and for us to say, "I love you." I like the expression "I love you—warts and all." Whether I say it to you or you say it to me, the message is one of blessed acceptance: I accept you and you accept me. Blessed be the name of our Lord and Savior, Jesus the Christ.

*The humility to ask for forgiveness in love is the fourth way.*

Christians, especially those in leadership roles, are not to be weaklings perambulating on all fours, but we are to be humble. Sometimes we seem to walk a tightrope. We cannot be running about giving leadership to this and that in the Church projecting weakness. We are not to grovel. We are not to fake competence, because sooner or later we are found out. However, our Lord wants us to be convinced it takes a humble attitude willing to ask for forgiveness in order to fulfill our calling to be pure.

You and I are not exempt from the spiritual law emphasizing even those safely within the fold are to seek forgiveness on bended knees. Assuredly, this is one of the things the new birth teaches us right away. We may soar through the heavenly breezes with joyous dexterity. There come times when we are to repent. This nearly always takes the form of a dual asking. For to be out of harmony with God is to be in a fix with man and hurting. The remedy is forgiveness, but we are to seek it. The willingness to knock on the door of God's mercy and that of man is more than half the battle. God will and does forgive. If the man, woman, or youth refuses to forgive, we enter a period of special dependence on Christ to supply direction. We may not need to ask again and again. Our Lord may release us and leave the burden with the one whose life may soon be blighted because of exercising a closed and negative attitude.

*The drive to want to be a growing Christian in love is the fifth way.*

Our Lord gives us a Faith with a built-in growth potential. I suppose one can sense this in every recorded word of Jesus. To become a Christian is to be put in touch with spiritual forces conducive to growth. We deny such forces at our own peril. To let love have its way is nothing more or less than to be a growing Christian. The washing away of the impurities on the inside and the replacement of them with purity is a matter-of-fact occurrence for those experiencing it. We should not be astonished it happens. Better still, we should expect it to happen.

To live in the channels of grace provided by Him is a growing adventure. It is stimulated by the call to be pure. These channels are not what we always expect. There are some spectacular and very special surprises. Praise God, there is seldom a dull moment in the Faith of one born again! The Christian is aware that every day is a great day to be alive, and I do not mean a continual parade of the novel and bizarre every twenty-four hours. Ours is an optimism that ultimately never gives way to any happening including death. Our Lord conquered even that and promises the same for us.

Yes, sometimes we get the impression that an individual's experience with the Christ is frozen, fixed, and finalized. I doubt this impression is inaccurate in reality in many cases. It is more than a shame. It is an affront to the Christ who calls him to be growing in love. What will it take to thaw, untie, and make viable some professing His name? One excellent answer is to keep reminding them by various means in love that Christ's call is not to the rocking chair, the affluent but unproductive castle, and the morbidness that comes with potential goodness rotting before our very eyes. Those professing His Blessed Name are the Body of Christ or the Church, a living and ever-growing organism to whom He gave and continues to give Himself.

## 4.

Indeed, you and I are called to be pure.

The Gospel of Matthew relates: "You have heard that it was said to the men of old, 'You shall not kill; and whoever kills shall be liable to the judgment.' But I say to you that every one who is angry with his brother shall be liable to judgment; whoever insults his brother shall be liable to the council, and whoever says, 'You fool!' shall be liable to the fire of hell."

It is a call to let love have its way, and spelled out in particular it means: the ability to turn the other cheek; the confidence to speak the truth; the honesty to admit mistakes; the humility to ask for forgiveness; and the drive to want to be a growing Christian.

You and I have accepted Him and now He calls us to be pure. Why tarry? Why even question the proper timing? The call is as transparently clear as the virgin streams of water in the Himalaya Mountains.

## ❊CALLED TO BE RESILIENT❊

1.

"HANG LOOSE" and "Be able to bend or you will break" are timely pieces of advice.

They say Christians must be resilient or able to respond affirmatively to all situations in the highest and best sense. The world would tell us there is an element of compromise in life that would necessitate our "giving in" at some important points. Of course, that is not in keeping with the "highest and best." The world has a way of twisting and turning our Faith into the expedient, not the excellent. You and I are bought with a price, namely the sacrifice of Jesus upon the cross, and we must not allow the world to intervene and weaken. The truth in homey jewels of wisdom is invariably open to a reduction in spiritual insight. It would seem there are those who have mistaken such common sense approaches for the real thing which is the blessed gift of Christ to us in the form of right living. So there is often a delicate balance between the person who knows how to apply a gentle but manipulative humanism and the one who is a Christian seeking to grow in the Faith.

Admittedly, it is a day when schedules, modes of thinking, etc., can be changed at the twinkling of an eye. Unless we can make some sort of reasonable adjustment to these integral parts of our lives, we had best find a cave . . . of course, it might be subject to being covered by a new reservoir or blasted away to make room for a new industry. Christians are copers, that is, they can take such things in stride, not because of their brilliant techniques but because their Lord overcame the world. Our Faith is not dependent on geographic location or just the right set of circumstances. Our Lord comes to terms with both and yet is above both. Otherwise, our Faith would be severely limited and perhaps made into just another mediocre attempt to deal with the precariousness of human existence.

Our blessed Lord points the way to a victorious life unfragmented and not cursed by the keeping of "love-hate" records.

In Matthew 5:43–45 a clear course is set before us: "You have heard that it was said, 'You shall love your neighbor and hate your enemy.' But I say to you, Love your enemies and pray for those who persecute you, so that you may be sons of your Father who is in heaven; for he makes his sun rise on the evil and on the good, and sends rain on the just and on the unjust." These are not easy words to implement. This is often true of Jesus, isn't it? Yet, He does not open the way to do something and then tell us it isn't possible.

These few words showed a pagan world what it was not and His Jewish brethren what they could be.

### 2.

You and I are called to be resilient.
We all like to see where a decisive decision leads us.
Just where does our Lord's call take us?

### 3.

It *resists* the temptation "to right wrongs."

"An eye for an eye and a tooth for a tooth" was an improved way of dealing with wrongs long ago. But it is not the final and lofty revelation given to us by the Christ. Our Lord caringly nudges us to move beyond a mere calculation of justice. His way brings love into the dynamics of human relations. It does not seek an equal hurt for an equal hurt. When we stop to ponder, that sort of system leads no place beyond a strict keeping of records in the real and/or imagined injuries of life. That within itself is enough to keep our minds focused on judgment. Saint Paul says in Philippians 4:8, "Finally, brethren, whatever is true, whatever is honorable, whatever is just, whatever is pure, whatever is lovely, whatever is gracious, if there is any excellence, if there is anything worthy of praise, think about these things." Notice that while the word "just" is mentioned, it is among the true, honorable, pure, lovely, and gracious. Lincoln caught the vision of the Christ's message in his Second Inaugural Address: "With malice toward none; with charity for all; with firmness in the right as God gives us to see the right . . ."

Perhaps the most detrimental spirit is that which applies a keen eye into making everything come out even in life. To be sure, that is an improvement over anarchy. Yet, it has so many loopholes because I cannot walk in your shoes and you cannot walk in mine. Our Lord maintains victorious living—yes, right living—cannot be found in keeping score. Some seem to have a filing cabinet overflowing with folders listing and categorizing wrongs. Then upon what they consider suitable occasions they drag out their dregs in an attempt to drive home a point. Christ must shed a tear when He sees this happening. It is so opposed to His Sermon on the Mount, especially the test before us.

Our call entails a resiliency which enables us to bounce back at a person who has wronged us and say, "I love you." This is what Christ's life was all about. It is what ours—within the Faith—is all about. When we are stripped and beaten figuratively or literally, we are to love and pray for those committing such acts. The spirit of Christ in each of us always has the power to spring back, not in hurtful retaliation, but in loving consideration of the gospel message.

Where does the call to be resilient take us next?

It *resolves* to move beyond the mere keeping of a set of rules.

Many writers and seemingly much of the media make light of our time having few moral standards and keeping even fewer. While this appears to keep us in a twilight zone morally, I am not sure it is all bad. Sterility in the religious life is often marked by spending a lot of time deciding into which column particular actions and thoughts belong. From time to time we may need to do some analyzing. However, as a style of living we can approach the dangerous levels attained by some whose self-righteousness is a contradiction of our Lord's life and message. It is possible to be the epitome of a highly respected morality and know nothing of the saving grace of God through Christ. You might argue that this state of affairs is rare, but I am not so sure that it is. A person has to acknowledge his or her sins before repentance can take place. Saint Paul tells us in Romans 3:23 "since all have sinned and fall short of the glory of God." That doesn't leave much room for exacting regulations—regardless of how noble they appear to be—separate and apart from the conversion experience through Christ, does it?

Our Lord's way is away from rigidity and toward a saving resiliency. He doesn't say, "Now, here is our neighbor; love him. Over there is your enemy; hate him." To utilize a common phrase today "he puts it all together." Well, doesn't He? Some might even go so far as to say, "Jesus had His head on straight." Our Lord was in touch with the depths of human nature, even that part which appears to intend the very best. He knew there were many who, if given a favorable environment, would and could exercise the willpower to be moral giants. He also knew that created a situation which led to only one conclusion: righteousness before God, self-achieved. We are reminded of His word to us in Matthew 23:13: "But woe to you, scribes and Pharisees, hypocrites! because you shut the kingdom of heaven against men; for you neither enter yourselves, nor allow those who would enter to go in."

So, our Lord's teaching is in a real sense a resolve to keep changing man from the inside out with an ongoing, evident marriage of faith and works.

Where else does the call to be resilient take us?

It *respects* the new dimensions Christ brought to the Judeo-Christian faith.

Often Jesus begins with "You have heard it said . . ." He is updating His followers. He brings them something better. The old ways don't allow for the right priority; the right one is, of course, to love in all situations. While Jesus has been depicted as a revolutionist by many, in reality He was probably an evolutionist. His teaching stretches that already in existence and thereby brings to His people, the Jews, a new and dynamic way of looking at life.

Today as Christian members of the Church it takes you and me into those blessed but sometimes very unsettling heights. What if we love our enemies and pray for our persecutors . . . then they turn on us with renewed hostility and kill or mutilate us? Our first reaction may be, "Well, that just isn't the way it is supposed to work." To react that way is to second-guess what our Lord has in mind. My, how we do get in the way of the Faith revealed to us! Lest we forget, the latter part of the text reads: "for he makes his sun rise on the evil and on the good, and sends rain on the just and on the unjust." You and I are not a favored people—"a royal priesthood"—because we are exempt from God's overall and everlasting purposes. We are favored because we have seen the light of Calvary and accepted His Son, regardless of where we are led. The blood of martyrs is always a part of the landscape as we survey our Faith. You and I may need to have our memories refreshed that we are in truth also parts of that landscape. Even while the clergy read accounts of the Church through the ages and are thrilled by the sacrifices of those gone before, they are summoned to the altar of accountability for they too are now in their own lives writing Church history.

There is a tendency after the exhilaration of the conversion experience of commitment to Christ has dimmed for us to nestle down into pathways most conducive to our comfort. Indeed, we might even skip over our text. God forgive us! The crown is never ours without the Cross. I fear some will attempt to claim a crown, tainted by the refusal to be responsive and responsible to this portion of the Sermon on the Mount.

In 1887 for his graduating class at Andover Theological Seminary, Ernest Warburton Shurtleff wrote:

Lead on, O King Eternal,
We follow, not with fears,
For gladness breaks like morning
Where'ere thy face appears.
Thy Cross is lifted o'er us;
We journey in its light;
The Crown awaits the conquest;
Lead on, O God of might.

Finally, where does the call to be resilient take us?

It *restores* a basic integrity necessary for us to be authentic witnesses.

Mainline denominations have been hit often and hard by the modern proverb "We are just like everyone else trying to serve man and reach the same destination." While such a saw may have been essential for a time to keep our feet on the ground and in touch with humanity, it has now, in my opinion, neared the end of its usefulness. Christians are not "just like everyone else." They are a special people—"called out"— who do not set out to lord it over others because of their superior way of life. They (you and me, if you please) call upon their Lord to lead them that they may be known for their authenticity before their brothers and sisters, some within and some outside of the fold. The great theologian Soren Kierkegaard attacked the Church of his day in a sense because everyone was like everyone else, members of the Church for the most part, but unwilling to come to terms with the Word which called for undivided loyalty to Christ.

A well-known Episcopal layman, William Stringfellow, says in his book *Conscience and Obedience*: "A most obstinate misconception associated with the gospel of Jesus Christ is that the gospel is welcome in the world." That is prophetic! Christian laity and clergy alike should listen and give thanks someone that has the courage not only to say it but put it into print. Our call to resiliency is not one that promises attractiveness, popularity, success, or even progress as the world understands those inviting, nice terms. Saint Paul comes on strong in Ephesians 6:14 when he says, "Stand therefore, having girded your loins with truth, and having put on the breastplate of righteousness." That does not in any way, shape, or form lay before us the requirement to get lost in a crowd of pilgrims pushing and shoving us towards goals of peace and goodwill given definition and made sacred by a very surface kind of Faith, hardly worthy of the name.

Our voyage is nearly complete for now.

4.

Christians are called to be resilient.

Listen again to the glorious and always pertinent word from our Blessed Lord: "You have heard that it was said, 'You shall love your neighbor and hate your enemy.' But I say to you, Love your enemies and pray for those who persecute you, so that you may be sons of your Father who is in heaven; for he makes his sun rise on the evil and on the good, and sends rain on the just and on the unjust."

To decide decisively on the call for our lives lays before us not the routine "three Rs" but the majestic appeal of four which contain a built-in selling quality for those genuinely seeking a closer walk with the Christ: *resisting* the temptation "to right wrongs"; *resolving* to move beyond the mere keeping of a set of rules; *respecting* the new dimensions Christ brought to the Judeo-Christian faith; and *restoring* a basic integrity necessary for us to be authentic witnesses.

The serious (and joyous) followers of the Christ cope with today's living by hearing and obeying the call to be resilient.

## ✽CALLED TO BE SINGLE-MINDED✽

1.

THE FIRST OF the Ten Commandments is potently profound, over-shadowing the others.

Exodus 20:3 rings with thunder from Mount Sinai: "You shall have no other gods before me." This one sets the tone for those that follow. No person, animal, ideology, or thing is to come between a human being and God. The Commandment is made up of one- and two-syllable words. It cannot be mistaken. It moves to us with such divine directness and over-powering simplicity that it cannot be misunderstood. "That's the way it is," says our God, "and you take it lightly at your eternal peril." There is an awesomeness about it all upon which hangs your destiny and mine. Someone has said cynically with some derision, "Yes, the initial command of Moses is the Hebrew hard sell" to which you and I should reply, "Take off your shoes! You have entered hallowed ground and you treat it like a chimpanzee puttering around disrespectfully in a magnificent garden."

The survival and sanity of humanity are tied to this commandment. Mankind will have a god or gods of some sort. I suppose everything published in the social sciences would sooner or later confirm that state-ment. We have a need—not extractable—to look to a higher power within and without. No one or no generation of people can remain sane and ignore it. Perhaps the best of examples in this century thus far was the Nazi regime in Germany.

By now you may be saying to yourselves, "All well and good. We agree, but where do we go from here in a brief time frame?" Well, we move from the Old to the New Testament. We look to our Lord for a pointed directive.

Jesus the Christ builds upon this Commandment in a specific sense.

In Matthew 6:24, He proclaims a principle, piercing and pertinent: "No one can serve two masters; for either he will hate the one and love the other, or he will be devoted to the one and despise the other. You cannot serve God and mammon." We are called to be single-minded. We cannot have other gods before Him—in particular mammon—which translates into "riches" or material wealth. He does not say we have to be poverty stricken to worship and serve God. He says to place mammon ahead of God means we cannot possible serve God.

The call to be single-minded is to the Christian. Are we heeding the call? Will we?

## 2.

Christians who go all the way in the Faith are unique and an exception to the main currents of the world and some of the currents within the institutional Church. They hear a different drummer and His name is Jesus the Christ. We can elucidate by looking into four distinctive responses they make to their environment.

Such Christians wonder sometimes why they don't fit in as the world views happenings and events. Whoever said they would? You and I are called to be single-minded and that means *one* Master, God.

## 3.

*The first response is they have power in circumstances that others are powerless.*

What do we mean by this? Simply, God's love is the most powerful force in the entire universe. To those who are born anew He grants love in more colors than have ever been in all the rainbows put together. When asked which was the first of the commandments, His reply was, in effect, a final and fulfilling restatement of the first one given at Mount Sinai. He said, "The first is, 'Hear, O Israel: The Lord our God, the Lord is one; and you shall love the Lord your God with all your heart, with all your soul, and with all your mind, and with all your strength'" (Mark 12:31). The power generated in those lines is beyond our comprehension. Christians have direct access to it not because of their goodness but because of God's greatness evidenced in love.

The power which comes to us and works within us is due to our identity. 1 John 3:2 glows with glory: "Beloved, we are God's children now; it does not yet appear what we shall be but we know that when he appears we shall be like him, for we shall see him as he is." The Christian does not have an identity crisis, unless it is produced by an unwillingness to grow. The growing Christian knows who he or she is. Why fritter away our lives by playing the guessing game, "Who am I?" In love we belong to God. Saint Paul tells us, in 1 Corinthians 6:19–20, that ". . . You are not your own; you were bought with a price."

Are some muttering under their breath, "Preacher, that sounds good, but I don't now what you are talking about?" Your Lord and Savior says, "And I tell you, ask, and it will be given you; seek, and you will find; knock, and it will be opened to you" (Luke 11:9). Then He comes back in the very next verse in the same chapter and says, "For everyone who asks receives, and he who seeks finds, and to him who knocks it will be opened." Do you find that difficult to believe? Don't you think it is more difficult not to believe it?

Heeding the call to be single-minded brings to our attention something else peculiar to Christians.

*The second response is they radiate purpose in situations that others find purposeless.*

The Master says it so well and succinctly early in the Sermon on the Mount: "You are the salt of the earth . . ." (Matt. 5:13). Isn't that exciting? In the eyes of the world it looks like an ego trip. For those who are single-minded in serving one Master it is a natural course of events. We are the saving feature in situations. That doesn't mean we smooth out the rough places necessarily. There are those who regard anything less than 100 percent acceptance of their ideas as being ungodly. As a sage said, "Some persons will pay large sums for health and happiness; but they will give away everything they own to get their way." As Christians we are never always right; we bear witness to being in the right. Remembering the difference between the two often spells out failure or success in Christ's Kingdom.

During the years of my ministry I have observed numerous Christians who devalued and thwarted their Faith. There was so much more within them, but they refused to let the healing rays loose. Satan's subtle and sincere way of telling us, "Now you don't want to appear foolish" bears fruit. Too late we learn it is not only sour and beginning to rot, but worm-eaten as well. You and I do not come on like self-righteous gangbusters showing others how brilliant we are and how much of Christ we have. We don't have to do that. Our call is to be single-minded and that simply means we serve one Master. His name is Jesus the Christ.

In a day when people are constantly touching wills and spirits in a grating way, we learn just to be together largely in quietude may be more important than to come to any earthshaking decisions. The unhurried, unplanned, and unsophisticated interaction of precious sons and daughters of the Father may provide more real food for ongoing vital living than heavy agendas and hour-long reports. There is a word with which you may be familiar. It is *koinonia*, a Greek word. In an elementary sense it indicates a fellowship or sharing of Christians with the spirit of Christ present. The small group movement around the world in recent years gives example after example. There may be no greater purpose than just coming together as Christians. Then, to use a play on words, we rediscover purpose and take it into situations others find purposeless.

Taking to our hearts and minds, indeed our very wills, the call to be single-minded causes us to look again at the distinctiveness of Christians.

*The third response is they accept privilege in circles that others consider unprivileged.*

While we tend to feel more comfortable with those in the same economic and social categories, our Faith transcends and works through such imposing barriers. To have the mind of Christ is to move freely among all classes. The first-century Church dealt with the partiality issue in the Epistle of James. The second chapter tells of a man with gold rings and fine clothing and a poor man in shabby clothing. One is asked to please have a seat and the other is told to stand or sit at someone's feet. Distinctions of this type are seen as coming from a judgmental attitude with evil thoughts. In the same chapter, James relates point-blank, "But if you show partiality, you commit sin, and are convicted by the law as transgressors" (2:9). To be "one in Christ" is to obliterate that which separates and divides.

Now, the world does not understand such things. One of the biggest put-downs some can experience is to be found among those who don't meet certain worldly prescribed standards. They see nothing privileged in relating to others who simply don't have it economically and socially. In their thoughts Christ is divided and His Church is unequipped to handle various styles of living. The world sees nothing privileged about mingling and communicating with those who just haven't made it in this life. Conversely, there is a segment of the world that hates and envies the rich, cultured, and prominent in the Church even though they practice the Faith with concern and compassion.

How about you and me? While our lives naturally tend to be lived out at certain social and economic strata, aren't we privileged to be among those above and below? Just as we say "above and below," we are caught in the potential trap of denying the oneness in Christ that should keep us all on the same glorious and victorious spiritual plane.

Isn't the call to be single-minded with one Master, the Christ, stupendously thrilling? How privileged we are! How joyously free and healingly unrestrained we can be!

There is one more unique feature.

*The fourth response is they own promise in areas that others demean unpromising.*

In the Old Testament the writer of Ecclesiastes manages to give us a philosophical peek into our final point: "For everything there is a season, and a time for every matter under heaven" (3:1). He follows this with a lengthy list of life's events and their lingering significance for all. Prior to the advent, ministry, death, and resurrection of the Christ it was common for such words to end in futility and pessimism. What a difference the Savior and Lord makes! To be single-minded in His service is to cause this passage of Old Testament wisdom literature to be baptized in promise. Our Lord was a student of Hebrew Scripture and there is good reason to believe He was fully aware of Ecclesiastes. He moves the unpromising into the promising. We are led from the futile and pessimistic to the worthwhile and hopeful in the same areas of human existence.

From a somewhat different and yet closely related angle, our single-mindedness can and does provide for us the owning of promise for good. As someone in the public relations field has said, "If you keep turning a happening long enough, there is an interesting story someone wants to hear or see." Under the Lordship of Christ you and I have a similar experience. The history of the Faith is sprinkled profusely with those who said "Yes, Lord" in areas while the world was snickering, hissing, and profaning. The point of view was decisive. No one can serve both God and mammon. We are appalled sometimes by the worldly attitudes in the Church that downgrade precious persons who have heard the voice of the Lord ask, "Whom shall I send, and who will go for us?" and have replied, "Here am I! Send me!"

4.

Yes, you and I are most assuredly called to be single-minded.

There is no lack of understanding the passage in Matthew 6:24: "No one can serve two masters; for either he will hate the one and love the other, or he will be devoted to the one and despise the other. You cannot serve God and mammon."

Those who follow the call are rather easily spotted by four distinctive responses to their environment: they have power in circumstances that others are powerless; radiate purpose in situations that others find purposeless; accept privilege in circles that others consider unprivileged: and own promise in areas that others demean unpromising.

Are we willing to be different—even eccentric in the world's assessment—to live and spread the Faith? James tells us, ". . . for he who doubts is like a wave of the sea that is driven and tossed by the wind. For that person must not suppose that a double-minded man, unstable in all his ways, will receive anything from the Lord" (1:6–8). In prayerful resolve: Oh, God, we know we cannot serve two masters. We have determined today to serve One, Your Son the Christ.

# ✤CALLED TO BE ASTUTE✤

### 1.

IS THERE AN awareness or special sensitivity Christians have that others don't have?

Some would maintain that is an impossible question to answer. To be sure it is one that seems to be filled with audacity. Yet, I for one do not think it is impossible. My hesitancy comes at the point of offering proof in ways that would gain the approval and applause of the world. Into that trap, many disciples of Christ have fallen. We have said in the language and thought forms of the world, "Here is proof we have something you don't." It has spelled disaster upon occasion. Had we only listened to the Master say: "My kingship is not of this world . . ." (John 18:36), we would not have been on the brink of disillusionment. Statistical success does not and has not always indicated documentation for our select pipeline to God. In fact, the Lord was not successful in piling up numbers. Some years ago a denominational leader said that we cannot compete with television on Sunday nights, so why bother with church services? Of course, on that narrow basis he was right. The scary part is that he thought the Body of Christ was supposed to compete with the secular extravaganzas on the tube.

You and I as Christians are select and we do have access to strength and support others do not have. That is not an egotistical statement. It is simply one of truth. Saint Paul tells the Church at Colossae: "And let the peace of Christ rule in your hearts, to which indeed you were called in the one body. And be thankful" (3:15). Saint Peter makes it emphatic: "But you are a chosen race, a royal priesthood, a holy nation, God's own people . . ." (1 Pet. 2:9). Ponder that for a moment. That Scripture includes you and me!

Our Lord opens avenues to Christians unknown to non-Christians.

More specifically, in Matthew 7:7–8 He says to us: "Ask, and it will be given you: seek and you will find; knock, and it will be opened to you. For every one who asks receives, and he who seeks finds, and to him who knocks it will be opened." The fascinating glow to those words is seen in their openendedness. He doesn't indicate there are any exceptions.

Strange as it may sound, we are called to be astute. This does not mean in any way whatsoever the selfish pursuit and "success" orientation the world adores. It means: "I have been crucified with Christ; it is no longer I who live, but Christ who lives in me . . ." (Gal. 2:20).

### 2.

The call to be astute is one telling us to acknowledge and utilize gifts peculiarly ours.

This special relationship to God is seen in tapping truth in life's experiences, especially six.

### 3.

*In the time of trouble we can tap truth.*

In a land of affluence and a denomination of privilege we are prone to look upon trouble with disdain. The concept of sacrificial giving is foreign to our ears and perhaps has been all our lives, in or out of the Church. The very thought of giving 10 percent or more of income to Christ and His Church is disruptive and cause for a whole barricade of defenses. If we can give a pittance and maintain an image of respectability before friends and "those who count," we beguile ourselves into believing we are trouble-free. The fact of the matter is, of course, the longer we refuse to confront the real situation, the more trouble we have in the long run . . . indeed, the fires of hell become more unyielding. Our denomination today bears some of the marks of the Church of England during the period John and Charles Wesley ministered. It tends again and again to serve itself in thought and deed.

From a pointedly personal standpoint, our Lord says to you and me, "Ask . . . seek . . . knock." He does not do this just to say a few well-intended words or try to appease disgruntled followers. Life says we are going to have trouble. You and I need not be engulfed by it, settling back into a state of gloom and doom. It is true, some seem to have more than their share. However, before you and I claim such mistreatment, let's be certain it isn't a case of some person or situation merely fracturing a spoiled and pampered existence. Christ has called us to ministry not minutia.

So much for initial point.

*In the time of tragedy, we can tap truth.*

By most and perhaps all measurements, tragedy is a factor in our lives. We anguish in pain, sorrow, and disillusionment. During these disquieting periods do we "Ask ... seek ... knock?" I have heard individuals say, "Pastor, I have done that but there was and is no relief." When hearing this sort of response I am reminded of the scene shortly after the Resurrection. Mary Magdelene was weeping and asked where they had taken her Lord; the greatest of all tragedies appeared to be upon her. Then the resurrected Jesus said to her, "Woman why are you weeping? Whom do you seek?" (John 20:15). She thought He was the gardener. He was standing beside her and she did not recognize Him. When she recognized him, her relief came.

The tenacious Saint Paul had tragedy after tragedy. He says in Romans 8:18, "I consider that the sufferings of this present time are not worth comparing with the glory that is to be revealed to us." Again in Ephesians he says, "Therefore take the whole armor of God, that you may be able to withstand in the evil day, and having done all to stand" (6:13). Has it occurred to you and me that we do not "stand" because we do not "Ask ... seek ... knock" or if we do, it is with one knee on the floor and our eyes on the clock?

We must not tarry.

*In the time of triumph, we can tap truth.*

While we may praise God at first for a major victory, we tend to forget His loving care. Our heads get too big. We do not know our friends. We lord it over those who are less fortunate. We are prone to bask in the sunshine of our own merits and brilliance. A string of triumphs can make us virtually blind to those about us. While we may say to ourselves, "Oh, they are just jealous," a careful examination usually reveals it is often our overbearing sense of accomplishment provoking them. On the other hand, God does not expect us to downgrade an attainment there for all to see. How, then, do we rightfully handle moments of triumph? Our blessed Lord says "Ask ... seek ... knock."

The call to be astute is one which can and does make triumph a growing in grace for us and others. You and I are spiritually triumphant not because of what the world declares a triumph, but because we learn through the Master how to handle such glowing achievement. The winner in the world's sight can be a Christian and above all can manifest a Christian life at which others will marvel and—if not openly—at least secretly admire. In the world of show business, few have ever been so victoriously prominent over as long a period as Bing Crosby. I know of no one who has ever described him as arrogant, rude, or condescending . . . and that was noted long before his death. The roots of his religion ran deep. He must have found in the wellsprings of his faith that in asking he received, in seeking he found, and in knocking it was opened to him.

Join me as we look into another common experience.

*In the time of trivia, we can tap truth.*

Some dear soul said, "Life has its high points and low points but most of it is in between." Some of that "in between" seems to be trivial happenings, even boredom. What can possibly be occurring during such times that is productive for Christ and His work here on earth? Can it be that God forsakes us for a while and allows us to languish in apathetic moods with our spirits settled into drowsy neutrality? What can be good about the routine of taking two steps forward and two backwards, except that it keeps one from toppling over for having stood in the same place too long? The call to be astute is powerfully relevant in these states. We are not chosen by Christ to waste the gift of life. He lays before us the passageway of productivity even in the midst of mountains of miscellanea: "Ask . . . seek . . . knock."

Today the humdrum of living eats away in unexpected places. I am speaking, of course, of those professing the name of Jesus the Christ. Does this mean one's personal religious experience is doomed to dullness and the Master really has taken a long walk away from us? Hopefully, we know better than that. I believe feelings of useless monotony remain only as long as we refuse to "Ask . . . seek . . . knock," or because we make up our own recipe for astuteness filled with conceit and guaranteed to cure the weight of trivia on our own terms.

We tend to overlook the next event in life.

*In the time of travesty, we can tap truth.*

When life seems distorted, disoriented, and dislocated to the point of sheer nonsense, what do we do? Some slide into a kind of self-hypnosis that results in a dreamland, hoping their fragmentary existence can be made less harsh. Others cry out for positive threads that can give a reason for life to continue. Those under the most severe strains are convinced, at least momentarily, that suicide is the only answer. If we have lived very many years at all, we know of these unwelcome states.

When life just doesn't seem to make any sense at all, what do you and I do? Are we prone to go in the directions just previously mentioned? If we do, what does our Faith have to say to us? Maybe Satan is on such a rampage; he insists to "Ask . . . seek . . . knock" is only more of the same grotesque meaninglessness. In the Gospel of John, our Lord says of the Devil, "When he lies, he speaks according to his own nature, for he is a liar and the father of lies" (8:44). The most apropos time of all to "Ask . . . seek . . . knock" is when nothing seems to make much sense and there are more loose ends than anyone can count. We are called to be astute not to outsmart the Devil on his own turf, but to enter into those supports, strengths, and answers available only to those within the Faith.

You are incited to share the last point.

*In the time of tremor, we can tap truth.*

Foundations shake. The expression "all hell is breaking loose" fits at different places in our lives, doesn't it? Cherished and respected people seem to come unglued. Institutions develop large cracks in them. Organizations with time-honored reputations are found to be corrupt. The institutional Church has faltered and floundered to the extremes of outright apostasy and hypocrisy. A few times in the history of the Faith the earnest acts of asking, seeking, and knocking led persons and families out of the so-called visible Church.

God has never forsaken His people, even when tremors sent things and people in all sorts of directions. He has preserved a faithful remnant all the way back to Abraham whom He told, "And I will make of you a great nation, and I will bless you, and make your name great, so that you will be a blessing" (Gen. 12:2). At the time of Jesus' crucifixion there were many who would not have given two cents for the continuation of what He set in motion. How wrong they were! We cannot control or even accurately predict the quaking in life. Hallelujah, we have written in unerasable ink on an imperishable manuscript "Ask and receive . . . seek and find . . . knock and it will be opened!"

4.

The call to be astute is not to be underestimated or undervalued.

The Christ opens the way: "Ask, and it will be given you; seek and you will find; knock, and it will be opened to you. For every one who asks receives, and he who seeks finds, and to him who knocks it will be opened."

Our call is seen especially in six events of the tapestry of life in which we can tap truth: in the time of trouble, tragedy, triumph, trivia, travesty, and tremor.

We have the answers to life's most basic and pressing questions.

What are we doing about it? Are we quibbling over answers that are not really answers because they are not God's? Are we wishing the Christ would sit down and explain to us every detail so that we can see if we agree? Are we thinking, "How can we manipulate something we know as Christians into an advantage for financial gain in the secular business and/or professional worlds?" If you and I are doing any of these monstrous things or something similar, may God have immediate mercy on us!

The call to be astute contains an entree into God's storehouse of riches overflowing with miracles. Let us not be deceived into believing it is our astuteness that provides and produces. To do so is to make null and void Christ's promise that to ask is to receive, to seek is to find, and to knock is to have it opened.

Our Lord's promises are true, so true in fact, they do not respond to human misuse . . . and that's a great protection built upon an eternal Faith.

––––––––––

*Used by permission of CSS Publishing Company, Inc.,*
*517 S. Main Street, P.O. Box 4503, Lima, Ohio, 45802–4503.*

**Donald Charles Lacy**

*1979 and 1993*

*Our time calls for a determined evangelical spirit and an ecumenical orientation. The two belong together: "What God has joined together, let not man put asunder."* Mary and Jesus *was born from a warm heart, open mind, and willing spirit, with the joyous imperative, "woe be unto me if I leave these words unsaid," persistently present. The Advent season presents itself as a unique period of preparation. While it is deeply individualistic, it stretches across and into all lives.* Mary and Jesus *is a modest attempt to provide a preaching/teaching series for those clergy and laity who seek to worship and study seriously during this blessed season. Four of four sermons are presented.*

# CHAPTER 3

# Mary and Jesus

## ❧HAIL, MARY❧

### 1.

THE ANGEL Gabriel and Mary, the mother of Jesus, have quite a conversation in the first chapter of Luke, verses twenty-six through thirty-eight.

We call this brief section the Annunciation because of its function of foretelling our Lord's birth. It appears only in the Gospel of Luke. It elevates for us the person of Mary.

For pure excitement and a sense of wonder this passage ranks very high. Luke begins by telling us the angel Gabriel was sent from God to a city of Galilee called Nazareth. More specifically, he was sent to a virgin betrothed to a man named Joseph, who came from the house of David. The virgin's name was Mary. He addressed her with great respect: "Hail, O favored one, the Lord, is with you!" Mary was greatly troubled and began to wonder what he meant. He told her not to be afraid; she had found favor with God. Then he broke the colossal news to her. She would conceive and bear a son called Jesus. The son will be called Son of the Most High. He would have the throne of David, and reign over the house of Jacob forever, and there would be no end to His kingdom. Mary responded by saying that she didn't even have a husband. Then Gabriel told her the Holy Spirit would be upon her and the child would be the Son of God. The angel further pointed out Elizabeth in her old age would have a son, indicating all things are possible with God. The passage closes as Mary submits as a handmaid of the Lord, and the angel departs.

Many have borne the lovely and attractive name of Mary through the centuries.

In the Old Testament the most famous is the older sister of Moses and Aaron. She was called Miriam, the Hebrew equivalent of the Greek Mary. She played a part in the survival of Moses as an infant.

The New Testament mentions, at least, six different ones. In addition to the mother of Jesus there are Mary Magdalene, Mary of Bethany, the mother of James and Joseph, the mother of Mark, and a Christian woman mentioned in Romans 16. Of course, it is during Advent that our blessed Lord's mother deserves close and honored attention.

2.

Let's zero in now on those exciting—even awesomely bewildering—words in Luke 1:26–28: "In the sixth month the angel Gabriel was sent from God to a city of Galilee named Nazareth, to a virgin betrothed to a man whose name was Joseph, of the house of David; and the virgin's name was Mary. And he came to her and said, 'Hail, O favored one, the Lord is with you!'"

It has long been my opinion that Roman Catholics have made far too much of Mary and Protestants have made far too little.

Join me as we become proper and probing Protestants by asking, "Why should we hold Mary in high esteem?" The reasons are a minimum of four and all come directly from Scripture.

3.

*The first is her moral excellence.*

Is it possible that God would have chosen just any young woman to give birth to His Son? The heavens have resounded with a loud "No!" since this first episode with Gabriel. She embodied all of the ideals of young womanhood. There is a beauty about purity that is always inspiring above decadent minds and societies.

I am reminded of the young woman who came to the pastor's study saying she only wanted to stop by for a few minutes of light conversation. As she began to talk about the good times in her life, her eyes caught a small bouquet of snow white carnations on the desk. The longer she talked the more she became incoherent and began to sob. At last she broke the tenseness in low tones that carried the weight of grave seriousness. She said softly, "I am no longer like the flowers on your desk." She knew this did not undo what had taken place and she acknowledged that for her something uniquely beautiful was gone forever. In the realm of moral excellence some things do not change. You and I have not decreed this but God has; and this protects the decency and sanctity of marriage and family life.

Today's world with its grime, sordidness, and impudence either puts Mary on a pedestal and ignores her or snickers at stories that say she was less than what Scripture tells us. Of course, those women who choose—and it is by their choice—to live at lofty moral levels are invariably confronted by the clamor of freedom which translates into power. This is not new. If history teaches us anything on a consistent basis, it is in the words of the English historian Sir John Emerich Edward Dalberg-Acton "Power tends to corrupt and absolute power corrupts absolutely." The abuse of power, largely by men, across the centuries has filled millions of volumes, drenching them with blood and misery. Mankind has always sought for the ideals of Mary, perhaps below the conscious level. Why? The answer lies in the fact mankind must have a visible, real, and authentic symbol of purity or it resides on the quicksands of the totally mundane that sooner or later sinks into despair. Thank God He gave us Mary, that He chose a morally excellent woman to give birth to His Son, and He beckons to you and me to kneel before what she represents. Notice, I did not say she was, is, or should be an object of worship. Purity that is in truth purity deserves our respect and reverence. Indeed it has its own magnetism.

Let's turn our attention now to another reason.

*The second is she is chosen by God.*

The Scripture does not read in any way whatsoever that Mary is selected by a committee of elders or prominent religious leaders. Gabriel says, "Hail, O favored one, . . ." The supernatural and everlasting arms of God are intervening. No person or persons on this earth had the time, brilliance, or spiritual sagacity to pick the right young woman. God said, "I shall send My message through Gabriel to Mary," and—praise His name—He did! Can you imagine what sort of chaos would have been created had such a decision been left in the hands of mere men? They would have most assuredly bungled, bollixed, and besmirched the entire matter. It seems when some very crucial happenings are at stake God does not delegate to His children. He breaks into the natural course of events and simply says, "This is the way it is going to be."

Have you and I any doubt about her selection by God? If we—as Protestants—base our conclusions on what the biblical narrative tells us, how can we doubt? Even if we were to approach our text from a hyper-critical point of view, what can we do to explain away the Lukan account of her being favored by Almighty God? Well, we really have to stretch ourselves far afield to question seriously the reliability of Dr. Luke. This Gospel was put into its current form well before the end of the first century, which means it is removed not more than a couple of generations from the resurrection of Christ. Suppose we maintain verse twenty-eight is a clever editing job. Then, how do we explain the remainder of the Annunciation in Luke and similar verses in Matthew? Perhaps we have hypothesized long enough. Why don't we just worship in humble adoration the recorded Word, admitting Mary's select place for all time in the story of our Faith?

To build a case for Mary being miraculously chosen by God is to rule out His choosing of others. In the Gospel of John 15:16, for example, Christ indicates: "You did not choose me, but I chose you and appointed you that you should go and bear fruit and that your fruit should abide; so that whatever you ask the Father in my name, he may give it to you." Let us move back much further to Deuteronomy 7:6 where Moses spells out the unique relationship of the Hebrews to their God: "For you are a people holy to the Lord your God; the Lord your God has chosen you to be a people for his own possession, out of all the peoples that are on the face of the earth."

Now we move to the reason showing the eternally exquisite nature of her motherhood.

*The third is she is the mother of Jesus the Christ.*

Will you project yourselves for a moment to that long ago time and faraway place of our Lord's birth? What details we have are in Scripture and most are familiar with them. Just to read them with a little care tells us Mary was the mother of a son, Jesus by name. There is no reason to believe there was anything extraordinary about her motherhood, except to say she knew in advance He would be the Messiah and the Holy Spirit would be the Father. You may react, "Well, preacher, that is quite an exception!" True, but the period of pregnancy with its many trials and joys, the labor pains, and the delivery must have been little—if any—different than those numerous other Jewish women at the time. It seems to me that to maintain she did not experience all of those things is to call into question the authenticity of His birth by a woman. I do not believe she was spared any of the physical pain and mental fears that have perpetually been a part of becoming a mother. There are those who have seen her motherhood as a mere acting out of history and prophecy. Of course, there are those who have said the same things about our Lord's crucifixion. You and I were not there those nearly two thousand years ago in a place called Bethlehem, and yet in a strangely joyful way we were, along with the rest of mankind.

Attitudes have been and are at present relegating the matter of human birth to a strictly biological category to be handled much like a plant superintendent would handle parts, pieces, and machines. I am sorry for this. I am sorry for those who feel that becoming pregnant and giving birth to a child is a singular process that involves just two human beings. It seems to me—with very few exceptions—to abort life is to shake our fists in the face of God, telling Him in no uncertain terms we will run our own lives and He can go "jump into the lake" or sit powerlessly on His faraway heavenly throne. In pregnancy and childbirth there are always more than two persons involved. In a profound sense the entire human race is involved. Have we forgotten so quickly how we came into this world? Life is a gift. We always get into trouble when we try "to play God." There are those who demand the control of their bodies, especially when it comes to allowing a child to live or die they are carrying. It seems to me they are invariably those who have not answered the prior question, "Why—with all the so-called liberating preventatives—did you become pregnant in the first place?" Sexual freedom can be nothing more than a license to tell the human race to go to hell. In fact, sexual freedom is never really found outside of the bonds of marriage. That slightly risque cliche "sowing wild oats and praying for crop failure" continues to be relevant.

Mary, the mother of Jesus, has something very important to say to women, men, youth, and children. Think about it. Don't deny her that mission . . . and I said nothing about worshipping her.

There is, at least, one more reason we are to hold her in high esteem.

*The fourth is she is a willing servant.*

Compare her response, for example, to that of Jeremiah who was a young man. In the book that bears his name the Lord said to him: "Before I formed you in the womb I knew you, and before you were born I consecrated you; I appointed you a prophet to the nations" (1:5). He told the Lord he didn't know how to speak because he was only a youth. Then, the Lord told him in no uncertain terms: "Do not say, 'I am only a youth'; for to all to whom I send you you shall go, and whatever I command you you shall speak" (1:7). It seems that Jeremiah wanted to debate or argue the issue. He had his excuse and therefore would not be willing to do what the Lord asked. Well, we know who won that skirmish! Mary didn't put up a fuss. All she does is to ask for clarification of what at first appears to be the unbelievable; she gets it.

We can all learn from Mary's acquiescence to the will of God. You and I are so very stubborn at times in our relationship with Him. We want our way. Christian members of the Church can be the most rigid and obstinate of all because each may feel God is solely on his or her side. The sanctity of each distinct and separate person is a precious concept that belongs in the Faith. Yet, it is only in our relationship with God that it has legitimate and worthwhile meaning. God does not want us to deal and trade with Him in order to serve Him on an ongoing, compromising basis. We cannot really serve Him that way . . . and to be painfully honest, we are all very restricted in our vision and perception. The horrendous arrogance of our time seems almost always centered on our self-sufficiency and God's deficiency in understanding us.

4.

The full Gospel message demands we not make less of Jesus the Christ but more of Mary, His mother.

You and I tend to hear and see only in portions and fragments. This has been true among Christians and would-be Christians far longer than any of us can remember. Some have spent their lives picking and choosing among the books, chapters, and verses in the Bible to substantiate preconceived notions. May God be merciful!

Are you and I among those who should have been learning of Mary's select place in our Faith but have not bothered to do so?

Mary was and is not God. In fact, our Lord did not even make her one of His Apostles. She was and is, nevertheless, someone very special. "Hail, O favored one, the Lord is with you!"

# ❧DESCRIBING THE BABY❧

1.

DESCRIBING A baby and dreaming about what he or she will become are parental pastimes beginning in the dim, distant past.

Will he (or she) become President of the United States? There's always that possibility, isn't there? A father's eyes twinkle as he visualizes the baby some day with hand on Bible being sworn into the presidency. Mother muses as she visualizes herself kissing her baby of fifty-five before the entire world via television.

Will the baby be rich and powerful? Would parents wish this upon a child? You know as well as I that the answer is "Yes." Generally, we want our offspring to be prominent.

It would be fascinating to know all the dreams dreamed and all the prayers offered by parents for the tiny bundles of humanity that have entered the families of the world. Think of those you and I have already dreamed. Yes, and think of all those prayers—some with logical precision and others with emotional pleas—offered to Almighty God.

How do we describe our infants? "He's such a handsome little fellow. He looks just like his father" . . . or "He's such a handsome little fellow. He doesn't look like his father at all." "She's a beautiful child. She already shows human relations skills that will enable her to marry a fine executive" . . . or "She's a beautiful child. She already shows human relations skills that will enable her to become a fine executive."

So much for the infants of the world, including yours and mine.

How would you go about describing Mary's baby?

Would the adjectives be: unique, divine, Jewish, Savior, wonderful, God, etc? Well, that's a beginning list, isn't it? Let's back up a step and ask, "How do you define the descriptive words? In what way was He unique? How was He divine? To what extent was He Jewish? What does it mean to be a savior? He was wonderful, but so what? What do we mean by labeling Him 'God?'"

We Christians have used many words over the centuries to tell who and what He is. We have not done much of a job in defining or spelling out what we mean. Have you thought through what you understand Mary's baby to be? In a sense this is a joyful task of a lifetime. In another sense it is a present imperative.

Fortunately, Gabriel in the Annunciation in Luke briefly—but brilliantly—weaves for us a description.

### 2.

What does Gabriel say about Him?

Luke 1:30–33 records: "And the angel said to her, 'Do not be afraid, Mary, for you have found favor with God. And behold, you will conceive in your womb and bear a son, and you shall call his name Jesus. He will be great, and will be called the Son of the Most High; and the Lord God will give to him the throne of his father David, and he will reign over the house of Jacob for ever; and of his kingdom there will be no end.'" So, in a nutshell Gabriel describes in seven different but cohesive ways Mary's baby.

### 3.

*He will be of the male gender.*

Mary will "bear a son." There are hundreds of allusions to sons in the Old and New Testaments. It was upon the son the perpetuation of the clan, tribe, and nation rested. To be without one was considered to be a matter of reproach.

"Son" is also used in a figurative sense. They might be the more remote relatives, such as grandsons and other male relatives. They might be members of musical guilds, such as "sons of Korah." For example, between Psalm 46 and 47, we discover the words: "To the choirmaster. A Psalm of the Sons of Korah." There are sons of apothecaries. There are sons of prophets. There are followers of certain deities, such as "sons of Chemosh." There are sons of dwellers in specific places; for example, Genesis 10:4 speaks of "the sons of Javan" or Greece.

In the Old Testament one of the most profoundly moving stories of sonship is that of Joseph's love for his father, Jacob. In Genesis 45:13 Joseph says, "You must tell my father of all my splendor in Egypt, and of all that you have seen. Make haste and bring my father down here." He could have allowed his father to finish his life in misery and destitution.

The Parable of the Prodigal Son is a beautiful message of broken and restored sonship. How it speaks to all of us! Sooner or later we all experience far countries.

So, Mary's baby was a male child and entered a world that had already made provision for His maleness.

*His name will be Jesus.*

Mary "shall call his name Jesus." Of what significance is this? The word means "God saves" or "He will save." It is Grecianized form of the Hebrew "Joshua." We might even replace the word "Jesus" with the word "savior." It is also revealing to note that Isaiah has the same basic meaning in Hebrew, and who gives us the most clear and prophetic words of Jesus' coming in the Old Testament? That's right. Isaiah. So, we begin to see immediately why Mary is told to name Him as she does.

When you and I call Him "Savior" we do so for good reason. That's His name. Isn't it amazing the way God speaks to His people? For every doubt there is a verifiable reason within the Faith. We skim along the surface of our Faith oftentimes because we do to study it. Even in the very name given to Him we discover His prime function. He is "Savior."

While in America parents have been very reluctant to name a child Jesus, in other parts of the world that is not true. Spanish-speaking countries have utilized it again and again. In our own culture to use the name is immediately to mean one person and one person only. Perhaps there are those among us who know the "whys and wherefores" of such language differences better than I.

He was perfectly named.

*He will be great.*

Have you ever felt like saying to the biblical translators, "Why can't you be more imaginative?" That was my instantaneous reaction to the brief sentence, "He will be great." So, I decided to look some place other than the Revised Standard Version. Well, to make a long story short I looked into the *King James*, *New English*, and *Jerusalem* Bibles; do you know what I found? I found exactly the same wording, except in the King James which says "shall" in place of "will."

"Great" seems such an overused word. Yet, who am I to superimpose my desire for literary variety upon men who have spent their lives translating the Word of God? That question alone is enough to bring any pastor to his knees in gratitude for the dedication employed over the centuries in bringing the Word to us. Of course, we don't dare make an even bigger mistake by passing over Gabriel's little sentence labeling it "trite but necessary."

Gabriel, by way of Mr. Webster, must mean "markedly superior in character or quality." That's it, isn't it? Mary's baby will have no equals. He will be above all. Other wise and saintly men will sparkle with wisdom and serve mankind; but they will have dull times and refuse to serve unconditionally. He will sparkle, regardless of how we approach Him; He will serve, regardless of the circumstances.

Great? To be sure!

*He will be called the Son of the Most High (or God).*

Throughout His career Jesus spoke in simple directness of God being His Father. We come face to face with a relationship having no precedents in the Old Testament. "Father" is used hundred of times in the Old Testament but never in the stirring personal Father-Son relationship that Jesus uses it. Recall Matthew 7:21: "Not everyone who says to me, 'Lord, Lord,' shall enter the kingdom of heaven, but he who does the will of *my Father* who is in heaven." Then note from Mark, an even older Gospel: "and a voice came from heaven, 'Thou art *my* beloved *Son*; with thee I am well pleased'" (11:1). The Gospel of John is virtually saturated with the phrases "the Father" and "my Father." In fact John 10:30 says, "I and the Father are one." When He said that, the Jews around Him "blew their cool" and prepared to stone Him for blasphemy.

Up until now in Gabriel's description we might have made a case for Mary's baby being less than a full expression of God. Now the preponderance of biblical record assures us of His deity. He is a part of the Trinity, working in perfect harmony with the Father and the Holy Spirit.

Think of it! God's Son came and lived among us!

God will give to Him the throne of David.

The kings that stand out in Hebrew history are Saul, David, and Solomon. The one who ranks above all is David. His rule of approximately forty years is considered the high point. From the time he slew Goliath until his death his shadow covered all the kingdom. Seventy-three of the one hundred fifty Psalms bear the title "To David." He was above and beyond any other national hero. While his personal life and leadership in killing enormous numbers in battle may cause us to back away from him, his devotion to his God is remarkable and at times inspiring. In depicting him, Samuel says, ". . . the Lord has sought out a man after his own heart . . ." (1 Sam. 13:14). One could go into volumes, and some have, documenting the greatness of this multitalented man. The Messiah was to come from his lineage and He did.

In the eyes of many—perhaps most—Jews, Mary's baby should have matured into a political-religious figure bringing the Jews full independence from the Romans and a reign surpassing David's in worldly power and prominence. Obviously, that did not occur. Yet, David's throne was His in a sense no one could take away from Him. His Jewish brethren needed to read Isaiah 9:7 over and over again: "Of the increase of his government and of peace there will be no end, upon the throne of David, and over his kingdom, to establish it, and to uphold it with justice and with righteousness from this time forth and for evermore. The zeal of the Lord of hosts will do this."

Indeed, the throne of David was and is His.

*He will reign over the house of Jacob for ever.*

The beginning of Jesus' people is with Abraham, Isaac, and Jacob. After his battle with an angel Jacob was renamed "Israel" (Gen. 32:28). In Genesis 35:10 is recorded: "And God said to him, 'Your name is Jacob; no longer shall your name be called Jacob, but Israel shall be your name.' So his name was called Israel. And God said to him, 'I am God Almighty: be fruitful and multiply; a nation and a company of nations shall come from you, and kings shall spring from you.'"

I believe what Gabriel is attempting to communicate is that Mary's baby will be the real leader of God's chosen people, regardless of the revolutions and evolutions that they experience. The vast majority of them may deny Him as Savior and Lord, but that does not change God's decree. Praise God, you and I as Gentiles may know spiritually what it means to be of "the house of Jacob for ever!"

Thus, the Babe of Bethlehem always will have dominion over the house of Israel.

*There will no end to His kingdom.*

We simply take this statement at face value. The words "Everlasting Father" found in Isaiah 9:6 help us to understand this truth. When I say "simply," this is obviously exaggerated. How can you and I possibly understand a rule which has no ending to it? Nevertheless, that is what Gabriel places before us for our acceptance and reverence. As Christians our hope of life beyond the grave is built upon it because He has powers beyond any life or death cycle found on this earth.

This measurement is such a convenient and expedient tool for our vaporous existence. Mary's baby breaks that barrier. When the clock strikes twelve midnight, He will refuse to be declared null and void. When the hourglass has released all of its grains of sand into the lower part, the termination of His rule will be no closer than it was centuries ago. When the sun dances in the heavens at high noon, his kingdom will continue to move toward a limitless number of high noons.

Hallelujah, you and I serve One not held captive by the disappointment, disease, despair, and death afflicting mankind since the dawn of history!

4.

With the evidence so overwhelming in describing Mary's Son as the Christ, why hasn't the bulk of mankind said "yes" to Him?

It seems such an easy thing for us at this moment, doesn't it? Surely the proof is there. The rejection seems not only unintelligent but bordering on the asinine. Just now it is hard to believe that millions have never received Him. It seems such a free and right response. The depiction Gabriel gives us is more than a hundred generations old.

Perhaps we have had our answer all along. To accept Mary's Son is to become a new being. To ask Him to come into our hearts and minds assumes needful changes internally and externally will take place. We are afraid. We want to set the conditions and have our own way; we want Him to fit into our plans or stay away.

Advent says we are not only to describe the baby; we are to devote and dedicate ourselves to Him. In the second chapter of Luke an angel says to the shepherds: "for to you is born this day in the city of David a Savior, who is Christ the Lord" (2:11). The crux of the whole matter of Advent and Christmas rests upon whether you and I can proclaim, "He is *my* Savior, who is *my* Christ the Lord."

# ❋YOU HAVE TO BE KIDDING❋

### 1.

TODAY'S MOOD generally would call the Virgin Birth (conception) of Christ either irrelevant or unbelievable.

I suspect a large—very large—sector of society would react much like the title of the sermon, "You have to be kidding!" The reason for that is simple: we live in a secularized society. Those who watch carefully the movements in American life point to the signs. It seems this happened to us as long ago as the 1950s. Perhaps the best indicator is the way we treat Sundays. In most—if not all—of our large cities and metropolitan areas it is very difficult to tell Sunday from Monday or Saturday. This is not a revolt against the straitlaced Sundays of many years ago; our country went through that quite some time ago. It is a feeling apparently backed with steely rationale that the Judeo-Christian Faith just isn't that important. Of course, there are other indicators.

An even more provocative tenor of the times was and is a liberal theology whose reaction is about the same but distinguished by a "brotherhood of man" stance supported by lengthy arguments. As I make that statement, there are those who would label me as an alarmist and fuddyduddy, overreacting and concerned with mere trifles. Their case actually is built upon a very simple declaration: Let's get serious about living the Faith and stop believing the Virgin Birth has any real relevance to the Gospel. The trouble with that is what we believe shows the way we live out our Faith. To be sure there are those who pound pulpits and make emotional appeals that remind one more of a hate campaign against those who disagree with them. Often they are the ones who tell us either believe in the Virgin Birth pronto or you will burn in hell tomorrow. That may very well be true but—thank God—such radicals do not have the judgmental powers to send us to that awful location; that's reserved for God to decide!

Here and now what do you and I think or believe about His birth?

Maybe your first reaction is that you would not like to do such serious thinking at this hour. If that is your response, I trust—yes, hope and pray—that would not remain. Our day calls us to be studious and conscientious in the living of our Faith.

Please don't underrate your capacity for coming to grips with doctrines of the Faith. Surely you have heard of the "priesthood of all believers." Surely you know *The Book of Discipline* of our denomination lifts up the following: "general ministry of all Christians in Christ's name and spirit is both a gift and a task."

### 2.

Join me as we look at key words from the Scripture: "And the angel said to her, 'The Holy Spirit will come upon you, and the power of the Most High will overshadow you; therefore the child to be born will be called holy, the Son of God. And behold, your kinswoman Elizabeth in her old age has also conceived a son; and this is the sixth month with her who was called barren. For with God nothing will be impossible'" (Luke 1:35–37).

My real objection to those who do not believe in Christ's Virgin Birth (conception) is found in that last line: "For with God nothing will be impossible."

If all things are possible with God, then what is His nature like?

### 3.

*In the first place is God's loving, complete care.*

Jesus captures this aspect of God's nature in Matthew 10:29–30: "Are not two sparrows sold for a penny? And not one of them will fall to the ground without your Father's will. But even the hairs of your head are numbered." Surely the Virgin Birth (conception) of His Son is not beyond His providence or loving, complete care! Sparrows falling to the ground do not escape Him. The number of hairs on our heads are known. If the Christ understands Him in this way, surely it behooves us to do the same.

Have you ever thought about the security this provides? We are not subject to fate or the whims of an uncaring God.

To get the full impact of His providence, we ought to lay out before us a large table with replicas of everything and everyone in detail in a small town. Then we should tell ourselves how incomplete this really is because after all we haven't nor can we number the hairs on the heads of persons. Then we should just admit that there is really an infinite number of things we do not and cannot know even on such a reduced scale. Finally, to further illustrate what God's care is like we ought to acknowledge that we are attempting to reproduce an infinitesimal portion of His universe . . . and we can't even do that, let alone show any complete care of it! Either God is God and cares for His creation in its totality or you and I are subject to fatalistic, futile, and forlorn forces. Such is all of mankind's predicament. It is through the Old Testament generally and the Christ with His Apostles specifically that we Christians know and experience a care having no bounds, permeated with love.

In the last century there lived a gifted Presbyterian minister by the name of Maltbie Davenport Babcock. He was an outstanding person that included being an athlete, a renowned college preacher, and eventually pastor of the famed Brick Church in New York City. Yet, I doubt there is more than a handful of persons—including Presbyterians—who remember him with one exception. He wrote the hymn "This Is My Father's World." Listen to the third stanza:

> This is my Father's world,
> O let me ne'er forget
> That though the wrong seems oft so strong,
> God is the ruler yet.
> This is my Father's world:
> Why should my heart be sad?
> The Lord is King: let the heavens ring!
> God reigns: let the earth be glad!

Do you really believe the God of which we are speaking—indeed the God we worship—is incapable of bringing His Son to the world by the Virgin Birth (conception)?

*In the second place we discover God's loving, complete power.*

The Apostle Paul writes in Romans 1:20, "Ever since the creation of the world his invisible nature, namely his eternal power and deity, has been clearly received in the things that have been made." Paul's expressive statement Christians know to be the truth. It may take time, energy, and even hardship to uncover it. To deny and suppress it is to cause a deformed, sluggish, and, at best, mediocre experience with Christ. We do not serve and worship a second-rate God. Rome needed Jupiter, Apollo, Mars, and others. Greece needed Zeus, Phoebus, Ares, and others. Christians don't need them and never have. Pagan gods sooner or later become ludicrous; they also show themselves in time to be an abomination.

What power do you and I have? It is an age of "doing your own thing." Sometimes this is practiced in a semi-pagan frenzy to let those around us know we have power. There are fabulously successful cults that tell us we can have anything we want because we have limitless power. Take a good look at the bookstalls and magazine racks. In one way or another most seem to build up our egos by communicating to us how much we can attain . . . if we use the "right" methods and pay for them. The Christian knows what power he or she has is from God and no other source. However, human nature does not change very much and most—I fear—actually are duped into believing everything can be manipulated for their benefit; some faraway God or weak grandfatherly-type deity could not care less. The terror of much of today's orientation to life is the shocking—yes, sacrilegious, even blasphemous—way precious human beings act and react as though they are ends within themselves, separate and independent of God.

The vicious monsters of the world have invariably been those inebriated by their own sense of power. God has had little meaning for them, except as a Being who recognized their greatness and would not miss an opportunity to allow the world to be blessed (damned) by their gifts. While that may sound as though it applies only to a handful, such mental illness and perverseness pointing to a continuous spiritual famine is quite prevalent. In the preoccupation with self and instantaneous gratifications, the power of God could actually be called an impertinence.

"Holy, holy, holy! Lord God almighty" is one explicit way we Christians proclaim to the world God's power that is loving and complete. Would or could such a god be bound by biological laws He shaped initially? Can we even seriously suggest that He did not have the necessary power to bring His Son to the world by the Virgin Birth (conception)?

What next can we identify about His nature?

*In the third place is His loving, complete knowledge.*

For some this is a difficult avenue of thought because it brings into play the dynamics of the past, present, and future in a unique way. The human mind cannot grasp such unbounded knowing. We say to ourselves, "Well, if God already knows everything that has, is, and will happen, we are nothing more than puppets." Not so, we just do not understand infinite knowledge.

Recall for a moment when God made you aware of something that happened—perhaps long ago—and you are now able to make sense out of it. Haven't we all had such experiences? At the time there was neither rhyme nor reason to the event(s). Weeks, months, or years later we discover the "why" and troublesome, recalcitrant parts fall into their places. Can this be anything other than God's knowledge—loving and complete—at work? For you and me to have all of the pieces in place and know exactly "who, where, when, why, what, and how" assumes the level of God or, at least, aspirations in that direction. You and I are created in the image of God and a little lower than the angels; that puts limits on us, regardless of how flatteringly we may interpret it.

Saint Paul in the way of love sings in humble adoration: "For now we see in a mirror dimly, but then face to face. Now I know in part; then I shall understand fully, even as I have been fully understood" (1 Corinthians 13:12). He saw our dilemma so clearly! At best we see only partially. Someday the knowledge of God will be revealed to us and we too shall have access to the fullness of God's knowledge. Note that Paul does not "beat his head against a brick wall," so to speak. He sings out with praises for and to the God who was, is, and shall know all about him and everyone else as well. He yields to his inferior capacity and looks joyously forward to the day God will share that which is reserved for eternity.

Can we in our right minds say God did not know the particulars of our Lord's birth in advance? Furthermore, can we doubt Him knowing that humanity—even those who call His Son Savior—would question the Virgin Birth (conception) of Jesus? Yes, and doesn't He watch even now our being driven to the basics of His nature in order to be convinced the Virgin Birth (conception) was very much in His thinking countless years ago?

*In the fourth place we come to terms with His loving, complete presence.*

Try to think of some place God is not. Ah yes, the Russian cosmo-naut in his famous words said he found no indication of God in outer space. If God is spirit as it says in John 4:24 ("God is spirit, and those who worship him must worship in spirit and truth"), then why would he be in recognizable form to a communist trained to think and feel strictly in materialistic, secular terms? The opening lines of Genesis record: "In the beginning God created the heavens and the earth. The earth was without form and void, and darkness was upon the face of the deep; and the spirit of God was moving over the face of the waters" (Genesis 1:1–2). Just a glimpse of this aspect of His nature should be proof enough that our puny minds and limited visions are able only to recognize His omnipresence and not fathom it.

With the "eyes of faith" Saint Paul speaks in the Second Letter of Corinthians: "But thanks be to God, who in Christ always leads us in triumph, and through us spreads the fragrance of the knowledge of him everywhere" (2:14). Isn't that a sublime truth! We—you and I—are made partners with God in allowing the world to smell the scents of Jesus the Christ. It is not by our will but through His will. Just a verse later Paul says, "For we are the aroma of Christ to God among those who are being saved and among those who are perishing" (2:15). We are not to overextend ourselves by sentimentalizing, "He only has our hands and our feet to spread His message." God always has other means for His will to be done, but it so happens He selects you and me to do it.

Is there any possibility God, Who moves in and through all of His creation, could not have brought His Son to earth by the Virgin Birth (conception)? It seems to me that question borders on being nothing more than academic. The whole creation shouts, "And the Word became flesh and dwelt among us, full of grace and truth; we have beheld his glory, glory as of the only Son from the Father" (John 1:14). Surely, the words "Joseph, son of David, do not fear to take Mary your wife, for that which is conceived in her is of the Holy Spirit" (Matthew 1:20) are gloriously true!

### 4.

Language is a very significant force in religion.

The Hebrews recognized this at the dawning of their Faith. The name of God was so sacred it was not even spoken. A person's name was far more than just a handle to summon him or her; its meaning was in depth.

As we speak about God, language is crucial. To approach Him as a Being with loving and complete care, power, knowledge, and presence spells out an elementary and eternal relationship. In defining Him we define ourselves; that's what the Word of God does from cover to cover.

Decisive to our time is regaining our belief in the nature of God. Do you and I "have no other gods before Him" and "love Him with our whole heart, soul, and mind?" If the answer is an unconditional "yes," the Virgin Birth (conception) of Jesus becomes a beautiful, blessed story of the way God chose to bring His Son into the world.

## ❋A FAMILIAR TEXT REVISITED❋

### 1.

WHAT HAS BEEN the most used text for a Christmas sermon in the twentieth century?

Some seminary professors and, I suspect, a very large number of regular worship attenders would tell us it is Luke 2:7. The words read: "And she gave birth to her first-born son and wrapped him in swaddling cloths, and laid him in a manger, because there was no place for them in the inn." The emphasis invariably falls on there being "no room or place in the inn." The theme is nearly always the same: the world didn't and doesn't have any decent place for Him. I suppose none of us would quarrel with the validity of that.

It is interesting how preachers and laity alike have fixed their attention on a single verse. It isn't that the verse is unimportant. As previously mentioned, quite the contrary is true. The problem comes at the point of sentimentalizing. We romantically rock ourselves to sleep in the glitter and glow of lights and tinsel in a blissful but beguiling lethargy. "There's no room in the inn" and that's nice and even Christmasy. There's not supposed to be any room in the inn!

Now that I have taken time to be lightly critical and mildly irreligious, I want to make a case for the symbolism the verse projects.

Let me start by asking, "Is there a place for Him in our hearts?" Remember the little verses that go: "Come into my heart, Lord Jesus, Come in today, Come in to stay, Come into my heart, Lord Jesus?" That's more than just a children's song isn't it? Yes, it is infinitely more than cute little ones with angelic faces and innocent voices lifting lyrics to God! It's a universal plea. Yes, at one time or another I suppose all of us who profess His name have sung it . . . perhaps in silence.

Today can you and I say without hesitation that we have received Him? Oh, I don't mean merely as an historical figure. There are few persons who would say He never lived. Every textbook on religion of which I am aware gives a place to Jesus as having been born, lived, and died in much the same way the Bible presents it. I also don't mean merely mental assent to Him as the founder of our religion. We do as much in a denominational sense for Wesley, Calvin, Luther, Campbell, and others.

Now, come aboard as we explore new possibilities and avenues.

### 2.

What new meaning can be gotten from revisiting a familiar text? How shall we go about mining new precious stones and plumbing uncharted depths? Well, let's do some respectful dreaming and positive speculating by making three inquiries.

### 3.

*The first inquiry is, "Why was there no room for them?"*

Surely there would be a decent, respectable place for a young woman to give birth to a child. How thoughtless could the guests be? Weren't there people around who could have pressured the manager into finding a nice room for them? If others in the motel had known, surely they would have given up their pleasant and comfortable surroundings. Didn't the holy family—Joseph, Mary, and Jesus—deserve color TV, shower and bath facilities with hot and cold water, free coffee, clean linens, access to a pool, and a scenic view? Were there other women on the verge of bringing a child into the world at the same motel? That's very unlikely. Well, what happened to the hospitality at the Bethlehem Holiday Inn? I can't imagine such a thing happening today, can you?

Bethlehem literally means "house of bread." It was a small city of narrow streets and flat-roofed stone houses. It was a prosperous settlement. It was the "city of David" because the king was born there. The inns in those days had hillside caves for their stables with low stone mangers lined with warm straw. Very likely this was the setting for our Lord's birth. But the Messiah was supposed to be born in Bethlehem! Didn't everyone around there know that? Micah 5:2 says, "But you, O Bethlehem Ephrathah, who are little to be among the clans of Judah, from you shall come forth from me one who is to be ruler in Israel whose origin is from of old, from ancient days." Matthew 2:5–6 and John 7:42 substantiate this Scripture. Didn't they know the Messiah was to be born in their city? Maybe there were just too many out-of-town guests, and Messiah or no Messiah, there just wasn't a room available. Maybe Joseph didn't have a credit card and would have been a poor risk anyway. The carpenter's union didn't guarantee very much in those days.

You would have thought some wealthy person who knew the situation would have come along and offered the manager a tidy tip so that a really bad situation could have been improved, regardless of the means. It seems very reasonable that could have been done. In the long run everyone would have understood. The Son of God was coming into the world and He didn't have a decent place to be born. Surely mankind could cooperate a little bit. To ignore the predicament and plight in which Mary and Joseph—plus Jesus—found themselves couldn't be considered humanitarian. The Jewish people had had ingrained for centuries a sense of brotherhood, which certainly meant service to the needy. Joseph was from the house of David, so he wasn't just any Jew. Surely some prominent Jew of means could bail out this couple in distress about to have their first child. In the name of human kindness someone of influence should have stepped forth and relieved their embarrassment. The very idea! God's Son born in a cattle trough! Well, there's more respectful dreaming and positive speculating to be done.

*The second inquiry is, "If you had been an innkeeper, would you have made room for them?"*

"Boy, I sure would like to do something for that young couple, but I really can't." That's a businesslike, humanitarian point of view, isn't it? Yes, and isn't that just about what most of us would do? Here is the young woman with labor pains already started and her husband in a dither as to what he is going to do with someone so helpless. He's probably wondering if he will have to aid her in some open area where the child's life could be at stake. I still remember vividly taking a young woman across town with the gas gauge showing empty, running two stoplights, and wondering in a cold sweat if I would be called upon some place en route to the hospital to help deliver one of our four daughters. I didn't remember either Ball State University or Christian Theological Seminary preparing me for such an awesome task. I still speculate if we had run out of gas or been in an accident if there would have been those who would liked to have helped but really couldn't.

Well, what responsibility would you have had to them as an innkeeper? Would you have known them and immediately been sympathetic? That's not very likely. Joseph and Mary had just traveled from Nazareth to Bethlehem, a distance of eighty-five miles to meet the enrollment requirement of Caesar Augustus. The small city must have been overcrowded with persons trying to meet the Roman Emperor's mandate. You are harried and ready for your shift to be over. Indeed, why can't the next person handle this problem that Mary and Joseph pose? After all, a regular customer needs attention. The maid forgot to leave the proper number of towels and washcloths. And yes, that new overseer for the olive groves has to have an extra pillow and another bottle of fine wine; he will become a permanent resident soon. He and his family will be real assets. The young lady in distress will probably have a cute little tyke, and then she with her older husband can go back to Nazareth.

Let's suppose as you go about your duties you become suspicious about this couple's soon-to-be-born baby. You have a feeling something everlastingly thrilling is about to happen. Maybe you even probe the possibility of him being the long-awaited Messiah. In fact your body is tingling with something you can't explain. Then it dawns on you when you are under pressure and eat too rapidly, especially those spicy foods, your gallbladder acts up and makes you ill all over. About the time the Liar of liars says, "That's it! It's that pesky old thing and why didn't I have it taken out before Caesar brought all these people to be enrolled?"

A final time there is some respectful dreaming and positive speculating to be done.

*The third inquiry is, "Could this part of the story have turned out differently?"*
God could have decreed that the best accommodations in Bethlehem would be for the birth of His Son. If He is all-powerful, this is no big deal. I doubt there is a steadfast Christian that believes otherwise. A place could have been prepared in advance with all the fanfare that goes with the birth of a king. The royalty could have been summoned from all over the world to ooh and aah over Mary's baby. It could have been a celebration no one would ever forget. All rulers would have gladly paid their expenses to and from Bethlehem. Think what a colorful event it could have been! Parades of people and animals stopping traffic. It could have been far in advance of the Lindbergh and

MacArthur receptions in New York City. God could have made little Bethlehem the "Big Apple." Well, it didn't happen that way, did it? I suppose there are those who would maintain if it had, His birth would really have carried more authenticity with it. It was only later that some understood what Jesus meant when He said, "My kingship is not of this world . . ." (John 18:36).

Why didn't God just simply ignore Old Testament prophecy and say to the Jews, "I have chosen to bring my Son into the world in a spectacular way," and place Jesus a full-grown man of thirty years of age in the Holy Land? That would have saved a lot of discussion, debate, and dallying about the Virgin Birth and the silences of His early years. Doesn't it seem to you that would be a much more smooth way of handling the entry of Jesus on planet Earth? I suspect you and I would have done it that way "presto." He is here and ready to begin His ministry. That would have even beat the quickness with which some Methodist appointments are made! Think of all the doubts that would not have come up and the struggles that would not have had to be encountered.

Perhaps God should have been more democratic. He could have brought this business of Jesus' appearance to a vote before the peoples of the world, especially those who already had such rights. Please raise your hands or cast your ballots for or against the coming of the Savior. Would there have been politicking, pro and con? I think so. Some would have said, "Sure, we want and need him." Others would have said, "But we already have the Greek philosophers, the Old Testament, and numerous sages in other areas of the world." Still others would have discreetly asked, "Well, what kind of a leader will he be? Can we control him or will he be his own man?" Under such circumstances how would you have reacted?

Yes, and the beat goes on as to how it could have happened.

4.

How will your day turn out?

Will you feel good about there being "no room in the inn" because that's the way it has always been? There is such a thing as frozen, death-like orthodoxy which only condones the comfortable, the compromising, and the complimentary. Some potentially beautiful, radiant personalities have been locked-in by this easy conformity. Santa Claus or football or food or drink have been known to be replacements for Christ . . . and for many that is an easy way out also because that is the way it has always been in their lives.

From time to time you and I desperately need to do some respectful dreaming and positive speculating. Why? For the simple reason we have to be jarred loose from patterns that only tell us what we want to hear in the way we want to hear it.

What is the cutting edge provided by revisiting a familiar text? Is it not to be found at the point of accepting and celebrating the birth of Jesus in a manger as a God-ordained preliminary to His ministry, death, and Resurrection? Aren't you and I—above and beyond any Christmas story—called to minister with Him, die with Him, and arise with Him?

JOHN
XVII

DONALD C. LACY

*1983*

*Our Lord's "high priestly prayer" comes to us in all of its uniqueness, mystery, and hopefulness in the Gospel of John. The chapter is more than a literary classic and a magnificent portion of Holy Scripture. The words glow with the Holy Spirit beautifully at work in our time.* John Seventeen *is not written primarily for the academic whose main concern is theological technicalities with voluminous footnotes. It is written for the pastor and layperson of every church and persuasion who yearn to be absorbed by this chapter and live out its implication. It is my firm conviction that Christ through His prayer calls us to be both evangelical and ecumenical. A divided Church cannot afford the tainted luxury of two camps throwing darts (and worse) at one another. You and I know in the depths of our beings that there is One Gospel just as there is One Savior and Lord of us all. Two of six sermons are presented.*

# CHAPTER 4

# John Seventeen

## ❋I DO NOT PRAY FOR THE WORLD❋

### 1.

THERE IS nothing quite like the closeness of a strong, healthy family unit.

Support and caring are typical of a tightly knit family. Oh, the members may fight among themselves. In fact, they probably do. Just let an outsider try to hurt one of them! They will close ranks and wisdom dictates the interloper had best retreat. Johnny is having trouble at school. Other family members let him know by word and deed they are with him. Sally is having a great time being queen of the junior prom. Other family members share in her success and want others to know they are proud of her.

Some of the finest, most dedicated, and religious persons today are fighting hard for preservation of really strong families. It is a very worthy theme. Yes, it is an essential theme to preserve the Judeo-Christian foundation of morality in our society. There are those who have recognized for several years the slippage in the importance given families. Many that I hear have come to grips with the biblical insistence on the sanctity of marriage and the indispensable nature of a healthy family life. Some of the so-called modern and enlightened foes of the traditional ideals of the family claim cultural lag is a main reason why many have not seen the light. Those who would destroy the preciousness of faithfulness in marriage and respect in a home where family members reside in closeness and concern have their own ax to grind. It's a satanic bit of rationale more deadly than the guillotine and it's spelled "h-e-l-l."

Just what does this have to do with our blessed Lord's priestly prayer? In the closing days of His stay on earth Jesus prays for his family. Oh, we are not speaking of Mary, Joseph, and others in the carpenter's home. Unquestionably, they were important to Him. The way He treated his mother show His loving concern from that viewpoint. We are dealing with a dimension that includes you and me.

In John 17:9 Jesus says to his Father: "I pray for them. I do not pray for the world but for those you gave me, for they belong to you." His followers are his family. They are now—as the Cross looms ever larger—

to be pulled together into a fellowshipping and worshiping covenant. The binding cord was and would be God's love sealed with blood. At the Supper—where His intimates were present—in a portion of Luke 22:20, we read Jesus saying, "This cup is God's new covenant sealed with my blood, which is poured out for you."

### 2.

So, Jesus moves towards solidifying His disciples; in doing so He takes a stance apart from the world. The world or evil is in opposition to God's kingdom. Until the end of the age they must coexist and communicate, but his family must not be contaminated and controlled.

As His family is lovingly cemented together, five realizations filled to the brim with hope speak to all who profess the Christ as Savior and Lord.

### 3.

*First: there is sensation apart from the world.*

The heartfelt expression from a Christian or Christians, "Oh, we are just having a good time in the Lord" is foreign and ridiculous to the world. The pleasures of a sin-drenched and drowning world are not necessary for the Christian. In fact, they only tend to confuse members of Christ's Body. We must not be too narrow, bordering on the self-righteous, and make a list of "don'ts" stretching from here into outer space. Frequently, it is not a matter of something being inherently wrong; it is the method of misusing and abusing it. What is of far greater significance is to experience the Christ-centered sensation God has for us. Saint Paul makes the issue very clear in Galatians 5:22–24, "But the Spirit produces love, joy, peace, patience, kindness, goodness, faithfulness, humility, and self-control. There is no law against such things as these. And those who belong to Christ Jesus have put to death their human nature with all its passions and desires." In short, the Christian just doesn't need the world to be happy, content, and joyous.

A keynote in congregational worship is celebration. The Holy Communion is often called "the Eucharist." This comes from *eucharistia* and simply means "the giving of thanks." There was a time when the long face and serious religion went hand in hand. Praise God we have learned that just isn't necessarily true!

The hymns of Fanny Crosby have been criticized by some for not having polish and depth. However, she captures the essence of our first point in a couple of them. In "Blessed Assurance, Jesus Is Mine," she says:

Perfect submission, all is at rest;
I in my Savior am happy and blest,
Watching and waiting, looking above
Filled with his goodness, lost in his love.

In "Jesus, Keep Me Near the Cross," she says:

Near the cross, a trembling soul,
Love and mercy found me:
There the bright and morning star
Shed its beams around me.

Let's look to another realization.

*Second: there is security apart from the world.*

In the Sermon on the Mount Jesus says "... be concerned above everything else with the Kingdom of God and with what he required of you, and he will provide you with all these other things" (Matt. 6:33). While all of Christ's words are immensely important, these glow as a perpetual beacon to us. It is not that food, clothing, shelter, and other necessities are considered unimportant. It is that they must be seen in a rightful perspective. To be really secure is to be found in exactly what our Lord says. It is the movement away from the world to God that must first saturate our lives. Then the necessities in which both the Christian and world share are provided in just the proper amounts. To get this one guideline implanted and operative in each of us promises spiritual greatness.

Do you and I experience the security Christians have known to a greater or lesser extent since the glorious days our Lord walked and taught among His people? Are we still hungry and thirsty first of all for what this world has to offer? Is our religion what one person labeled "a tacked-on Christ"? Have we put our lives in order with neatness in an absorption with what the world considers important and then said almost as an afterthought, "You are blessing everything we are doing, aren't you Lord?" Is our motivation for worship to hear a preacher give his churchly approval to a priority list in our lives resembling a mild but nonetheless strangling hedonism?

The prodigal son traveled to a far country and became destitute; then he returned home. When he returned not only did his father welcome him, he provided him with food and drink. He had to return to the father's house before such needs could be properly met.

Join me as we learn from the next realization.

*Third: there is self-fulfillment apart from the world.*

There is a point of view that maintains, "How can I be a sinner unless I go out and sin?" The answer to that is quite simple. We are already sinners by the fact that without exception we are all tainted by original sin. To show oneself as a sinner takes no effort. It was written upon us with permanent ink by our first parents. So, immersion or even participation in the ways of evil or the world doesn't give one credentials to announce one now is in better position to grow spiritually. Quite the contrary may be true. One may be able to improve upon sinning and show others new roads to hell. Of course, the Lamb of God is able to cleanse us, but let us not strain His mercies! Matthew 8:12 speaks a hard but necessary word from the Lord: "But those who should be in the Kingdom will be thrown out into the darkness, where they will cry and gnash their teeth."

In Paul's Second Letter to the Corinthians, he tells his readers: "It is God himself who makes us, together with you, sure of our life in union with Christ; it is God himself who has set us apart" (1:21). In the first century church as today this has spiritual meaning, especially in Koinonia or Communion on equal terms with those whose lives are Christ-centered. Talk about self-fulfillment! The natural results of such living in a wider sense come to us from 1 Peter: "Your conduct among the heathen should be so good that when they accuse you of being evildoers, they will have to recognize your good deeds and so praise God on the Day of his coming" (2:12).

When speaking of the promise of the Holy Spirit, our blessed Lord says to His followers: "He is the spirit, who reveals the truth about God. The world cannot receive him, because it cannot see him or know him. But you know him, because he remains with you and is in you" (John 14:17).

Let's pursue the matter by exploring a further realization.

*Fourth: there is serenity apart from the world.*

In the fourteenth chapter and twenty-seventh verse of the Gospel of John, the Master says: "Peace is what I leave with you; it is my own peace that I give you. I do not give it as the world does. Do not be worried and upset; do not be afraid." That's as clear as the azure skies after a hurricane. It just doesn't leave any room for gloom. Within the faith the highest form of serenity that man can experience is present. As is too often the case, words can't quite explain and picture this wondrous promise that

Christians through the ages have found to be true. When hell seems to be boiling over and the devil is gushing with hateful vindictiveness, there is the calmness and patience Christians evidence.

There is much talk in our day about various forms of mysticism and meditation—and I might hasten to add, enormous amounts of money being spent on them. Transcendental meditation is perhaps the best known. It promotes and provides some documentation that its program gives increased learning ability, broader comprehension and improved ability to focus attention, relief from insomnia, reduced use of alcohol and cigarettes, improved relations with coworkers, and increased job satisfaction. Well, who doesn't want all of that! It—like all the others—runs the dangerous course of becoming an end within itself, devoid of salvation and the grace of the living God.

There is a final realization Christ gave to His followers during those few remaining days of His life as he was pulling them together into a closely knit fellowship and worshiping community.

*Fifth: there is servanthood apart from the world.*
Saint Paul in Galatians 6:10 says, "So then, as often as we have the chance, we should do good to everyone, and especially to those who belong to our family in the faith." We tend to overlook the latter part of the Apostle's words. There is something very precious—even with an eternal ring about it—that you and I are Christians in the United Methodist tradition. We are to serve and be served. There seems to be an exclusiveness about all of this and for me this is ingrained in the truth of the matter. Our problem may be that we feel to exclude others is always bad. If we believe that, it seems to me we are moving in the opposite direction of what our Lord intends. There is an obligation to serve within the Faith, separated from the world. Did Jesus favor His followers? Of course He did, in the highest sense possible. We get a glorious glimpse into this relationship in John 15:16 when He tells his disciples, "You did not choose me; I chose you . . ." Further, in the same chapter He says, "If you belonged to the world, then the world would love you as its own. But I chose you from this world, and you do not belong to it; that is why the world hates you" (15:19).

Christians have always appeared to have the precarious predicament of grouping themselves denominationally, by local churches, and even within local churches in ways that have tended to fragment the Faith. We know this has reached scandalous proportions on some occasions. May God forgive us! Saint Paul reminds us, "There is one body and one hope to which God has called you" (Eph. 4:4). In 1 Corinthians 12:12 the Apostle says, "Christ is like a single body, which has many parts; it is still one body, even though it is made up of different parts." He further elaborates these parts are all dependent on one another to make a complete body; this entails service "within." He says nothing about competition.

4.

Isn't our choice to be either in our Lord's family or out of it?

In the closing, climactic days of His ministry, Jesus most certainly was pressuring with love His disciples into a group that found him unequivocable to be Savior and Lord. Fence sitters almost had to fall one way or the other. They could not give allegiance to both the world and His kingdom. Isn't He pushing you and me for a decision on the matter during Lent? If we are clearly with Him, we are called to aid in bringing others to that place in their lives. If we are not sure or clearly with the world, we are potentially in the worst possible state; I mean, of course, there is the terrible prospect of death without the saving grace of God.

From time to time our blessed Lord pressures us. While we may react negatively to such a thought and feeling, we must remember we are confronting Him who alone ultimately controls our destinies. To resist His pressure is perilous to say the least.

Have you drawn the lines that you might stand with others in Christ? You can't have both Him and the world. Either He is or He isn't your Savior and Lord.

# ✻RIGHTEOUS FATHER! THE WORLD✻ DOES NOT KNOW YOU . . .

1.

"I DON'T KNOW you" can be used with different shades of meaning.

A mother may say it to an eleven-year-old son. He arrives at Sunday School ten minutes late. He is wearing his favorite shirt. The only problem is that he just finished fishing it out of the weekly wash. He has the latest comic in hand; it has nothing to do with the teacher's lesson. His mother drops her head and in pain mutters, "I don't know you."

A woman walking to work may say it to a man. She has begun to feel raindrops. A car stops and a man offers her a ride to the office. The offer is very attractive because she didn't bring her raincoat or umbrella. She pauses, sees if she recognizes him, and decides she can't. She says, "I don't know you" and walks a little more hurriedly.

A man may say it to a high school sweetheart. They meet at a gala wedding reception by coincidence twenty years after graduating from high school. He is in love with his wife but remembers other times when he was also romantically happy. The situation is awkward as she greets him by his nickname. He looks at her in disbelief after all those years. Then he says the only thing that seems to make sense at the moment: "I don't know you."

A lady mentally disturbed may say it to a dear friend. The friend drops by for some tea and conversation. Cordiality is strictly a one-way street. After a few minutes of sharing good and pleasant memories, the friend seats herself in a bit of amazement. The lady stares at her with a glassy look. Then she says, "I don't know you."

While all of these incidents are important and not necessarily unrelated to our major thrust, let's move to a thought both highly challenging and saddening.

Many do not know God through Christ.

Our Lord tells us in the priestly prayer: "Righteous Father! The world does not know you, but I know you, and these know that you sent me" (John 17:25). Your immediate question might be, "Well, how many are we assuming—one million, ten million, a hundred million?" The only answer I would give to such an inquiry is found in the Sermon on the Mount: "But the gate to life is narrow and the way that leads to it is hard, and there are few people who find it" (Matt. 7:14).

The real or authentic Church is the Body of Christ. The world is not a part of this worshiping fellowship. Yes, there is a separation line—known ultimately only to God—between the world and Christians.

## 2.

Not knowing God through the Christ calls attention to a series of seven situations. Those not knowing Him are caught in the following perplexities.

## 3.

*Being a Christian is hearsay and not firsthand information is the first.*

"Hearsay evidence" is based not on a witness's personal knowledge but on matters told him by another. While we might think of times this would be reliable, it always remains secondhand. We can also think of times when reliability isn't present by applying large doses of imagination! Most of us have played the game of sitting in a line, whispering a story to the next person. The results are humorously similar; the story undergoes quite a change. So, it is true with those perplexed by knowing our Lord by rumor; they are removed from the vitality of the Faith or the seal of Jesus the Christ.

In the early years of the Church, Peter and John were brought before the Jewish high priest and the religious ruling elite to defend their actions. Acts 4:20 records them as saying, "For we cannot stop speaking of what we ourselves have seen and heard." Both had been with Jesus in a physical and historical sense. Now He was with them through the Holy Spirit. To be sure, you and I cannot be as fortunate as Peter and John. Yet, we do not have to depend on hearsay to know Him spiritually. The Apostle John makes this abundantly clear in his First Letter: "What we have seen and heard we announce to you also, so that you will join with us in the fellowship that we have with the Father and with his Son Jesus Christ" (1:3).

*Being a Christian is academic and not a basic experience is the second.*

I know, and so do you, those who have probed the Bible in detail and can quote related sources with expertise; yet, they know virtually nothing about the saving power and essential lordship of the Christ. While I believe in the value of studying comparative religions, to lecture by the hour on the Bible, the Koran, and other sacred writings may simply be an intellectual exercise bearing little resemblance to the deeply personal Christ. This is not always true. We have all known intellectuals in our Faith who appreciated other religions and were great Christians. The late C. S. Lewis is an inspiring example. He moved from atheism to a glorious stalwart of the Faith. Francis A. Schaeffer is another thoroughly committed intellectual kneeling before his Master. He closes his book *How Should We Then Live* with those words: "This book is written in the hope that this generation may turn from that greatest of wickedness, the placing of any created thing in the place of the Creator, and that this generation may get its feet out of the paths of death and may live."

"Academic" may carry the meaning of a significant set of facts or truth remaining at surface level. To memorize the Ten Commandments does not mean one keeps them. To read carefully the Sermon on the Mount does not mean one believes what is being read. Yes, it is possible to be a regular churchgoer and not know the Lord of the Church! While perfect attendance at Sunday School may mean an elementary encounter with the Christ, it may also mean nothing more than time spent relating to others socially.

*Being a Christian is fictional and not autobiographical fact is the third.*

How many times have you read something and reacted, "Oh, I wish that were true!" Great novels have a way of doing that to us, don't they? We are led into a wonderland where we wished many of the things were happening to us. If we find a novel that really meets our emotional needs, we can become the character(s) or seemingly so. Then sooner or later we come back to reality and know the make-believe realm we had entered was just that: make-believe. Movies, plays, and many other arts have the same effect on us. They may all be marvelous entertainment. Yet, we are always on the outside looking in. How like those who do not know God through Christ!

We can dream about our faith and good works, but of what real value are they in a fictionalized form? We can build gorgeous castles of righteousness in the air only to discover they evaporate upon our awakening. What counts and ultimately the only thing that counts is whether or not we can be called His disciples by Him at all times and in all places.

*Being a Christian is valueless and not a prized relationship is the fourth.*

Wisdom, styles of living, and codes of ethics are sought elsewhere. There is much to be said for the Greek philosophers Socrates, Plato, and Aristotle. However, they were and are not the Christ. Confucius was a very bright fellow. He was not the Christ. Buddha was enlightened. He was not the Christ. Machiavelli was a shrewd operator. He was not the Christ. The Frenchmen, Rousseau and Voltaire, were gifted. They were not the Christ. Karl Marx was not the Christ. John Dewey was not the Christ. The list could get quite long, couldn't it?

The world searches feverishly and in desperation for answers as it discounts the lowly Galilean at each and every point. A relationship with Him is not considered of worth. It is often held up to ridicule, pictured as being regressive, and bluntly rejected. Who wants to mess around with a Jewish fellow who says, "Go and sell all you have and give the money to the poor, and you will have riches in heaven; then come and follow me?" (Mark 10:21). In the eyes of the world that just can't be much of a relationship!

*Being a Christian is expedient and not a lifelong love affair is the fifth.*

There are those who will survey their various worlds of movement and decide it will pay off to become a Christian. Some will assess their occupational status. Others will see the advantage from a professional standpoint. Others will note the business possibilities. Still others will see the social potential. Being a Christian is just simply the best thing to be until something better comes along. If you were to suspect and even suggest to them their motives, they might become furious. In my opinion, however, it is better to be furious now and confront one's real state than to face the just God saying, "I never knew you. Get away from me, you wicked people!" (Matt. 7:23).

Some of you about now may be reacting, "But, preacher, you are cruel and seem to be judging." My response is, "There are those who will use anything and anyone to get what they want and that includes the Christian Faith." In addition I find Matthew 12:33 speaks a timely word: "To have good fruit you must have a healthy tree; if you have a poor tree, you will have bad fruit. A tree is known by the kind of fruit it bears." Being a Christian is for a lifetime; the Shepherd knows and loves His own during all the highs, lows, and in-betweens.

*Being a Christian is cultural and not eternally valid is the sixth.*

Some have said the most detrimental act against the Faith was that delivered by the Roman Emperor Constantine in the fourth century. He made Christianity the official religion of the empire! Up until that time Christians had lived in danger of mob violence. In fact, the initial several decades of the Faith were times of persistent and consistent persecution. Some say Constantine acted on sheer political shrewdness; he couldn't beat them, so he joined them. At any rate, Christians almost overnight received status. Who can be sure whether or not this was good for the Faith? We do know from then until this very hour the Faith is entwined in the culture of our country and most others. The serious issue at hand is that voiced with vehemence by the great Danish theologian, Kierkegaard; he said when the Faith is thoroughly accommodated to the culture, Christianity ceases to exist.

You and I during Lent are called to ponder whether we have allowed the culture of the times or an era dictate the message of the Christ or if the message of the Christ speaks to a culture with the purity and integrity it must have to be eternally valid. We cannot hurry such an exploration. The subtleties are staggering!

*Being a Christian is childish and not childlike teachability is the seventh.*

A funny thing happens to some people; they think they outgrow the Faith. This takes many forms of expression. A man says, "Well, I was forced to go to Sunday School until I was sixteen years old. Just try to get me in church now!" His failure to acknowledge his continuing and ever present spiritual needs of course makes him the "childish" one. Sometimes, too, let's admit a church will fail to provide opportunities for further growth. It can get so hidebound that whatever spiritual creativity is at work suffocates. The very possibility of growth in the ways of our blessed Lord assumes enough openness for His teaching to be given a chance.

Communism has poked fun at those coming before the Christ with hands open and arms outstretched to receive His Word. Karl Marx said that religion is the opiate of the people. Perhaps nothing in modern times has been so close in appearance to the Antichrist. It sneers in derision and growls in anger at Matthew 18:2–4:

> So Jesus called a child, had him stand in front of them, and said, "I assure you that unless you change and become like children, you will never enter the Kingdom of heaven. The greatest in the Kingdom of heaven is the one who humbles himself and becomes like this child."

4.

A couple of little true and false quizzes may be the most beneficial inventory you can take during Lent.

Is being a Christian for you hearsay, academic, fictional, valueless, expedient, cultural, or childish? I hope your score is very low. Only you, of course, can provide the answers.

Is being a Christian firsthand information, a basic experience, autobiographical fact, a prized relationship, a lifelong love affair, eternally valid, or childlike? I hope your score is very high. Again only you can provide the answers.

The Lenten season says first and foremost all other things fall a far distant second to knowing the crucified and resurrected Christ.

In Matthew 13:44 our Lord says: "The Kingdom of heaven is like this. A man happens to find a treasure hidden in a field. He covers it up again, and is so happy that he goes and sells everything he has, and then goes back and buys that field."

The world would not do such a thing or if it did, it would attempt to parlay the investment into power that leads to a hellish ending.

**Healing Echoes:**

**Values for Christian Unity**

DONALD CHARLES LACY

**SERMONS FOR THE LAST THIRD
OF THE PENTECOST SEASON**

(SUNDAYS IN ORDINARY TIME)

*SERIES A FIRST LESSON TEXTS FROM
THE COMMON (CONSENSUS) LECTIONARY*

*1986*

*The universal Church of which we are a part did not just come on the scene nearly 2,000 years ago. Indeed, some would even date all-important happenings from the time of their denominational founders who may have lived centuries after Peter and Paul! It is likewise true that salvation history is much older than when the historical Jesus walked, talked, and ministered among precious human beings. To say, in a sense, He emerged out of a rich Judaism is simply to acknowledge what careful study shows us. Dare we overlook the fact, for example, He quotes Deuteronomy 6:4 when asked about the Great Commandment? Jesus and the Apostles did not come into, and minister in, a vacuum. The way was prepared and it began as far back, at least, as Abraham. Therefore, to preach on Christian unity is indeed not only apropos but also provides a cutting and creative edge that many seem to overlook. Two of nine sermons are presented.*

# CHAPTER 5

# *Healing Echoes: Values for Christian Unity*

## ❋LOYALTY: IMPERATIVE INGREDIENT❋

CHRISTIAN UNITY assumes loyalty. In our present passage, we read a classic statement of loyalty (Ruth 1:1–19a). There were no circumstances too hostile or potentially dangerous to keep Ruth from being with her mother-in-law. It is an ancient story, and every time it is told for the first time to a new generation, its worth to motivate loyalty shines with a majestic simplicity.

Our blessed Lord demonstrated it over and over again. He was loyal to His mission, even to death upon the Cross. He calls His disciples to follow Him in faithful obedience. He beckons to you and me right now to place our beings with His being. Our faithfulness, translated into loyalty for a cause centuries old, is to be given top priority. Christian unity must not be betrayed. Life is too complicated and precarious for His followers to go their own ways, frustrating the highest and best in ideals known to humankind. We can hear His voice saying, "Pull together, My friends, pull together."

I invite you to ponder the story from Ruth and note some highly significant reflections which come from an adherence to loyalty. Universality is present and Christ's church can benefit.

### *Tragedy Can be Overcome*

Volumes have been filled with the betrayal of Christians against Christians. This tragedy has an early beginning. We only have to open the pages of Holy Scripture which tell about Judas Iscariot's *sell out* and Simon Peter's denial. Why Peter made it and Judas didn't dwell in the mystery of the Godhead.

What we do know is, as brothers and sisters march with Christ, tragedy can be overcome. All of the problems, hypocrisy, and even apostasy cannot separate us from the love of the Galilean. As we meet opposition—sometimes vicious—in the cause of Christian unity, we need to read with care Romans 8:38–39, "For I am sure that neither death, nor life, nor angels, nor principalities, nor things present, nor things to come, nor powers, nor height, nor depth, nor anything else in all creation, will be able to separate us from the love of God in Christ

Jesus our Lord." Roman Catholics have a spiritually beneficial series entitled "Romans 8" and any sensitive and serious Christian can profit by it.

As one views the past, the Lutheran/Roman Catholic relationship would seem to be a tolerating isolationism, at best. Yet, with both, who represent hundreds of millions, we know tragedy—even centuries of it—is not decisive. "Ecumenism: A Lutheran Commitment," which is an official statement of the Lutheran Church in America (1982), lifts us the fact that "relations of the Church of Rome with the churches of the Reformation" will be one of the central themes of ecumenism. This is followed by the declaration: "This is observable in the agenda and success of the Lutheran-Roman Catholic dialogues, carried out both nationally and internationally since 1965." On June 25, 1980, on the 450th anniversary of the reading of the Augsburg Confession, Pope John Paul II declared: "With all my heart I greet all the Christians who, today and in the next few days, will be gathering at Augsburg to confirm, in the face of the fears and pessimism of a troubled humanity, that Jesus Christ is the salvation of the world . . ."

Where does the so-called average pastor and layperson fit into all of this? At the point of jubilation and thanksgiving! It is in the local setting, where parishioner relates to parishioner, pastor to pastor, pastor to parishioner, and parishioner to pastor, that Christian unity comes to fulfillment. We must do our ecumenism well, especially in the thousands of parishes around the globe.

Now, we move to real challenge.

### Nationality Not Decisive

It makes no difference whether you are from Judah or Moab. A higher loyalty is suggested.

Christian unity respects, honors, and appreciates nationality. However, there is the recognition that Christ's cause is universal.

The conversations which involve church/state relations are increasing. Fortunately, we are able to do this in our country and not be submerged into a detrimental debate that dooms one institution as a loser. History lays before us many examples of the state being victorious over the church and vice versa. I believe it is due to the sagacity of the Founding Fathers that we have lived in peaceful coexistence. They, in most cases, were religious men who understood the Church and State, as institutions, could and should remain separate. However, they were well aware, as persons related to each other, that religious and political ideas were bound to intermingle. Ben Franklin could write and pray his own version of "The Lord's Prayer" but this did not mean he would recommend it as an official prayer for the new nation. Thomas Jefferson came up with his own version of the New Testament, entitled *The Life and Morals of Jesus of Nazareth*. However, there is no record of him even remotely suggesting it should become *official* for the United States of America. Our illustrations could continue with John Adams, George Washington, etc.

No one likes to be referred to as a traitor to his/her country. Men and women have died protecting the USA. To consider, for one moment, they died in vain, is to become impudent and ungrateful to the point of sacrilege. Yet, we are prodded not to close our eyes to the gross injustice and demonic manipulation which can produce a stench so powerful the word *patriotism* becomes a questionable commodity.

*The Early Church and the State*, translated and edited by Agnes Cunningham, tells us the earliest Christian prayer of the church for the state is found in the "Letter to the Corinthians" of Clement of Rome. She indicates "it reflects clearly the conviction that earthly power and authority are bestowed by God on civil leaders. . . . an awareness, born of experience, that earthly princes can demand submission that stands in opposition to the will of God. . . . that grace for wise and peaceful governance be given to rulers, so that obedience to their commands not necessitate disobedience to God;" and meaning, therefore, "the Creator's purposes will be fulfilled."

Those advocates of Christian unity who support and affirm the World Council of Churches have been bombarded with rhetoric which insists this expression of a world organization is anti-nationalistic and, in fact, communistic. What many such diatribes never seem to consider is an adequate substitute, should it cease to exist. A common-sense approach to our global village makes necessary some such organization to communicate among Christ's flock. The World Council of Churches is a fellowship of "churches which confess the Lord Jesus Christ as God and Savior according to the Scriptures, and therefore, seek to fulfill together their common calling to the glory of the one God, Father, Son, and Holy Spirit." Even the Protestant fundamentalist would be hard-pressed to improve upon that! A new appreciation has come about for the Orthodox Churches as they work through the World Council of Churches. They know directly what it means to suffer for Christ and His church. One of the two keynote addresses at the recent Sixth Assembly was given by Professor Theodore Stylianopoulos, a Greek Orthodox Professor of New Testament from the United States.

The National Council of Churches of Christ in the USA is another vehicle receiving its share of abuse. Again, critics seldom—if ever—confront the question, "Suppose we do dump it, what do we put in its place?" Throughout its history we have seen the age-old tensions of church and state at work. At present, the level of accountability appears to be very high.

Christian unity says nationality is not the last word. The only word that really matters is given to us by Christ in His plea before His crucifixion that we be One. This is where our loyalty lies.

To return to our Scripture, we now move to an expression of the ultimate in loyalty.

### *No Strings Attached*

Ruth is firm with her mother-in-law, "I want to be with you . . . regardless." She was determined and would not be denied.

This same attitude is found in those involved with Christian unity. It is hoped there is never cause for embarrassment by those who become adamant about certain areas of theology and/or administration. Of course, the adage "agreement on essentials and charity on non-essentials" does not help us much, especially if there is widespread disagreement about definitions. We are rescued again and again by the work of the Holy Spirit. "Toward an Agreed Statement on the Holy Spirit," report of joint commission between the Roman Catholic Church and the World Methodist Council, aids us at this juncture. It maintains: "The Spirit guided each stage of the development of the early church. In every age, as the Paraclete, he reminds us of all that Jesus said, guides us into all truth, and enables us to bear witness to salvation in Christ."

Our blessed Lord, in Matthew 10:37–38, claims us on His terms: "He who loves father or mother more than me is not worthy of me; and he who does not take his cross and follow me is not worthy of me." Our first loyalty is to Him; all else is secondary. If we both believe and practice this, it follows that the unity of His disciples is a cross to carry which, at times, may become very heavy. To serve Him with *no strings attached* is to live with Him and die with Him. The Crucifixion cannot be separated from the Resurrection or vice versa.

*Loyalty is not an option* in Christian unity. As the close of the century comes upon us, ecumenists, loyal to their Lord, are seeing signs of a harvest, rich in all aspects of the Faith, as it was delivered to us centuries ago and evolved to this very hour. The World Missionary Conference was held in 1910 at Edinburgh, Scotland. Much of what it set in motion is now with us in more concrete ways. We are to know them by their fruits, and many of us believe the fruit is tasty, even, in some cases, luscious. Saint Paul was and is right: "But the fruit of the Spirit is love, joy, peace, patience, kindness, goodness, faithfulness, gentleness, self control . . ." (Gal. 5:22–23).

This inviting and infectious story from Ruth underlines the ancient/new truth that loyalty is an imperative ingredient for those who set out on the Judeo/Christian pilgrimage. Christian unity is undergirded by knowledge which maintains tragedy can be overcome, nationality is not decisive, and authentic loyalty is eventually summed up in *no strings attached*.

# ❈SECURITY: DEEPLY PERSONAL❈

CHRISTIAN UNITY proclaims security in a personal King, Jesus the Christ! The whole concept of security has taken on new connotations since the Second World War and especially with the news other nations besides the United States have the atomic bomb. Relatively speaking, it has not been too many years that individuals or even nations could cross mountains and/or oceans to gain security from enemies. Our own nation, for generations, was free from direct interference of the ongoing wars and intrigues of Europe, Asia, and Africa, largely because of being separated from them by thousands of miles of water. Obviously, this is not true today and has not been so for decades.

Ezekiel 34:11–16, 20–24 relays to us the message that God alone can provide security and He will do so through a messianic king, another David. Christians, generally, and those espousing Christian unity, in particular, have seen this in the coming of Jesus Christ. He will provide what others have been unable to do. While He will come with the great ruler in the background both literally and figuratively, He will also be different in His direct and powerful spirituality. His rule will not be distant and impersonal, but close and deeply personal.

In our passage, Ezekiel offers a far-advanced look at Christ the King. He was much more than the prophet could understand, but He inspires us with enough details to know God came in the flesh, bringing a security never before known. He catches a glimpse of God's personal presence in four easily recognizable ways.

## God Is Personally in Charge

Away with the old failures of men and their weak ways! Away with those who believe physical and material might are responsible for security! God is in charge, not distantly and forbiddingly, but closer than one's breath.

Since the dawning of the twentieth century, Christian unity or the ecumenical movement has witnessed and relished the personal way God has broken into the old ways and all their strangling complexities. The movement, of course, has not and is not free of problems, mistakes, and human sin. However, God is breathing life into it and this makes the decisive difference. In reflection, what has appeared to be floundering has only been that God's timetable is different from ours. Saint Paul lends a helping hand in Ephesians 2:19–20, depicting the new life in Christ: "So then you are no longer strangers and sojourners, but you are fellow citizens with the Saints and members of the household of God, built upon the foundation of the Apostles and prophets, Christ Jesus himself being the cornerstone." The universal church is composed not of strangers and sojourners, but fellow citizens with the saints and members of God's household.

The "Decree on Ecumenism" from Vatican II calls our attention to God's personal administration: "What has revealed the love of God among us is that the only-begotten Son of God has been sent by the Father into the world, so that, being made man, He might by His redemption of the entire human race give new life to it and unify it." There is nothing left to chance; with the only God of the universe at work, security bringing wholeness and holiness is evident.

In the same document, it is written: "The Lord of the Ages nevertheless wisely and patiently follows out the plan of His grace on our behalf, sinners that we are. In recent time He has begun to bestow more generously upon divided Christians remorse over their divisions and longing for unity."

Even with their philosophical brilliance, the Greeks knew little about a personal God. As Paul said, the "Greeks seek wisdom" and they experience the Cross of Christ as "folly." We are often prone to polish manuscripts with much of the same brilliance Socrates, Plato, Aristotle, and others taught us; more often than we like to admit, we, too, are locked into our categories, and discover only a personal God can break into them and grant a holy transcendence. A friend of mine maintains the biggest problem of those who grow older in the faith is sometimes not hardening of the arteries, but hardening of the categories!

A second way we can spot God's personal presence is open for all to see.

### *God Personally Looks after His People*

Christian unity proclaims these sublime words from Saint Peter: "But you are a chosen race, a royal priesthood, a holy nation, God's own people, that you may declare the wonderful deeds of him who called you out of darkness into his marvelous light" (1 Pet. 2:9). Think of it; we are *God's own people!* Why can we say this with such optimism? Let us return to Peter. In 1 Peter 1:3–5, we read: "Blessed be the God and Father of our Lord Jesus Christ! By his great mercy we have been born anew to a living hope through the resurrection of Jesus Christ from the dead and to an inheritance which is imperishable, undefiled, and unfading kept in heaven for you." What security! If there is something (Someone) better than that, let us lose no time bringing it to humankind.

Coming from *The Imitation of Christ*, by Thomas à Kempis is the straightforward, simple gem: "When Jesus speaks not inwardly to us, all other comfort is nothing worth; but if Jesus speaks but one word, we feel great consolation." This points to the almost unbelievable insecurity in our society. We do all sorts of things, some of them bordering on the miraculous, in search of security, discounting the God who comes to us personally, and learning, in shock and amazement, we have just been *spinning our wheels*. Yet, let the King say *one word*, and we sense in our totality a security beyond human achievement. The same great spiritual work captures the dynamics found in all of us: "Without a friend thou canst not well live; and if Jesus be not above all a friend to thee, thou shalt be indeed sad and desolate."

The personal touch of Christ cannot be over-emphasized in times when we grope for meaning that brings security. It is hoped that we have learned we do not have to ask, "To what church do you belong?" or "To what denomination do you hold allegiance?" or "Do you subscribe to my version of the faith?" before we allow the Savior and Lord to work among us. Christian unity knows, in its depths, in Christ there is no separation. It is in sin and sins we separate ourselves.

"But now in Christ Jesus you who once were far off have been brought near in the blood of Christ. For he is our peace, who has made us both one and has broken down the dividing wall of hostility" (Eph. 2:13–14), speaks to our plight with gravity and yet tremendous hope. "He is our peace" is the keynote for all immersed in our Lord's call to be One. We are not being cared for by institutions or the most finely-tuned committees and executives. *He* looks after us and thereby gives us a secure approach to all that life offers.

Join me for another sign.

### *God Personally Will Judge*

"Behold, I, I myself will judge . . ." gives no room for dubious thought and feelings. The Son of David judges simply by being Who and what He is. As He went about ministering, I find it inconceivable that most were left in doubt about their relationship with God. History seems to indicate *the Jews* fought Him at every turn, repudiating His message at every opportunity. Yet, we dare not be too absolutist and gloss over the details of the early history of Christianity. The fact is Jesus was a Jew, came to the Jews, and His earliest followers were Jews. By turning a deaf ear to our Lord, according to Saint Paul, ". . . through their trespass salvation has come to the Gentiles . . ." we are faced with the God of us all who saw fit to harden their hearts in the majority. Clark M. Williamson, in his very important work, *Has God Rejected His People?* sets the record straight for us in a discussion of the Pharisees: "Both Christianity and Judaism arose from within the matrix of the emergent new sensitivity expressed by the Pharisees." It is humbling, but growth-producing, to admit the historical Jesus did not give us Judaism but, in a sense, Judaism gave us the historical Jesus. Christian unity affirms that the personal God comes judging us through a real context of flesh and blood, namely Jews and a Jewish Jesus.

The corporate style of living many experience today renders judgment in ways reminiscent of a bulldozer crushing whatever is in its path, for no other reason than it is just in the way. There is nothing personal. While we may say it makes little difference how judgment is administered, pain and destruction result. That really is not the case. The corporate methodology breeds disillusionments and outright despair. The political machinations might as well be blobs of oppressive steel. The institutional church is not an exception. True, it can care for persons but, all too often, such care is determined by the exigencies of the system. We are pragmatists. If we cannot get along in the corporation, we seek those *components that will work*. Christian unity has a timely message—it believes clergy not only should be able freely to cross denominational lines for service, but in many cases should do so. God does not judge polity; He judges persons.

Finally, our journey takes us to the indescribable moment Saint John calls "The Word became flesh and dwelt among us."

### God Personally Appoints the New David

Ezekiel says, "He shall feed them." Christian unity understands the need of being fed by Christ. Our Lord is the focal point for food and, in fact, unless He does the feeding, malnutrition and even starvation result. Not only are we unable to save ourselves, we are unable to feed ourselves, separate and apart from Him. William Williams was a dissenting preacher in eighteenth-century Wales, but we remember him largely because of a single hymn that he wrote, entitled "Guide Me, O Thou Great Jehovah." With sustaining power those lines come to us:

Bread of heaven,
Bread of heaven,
Feed me till I want no more,
Feed me till I want no more.

This refrain could easily catch on as an ecumenical marching song.

The new David gives to us food that the old one could only fore-shadow. To specify, we immediately focus on the Eucharist. Alasdair I. C. Heron, in *Table and Tradition*, which is subtitled *Towards an Ecumenical Understanding of the Eucharist*, helps us come to grips with terminology by saying, "Very early in the ancient church, 'Eucharist' became the established name for the sacrament . . ." *Eucharista* means *thanksgiving*. Bernard Cooke, in *The Eucharist: Mystery of Friendship*, says quite simply, "The Eucharist is the supreme expression of man's unity with Christ and with his fellow man." In the classic *Introduction to Christian Worship* by James F. White, there is further acknowledgment: "The eucharist is the most characteristic structure of Christian worship. It is also the most widely used form of worship among Christians, being celebrated daily and weekly in millions of congregations and communities all over the world." It is in thanksgiving that the ecumenical movement goes forward, agonizing over our separation in the understanding and partaking of the Eucharist and, in the same moment, enjoying the unity we already have with the promise of more—much more.

As Christians, we have a gift which defies measurement; it is called a security that is deeply personal. We have been living in the King's castle all along, at times insensitive to our privileged place. Christian unity views that castle much as Thomas Ryan in *Tales of Christian Unity*, with a great house all on one level and rooms situated around a common dining room with one table. The doors are all open and people come and go as they please; the common table is the Eucharist. He adds, "I want to be able to say, as a Christian, that the whole house is mine, and that I live there, with my brothers and sisters."

God is in charge, looks after His people, will judge, and appoints a new David; all are done personally. This is a message of living hope for Christ's Body, the Church. The security that is inherently imbedded bids us to come and die—if need be for the cause of Christian unity.

The times are exciting and our blessed Lord has timed the excitement of the fulfillment of His call to be One perfectly. In a modest way, these values for Christian unity provide a lighted candle in the darkness which remains with us, intended to keep His Body torn asunder.

Come with your cross and follow Him on the pilgrimage that leads to a visible "one, holy, catholic and apostolic Church."

———

*Used by permission of CSS Publishing Company, Inc.,*
*517 S. Main Street, P.O. Box 4503, Lima, Ohio, 45802–4503.*

## Reactivating Acts

**"A Preaching,
Teaching Program
for the Pentecost Season"**

**Donald Charles Lacy**

Second Printing

*1991*

*It is so important that our scriptural, homiletical, and theological work be
"field-tested." Entirely too much of what is done at the parish level does
not speak to the needs of parishoners. The problem is common. What
looks good on paper doesn't work! My own experience is that laity will
plan preaching and teaching events with their pastors. This points the way
to an exciting, worthwhile, and practical event in the life of a local
congregation. Reactivating Acts is a field-tested preaching/teaching event
that will enable a congregation and pastor to focus on Church history for
all of the Pentecost season. Week after week the congregation and pastor
will study together. Four of twenty-four sermons are presented.*

CHAPTER 6

# Reactivating Acts

## ❦EXPLORING THE ESSENCE❦

### Background

THE KEY FIGURE throughout Acts 6:8–8:3 is Stephen. We get a clear picture of him as a Christian. We note some of the stories often included in early Christian preaching. We see what forthrightness and bravery produces: death in the hall of stones.

Our story begins with a man empowered by the Holy Spirit. Stephen was "full of grace and power." He "did great wonders and signs among the people." There were those of different synagogues who arose and disputed with him. They couldn't accomplish much that way, so they got together and conceived of a plan to destroy him. They charged him with blasphemous words against Moses and God. They stirred up the people, including some elders and scribes, and brought him before the Sanhedrin. They made official charges, but noticed "his face was like the face of an angel."

Now, our narrative shifts as Stephen presents his defense. He addresses the group as "brethren and fathers." He summarizes the beginnings of the Hebrew faith by telling of Abraham, Isaac, and Jacob. The emphasis is on Abraham. Then he moves to Joseph, telling of him being sold into Egypt and how God rescued him as he found favor in Pharaoh's sight. Joseph is seen as one who brings his brothers, his father, and "all his kindred" to Egypt to escape starvation. Egypt gets a new Pharaoh. The new one does not deal with the Hebrews as a humanitarian; in fact, the infant Moses barely escapes death and is brought up by Pharaoh's daughter. Stephen then launches into a lengthy narrative about Moses. Moses, a trusted and privileged leader among the Egyptians, sees his people being wronged. He attempts to go among them as God's instrument but is refused. Moses is baffled and probably bitterly hurt; he goes to the land of Midian where he becomes the father of two sons. Forty years passed and an angel appeared to him in the wilderness of Mount Sinai. The voice of the Lord came. It told him to take off his shoes and be ready to go to Egypt to deliver the Israelites. Moses did his work, performing wonders and signs. While he was at Mount Sinai receiving "living oracles," his people disobeyed and worked with Aaron to make a calf to worship. Stephen quotes Amos 5:25–27 and implies idolatry has been a continual problem. Then he moves quickly to tell them of the "tent of witness in the wilderness," Joshua, David, and Solomon. Stephen wants it understood that "the Most High does not dwell in houses made with hands." From that viewpoint the tent or tabernacles which moved about were superior to Solomon's temple.

There is at this juncture a notable change in tone, cutting and keenly judgmental. He begins to level charges himself. The Sanhedrin is labeled a "Stiff-necked people, uncircumcised in heart and ears." They are also told ". . . you always resist the Holy Spirit." He points to Jesus as he says, ". . . whom you have now betrayed and murdered." They are enraged! Stephen looks into the heavens and sees Jesus at the right hand of God and he proceeds to tell them so. That was the last straw, as they throw him out of the city and stone him to death. Saul, later to be Saint Paul, is overseeing the murder. As Stephen dies he prays for his spirit to be received and asks for forgiveness of those responsible for his death.

## Introduction

Our text is like a mighty steel cable, connecting heaven and earth, that contains the essence of the Christ's ministry. Acts 7:60 says: "And he knelt down and cried with a loud voice, 'Lord, do not hold this sin against them.' And when he had said this, he fell asleep." These words point to something beyond the human; you and I know we are in touch with why Christ came and dwelt among us.

There are three lofty and abiding truths humanity had to see and must continue to see.

## Application

*In the first place to be innocent and greatly wronged makes forgiveness the supreme gift that only God can grant.*

There is a sense of justice and fair play in all of us. Granted it is in varying degrees, but it is present. We like for things to add up. For every wrong there ought to be a right. On the scales of life the two sides should eventually come close to being at the same level. Equal treatment, opportunity, and sacrifice are ideals we hold near and dear. Most people I meet have a built-in computer, which for want of a better way of saying it, emphasizes the rightness of an "eye for an eye and a tooth for a tooth." For every bad thing that happens there is a silver lining. Most of us go through life proclaiming openly or whispering quietly life has its ups and downs but at the end they balance out. It is a rather comforting value, isn't it? How does this apply to Stephen . . . or Christ? What sort of fair play was at work as they died in agony?

We must move out of the usual patterns of justice and morality. Every bone within a "good" man or woman may say, "Stephen was an innocent person, terribly wronged, and his killers should be put before a firing squad or something worse." Is that what he says? Quite the contrary. Bruised, battered, and beaten by various sizes and shapes of stones he falls on his knees and cries out, "Lord, do not hold this sin against them." He isn't negotiating through an attorney to see if a restraining order can be implemented. He doesn't shout curses indicating he or his family will "get back . . . regardless." He doesn't blame God by crying out, "Why are you allowing this to happen? I am innocent and you know it. Is there no justice in Your world?" Does he question the necessity of his death? Does he wonder if he is dying in vain, which is an insult to our being created in God's image? We have reason to believe the answer is negative in both cases.

So, held up before us is an innocent man who is greatly wronged. After all, he was only stating the case for the primitive Christian Faith. He was filled with the Holy Spirit from God and that enabled him not only to die by the hands of those who despised his Christ but to ask they be forgiven for their horrendous deed. You and I today do not have the powers within ourselves to do what he did (or for that matter did he); God working through the Holy Spirit makes the impossible possible. Christ was "the" Sacrificial Lamb. Stephen was a sacrificial lamb. Every generation must have its sacrificial lambs. Blameless and praying for the forgiveness of their persecutors.

We turn now to another lofty and abiding truth.

*In the second place to be Christ's person is to acknowledge the possibility—even the probability—of martyrdom.*

In a sense Christ literally beckons all His followers to come and die with Him. While at first that sounds like a beautiful and enticing challenge, it loses its glitter and glow for those who discover it also means to ask for forgiveness for those who do the killing. The attraction of being a martyr has been with the Faith since its inception. One can easily build all sorts of future monuments in one's mind. It is when our martyrdom becomes really Christlike with Stephen as a model that we explore the essence of what it means to be Christ's person.

Indeed, the human and the divine are wedded together in the kind of dying we are talking about. The Holy Spirit has made and does make it possible for us to die at the hands of our enemies and in turn put upon our lips a cry that they be forgiven. Just as man cannot save himself, so man cannot suffer martyrdom in the manner of Stephen on his own strength. The Holy Spirit from God must come upon the scene!

In the Sermon on the Mount our Lord says, "Blessed are you when men revile you and persecute you and utter all kinds of evil against you falsely on my account (Matt. 5:11). Note the closing prepositional phrase: "on my account." It was "on behalf of his Lord" that Stephen got himself into serious trouble and died in a barrage of stones. It is decisive to our own religious growth that we see clearly if a martyr's death is to come to you and me, it should be because of Jesus the Christ. That deserves pondering beyond today; it touches the heart of our faith. Saint Paul says, "For I decided to know nothing among you except Jesus Christ and him crucified" (1 Corinthians 2:2). As strange gods huddle around us and plead for our attention and devotion, we had better claim Him as Savior and Lord once and for all. The dreariness and drabness of our lives may well be that we have already decided we must die properly in the eyes of the world, which rules out anything resembling Stephen's martyrdom.

There is a final lofty and abiding truth.

*In the third place to be an agent of God's love is an offering of reconciliation to a sinful and lost world.*

Our blessed Lord says, "Come to me, all who labor and are heavy laden, and I will give you rest" (Matthew 11:28). That seems almost in direct contradiction to a lifeless figure half-covered in a pile or rocks that has just been claimed by the Death Angel, doesn't it? It is a stunning verse in light of what has happened to an innocent man. Yet, notice how that verse and the scene of Stephen's corpse meet in the higher realms of religious understanding. We are weak and heavy laden in a multitude of ways until we kneel at the foot of the Cross. To kneel at that cross may very well mean death at the hands of those shouting slurs at both us and our Christ. Nevertheless, this may be the only way we can arrive at perfect wholeness or holiness and in turn find rest. Our mission is that of being a giver of a magnificent gift to those despising the lowly Galilean and considering us interlopers in a world loving its own; indeed, we are to be a reconciling example in miniature of God's love. Saint Paul captures the living ideal in 2 Corinthians 12:10: "For the sake of Christ, then, I am content with weaknesses, insults, hardships, persecutions, and calamities; for when I am weak, then I am strong."

You and I as Christians are by definition reconcilers. What do we mean? Again Saint Paul puts it into words for us; ". . . in Christ God was reconciling the world to himself, not counting their trespasses against them, and entrusting to us the message of reconciliation" (2 Corinthians 5:19). You and I are participants—yes, agents—in restoring sinful and lost human beings to friendship and harmony with God. Have you ever thought of yourself in that way? Praise God, that's our honored place of service as we march victoriously in life or death under orders from the Christ!

You and I as Christians cannot simply blend into the fabric of the world and go on our way unnoticed. We are marked by the Cross of Christ as well as Stephen and others like him. In our own unique ways we are intermediaries carrying the message that Christ died for humanity and we—if need be—are also willing under the anointing of the Holy Spirit to die because of Him.

### *Conclusion*

Do you back away from thoughts of Stephen's death? I do. I want to recoil from such martyrdom. It seems so out of place in a time when so much of our nation registers a belief in God. Why should there be any need to think in terms of some innocent person dying and praying for forgiveness for his or her killer(s)? Doesn't most everyone give respect and reverence to the Christ today? Such honest probing eventually leads to an unvarnished and blunt confrontation with our own relationship to the Christ. It is only as the Faith really begins to mean a great deal to us that we catch a glimpse of the eternal greatness of being killed without just cause and calling upon God to forgive those responsible for our murder.

When "all of the chips are down," truth visits us. Stephen gives us a gift we may need to give someday. No age is exempt from the need for martyrdom patterned after Stephen. You and I are ministers of reconciliation in a world always wanting Christ to be less than Who He is.

## ❊THE IMPARTIAL GOD❊

### *Background*

ACTS 9:32 through 11:18 is lengthy and we discover Peter again becomes the dominant figure.

In the early verses the story of Dorcas is told. The Scripture says, "she was full of good works and acts of charity." She died and was prepared for burial. Peter was in the vicinity so they sent word for him to come. When he arrived, widows were standing about showing tunics and other garments Dorcas had made while alive. Peter put them outside the room in which she was lying and told her to rise. She did and Peter presented her alive to the saints and widows. This miracle became known and many believed in the Lord in Joppa, a seaport on the Mediterranean coast.

Much of the section, of course, is about Cornelius.

Cornelius is delineated as a centurion, "a devout man who feared God with all his household, gave alms liberally to the people, and prayed constantly to God." An angel greeted him and told him his prayers and alms had "ascended as a memorial before God." The angel then told him to send for Peter and he did.

The next day Peter went to a housetop to pray about noon and he fell into a trance. The heaven opened and something like a great sheet descended. In it were "all kinds of animals and reptiles and birds of the air." A voice told Peter to rise, kill, and eat. Peter's response was "No" and that he had never eaten anything common or unclean. The voice was persistent; it came to him a second and third time.

Peter was inwardly perplexed by the meaning of the vision. About that time the men arrived that were sent by Cornelius. The Spirit told Peter three men were looking for him and to go with them without hesitation. So, Peter introduced himself as the one they were looking for and they spoke of their mission. They remained overnight.

The next day Peter, the men from Cornelius, and some of the brethren made their way to Caesarea. Cornelius had called together his kinsmen and close friends. Upon Peter's entry, he fell down and worshiped him. Peter would have none of that, so he told him to stand up because he too was a man. Peter told them that they already knew it was unlawful for him to associate with or to visit anyone of another nation; God had shown him no man was to be called common or unclean. Peter then wants to know why they sent for him.

Cornelius describes his visit with a man in bright apparel. The man told him to send for Peter and he did. He tells Peter they are now ready to hear what has been commanded by the Lord.

Peter launches into a brief but bold sermon. He says that he perceives God shows no partiality; He accepts all who fear Him and do what is right. He then spells out in summary the message of God through Christ. While Peter was preaching, the Holy Spirit fell upon them. Those with Peter who were circumcised were amazed because the Spirit fell upon the Gentiles as well. They spoke in tongues and extolled God. Baptism by water then was administered. Peter stayed with the household of Cornelius for some days.

The closing part of the section tells us of Peter's confrontation with the so-called "circumcision party." This was the group that did not feel Gentiles or non-Jews had a part in the Faith. Peter explained to them all that had taken place. Their response was, ". . . to the Gentiles also God has granted repentance unto life."

## Introduction

The peak of significance is reached for you and me in the text. Acts 10:34 reads, "And Peter opened his mouth and said: 'Truly I perceive that God shows no partiality.'" That has the effect of letting you and me in!

Christ came through, to, and for the Jews, but now He is for everyone. This gives rise to four glorious affirmations.

## Application

*The first is that the God of Jesus the Christ cares about all of humankind.*

You and I may react to this affirmation quickly by saying, "Well, of course, He does." It looks fairly simple to us. It is an open and closed case. However, to the Jews who proclaimed Jesus as the crucified and resurrected Christ it was a much different matter. As has been mentioned, He came "through, to, and for them." That's biblical. "Did God intend that His Son be Savior and Lord to and for others?" was not a silly or light inquiry. Note that even Saint Peter had to be shown that God was not partial. It is to the credit and honor of the Jews to whom Peter is speaking that they accept his vision and viewpoint. Of course, the problem did surface upon occasion all through the first-century Church.

There is a hurtful and uncharitable possessiveness in denominationalism that bears resemblance to the issue at hand. Church history has examples galore in every century of a body of Christians believing and maintaining they had the only clear pipeline and perfect revelation from God. "Circumcision party" is really the name of a sect that said one had to become a Jew in order to be clean and acceptable to God. Ponder for a moment the persons and groups you have known or known about whose major thrust was that they were the only ones who "really" knew what the Faith was all about. Some of the sad moments in the march of the saints across the centuries are with us. Sects took the attitude, "Well, you people over there are common, unclean, and don't know the Christ as perfectly as we do." Yes, and recall those then and now who have already condemned some of us to the fiery furnaces, screaming for cold glasses of water. The unity of the Church in the sense of a body of believers working together as brothers and sisters in Christ has been ludicrous from time to time. It is the attitude of "we are not going to give up this, we are not going to accept that, and we are right" that divides us. Too many have and do take their eyes off the Christ and just crassly want their own way, regardless of the fallout.

There is more to be affirmed.

*The second is that the God of Jesus the Christ reaches out to all human beings.*
This affirmation is perhaps the most comforting you and I can enjoy. God does not turn a cold shoulder. God does not allow precious people to languish indefinitely in the quagmires of lostness and futility. All barriers are crossed. At whatever point you and I see walls He is there to break them down or circumvent them. Saint Paul captures this mood in Ephesians 2:17–18 as he speaks to the Jew-Gentile separation: "And he came and preached peace to you who were far off and peace to those who were near; for through him we both have access in one Spirit to the Father." Who is the key figure in God's "worldwide outreach program?"

His name is Jesus the Christ, isn't it? Gone are the days of imperfect manifestations. God comes to us in the flesh with outstretched arms. He is not partial. No category defies Him. No one is beyond the healing rays of the Great Physician. No one dare says, "He is our Christ and you can't have Him." No one controls access to God, except Jesus the Christ. He is the Christ for all humanity. He tells us in John 12:32, ". . . and I, when I am lifted up from the earth, will draw all men to myself." The death of His Son was and is the means God utilizes to reach precious persons. There is no symbol as powerfully productive and eternally essential as the Cross. Impotent Christianity is invariably that brand which attempts to tell others of God's love but refuses or forgets to mention and elevate the Cross— splattered, splotched, and sprinkled with sacrificial blood.

We move to our next affirmation.

*The third is that the God of Jesus the Christ tells us to tell others salvation is intended for all.*
The impartial God through His Son says, "Go therefore and make disciples of all nations, baptizing them in the name of the Father and of the Son and of the Holy Spirit" (Matt. 28:19). In our own country during the nineteenth century these were probably the most often quoted words in the *New Testament*. American Christians moved out and into every nation in the world. It was almost like another crusade, this time seeking to conquer the spirit of those to whom the Christ was unknown. Only the God who shows no partiality could inspire His people to tell and teach others of the Faith beyond the narrow confines of white Protestants in a particular place at a particular time. Today it is a different story, isn't it? Many areas of the world are closed—indeed, the doors are bolted—to the message of the Christ. Of course, that is no cause for going on an indefinite

binge of gloom and doom. In the last century and the early part of this one large numbers of missionaries did their job well. Third, fourth, and fifth generation Christians in those lands are now—for the most part—giving leadership to their people. While reports tend to be garbled and those with political axes to grind attempt intimidation, there is much good news about the witnessing to the Good News on the continents of Africa, Asia, South America, and elsewhere.

What is our mission today as we survey the world and the command to take the Word to all peoples? Don't we find ourselves much like the proud parents who have given birth to successful sons and daughters; yet, we would like for them to continue to listen attentively to us and conform to our cultural molds? Is it a matter of giving the gift of the Good News to others and wanting to remind them how they got it and they had better be grateful for our generosity and sacrifice? Does it ever occur to us that every body of people—including you and me—on the face of the earth could be confronted in the same way?

Lastly, what do we affirm?

*The fourth is that the God of Jesus the Christ is universally responsible.*

Pagan gods were fickle. Some of the stories out of Greek and Roman mythologies, as well as many others, give us tales that are not only entertainingly funny but downright tragically hilarious. As we read about the antics of Jupiter, Juno, Zeus, Hera, Bacchus, Osiris, Isis, and many others we may wonder how people could be so stupid. Then we may begin to feel compassion for them because they did not know of the Good News. I wonder if it were possible for the people in those days and times to look on us, what their reactions would be? Oh, it's a bit of hazy theorizing, isn't it? Yet, we just might find them—if such a thing could happen—wondering how any body of people so privileged could be taken in by the gods that science, acculturation, and secular humanism have foisted upon us. Indeed, how can an impartial God who is responsible to His universe and vice versa avoid justice and judgment on the basis of you and I being held accountable for the light given to us? Our day in the Church is afflicted with the "consumer-entertainment" syndrome. One wonders if Christ were to die in our midst today if we would clap our hands, stomp our feet, and shout "Bravo!" . . . then go off to look for a better act? We can almost hear Peter saying, "God shows no partiality and while that means the Gospel is intended for everyone, it does not annul Christ's word on responsibility to me in Luke 13:48: 'Everyone to whom much is given, of him will much be required.'"

### Conclusion

Our Faith was and is catholic or worldwide; just as Peter declared centuries ago, God shows no partiality. The door of salvation is ajar for everyone. That's sobering isn't it? By thought and deed various branches of Christianity have practiced partiality persistently. Each has been a member of a "circumcision party" and possibly continued unaware of it.

You and I are special in God's sight. Would you believe—so is everyone else? His blessed Son, Jesus the Christ, reminds all of humanity, ". . . I am the way, and the truth, and the life . . ." (John 14:6).

## ❋A PARTING OF THE WAYS❋

### Background

IN ACTS 15:36–16:10 we are met with Paul's expressed need to visit the cities where he and Barnabas had proclaimed the Word to see how they are doing. Barnabas wanted to take along a fellow John called Mark. However, Paul was not in agreement and thought it best he not go along. Apparently, he had withdrawn from them in Pamphylia, refusing to cooperate in the work there. Now, we have some of the sharpest words in the Book of Acts because they involve two brothers in Christ who have labored together through "thick and thin." The author of Acts calls it "a sharp contention." Barnabas took Mark and went to Cyprus. Paul chose Silas, going through Syria and Cilicia, strengthening the churches. The record says Paul was commended by the brethren.

Paul visits Berbe and Lystra; Timothy comes into the picture. He must have already been a disciple, probably an earlier convert of Paul. Timothy was the son of a Jewish mother who was a believer; his father was Greek. Paul wanted him to accompany him in his ministry. To avoid any question of his authenticity, Paul circumcised him. Then, they went on their way to different cities, delivering decisions which had been reached at Jerusalem by the apostles and elders. This series of verses closes by saying the churches were strengthened in faith and they increased in numbers daily.

It is significant that we say a few words about Timothy before moving into our next portion of Scripture. He became Paul's secretary and helper or assistant. He must have been quite young at the time. In 1 Corinthians 4:17 he is referred to by Paul as "my beloved and faithful child in the Lord." Two

New Testament books bear his name. Some traditional strands of information have said he was the first bishop of Ephesus. He not only becomes a prominent figure in Acts, he is mentioned a number of times in Paul's letters.

Their travels take them through different places, but they do not tarry to speak the Word. The Holy Spirit had told them to keep moving. Finally, they stopped for a time in the Troas (Alexandria) which was a chief city and port, located southwest of the ancient city of Ilium or Troy of Homer's *Iliad*. There a vision appeared to Paul in the night to go to Macedonia, a Roman province located on what we call the continent of Europe in the nation of Greece. They immediately decided to go; they concluded God had called them to preach there. So, our current section concludes with them ready to go to Macedonia.

## *Introduction*

Now, we come to terms with a text both alarming and fraught with emotion. Acts 15:39 says, "And there arose a sharp contention, so that they separated from each other; Barnabas took Mark with him and sailed away to Cyprus." I suppose it is one of those verses in the Bible we would just as soon conceal or gloss over. Spiritual integrity born of being a serious follower of the Christ demands that we not do that.

Candidly, what does this verse teach us?

## *Application*

*Disagreements need not lead to failure.*

We have all seen individuals and groups fight with hostility—even hatred—being given a field day. Healing necessary to bring them into a loving relationship just never seems to take place. Sometimes this sort of thing eats through entire families for more than one generation. Sometimes groups never recover and as individuals are so soured they refuse to be a part of anything. It seems to me these instances show us a "disagreeing attitude" is more than that; it is an unforgiving spirit that cannot move into other relationships calling on God to heal past wounds. Does it have to be that way? No.

We are all entitled to our points of view. Obviously, Paul did not think Mark was the man to be a part of his next journey; Barnabas just didn't see it that way. We could read all sorts of things into this. Perhaps it was a power struggle between the two. Maybe Paul was emerging as the dominant leader (there is evidence to support this) and Barnabas was trying to hang in there at least as a near equal. Speculation of this type could be unending, especially for a novelist who might have dollar bills dancing around in his or her head. The truth of the matter is they just didn't see Mark in the same light and who can blame either one or the other for that?

I do not see the "sharp contention" as a failure, even though the two did have a parting of the ways. It sounds like they departed in a huff. Nevertheless, it says nothing of a renunciation of the Faith on the part of either Paul or Barnabas. There is no indication they shouted threats at one another. There is no indication they promised to ruin one another as they met on some competitive field of ministry. While we hear a lot more about Paul from here on, Barnabas must have done a great job in supporting and strengthening Mark; otherwise, we would not likely have the Gospel according to Mark. It sounds as though the disagreement led to far more productivity, indeed success and not failure.

What next are we taught by the text?

*God's wisdom must have dictated the two workers go separate ways.*
There is purpose in what happened. Do you think it was by accident this takes place between Paul and Barnabas? I don't think so. Let's ask a much larger question: do you think that anything that happened or is recorded in the Bible was by accident? Again, I don't think so. The providence of God is at work. The dissemination of the Gospel is at stake and do you think God for one moment would allow that message to go uncommunicated? Heavens no! Paul and Barnabas in their separation were a working out of God's will, even though they may not have sensed it at the time.

Have we not seen this in our own lives? Some persons transfer to other churches in the same community and at the time it causes hurt and no small amount of gossip. It has been my experience that often this works to the benefit of everyone concerned. To be sure our God is not divided and unsure. However, our perception of Him often is. We may even blame Him—if we are brave enough! There may be a parting of the ways with one's best friend. So what? Does that mean that there are no other best friends down the road? Does that mean you entered into some sort of lifetime contract with a friend(s) that is unbreakable? Does it mean hurt feelings and "tons of tongue wagging" have to blight the future? Does it ever occur to us that God just might like for us to see and appreciate friendship in a broader context?

There is seldom—if ever—any strong Christian relationship devoid of trust and credibility. While we may know this in our daily walk with others and attempt to live by it, what about God as He relates to us through the Christ? Do we have trust in Him and does He have credibility? How many times have we second-guessed Him in recent days?

We move now to a practical truth.

*Sometimes two personalities just don't jibe.*

We do not have to be apologetic for this. It's a fact of life, isn't it or is it? Is there anyone receiving this message who has never had a personality conflict? Do you know someone whose personality has always meshed with everyone else's? There are those who say an unobtrusive person who continually yields with graciousness at points others are assertive, really has no conflicts. That's fallacious though, isn't it? There comes a time that person is supposed to stand up and be counted in the eyes of some and it doesn't happen. What occurs? Conflict.

Are we dealing with a basically negative phenomenon? That is, when two personalities just can't get along, is it all bad with no positive effects? I hardly think so. Peace and tranquility can be counterproductive to upward movements in the Faith. We can become lulled into a feeling of all is well to the extent sheer inertia, ineffectiveness, and inefficiency take over. That sort of ministry, lay or clergy, is an embarrassment to those serving the Christ on the firing line and surely must be a disappointment to the Christ, who seems to have had an abundance of personality conflicts in a brief time.

Our text continues to speak to us in an instructive way.

*There must have been a powerful sense of ministry in all four men.*

Paul, Barnabas, Mark, and Silas must have all felt deeply what Paul says in Romans 1:16: "For I am not ashamed of the gospel: it is the power of God for salvation to everyone who has faith, to the Jew first and also to the Greek." There was not a falling away from the Faith as each man by turns disowned his call from God. Quite the contrary. All continue to serve their Christ and it would appear in an even more gloriously productive way. God does not cease to bless them as things work themselves out. A verse much later in the book of Romans quickly comes to mind: "For the gifts and the call of God are irrevocable" (11:29).

Authentic ministry is following in the footsteps of the Christ, His Apostles, and His disciples which means we have a servant model. Would our sense of ministry quickly dissipate under the circumstances these four faced? Would we find our sense of service directly dependent upon no contention and upsets? As we ask that question, we are awakened to the fact some seem to equate service with usability. While value judgments tend to put us in hot water, we cannot preach and teach the Word of God apart from them. This leads me to say those with the problem tend to see life in terms of using and being used. To be aware of such factors is necessary, but to view life in such a manner is generally catastrophic, breeding unnecessary emotional hurt and warped mental pictures. Paul says to you and me today as he did to Archippus: "See that you fulfill the ministry which you have received in the Lord" (Colossians 4:17) . . . and that may mean we must rise above some set patterns influencing our entire lives.

A final point speaks to us.

*Some doors have to close before others can open.*

That's a cliche, but there is spiritual truth in it. Have we not seen it in death? One person's life must go the way of all flesh and return to dust before another can blossom. That's perhaps the most basic of all illustrations, but look deeply into your life unhurriedly. Truth is at hand, is it not? Upon some occasions we can almost see the doors closing and opening . . . opening and closing. They may be large or small, steel or wooden, with or without a knob, and thick or thin; but they are very much a part of our lives . . . and deaths.

Paul didn't want Mark to go with them and a door closed but Barnabas did and a door opened. To carry our insight further note that all four were involved in the process. The grouping and ministerial forms could have been much different. Indeed, there were several possibilities. I can't help but feel that God had a direct hand in all that was taking place . . . even to the point of when it appeared Paul slammed the door on Barnabas's fingers!

## *Conclusion*

Indeed, our text is one of the great teaching verses of the New Testament, provided that we are open to it. In summary: disagreements need not lead to failure; God's wisdom must have dictated the two workers go separate ways; sometimes two personalities just don't jibe; there must have been a powerful sense of ministry in all four men; and some doors have to close before others can open. In all cases there is cause for healthy optimism.

Are Christians such as Paul, Barnabas, Silas, and Mark ever losers with anything resembling finality? No. If you and I are steadfast and yet open to learn in the Faith regardless of upheavals and contention, are we losers eventually? No . . . praise God!

## ✤REACTING TO A STORM✤

## *Background*

OUR SCRIPTURAL backdrop, Acts 27:1–28:16, divides itself up into three segments. The first is Paul's voyage to the island of Malta. The second is an unusual look into his stay on the island. The third is his voyage to and arrival at home.

Paul and some other prisoners embarked in a ship of Adramyttium. Their first stop was at Sidon. A man by the name of Julius had responsibility for Paul and allowed him to be with his friends at Sidon. Then they set sail north and westward in the waters south of the present country of Turkey. Their next stop was at Myra in Lycia. They changed ships, this time one "of Alexandria." From there they arrived a number of days later at Cnidus. Their next stop was at Fair Havens near the city of Lasea on the very large island of Crete. By now the voyage had become dangerous and Paul let it be known that was how he sized up the situation. The centurion paid more attention to the captain and the owner of the ship than to Paul. So, they set sail again in hope they might reach Phoenix on Crete, a more suitable harbor for winter. The ship moved along close to the island, apparently with some ease at first. However, they were struck by a tempestuous wind and driven far from land. The ship floundered badly. They began to throw the cargo overboard. Neither the sun nor the stars appeared for many days. Hope was abandoned. Paul comes forth and tells them they should have listened to him earlier, but not to worry because there will be no loss of life. An angel had spoken to him. The sailors thought they were nearing land and lowered a boat into the sea to escape from the ship but on Paul's advice they were not able to do so. Apparently everyone ate some food on the fourteenth day of their suspenseful ordeal. Paul must have made a worship experience out of it because the Scripture says, ". . . he took bread and giving thanks to God in the presence of all he broke it and began to eat." They spotted a beach and headed for it. The ship ran aground. The soldiers planned to kill all the prisoners, but the centurion, wishing to save Paul, would not have it that way. By swimming or on pieces of the ship everyone escaped to the land.

They found out they had landed on the island of Malta, directly south of Sicily. The natives welcomed them and built a fire. Paul gathered a bundle of sticks to put on the fire. A viper fastened on his hand and the natives immediately assumed he was guilty of murder. Paul shook off the creature into the fire and suffered no harm. They waited for him to swell up or fall dead. Neither one nor the other happened, so they said he was a god. Paul healed the father of the chief man of the island. Others who had diseases were also healed by Paul. They were given many gifts and provisions as they prepared to embark.

They were on Malta three months and set sail for Rome. The ship stopped at Syracuse on Sicily for three days. It moved to Rhegium on the southern tip of Italy and on to Puteoli, where the Apostle found Christian friends. The record says, "And so we came to Rome." In Rome the brethren came as far as the Forum of Appius and Three Taverns to meet Paul. Paul thanked God and took courage. He was allowed to stay by himself with the soldier that guarded him.

## Introduction

In the midst of darkness and hopelessness at sea Paul speaks: "I now bid you take heart; for there will be no los of life among you, but only of the ship" (Acts 27:22). His word is one of authority. Why? An angel of God had spoken to him.

If you and I were in like circumstances, how would we react to Paul's words? Let's take a look. It will do us good.

## Application

*"The man is mad from the experience; let's prepare for a watery grave."*

We hear him and turn him completely off. There is no object in delaying the inevitable. Others have gone down and we are going to join them. It's time to be stoical and take what fate has handed out. To give his words any chance at all is to get our hopes up, only to discover we are being plunged into waters that will not be denied. Maybe as a last thought we ought to recognize Paul's great career. Maybe he was right about Jesus arising from the dead and he will go to meet his lasting reward. That doesn't mean he is going to conquer this terrifying storm.

Storms at sea are really something. I remember one vividly. It was in the Atlantic a couple hundred miles off the coast of the USA. The one hundred and fifty or so that were aboard the ship during those three days must have all wondered at some point whether or not we would return to a comfortable harbor in Newport, Rhode Island. I don't recall anyone telling us there would be no loss of life. There was no Chaplain aboard. What one could sense was the feeling our technology and the captain's experience would save us. Had we been faced with the same vulnerability as the sailors and soldiers on Paul's ship, I am convinced that if someone had said, "The ship won't make it but all the crew and passengers will" he would have been declared an oddball and ignored by some.

Saint Paul was right and yet we see him in the context of a proven hero of the Faith. He must have been a complete stranger to some on board during those very violently dark days and nights. Perhaps you and I would have thought he was mad. Maybe we would have turned him out and acquiesced into an unemotional acceptance that death was at hand and there is no purpose in fighting. . . . God or no God.

There are other reactions, aren't there?

*"At least there's one with courage, regardless of his lack of realism."*

That's the old pat on the back for effort but with no actual faith, isn't it? That sounds so typical! We admire a person's dedication to the Faith but deep down question his or her coming to terms with reality. It's "OK" to be brave and live sacrificially but what good does it do? Anyway how can we be sure it isn't just a waste of time to be courageous? Why not rest easy in a mild—if not exciting—fatalism? In the life of the Church some admire those who practice certain disciplines such as tithing, regular worship attendance, hours of service, and daily prayers. Yet, they can't quite swallow and certainly cannot digest the worthwhileness of that which just doesn't seem to pay off in the realities of this world. The stark truth of the matter is there are those who commend the Cross openly but under their breaths say its all for naught because of the kind of world we live in.

It is very important to recognize not only that Saint Paul speaks with courage but that such courage comes to the surface from a vast reservoir of Christian experience. He was not out of character. When the Holy Spirit (an angel more specifically) gave a revelation, he passed it on. It's really a matter-of-fact situation. The Christ, crucified and resurrected, made up who and what Paul was. In that sense he wasn't a complex man. He was a religious genius but that could scarcely be traced to inborn traits. He was such a genius because he found his identity—past, present, and future—in the Christ. Those who have not entered the intimate relationship Paul had with Christ do not comprehend that being courageous was not only optimistic but realistic. He lived with real dangers around him. Yet, his reactions to them were spiritually realistic. He could be drowned at any minute. Of course, that was not going to happen because God through an angel said it wouldn't.

Let's look at the text in light of ourselves again.

*"Why doesn't he just let things happen and keep his mouth shut."*

Paul stuck his neck out. He's telling everyone to "hang loose"; an angel has told him the ship will be wrecked but no one will drown. That's pretty silly, why didn't he just "play it cool" and keep his prognostications under wraps? That way he could announce how right he was by adjusting revelation to whatever took place. Those foregoing words have a satanic ring to them, don't they? It's as if the Apostle doesn't have an ounce of real integrity. He is little more than a cheap finagler that will come forth at the last moment and display his genius. Are our projections a bit too severe and awkward? I think not as long as we keep in mind the predictability of human nature. If Paul were living among us today, would it be any different? We know the answer to that! There are always people in like situations who want no part of God's man or anything he says . . . even in the time of great peril.

Pastors and key laity are sometimes faced with experiencing storms and loss of some type being imminent. Sometimes they think the best and easiest thing to do is exactly what our reaction says: see what develops and don't utter a word. However, when precious human beings are aboard a ship marked "the Church" and that ship is being driven to and fro on vicious seas and a word from the Lord does come, shouldn't it be forthrightly shared? Private revelation given to those who provide leadership for Christians that goes uncommunicated is much like the person with a key to the door of a shelterhouse who doesn't let on while everyone nearby is drenched by a rainstorm and bruised by hailstones.

There is more.

*"He is a wonderfully strong and sincere human being; I hope he is right."*

That's more than a pat on the back; that's an unqualified vote for success. There are those who respect us and really want us to succeed, even our prophecies. They will tell us how much they appreciate us and how talented we are. They will share their complimentary words with others. Who can find fault with such heartfelt outpouring? Probably only the few who are out-and-out hostile. Clergy feel comfortable with such persons. There is no doubt about what they want to happen.

There is only one thing wrong about this reaction. We turn to the book of Jonah. Jonah, you recall, was sent by God to Ninevah to tell the people they would be destroyed because of their wickedness. What happened? They sought forgiveness! When God saw their repentance, He decided not to do away with them. Now Jonah was very upset. He wanted God to destroy them. He thought he had failed! He saw himself as wrong and said, "Therefore now, O Lord, take my life from me, I beseech thee, for it is better for me to die than to live" (4:3). If man's repentance causes another word to come from God and it disappoints us and our sympathizers because of the secret desire above all to be right, now what happens? You guessed it! Repentance for seeking primarily to be right and draw attention to one's greatness in place of doing God's will first, last, and always.

There is another reaction.

*"He is a servant of God and if he says it, I believe it."*

I suppose all Christian leaders—if they were subjected to the circumstances of Paul—would find this music to their ears. That's an attitude of faith and trust par excellence in God through one of His servants. It has no strings attached. It is a reaction that thrills even the soul maintaining a noncommittal stance. Credibility is at a very high level, perhaps the highest attainable. Debate, discussion, and even clever deductions are out of place. No apologies necessary. God has given strength and guidance through His servant Paul, a man spiritually intoxicated with the Christ.

All clergy earnestly desire this sort of reaction to them and their ministry. If they don't, they had best be someplace other than ministerial service. We hope—almost in agony at times—that we can be worthy of such response. It is not because we have earned the favor of God but that He has called us into obedience and that obedience to Him gives us the right to seek and expect such response. Indeed, the Apostle Peter was correct: ". . . chosen and destined by God the Father and sanctified by the Spirit for obedience to Jesus Christ . . ." (1 Peter 1:2).

## *Conclusion*

It is difficult, to say the least, to take Holy Scripture and ask it to speak to our situation . . . or is it? Aren't the reactions pulled from absorption in the text as practical and truthful as any expertly documented report of the hour's news? Sometimes—yea, more than we like to admit—we underestimate the power of Holy Scripture to speak to us with vividness. Were you there with Paul during that savage storm? I hope so. I was.

Saint Paul had learned as you and I must:

> Trust and obey, for there's no other way
> To be happy in Jesus, but to trust and obey.

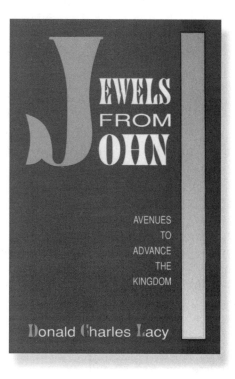

JEWELS FROM JOHN

AVENUES
TO
ADVANCE
THE
KINGDOM

Donald Charles Lacy

*1992*

*The gospel of John is delightfully compelling and uniquely fulfilling! This is especially true during the Lenten season as we tend to look for a change of pace in the material presented by Matthew, Mark, and Luke. This gospel has a way of pushing our homiletical skills to the hilt. Only both a rational and mystical approach can do justice to its magnificence. These sermons were originally preached as a part of an all-church Bible study series. The sponsoring group was the United Methodist Women. We broke the gospel down into six major sections and studied each, week by week. Then, on Sunday, a particular text was chosen from the passage, was studied, and a sermon was preached. The value of such an approach is simple and basic: an entire church is focused on an assigned book of the Bible and sermons that elucidate a key spiritual truth are preached. Two of six sermons are presented.*

CHAPTER 7

# *Jewels from John*

## ❋ADULTERY: FORGIVABLE BUT NOT❋ TO BE REPEATED

1.

THE GOSPEL OF John 8:1–11 tells of a woman caught committing adultery. According to the story Jesus went to the Mount of Olives for the night, probably to spend long hours in prayer. Early the next morning He went to the Temple. There the people gathered around Him, He sat down, and began to teach them. His teaching was disrupted by the teachers of the law and the Pharisees. They brought a woman who had been caught in the act of adultery. They made her stand before everyone and confronted Jesus with her sin. They pointed out that in their law, Moses commanded such a woman was to be stoned to death. Our Lord must have known exactly what they meant for He was a student and teacher of His own rich religious heritage. Then they asked Him for His teaching on the matter. It was a trap for Jesus, so they could accuse Him. He could quickly be in trouble with the Roman and/or Jewish authorities. He seems to have ignored them for the moment by bending over and writing on the ground with His finger. They continued to pose questions and then He straightened up. His answer is one that still rings in the corridors of every real or imagined court house in the country dealing with such a matter. He said, "whichever one of you has committed no sin may throw the first stone at her." Then He bent over again and began to write on the ground. When they witnessed our Lord's response, they left the area. Jesus was left alone with the woman still standing in His midst. Then He straightened up again and said to her, "Where are they? Is there no one left to condemn you?" She answered, "No one, sir." Jesus closes the story by saying, "I do not condemn you either. Go, but do not sin again."

The problem is one that is age-old.

For centuries the Jews had dealt with it in the law of Moses. We commonly understand this Law to be found in the first five books of the Old Testament; Genesis, Exodus, Leviticus, Numbers, and Deuteronomy. In addition to the Ten Commandments, Leviticus chapter twenty and Deuteronomy chapter twenty-two specifically deal with adultery. For an ancient people their thoughts are at a lofty level. They recognized the wrong involved, defined it, and prescribed punishment.

On other occasions Jesus speaks to the matter in ways that cut across the ideas of the ruling religious groups. The one that really must have "blown their minds" is found in Matthew 5:27–28. Jesus said, "You have heard that it was said, 'Do not commit adultery.' But now I tell you: anyone who looks at a woman and wants to possess her is guilty of committing adultery with her in his heart." Most men, I suspect, have difficulties with this one.

But let's not unduly digress from our initial story.

Notice in the narrative the attitude of Jesus the Christ as compared to the teachers of the law and the Pharisees.

There is a *trio of comparisons* meant for our enrichment and enlightenment.

*They exposed her, but not Jesus, to public ridicule.*

One sees a group, really a personification of self-righteousness, not only making charges but doing so in the most embarrassing way possible. There isn't much doubt about her guilt. The story does not argue for her innocence. If questioned, one has the feeling those pressing for prosecution can give all of the naughty details. They are a sophisticated lynching squad ready, willing, and able to make her a spectacle for all to view. It has a kind of carnival air about it. If they had thought about it, tickets would probably have been sold to watch the event! No doubt there would have been many takers. Parts of the Old West must have taken their script from these men without knowing it.

While moral standards have to be upheld in order for civilization to exist, one has the uncomfortable feeling they were after more. The poor soul may have been guilty many times. We do not know. We know they wanted to put Jesus on the spot. If they could just get Him into serious trouble with the majority of the Jewish religious authorities or, better still, the Roman rulers, their little staged event would be successful. In fact, the Romans did kill Jesus. Remember He died by crucifixion and not by stoning. Perhaps of even greater significance was their own need to be above others. As upholders of the law placed over against her illicit, amorous escapade, they looked quite good. A perceptive cartoonist could have a field day using such an idea. Of course, you and I would not want to carry that too far because we cannot actually know all the motives of such men at this point in time or can anyone else for that matter. At any rate, the worse she could be made to look the better they looked. That sounds familiar, doesn't it?

Now, Jesus doesn't say to His brethren—and these men were in a sense His Jewish brothers—"You fellows are exactly right." He could very easily have given His approval to their actions and proceeded with the execution in an appropriate place. Maybe they were anxious to have His "blessing" and didn't know it. Often if a layperson can get the "blessing" of his or her pastor then that covers a multitude of sins. Of course, he can be given just the tip of the iceberg which looks innocent, inviting, and worthy. I think it would have been so easy for Jesus to have told them how great, pure, and virtuous they were for having spotted her yielding to temptation and bringing her forth for judgment. This would have confirmed their under-standing of the Mosaic Law and left Jesus a comrade in arms. Of course, He doesn't do this. In fact, He does quite the opposite. From one stand-point our Lord was an exceedingly poor politician. Surely He could have agreed with their actions and at some later time brought them around to His way of thinking. Not Jesus! He must do the work of the Father and the Father was saying things they couldn't or wouldn't hear.

So much for the first third of the trio.

The second of the three comparisons merits our attention.

*They suggested she be stoned to death, but not Jesus.*

While stoning may appear to you and me to be a terrible way to die, it had been common among the Jews for centuries. It was their form of capital punishment. Blasphemy, idolatry, and adultery were all punishable by stoning. Not everyone died that was singled out. For example, later in the eighth chapter of John, Jesus claims to have been a part of the creation before Abraham. His opponents found this blasphemous, so they picked up stones to throw at Him. He managed to slip away. In the fourteenth chapter of Acts in Lystra crowds turned against Paul. They stoned him and dragged him out of town. They thought he was dead. However, some believers gathered around him and he got up.

The teachers of the law and Pharisees were only doing what they felt necessary. Sure they were attempting to put Jesus on the spot, but their ancestors had been stoning people for centuries. They thought they were doing so for good reasons. Their actions were very consistent, legalistic, and predictable. The irritating problem was Jesus who was working beyond their understanding of consistency, legalism, and predictability. For their day and time they were models of religious thought and idealism. The flowering of their Faith into Christianity was something most of them refused to accept. The faith of Abraham, Moses, David, and the prophets was aborted. They just didn't allow the essential, total fulfill-ment to come into their hearts and minds in the person of Jesus the Christ. The centuries since that time have been filled with sadness and desperation because the Lord's people by and large rejected Him. Symbolically, their own adultery can be seen in the refusal to become a faithful part of the Church or the bride married to her husband, the Christ. Paul tells us in Ephesians 5:23, "For a husband has authority over his wife just as Christ has authority over the church; and Christ is himself the Savior of the church, his body."

Jesus doesn't inflict the woman with a tirade on the awfulness of her sin, let alone stone her. He knows that she knows adultery is wrong. Sometimes you and I point a critical finger at people's lives simply telling them what they already know about themselves. They need the Savior and not our low-grade lectures. Anyway, if we talk long enough and critical enough we are probably saying more about ourselves than them. Our blessed Lord knows all of this infinitely more. Praise His name, He does not come at us with flaming nostrils and a wailing voice reciting our sins chapter and verse! Praise His name, He is not ready to shame us into submission by cataloging our infractions! Praise His name, any stones He may throw are those that have love in the center with compassion and mercy for outer layers.

So much for the second third of the trio.

The final of three comparisons speaks to the meeting of a universal need.

*They left her alone, but not Jesus.*

When it became obvious Jesus would not be caught by their snare, they pulled out. Perhaps it was also due to their lack of genuine concern for the adulteress. Perhaps it was also a matter of lost prestige before the people. If you and I don't get our way, it's very easy to leave the situation or person. Our concern is often noticeably lacking for those caught in sin. If our judgment is questioned about a person(s) or situation(s), we most likely feel the prestige factor slipping and we excuse ourselves. You and I might qualify as "teachers of the law and Pharisees."

To be left alone with Jesus must have been awesome and filled with joy. We don't know whether or not she shed tears. I think she did. We don't know that she audibly said, "I'm sorry. Forgive me." I think she did. I see her as a "fallen woman" in the presence of total purity whose tears are trickling down both cheeks . . . who prays for forgiveness and means it for the first time in her life . . . who has those awful images brought to mind of her betrayal of the marital vows . . . who knows firsthand the meaning of liberation in the only sense that it ultimately matters . . . who forgives not only her accusers but her willing lover(s) as well . . . who leaves the presence of Jesus knowing she is important in His sight . . . who accepts herself as a child of God, guilty of the sordid and licentious to be sure, but at last washed in the blood of the lamb . . . who now can be just as saintly as any woman having never broken her vows of marital faithfulness.

I wonder about you and me. Do we walk off and leave such persons to fend for themselves? Do we ignore them as just so much trash to be avoided? Maybe we like to be around them to hear their tales of exploitation, explicitness, and expletives. Indeed, what are our attitudes? Maybe we feel good, even superior, knowing we have not physically been guilty of the act . . . until a voice whispers, "How many times have you wished for the right person, at the right time, and in the right place to make love?" Our Lord knew that her problem was not unique. He knew long before you and I that we seem to have a bad habit of condemning those whose sins do not tempt us very much. After all, it is so easy to say in our later years, "Isn't adultery a terrible thing!" It is so convenient, even smug, to say when we are happily married, "Good heavens, what a crime!" You and I do well to remember the words "except for the grace of God . . ."

Thus, we complete the trio of comparisons.

Adultery is not the unpardonable sin.

Having said that, however, let's keep a certain perspective. Nothing destroys a marriage quite so thoroughly as adultery. It is a sin that can be and often is forgiven, but it really isn't often forgotten. Satan will say, "Well, it happened once and it will happen again." If we do not begin the day with a forgiving attitude that places God's love first, the memory of the act will destroy the marriage through real or imagined infidelity.

Perhaps an even more wicked sin is the innocent spouse who "uses" the guilty one long after it has happened. I wonder how many men have "towed the line" under the threat of ruinous divorce settlements, becoming little more than four-year-old boys living out their lives in quiet desperation? I wonder how many women have buried themselves in liquor, drugs, and other escape hatches because their husbands threatened to expose them to their children, relative, and friends? There isn't a single drop of Christ's forgiving blood in such attitudes!

You and I are to be forgiving but certainly not condoning.

Periodically, and at the time of temptation, it is well to repeat the questions, "Wilt thou love, comfort, honor, and keep, in sickness and in health; and forsaking all others keep thee only unto your mate so long as ye both shall live?" and then answer, "I will" as many times as it takes to be confident faithfulness is right.

Really there is little that can be said about adultery which goes beyond our Lord's closing words to her. He says, "Go, but do not sin again." *Adultery is forgivable but it is not to be repeated.*

# ❋JESUS WASHES FEET: AN ACT OF HUMILITY❋ WORTH IMITATING

THE GOSPEL OF John 13:1–20 tells of Jesus washing the feet of the Apostles. It was the day before the Passover Festival, commemorating God's deliverance of Israel from Pharaoh's oppressions. Jesus knew that His time had arrived to leave the world. He and His close disciples were having supper. The Devil had already suggested to Judas Iscariot the betrayal. Jesus arose from the table, took off His outer garment, and tied a towel around His waist. Then He poured some water into a wash-basin. He washed their feet and dried them with the towel around His waist. Then He and Peter had a brief encounter with Peter eventually saying, "Lord, do not wash only my feet, then! Wash my hands and head, too!" Jesus then announced all were clean except one, meaning Judas Iscariot. Having finished the task, He put on His outer garment and returned to His place at the table. He confirmed the validity of them calling Him "Teacher and Lord." Then He explicitly told them they should wash one another's feet and that He had set the example. Furthermore, He says if they put it into practice they will be very happy. With a note of melancholy He relates how the Scripture "The man who shared my food turned against me (Ps. 41:9)," must come true. Our Lord closes the passage by indicating whoever receives anyone He sends receives Him also and whoever receives Him receives the Father.

Footwashing is not a new idea among denominations.

For example, the Church of the Brethren recovered the practice in the eighteenth century. To the best of my knowledge most, if not all, in that group continue it today in some form. It is normally done in the same service as partaking of Communion. While at a conference in the northern part of Indiana I was privileged to be a part of such a service under the leadership of the Church of the Brethren. In this particular instance we simply sat around tables, reading Scripture, singing hymns, partaking of light refreshments, and washing one another's feet. For several it was a first time! The service might best be described as one of some hesitation, a bit of perspiration, and a generous portion of inspiration. I had seen this done different times as a boy in a Congregational-Christian church in which I spent my early years. Of course, there are other Christian groups that also utilize it.

The United Methodist Church, in a few individual congregations, is involved in the service. The prime examples are probably Edgehill in Nashville, Tennessee, and Shiloh in Mahomet, Illinois. Our denomination has published a book called *Ritual in a New Day* which has a chapter on footwashing. While suggestions are given, it recommends each church do its "own thing," meaning we should shape and form our own rituals.

Now we are to ask the key questions, "Does or does not the New Testament make a strong case for footwashing?" It seems to me the answer has to be a categorical, "Yes, it does." Our Lord doesn't leave any doubt.

Let's make some careful observations about the narrative to test this point of view.

*There is a seriousness in the scene.*

One gets the impression this is about the most solemn occasion in the events of our Lord's life, except the Crucifixion. The Apostles are all there. His death is close at hand. Most or all of the "chips are down." His entire ministry and mission seem to be at stake. The air is scented with an ominous and even bewildering smell. Will the way of the Master triumph over and through the happenings of the next few days?

What the betrayer would or would not do is uppermost in their minds. The Devil had made his point with Judas Iscariot. It is interesting to note he was probably the only one who was not a Galilean. It is thought he was so clever, cunning, and deceptive the Apostles did not know for sure it was he until the deed had been perpetrated. His mercenary tendencies must have gotten the best of him. Apparently he thought Jesus was going to usher into existence an earthly political kingdom in which the Master would be King. He would be secretary of the treasury because he already handled the money for the little group. It is always well to use both names, Judas Iscariot, when referring to the traitor. The reason is simply that there are, at least, eight others mentioned in the Bible carrying the name of Judas.

You and I are privileged to know our Lord was successful. We know how the story ends. In the Upper Room that night it is very doubtful a single Apostle was totally convinced their Lord's Kingdom would gloriously survive a form other than what they had already been able to experience. We must not belittle them. Only God had the answers that mattered.

So, it is in this kind of an atmosphere that footwashing takes place.

It is a very special time in the lives of the Apostles.

Let's observe again closely.

*Jesus tells Peter it has to be done.*

In verse eight Peter declares, "Never at any time will you wash my feet!" and our Lord responds, "If I do not wash your feet, you will no longer be my disciples." We suppose Peter was prompted to say what he did by his reluctance to have his Lord do such a menial task. There is no mistaking his Lord's reply. It is direct, firm, and clear. Peter was such a lovable pest. Prior to the death and resurrection of Jesus he blew hot and cold. He had an affinity for either being the strongest or weakest of the group. He could be blatantly traitorous or admirable dainty. It sounds as though Jesus in this episode is "laying down the law" to him. If he wants to continue being a follower of Jesus, he must submit to having his feet washed by the Master.

Doesn't this also have something directly to convey to you and me? When speaking of the sacraments of Baptism and Holy Communion, a very large part of the Christian Faith points to the intention and command of our Lord. The Scriptures continually speak to us through the stories of the Lord's relationship to others. This is especially true of Peter, James, and John along with the other Apostles and a number of women. The Gospel's directness and relevance come to us not from isolated situations where the Christ is speaking to Himself! In brief, isn't He speaking to you and me through His word exchange with Peter?

So much for this amplification of the story.

It's time to move to another pertinent point.

*Jesus, as Lord and Teacher, washes their feet.*

He maintains at one place in the text, "I, your Lord and Teacher, have just washed your feet." It is as though He is saying, "This was not just anyone cleansing your feet. It was I, Jesus the Christ." Something of authoritative significance had taken place. It was not just another time of washing one's or another's dusty and oftentimes dirty feet, as was the custom in that part of the world upon entering a home.

Isn't it amazing how our Lord takes the common and ordinary unto Himself and sanctifies it? We would be hard pressed to find at any time in His ministry the use of the unusual or aristocratic to teach a lesson. He is continually immersed in the daily, even mundane, lives of the people. At most every home in Palestine there was a basin, towel, and water. A similar observation can be made in the case of water for Baptism and bread and wine for the Lord's Supper.

With our traditions and mind-sets it is laborious attempting to see the importance of one man washing the feet of twelve others, until we acknowledge that the ordinary has been made into the extraordinary. The passage reads in such a way that we can see some sort of official act has taken place. There is even the suggestion an ordinance or ritual has been given birth. Wile we should resist the tendency to build all sorts of proper methods and institute lengthy religious-sounding official language, what has occurred is of paramount import. Jesus is near the end of His stay on this earth and the weighty seriousness of His graciously beautiful act is for hundreds of generations to take into their hearts. That includes you and me.

Now we move to what some say is the clincher.

*Jesus sets an example for us to follow.*
Our Lord says, "You, then, should wash one another's feet. I have set an example for you, so that you will do just what I have done for you." Can you and I defend an opposing position? We would have to move words around in this passage in order to maintain Jesus doesn't speak pointedly and positively on the matter. In our churches we do many other things with far less scriptural prompting. In fact most of what we do has no direct command in the Bible. There isn't even anything about Sunday morning worship services, budgets, and suitable buildings. You and I might skim over the verses just read and explain them away as just so much information for the Apostles there and then. The trouble with that is we could do just about the same thing with the entire Bible. The United Methodist Church in its vows of membership requires we answer affirmatively the question, "Do you receive and profess the Christian faith as contained in the Scriptures of the Old and New Testaments?"

We could, of course, interpret this to mean Jesus was setting an example for the key leaders of the Faith for centuries to come. This would mean footwashing is reserved for the few. It might mean in our day and time only the ordained clergy are to participate. My own reaction to that is: There is a difference in the function of lay and clergy ministries, but our Lord's Spirit is not divisive among His own people. To put it another way, ordination does set the clergy apart, but it does not obliterated the oneness in Christ with laity. Our day especially calls for openness, even experimentation, among all professing Jesus the Christ . . . and I didn't say a liberal stance on every issue.

The example is set before you and me. Where we take it from here is up to us in an attitude of sincere prayer and intellectual processing. In the back of our minds and in the depths of our hearts we are called to be cognizant of the fact we are confronted with the recorded words of Jesus. The Gospel of John is not in the Old Testament and it is not an Epistle to a particular church.

We move to our final observation.

*Christians are equally significant.*

Our Lord's emphasis on the relationship of the master to the slave and the messenger to the one sending him has a leveling influence. While different personalities sparkle before our eyes in that Upper Room, all, except Judas Iscariot, seem to be of equal value. There is an interrelatedness between leader and follower that results in both being very important. Boasting, judging, and even estimates of worth are drowned in a series of loving relationships in which servanthood under God becomes the only major guidepost. Greatness is measured in service, especially that without fanfare and no promise of gain.

You and I in a leadership role would probably have delegated the awkwardness and grovelling posture of washing feet to someone not having the expertise to perform the really "prime duties" of the Faith. Well, our Lord didn't. Pride and/or lack of spiritual sensitivity would likely have been our real barriers. Isn't it uncanny how our Lord's ministry shows us so much about ourselves in ways we can only deny at our peril?

So, we conclude the last of five careful observations.

Should you and I wash one another's feet?

Maybe we ought to list reasons for and against. To follow that route requires strict honesty. We should not be ashamed of any reason, pro or con. To spend some time doing this enables us to think through the matter. Whichever list is longer probably doesn't matter as much as our willingness to come to terms with Holy Scripture and provide our own decisions. Of course, we should undergird the probings and findings with prayer.

For some, change in any way, shape, or form is painful. Even to be open to consider the possibility of doing some things differently can cause considerable pain. We like the old pathways or as someone has said we are "addicted to the comfortable."

Just now what is the Spirit saying to you and me about washing one another's feet in the future? That's a serious question. It is not apt to go away. Whatever we decide and/or do, Jesus the Christ calls us to love one another. In reality, this means letting Him have His way.

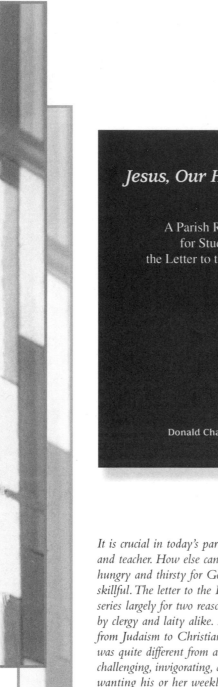

**Jesus, Our High Priest**

A Parish Resource
for Studying
the Letter to the Hebrews

Donald Charles Lacy

1997

*It is crucial in today's parish life for the pastor/priest to be both preacher and teacher. How else can we offer substance to our parishioners who are hungry and thirsty for God's Word? Granted, one's delivery must be skillful. The letter to the Hebrews was selected for a preaching/teaching series largely for two reasons: 1. For some reason, it seems to be avoided by clergy and laity alike. 2. Its unique magnificence, especially as a bridge from Judaism to Christianity, cries out to be heard. I quickly noted that it was quite different from any other book in the New Testament. It was challenging, invigorating, and motivating. Of course, it is not for one wanting his or her weekly injection of "feel good" theology! Three of fourteen sermons are presented.*

CHAPTER 8

# Jesus, Our High Priest

## ❋HOW SHALL WE ESCAPE?❋

### Background

ANGELS HAVE made quite a comeback! (Heb. 1:5–2:18). There seems to be widespread interest in them in our contemporary society and, of course, opportunists seeking to use them to the hilt. I guess we all believe in angels in some sense.

The biblical world was dominated by the presence of angels, some good and some bad but mostly good. The writer of Hebrews wants his readers to know Jesus is far more important and powerful. Various quotations from the Hebrew Scriptures (Old Testament) are skillfully used to build his case. This is especially true of the Psalms, the prayerbook of the ancient church.

What the author wants us to know very pointedly is that Jesus brings us the ultimate in salvation. Regardless of their special place, such as Gabriel, angels are not our saviors. They were never intended to be and to understand it that way is a serious mistake. This is why his question has a powerful cutting edge to it that points to punishment and even damnation, unless one is open to God's outstretched hand through His Son.

### Focus

Indeed, how shall we escape if we pay no attention to such a great salvation? I suggest to you areas that deserve our full attention. There may be more but there are, at least, four that quickly come to mind.

### Application

*First, how essential is essential?*

The word "essential" just doesn't give us much leeway, does it? Upfront we are called to deal with more than an idea or suggestion.

Salvation has to do with who and what we are. Not to pay any attention is self-defeating and even spiritually suicidal. To back away from it is not to make it null and void but simply to say, "I am not going to deal with that now." In short, it will still be essential today, tomorrow, and forever. No reworking of one's life really changes the gift of a great salvation.

We have all known fairly early in life that in order for human beings to exist certain essentials have to be in place. For those of us who have little scientific training we begin with air, food, and water. It is really not that much different in one's spiritual life. There are philosophers who tell us everyone has a philosophy of life or—in effect—some form of salvation that gives meaning and purpose. It may hardly resemble a Judeo-Christian understanding but nevertheless is seems to be the glue that holds people together. The message from the letter to the Hebrews is unmistakable: a great salvation, first announced by the Lord Himself, beckons to be received.

Anything essential means it is not going to disappear. It is here to stay. Sooner or later we are going to deal with it one way or another. Not to deal with it is to deal with it! For many—yes, perhaps the vast majority of people—discover late in life what they thought had been resolved or at least, put permanently on a "back burner" is there for consideration. Some politicians have used the term "deferred repentance," apparently meaning "as soon as I get through with the dirty work, I'll get right with my God." That may sound very shrewd but suppose the Lord calls you home before the dirty work is finished?

The infinite love of our great salvation saves us from becoming rigidly legalistic that leads to an unforgiving attitude, damning everyone in our way who doesn't conform. Having admitted that and the glory in this love, we return to the same piercing and unmovable question: How shall we escape, if we pay no attention to such a great salvation? Think of the many who tried to eradicate it, were claimed by the death angels, and another generation discovers God hasn't changed His mind!

*Second, how serious is serious?*

Physicians are those who tell us how serious something is about our bodies or act as channels so we are able to find out. It would be difficult to imagine a society in which they did not exist and we could not count on them. Often they have been friends, counselors, and even religious-like figures in which we put much trust. But who tells us how serious spiritual matters are? Hopefully, these are the clergy in parishes who are about the last of the general practitioners. In a way their cause and calling are always the same: act as a means to give people the salvation of Christ. It is always a serious matter that asks often silently, "how shall we escape . . .?"

I wished, as you probably do, that everything didn't have to be so serious today. We become overloaded—it seems—by trivialities superimposed upon us by persons we do not know and probably never will. If you are like I am some days, you just wish it would all go away and a much more simple lifestyle were instituted. That gives us the opportunity to ask "how serious is serious?" as we seek to practice the Christian Faith. After sifting and sorting attitudes, hopefully we can still maintain with utmost integrity and commitment that what is done with Christ's salvation is serious at levels nothing else is.

The cliche "all we have to do is die and pay taxes" may say something more important than we realize. They are both serious! The time we spend dealing with our deaths, consciously and subconsciously, would probably boggle all of our minds. It is even said by some that after childhood we begin to prepare for death. I suspect most of us well before sixty-five have pictured our funeral scenes. Who will be there? What will be said? How will I look as a corpse? Who will be sad? Who will be glad? What about the casket and flowers? Will there be memorials and from whom? Will I be appreciated? Will I be able to know the answers to the questions I am asking? There really is no denying this is serious business and our passing inevitably deals with "salvation."

*Third, how pressing is pressing?*

"Pastor, if you are just trying to put the pressure on, forget it" may very well be your response at this stage of our visit together. In fact, you feel as though it has been a really tough week and anything even slightly resembling pressure should be immediately forgotten. I am in sympathy with that and know some of your struggles. I also know how weary we can become if we continually feel the weight of unrelenting heaviness. It isn't healthy! Of course, it is not healthy to move away from the ultimate questions our faith asks and that's why the question the letter to the Hebrews poses is ever with us.

The unmatched beauty of our Faith needs to find its way through the heavy loads today's living brings to us. Believe it or not, we can discover that's why we feel pressured! Christ wants a word with us. He is standing at the door knocking and until we realize we are not going to feel better until we open the door we are caught in a bind. He wants to eat and drink with us. Yes, pressure does build from continually hearing the knocking and our refusal for whatever reason(s) to open the door. How can it be any other way? Indeed, how shall we escape if we pay no attention to such a great salvation? There have been, are, and will be those who prove it is true. Is this not positive pressure solely intended for our good?

You have likely heard the prayer at sometime or another that says, "Do not pray for easy lives. Pray to be stronger men! Do not pray for tasks equal to your powers. Pray for powers equal to your tasks." Making that an integral part of our personal religious systems is very helpful and offers wonderful freedom. For one thing it brings a much-needed dimension to our prayer lives and for another moves us away from "poor little weak me." The greatness of God begins to be seen and especially His unlimited power given through the Son to change us; this becomes the difference between burdens that bury us and a salvation that literally saves us.

*Fourth, how urgent is urgent?*

"How shall we escape . . ." rings with urgency. The question leaps out at us and gets our attention. Not only once does this happen but over and over again as a reminder that putting it off leaves a jeopardy in our lives over which we have little control, except to deal with it. It doesn't help to complain about the contrived scare tactics of questionable revivalists. It doesn't help to work at an attitudinal change that tries to neutralize or even make irrelevant the solemn inquiry. It doesn't even help to look at other translations and revisions of the letter to the Hebrews. The substance and pointedness are there for all to see!

What does this say about the integrity of our preaching and teaching? Perhaps it makes a lot of pragmatic sense to rephrase in such a way that the sting is taken out of it and it becomes more palatable as a suggestion or implication. There are those who say we continually attempt to make the Ten Commandments the "ten suggestions." That way we can still have it "our way" by insisting on the right to define revelation in ways conducive to our temperaments and tastes. May God be merciful! What does all of this say about the accountability of the one doing the preaching and teaching? It really gets down to asking "are we called to please and appease our listeners or are we called under the yoke of Christ to be obedient stewards and vessels of the Word?"

If someone were to say that your house was on fire, I assume you would see the fire department was called. If your home was being burglarized, I assume you would call some law enforcement agency. If you were posed with the question of coming to terms with a "destiny or eternity" issue, I assume there would be no delay. Yet, that is not the way life and death seems to be played out among us is it?

I believe often the most kind and compassionate thing we can say to others as we go about living the Faith is, "the question is still being asked and I will pray that you deal with it *today*." Procrastination in serious spiritual matters takes its toll. Wholeness and holiness come to those who have dealt humbly with it, discovering the urgency was real and was not going to go away. Dear friends, it is not going to go away.

## Conclusion

In our voyage through the letter to the Hebrews we are not likely to deal with anything more important than the question at hand. The Gospel has been and is being presented to us. In our country that has been true since the earliest of times. For every generation and individual the awesome inquiry is answered. Our fate individually and collectively becomes whatever it becomes. Remember, not to deal with it is to deal with it!

I hope you will see that it is *essential, serious, pressing*, and *urgent*. Again, words are the means for delivering to us life and death issues. Words enable us to grasp who and what we are in relationship to the Gospel given to us by Christ and His Apostles. How about that slip of paper just waiting to be used for your spiritual benefit! Shouldn't the four be written down and pondered?

We are called to pay attention to the great salvation first announced by our Lord and proven in practice by those who followed. Sometimes in joy and sometimes in sadness the loving Christ sees our every move.

## *Reflection*

1. Is salvation in Christ accepted by you as being essential?
2. Have you shared with others the seriousness of Christ's revelation to you?
3. How do you deal with the pressure of knowing Christ is imperative?
4. Do you tend to avoid the urgency of the Faith?

## ❋FIXED ON JESUS❋

### *Background*

OUR AUTHOR begins this chapter (Heb. 12:1–29) by sharing with us the security and stability given to us by God our Father. To be real sons is to be "looked after" in a special Way by Him Who has created all. Human fathers punish us and so does our spiritual Father, God Himself. God does so especially that we may share His holiness.

Then, encouragement and instruction flow from the author of the letter to the Hebrews. We are to "lift up our tired hands and strengthen our trembling knees." We are to attempt "to be at peace with everyone" and "live a holy life." Holiness is intended to attract others to the Lord. We are intended to be "God's first-born sons, whose names are written in heaven." The blood of Jesus "promises much better things than does the blood of Abel." We are reminded we cannot escape "*if* we turn away from the one who speaks from heaven!"

The chapter is concluded with words of gratitude—reminiscent of Saint Paul's writings—even though there are overwhelming doubts among scholars that he was the author of Hebrews. Such gratitude comes from receiving "a kingdom that cannot be shaken." We are to worship our God with "reverence and awe." Why? Because He is "a destroying fire."

## Focus

As we move towards the end of the letter to the Hebrews the author wants us to know "we have this large crowd of witnesses around us" pointing to the Church triumphant and the Church militant. Above all, the living are to keep their "eyes fixed on Jesus," calling forth a foursome.

## Application

*First, when our eyes are fixed on Jesus, there is a permanent claim on us.*

Probably all of us have heard the expression, "Give him an inch and he will take a mile." Really, that's very much the way Jesus is! Is this being sneaky? Well, just maybe. There are occasions in the Holy Scriptures where the Lord certainly seems to have a sense of humor, even though it be cutting. For example, in the twenty-third chapter of the gospel of Saint Matthew He exclaims again and again about "teachers of the law and Pharisees." In fact, He bluntly calls them hypocrites. In one instance He exclaims: "you sail the seas and cross whole countries to win one convert; and when you succeed, you make him twice as deserving of going to hell as you yourselves are!" It certainly seems what they wanted to do was deny Him any permanent claim on their lives because they could see if they gave Him that proverbial inch, He just might—in time—claim them as His disciples.

Obviously, there are many claims on us. We can go down a family list or financial list and immediately bring to the surface people and forces that claim us. That's simply the way our lives are lived. We might say to a son or daughter at graduation time, "Sorry, I can't make the commencement. My eyes are fixed on Jesus." We might say to a creditor, "I know my bill is past ninety days due but my eyes are fixed on Jesus." I suspect at first these examples appear ludicrous but think awhile longer and I think you will discover something else: Religion can be an excuse for most anything. The adjective "permanent" is of assistance here. Sons and daughters will pass away as we do. Financial obligations will some day be of no concern. The Lord is the One with the "permanent" claim.

Those who have lived the Christian life with "love, joy, peace, patience, kindness, goodness, faithfulness, humility, and self-control" wear the "yoke" or the "claim" well. They would have it no other way! It is "permanent" and what could be better? Really, nothing. Such persons especially know joy to the full. How about you and me? Is this our experience of the Faith? If not, why not? Are you and I a part of the "crowd of witnesses" living on this earth, enjoying communion with those in heaven? If we are coming up with contradictory feelings and spiritual nausea, just maybe something is amiss.

*Second, when our eyes are fixed on Jesus, there is a meeting of heaven and earth.*

Some of us used to sing, "Just over in the glory land . . ." I have always held precious the insight, especially among Orthodox, that in our worship there is a mystical meeting with the saints who have gone the way of all flesh. You and I can, at least, taste "over in the glory land." We can know momentarily what heaven is all about. This is only possible by keeping our "eyes fixed on Jesus." He is not only our Savior and Lord; He is Savior and Lord to those who have gone before us and those who will come after us. Heaven needs to be "talked about and believed in" more than it is, even in most "church circles." When the Lord goes to prepare a place for us, I believe that is exactly what He means. The promise was not only made to the ancient Church but to you and me as well.

There are those, perhaps a majority, who maintain "when you're dead, you are dead." The implication of this is usually there is a radical difference and separation between the living and the dead. The casket is lowered in the grave or the ashes are preserved in an attractive urn. There are only the memories that linger. If we are only physical and/or material bodies, we are on the right tract. However, to keep our "eyes fixed on Jesus," tells me there is an ongoing and eternal meeting of our spirits. We pray, "May the Lord now welcome him (her) to the table of God's children in heaven. With faith and hope in eternal life, let us assist him (her) with our prayers." Does that sound like there is no connection between the "here and now and the hereafter?" We also pray, "Receive him (her) into the arms of your mercy, into the blessed rest of everlasting peace, and into the glorious company of the saints of light." If the dead are permanently gone from our midst and our aspirations are null or void, why do we pray such things? When we understand Christ's Holy Church comprises both the living and the dead, we know why there are prayers for the dead. Indeed, we know along with the ancient Church this Jesus we worship is Lord over both and at the same time!

There is so much to our Faith and we—even in the life of His Body, the Church—seem to experience so little of it. I believe this is because we just simply do not keep our "eyes fixed on Jesus." Maybe it is because we only weakly believe He lived, died, and arose from the dead. His people are both living and dead. His people are the Saints Peter and Paul. But you and I are also His people! It is when we lack concentration on Him, so many different things or people burden us and cause us to "tip our hats" at Him. He is nominal or titular. He is like a bishop without a diocese or area of people who is largely symbolic.

*Third, when our eyes are fixed on Jesus, there is a magnificent tunnel vision.*

Well, that's a change, isn't it? We usually think of "tunnel vision" as a handicap or detriment to thinking with intelligence. We don't need to give any illustrations because we all probably have so many it would be a matter of telling us more than we want to know. Now, we are dealing with an exception because the author of the letter to the Hebrews is asking us to do what we are taught not to do. "Eyes fixed on Jesus" suggests we don't look at anything or anyone else. Throw away, at least, one guideline in the rule book of clear thinking providing wisdom. Really that's much like our Faith that has to be lived in ways seemingly contradictory to what we have been taught. A case in point is the contemporary assertion, "Take good care of number one. He (she) is all you have." This, of course, not so subtly means look after yourself first and foremost; if you do look after others, be sure it still benefits you. This point of view is pervasive. But our Lord says, "For whoever wants to save his own life will lose it; but whoever loses his life for my sake will find it."

I want us to focus for a moment on the descriptive word "magnificent." In short, there is nothing quite like keeping our eyes fixed on Jesus. The word fails to give us all that is adequate but it does give us an excellent starting point. Entering into this is a privileged status at once humbling and strength giving. Jesus is the Masterpiece. You and I have the high honor of gazing upon Him "on whom our faith depends from beginning to end." For Him to matter that much to us is for everything and especially everyone to matter in our lives. We discover the magnificence really creates a miracle for accepting all of life. What at first appears narrow and suffocating becomes broadening and freeing. There is a simple explanation here: He was God who walked the earthly road of this world among us; He is now God who is in heaven, providing providence for all that was, is, and shall be. We should be driven to our knees in gratitude!

The "world" or those found outside of the community of serious believers find us pretty silly people! They will say, "You just can't lock out or freeze out other religious giants, philosophers, and powerful figures." That's true in one sense: we do not live in a controlled environment, isolated from good and bad. However, we can keep our eyes fixed on Jesus for so long and in such a way we are taught what part other greats are to play in our lives. It is a matter of disciplined perspective. He is the One and let's allow others to fit into their proper roles under His jurisdiction. We will serve some god(s) and it (they) will give us our outlooks. Why not Jesus the Christ?

*Fourth, when our eyes are fixed on Jesus, there is a sense of ultimacy in our lives.*
We know what counts! Again we return to the hymnist, Will L. Thompson:

Jesus is all the world to me,
I want no better friend;
I trust him now,
I'll trust him when life's fleetings shall end.
Beautiful life with such a friend,
beautiful life that has no end;
eternal life, eternal joy, he's my friend.

Note the powerful joy! Note that when Jesus is "all the world to me"
or I am fixed on Him there is a "beautiful life that has no end!" In a
way this is a simple logical progression to be fixed on the Lord is to
spend eternity with Him. Experiences will be different for everyone.
There will be successes and failures, joys and sorrows. Yet, we are in a
win-win situation. To keep "our eyes fixed on Jesus," means we are not
in a losing mode. Regardless of how the world or our "sometimes
friends" in the Church may slander and/or libel us, we are going to be
winners! Praise God!

A quick glance at the lives of many persons tell us that since their eyes
are not fixed on Jesus, their sense of ultimacy is some other place or with
someone else. We can call it tragedy of the first order and be almost immediately judgmental. However, take a good look in a mirror. Are our eyes
fixed on Jesus? Maybe we are spending too much time with the face we
see in the mirror. The spiritual disease of self-centeredness is widespread.
Believe me, it knows no race, gender, nationality, or creed exclusively. There
is plenty to go around! We serious and committed Christians do put all of
our "eggs in one basket." This is what Holy Scripture tells us to do, in this
case the letter to the Hebrews. Yet, how many persons do you know who
put their focus "on and in" political, social, and economic philosophies?
Perhaps that is where we and our friends find ourselves and we just at this
instant are coming to terms with it.

From another viewpoint there is a tendency in today's world to avoid
and even declare unimportant spiritual ultimacy. I believe the most appropriate term for this state of affairs is "nihilism." It is a denial of meaning or
purpose in existence. "Do what you want, when you want, where you want,
and how you want"; in the long run it won't make any difference anyway.
Why bother with morals and ethics? Of course, some of us who believe
strongly in the revelation of our Judeo-Christian tradition could say such
persons are focused on nothing and therefore end up with nothing! Indeed,

life does become meaningless and without purpose. There is no "attitude of gratitude" for God's grace, love, justice, and mercy. Do we hear an earlier word? "How shall we escape if we pay no attention . . . ?

## Conclusion

If you and I were asked to offer advice to a new Christian, wouldn't it go something like this: above all, keep your eyes fixed on Jesus? I hope so and trust that bit of advice comes from one who already knows what that is all about. The author undoubtedly knows in his depths that in order to become like Him, we do so only by keeping our eyes fixed on Him. Some critics might react by exclaiming, "How dare you be so literal!" My reaction to this is, "How dare we not be so literal." You and I know the spiritual truth embodied here.

We have called forth a foursome of helpful understandings, ideal and yet real. *When our eyes are fixed on Jesus, there is a permanent claim on us; a meeting of heaven and earth; a magnificent tunnel vision; and a sense of ultimacy in our lives.* Isn't this a grand—even resplendent—set of understandings? We have so much to share with the world. Are we witnesses in a seriously joyful sense? Oh sing at the top of your voices, "He lives, He lives, Christ Jesus lives today! He walks with me and talks with me along life's narrow way."

As we look forward to one more chapter, let us kneel in appreciation for what we have learned, clergy and laity alike, from an often avoided New Testament writing. I am learning to keep my eyes fixed on Jesus. Are you?

## Reflection

1. Do you believe Jesus has a claim on you that is permanent?
2. Why is it possible to believe that the here and hereafter form a whole?
3. How do you go about concentrating on Jesus so that you are attuned to Him?
4. In the last analysis is there anything or anyone more important than Jesus?

# ❊WHAT CAN ANYONE DO TO YOU?❊

## Background

THE CLOSING chapter (Heb. 13:1–25) presents us with a wrap-up that includes a number of commands. In fact, the initial verse says, "Keep on loving one another as Christian brothers." In a way that is the overall guiding objective to what has previously been said.

The author deals with a number of different imperatives, likely indicating the problems at hand. We are called to "remember." "Marriage is to be honored by all . . ." and adultery is very serious. Watch out for the love of money! Former leaders, who were faithful, are to be held in high regard. A difference is seen in the Jewish altar and the new altar for followers of Christ. Jesus, and only Jesus, is our sacrifice. We are to do good and help one another because this pleases God. Obedience to leaders in the Faith is necessary; they are held accountable for watching over our souls.

The closing prayer and final words bring the letter to the Hebrews to a memorable conclusion that pushes—yes, inspires—us into the future in service to and for our High Priest, the Son of the Father. Timothy is mentioned by name. "The brothers from Italy send you their greetings," probably pointing to the Saints Peter and Paul who were martyred there.

## Focus

The author closes with an implied understanding that is my favorite. "When we are right with God the Father through His Son, everything matters and yet nothing else matters." It is in that sobering and yet joyous context we are brought to the realization of four statements.

## Application

*First, there is the assurance of not needing to be worldly successful.*

Talk about freedom! Isn't that something wonderful! The text speaks of watching out for "the love of money." Translated into contemporary terms that seems to me to be proclaiming we don't always have to be bigger and better financially in order to be Christians. Furthermore, the text says to "be satisfied with what you have." That almost sounds like heresy in today's world, doesn't it? It is a catastrophic eye-opener to study with care our styles of living and attitudes as we begin to have revealed to us so much—very much—of what we do has success in dollar bills tied to it. We may say emphatically we don't love money but, then, why does it weigh so heavily in our lives? If you are not worldly successful, what can anyone do to you? Liberation is at hand in this simple statement! Your worth is not dependent—in God's eyes—on accumulating money or what it represents.

My purpose is not at all to condemn those who have done well in economic terms. Some of the most generous people I have known and do know have "considerable means." We might even ask, "Just what is the difference between a wealthy person who condescends to a poor person and a poor person who despises a wealthy person?" Just because you have not kept up with "Johnny Jones" or "Sally Smith" probably has no bearing whatsoever in regard to salvation. Obviously, those who work hard and are good managers, will likely have more in a material sense. Obviously, a person who inherits a million dollars or more, has greater opportunity in a material sense.

To have achieved in a given field of endeavor with worldly adulation doesn't necessarily have anything significant to say in a "so-called Christian sense." It might be a way to draw others closer to Christ and His Church or it might be a means to drive them away! Ambition is frequently a very positive thing. Wrongly exercised, it becomes a noose around one's neck and leads exactly to what the author is warning against. I have a strong feeling pride of accomplishment before God on judgment day will not carry much weight! On the other hand, we should not open the door to laziness and fatalism. All that's really being said is: to fail or succeed in a worldly sense is inevitably a secondary consideration.

*Second, there is the assurance of God's presence with us.*

Sometimes under very trying and difficult circumstances I humbly pray, "Please, dear God, just be with us." His presence always makes the difference, doesn't it? It seems we can undergo and survive most any set of circumstances as long as God is with us. Indeed, when He is present, "what can anyone do to you?" It's such an elementary thing and you would think most everyone would know that. Not so! There are those who appear to call upon God only as a last resort. It's like saying, "If we need Your presence, we will ask for it. Otherwise bug off and we will see what we can do." The ironic part of such an attitude is God is always with us anyway and we assume we can determine His going and coming! The part we play is "acknowledgment and invitation." We are to acknowledge the need and do the inviting. It's akin to the Scripture that indicates God knows what we need before we pray but we are to pray anyway!

When the doubts come, what do we do? If you are not sure of His presence, do a very simple exercise. Imagine a gloomy and depressing day. The clouds are seemingly omnipresent. Then say to yourself, "I know the sun is out there some place, even though I don't see it or feel the warmth. I will see it again soon. In fact, I will see it come up and go down. Therefore, for it to be hidden doesn't mean it is not there. In fact, I know from experience it is there." Now that is about as simple as we can put it but reflect on the truth presented. In a much more Christian context your Savior and Lord, Jesus the Christ, is there by your side through the power of the Holy Spirit.

So, "what can anyone do to you" that in the long run defeats you? How often we underestimate our Faith. How often we claim too little of what is rightfully ours. How often we run around in circles of desperation because we refuse the childlike request, "Lord Jesus, please be with us (me)."

Do we sometimes believe God does not live up to His promises? That's an honest question. Do we mutter under our breaths, "He says He won't leave or abandon us but I wouldn't bet on it." Of course, what gets into the event(s) is our agendas and His presence. Because some situation does not turn out the way you had expected or wanted does not prove the absence of God. In my experience and observation He never or seldom ever says, "This is what is going to take place because I have taken your agenda to heart and have chosen to be present to see it turn out the way you want." Frankly, too often we seek to bring His presence into the picture to prove the validity of what we want and attempt to make happen. Can we manipulate God?

*Third, there is the assurance of having permission to be bold.*

There is no mistaking the word from the author. "Let us be bold . . ." Why can we be bold? Simply because the Lord never leaves us or forsakes us. That being the case, "what can anyone do to you?" Boldness is an integral part of the picture. It's in our style of living the Christian life. We do not need to assume such a stance. It plainly says, "Let us be bold. . . ." We should move quickly to point out aggressiveness is out of place, unless it is thoroughly saturated with love. Even assertiveness is out of place, unless tempered by a Christlike spirit. It is the force of the Holy Spirit that does our work for us. To "run over people" and insist arrogantly of one's righteousness, of course, are subpar methods that give us just the kind of results we don't want! We can be right in the substance we know and wrong in the means we use to place it before others. Substance and means are related, in fact, necessarily in our Christian practice.

Only in harmony with the Holy Spirit can this permission to be bold give to us the fruit desired. Always underlying this *modus operandi* is the certainty and conviction of our right relationship with God the Father through His Son, our Savior and Lord. In short, don't go it alone! That's the surest way to create troublesome situations and upset people. Why? Because we become our own frame of reference and assume our strength is adequate. It reminds me of the cliche "He who seeks to be his own attorney to defend himself has a fool for a client." The first chapter of Saint John's Epistle speaks eloquently, ". . . we have someone who pleads with the Father on our behalf—Jesus Christ, the righteous."

When speaking of the Holy Spirit, he says in his Gospel, "I will ask the Father, and he will give you another Helper, who will stay with you forever." So, our boldness in the Faith is always "tied to and springs from" a strong and dynamic "right relationship." Having said this, be sure we are to be bold!

We are not called to be witnesses in an open and confident way lacking the equipment to do so. I share in the understanding that "to be called is also to be equipped." What is that equipment? Certainly it is varied as people are different. Yet, one spiritual characteristic stands out: it is a matter of being childlike or teachable. Lord, here I am, do with me what You will. Then, pay close—very close—attention and be willing to move out in faith. No situation is exactly alike but one thing is constant: an open mind, a warm heart, and a willing spirit. So, we see the equipment and the means to know it become virtually one and the same!

*Fourth, there is the assurance of not needing to be afraid.*

"Being afraid or fear" is an enigma for many people, perhaps most. The Scriptures seem to say, "Be afraid and do not be afraid." "Fear God and do not fear God." Of course, both are true. You see, in faith—as Christians—we must sooner or later be able to deal with Holy mystery, apparent contradiction, and obvious ambiguity. So, how can we be both afraid and not be afraid? To assist us we begin with the spiritual truth that when all is right with our souls we should fear no human being or anything. Furthermore, we then recall Jesus warning us in Saint Matthew: "Do not be afraid of those who kill the body but cannot kill the soul; rather be afraid of God, who can destroy both body and soul in hell." Such an understanding is like "deep calling unto deep." No person(s) can send us to hell. This is always God's business. My sense of this truth is we send ourselves to hell by deliberately and knowingly refusing to do what we know is right or doing those things we know are wrong. It is not too different from shaking one's fist in the face of God the Father and telling His Son He doesn't know what He is talking about!

Our text is actually quoting Psalm 118:6. In an ironic and yet glorious way in the prior verses of the same psalm the Psalmist emphasizes God's love is eternal four separate times! So, in the most profound and everlasting way love and fear are wedded in bliss forever. Don't miss the element of human nature. Just because we are His children does not mean a loving Father will tolerate our flaunting of revealed truth. If we are counting on His love in a "user friendly" sense with sinful lives and attitudes, beware of what Jesus tells us earlier! Fear is put to rest and even chased into oblivion as the Father's love encompasses us. To play at the game of hypocrisy and some blaspheming now and then will surely get us into serious trouble.

In the highest and best sense the author of the letter to the Hebrews gives a closing gift. We do have the assurance of not needing to be afraid. This comes not only from him but the wellsprings of the Judeo-Christian tradition found in the Psalms. Are you right with God our Father through the saving power of His Son? If the answer is unquestionably in the affirmative, then what can any human being(s) do to you? If the answer is shaky or in the negative, do you see the jeopardy in which you are placed? How joyfully precious is our Faith! How marvelously wonderful is the Church Universal—"one, holy, catholic, apostolic"—that gives us this gift, handed on by those who were obedient to the Holy Spirit! We have only begun to appreciate what we have as Christians!

## Conclusion

How blessed we are to share, laity and clergy alike, this magnificently brilliant letter to the Hebrews. Maybe even now you are asking yourself, "Why didn't I study this before?" or "Why haven't we as a church offered this as an opportunity for growth?" The riches of Holy Scripture continues to astound me, even in the New Testament that I thought I knew reasonably well! Praise God for our High Priest, Jesus the Christ, who shall forever be our one and only Sacrifice!

What can anyone do to you? Nothing that is permanently hurtful! This says to you and me *there is the assurance of not needing to be worldly successful; of God's presence with us; of having permission to be bold; and of not needing to be afraid.* I beg of you, please weigh each carefully—not only today but—in the days, weeks, months, and even years to come. There is a special kind of assurance here that transcends time and mortality.

It is in thanksgiving that I bring to a close these visits together. I have trusted throughout the series that the Holy Spirit would bless all thoughts, words, and feelings. Gratefully before you and God, I acknowledge in humility my role as preacher/teacher and pastor/priest in being a channel or instrument to lift up the letter to the Hebrews!

## Reflection

1. Do you believe God accepts you, even though you are not successful in worldly terms?
2. Is God's presence a gift you strongly appreciate?
3. How can you know it is right to be bold in the Lord?
4. Why is fear inevitably a possible issue in your life?

*A Taste of Glory*

*Explorations into John 6:53~58*

**DONALD CHARLES LACY**

2000

*This book seeks to reveal and appreciate the mysteries of the Holy
Communion or Eucharist. As the pilgrim says, "I believe that if I had
only the verses from John 6:53–58 the rest of my life would be meaningful
and fruitful. Of course, I know, dear Lord, there is much more to learn
from these verses. Please make me a blessing to every life that I touch.
Please continue to teach me. Please empower me at all times and all
places to be Your person, speaking the truth in love. Please keep me in
harmony with the Holy Spirit. It is true, Lord, that whether I live or die,
I belong to You and Your Supper provides ongoing spiritual strength. I
pray You will satisfy my hunger and thirst, now and for evermore." In
addition to the prelude and postlude, two of the six sermons are presented.*

# CHAPTER 9

# A Taste of Glory

## ❋PRELUDE❋

PILGRIM: PRECIOUS and loving Lord, I need a special visit with You again. For some time now I have been pondering the glorious words that come from Saint John's Gospel in the sixth chapter. I mean, of course, verses fifty-three through fifty-eight.

**Jesus**: You know I love you and will listen carefully.

**Pilgrim**: Dear Jesus, that's why I came to You again. Every time I read these words I am taken up into a magnificent world of powerful mystery. I just have a really tough time explaining how I feel. Your flesh and Your blood! O great and holy One, I kneel in humble adoration. Please help me to understand, at least, in an elementary fashion what this is all about.

**Jesus**: Remember, my son, it takes genuine humility and sincerity to begin to know Me better.

**Pilgrim**: So many times over the years I have experienced Your body and blood in Holy Communion as a dull act of scheduled worship, yearning to be free. There was so much more to be felt and appreciated! It is as though You desired deeply to be so much closer and meaningful but just couldn't. This makes me so sad. There was an awesome greatness and powerful love waiting to burst forth but, Lord, it just didn't happen! In agony I watched and waited. Decent people went through the motions. Some, including myself, even knelt in prayer but it just didn't happen.

**Jesus**: I gave and continue to give My body. I gave and continue to give My blood. Do you and others actually want to eat My flesh and drink My blood from My priests and pastors or deep down do you only seek a bit of solace for the moment?

**Pilgrim**: Please be merciful to me, Lord. I want all the spiritual grandeur these verses from Saint John's Gospel offer. I long for that perfect promised closeness. Sometimes in great pain I suffer to have this unique gift of Yourself that guarantees Your true presence. Lord, I beg of You, please hear me out. The Holy Spirit is moving mightily in my life and others. We believe our desire comes from undefiled motivation. I am not afraid, only frustrated and disappointed by the Holy Communion being so much less than what I believe You surely intended. Your children seem to be often sitting at a banquet table offering Your flesh and blood but they are starving, or at least, seriously malnourished!

**Jesus**: Do you remember what I said to you recently? Let me refresh your memory: "Do not judge others and God will not judge you. Do not condemn others and God will not condemn you. Forgive others and God will forgive you." Think on this and focus on My Crucifixion.

**Pilgrim**: Savior of my soul, please forgive again all my sins of omission and commission. I trust You with my life and death. I want somehow for Your body to become my body. I want some way for Your blood to become my blood. I give You myself—fully, totally, and completely. I really have nothing else to offer.

**Jesus**: Are you sure there are no reservations? So just what will you try to hide in hopes I will not notice? Will an old love and preoccupation entice you to treat My body and My blood as merely a means to the ends of self glory? Reflect upon My conversation with Simon Peter near the end of John's Gospel.

**Pilgrim**: Lord, be merciful to me, a sinner who wavers under pressure! I do not deserve what I ask. Even my spiritual riches are pitiful rags in Your sight. Even my most lofty motivations and ideals leave something to be desired. Even my humility and sincerity sometimes turn to pride. Even my thought patterns and ways of behaving reveal a life struggling just enough to be decent in the world's sight. I plead with You, be merciful and do for me what I can never do for myself. Yes, Lord, I truly want more than anything else Your body and Your blood. Lord, do what You will.

**Jesus**: Very well, my son. You have learned much. Today your spiritual journey becomes one of joyful obedience and sacrificial love. My body and My blood shall sustain you. Do not look back. My love will never let you go.

# ❋REAL PRESENCE❋

*Whoever eats my flesh and drinks my blood remains in me, and I in him.*
*—John 6:56 (NIV)—*

## Introduction

THERE IS A coming together and merging with the Lord that is awesomely mysterious and profound.

To receive the Sacrament indicates we remain in Him and He in us. So, we are brought to terms with something (someone) in more than a symbolic and figurative sense. Perhaps the best designation is *real presence.* This not only avoids such heavy terminology as transubstantiation and consubstantiation but gives a working, simplified way of understanding a very difficult idea. Our spiritual forebears, John and Charles Wesley, found this delineation appropriate. They were on solid ground because I believe it would also fit what is intended to happen since the time of Christ and the Apostles. *Real Presence* has a way of dispelling ideas that maintain only symbolism and/or figurative language are present. As is often the case in our pilgrimage, we strain for words to tell us some aspect of truth and discover some are better than others, but all are somewhat lacking! Yet, we do have beacons under the guidance of the Holy Spirit over the centuries and we are blessed!

## Focus

The special occasion or worship activity we label Holy Communion somehow and some way calls into being an incomparable oneness in Christ. It is as though to swallow the bread and wine is to allow Him to enter our bodies with His blood flowing through our arteries and veins, yes, and vice versa! Allowing for the inadequacy of language, let us name what we mean.

## Application

There is power transcending our understanding

Don't you feel like saying, "Are we dealing with nuclear energy or some primeval resource?" Maybe your true thoughts are along these lines: "This is just too irrational and I would rather hear about something else" or "Why deal with something so nebulous and probably unimportant?" It is said by some we should stay away from politics and religion because they always start arguments. We might even pursue this further but of what value would that be in light of the fact our Lord says, also in John's Gospel: "If you hold to my teaching, you are really my disciples. Then you will know the truth, and the truth will set you free." We are intended to struggle and yet rest assured in a peace that passes all understanding. There is a banquet on the altar of the Lord that promises eucharistic might. O sing of the greatness found in these words written by a contemporary Liberian: "Come, let us eat, for now the feast is spread" and "Come, let us drink, for now the wine is poured."

If you are like I am, I want things much more neatly put into an understandable package than this verse. After all, we know—for the most part—what is meant by our Master telling us to "love your enemies and pray for those who persecute you." Yes, and the whole idea of power is much more easy to digest, provided we can circumvent special terms like *real presence* applied to the Lord's Supper. I believe much of the time as clergy and laity we prefer power on the basis of something we can perceive as a worldly benefit. What will it take to push membership and worship, plus salary level, to a place where brothers and sisters say, "He or she is such a success?"

So, *there is a power transcending our understanding*. I beg of you not to turn away in frustration.

## THERE IS A LOVE THAT WANTS US TO BE CHRISTLIKE

Jesus doesn't just want to hug us tightly; He wants to become part of us and vice versa. His goal is that of His love penetrating us and encompassing us. In a sense we are Him and He is us. See how priceless the Holy Communion is! The world had never and has never known such love. We find the gift of His very life in the Sacrament. We are privileged to have His *real presence*. In a way this love is "in, among, for, with us." The heavens shout: "Love divine, all loves excelling" and "Fix in us thy humble dwelling." "Love" is such a misused term today, so we need with urgency to embrace fully what our wondrous Savior and Lord has in store for those who confess Him.

It needs continual repeating that "the" Sacrament is a means of spiritual formation par excellence. Why? Primarily because God is love and His Son comes to us in His Body and Blood. How can we be formed into His image without special—even miraculous—worship times that hold high the Lord's Supper? The truth of the matter is we probably cannot be; that does not put down those claiming Christ who find "sacrament" secondary to the preaching event and/or disciplined prayer.

The point is: Why digress from our Lord's command to remember Him in a certain way, especially when so deeply imbedded in Holy Scriptures?

So, *there is a love that wants us to be Christlike.* We are called to be like Him in thought, word, and deed.

### THERE IS A JOY BEYOND WORLDLY APPRECIATION

Perhaps we have all heard Christians are "in" the world but not "of" the world. It remains a helpful way of seeing ourselves as a peculiar people God has called. Saint Paul helps us when he says in Romans twelve: "Do not conform any longer to the pattern of this world . . ." Christians are a select—even an elite—group in the best sense of the word. Certainly a precious highlight and even defining moment is found in the Holy Communion. When we receive His Body and Blood, we sometimes weep in a joy that is so foreign to anything the world can appreciate. As we receive the elements, we can know in our innermost beings our sins are forgiven and heaven our eventual home! Why? He is in us and we are in Him.

In times of turbulence and travail our oldest daughter used to speak of her great desire for joy. It was that noteworthy moment(s) that the Father not only smiled from heaven on His children but especially upon her. As you and I are being blessed by the Eucharist, there is that Fatherly smile from heaven that is known only by His sons and daughters in the Body of Christ. When Saint Paul lists the fruit of the Spirit in Galatians 5, joy is second only to love. We are joyful about Christ's death and the death of our sins. Why? Because His Crucifixion means salvation, redemption, and resurrection. Our sins are no more, unless we choose to reembrace them. Sadness becomes joy. Indeed, death becomes life.

So, *there is a joy beyond worldly appreciation.* Celebrate your select place before the Father, the Son, and the Holy Spirit.

### THERE IS A GRACE OVERCOMING BUT UTILIZING OUR WEAKNESS

Times of sharing coffee and cookies with conversation are often helpfully soothing. Times of sharing soft drinks and pizza are just outright fun. Perhaps some even find beer and pretzels just "the ticket" to make life look better. If the Holy Spirit is present and who would doubt that possibility, we may very well be having a "grace filled" occasion. But, as Christians, if this is all we have in our lives, we have a colossal problem. Holy Communion provides a unique grace that in a way overwhelms and conquers. It is also grace that makes "the" Sacrament possible. In our frailty we need much more than the above mentioned pleasant times, as important as they may appear. Our deepest need calls for somebody or someone far bigger and better to do for us what we can never do for ourselves.

Grace enables me to remain in Him and He in me. What pitiful creatures we are without this favor of the Father though the Son! Jesus the Christ gives His all that we might have life and have it abundantly. The universal appeal of the hymn, "Amazing Grace," is that it seems to speak directly to all of us. Indeed, "How sweet the sound that saved a wretch like me!" Then, the first stanza goes on to say, "I once was lost, but now am found; was blind, but now I see." Our weakness is God's great opportunity. His Body and His Blood provide His *real presence*. Oh, sing to your Lord a new song of being a "very important person" in His sight, sealed by His unmerited favor.

So, *there is a grace overcoming but utilizing our weakness.* Christians call it His real presence.

THERE IS A FAITHFULNESS ALLOWING NO DEFEAT

*Real presence* strongly indicates that our Lord is faithfully present in a way that no one else is. "The" Sacrament is the centerpiece of understanding and appreciating the fact there is no ultimate defeat for those who cling tenaciously to His Body and His Blood. This is a glorious experience that is shared by those spiritual ancestors coming out of the First Century and continuing without interruption even to the moment we share now. In my own weak and ineffectual way I attempt to visualize my brothers/sisters across the ages receiving the Lord's Supper. They are from all races and nationalities. They come from every social and economic class. Their political sensitivities embrace every shade in a rainbow. They are saints and sinners. They are saintly sinners and sinful saints! Truly we are one in the Spirit and one in the Lord at His table.

Unless there is faithfulness over the long haul, there just isn't much else. Power, love, joy, and grace speak of *real presence*. Yet, what if there is a lack of faithfulness? So much tends to depend on so few! We speak of discipline and commitment. We speak of consistency and persistency. We speak of an attitude that maintains, "When the going gets tough, the tough get going." The eternal Son of the eternal Father became a man, born of the blessed Virgin Mary, and lived among us. Since that time He lives among us through His Body and Blood. He does so through the faithful ministrations of "the" Sacrament by the ordained clergy under the guidance of the Holy Spirit.

So, *there is a faithfulness allowing no defeat.* Persecute or kill us but we shall never be overpowered by the Evil One.

## Conclusion

The term *real presence* seems more and more to be coming into usage today among those serious about religion, especially the Holy Communion. I believe this is very healthy and spiritually wholesome. It is a term that certainly isn't new and yet it has such a contemporary ring to it. Furthermore, it communicates in ways beneficially across denominational lives. The promise of whoever eats His flesh and drinks His blood being pivotal in His residence in us, plus our remaining in Him, causes us to be thankful many times over. I like all of this just that way, don't you?

## Exploration

1. How do you understand the power in "the" Sacrament?
2. Have you ever experienced the love Christ intends in His Supper?
3. At what times in your life is joy most noticeable?
4. Why do you suppose we are all dependent on His grace?
5. When was the last time you were convinced it was "okay" to give up?

# ❖FROM HEAVEN❖

*This is the bread that came down from heaven. Our forefathers ate manna and died, but he who feeds on this bread will live forever.*
—*John 6:58 (NIV)*—

## Introduction

OUR BLESSED Savior and Lord wants us to know the holy sacrifice of Himself is of everlasting significance for humanity.

The closing words of this unusually awesome series of verses is placed before us. It is to show us that disciples of Jesus the Christ have available something (someone) to them—wonder beyond wonders—

that decidedly surpasses the manna of their forefathers. In the form of simple elements of the flesh of God, specifically the Son, is given to us to eat. He is *from heaven* and it is *from heaven*. It is another way of our Lord illustrating that He came "not to do away with the Law but to fulfill it." "Manna" was revelation in that day and time to the ancient Hebrews. It was not at all fully adequate and complete. Only His flesh (and blood) give us completeness and revelation which is definitive. Early disciples, especially Saint Paul, enabled the entire non–Jewish world also to have access to Him and consequently to the Holy Communion. "The" Sacrament is "a taste of glory" that comes *from heaven* and gives us a spiritual being and holiness of life our Lord's ancestors only dreamed about. Perhaps we want to maintain, "But this is only idealism"; I believe we must not do that!

### Focus

Our Savior and Lord places a capstone on His word to us about "the" Sacrament. We are not to look for something else as symbol and reality so powerfilled with love for those who seek to be like Him, indeed forever and ever. It seems to me our very best response is to state carefully affirmations that bring truth, life, and promise.

### Application

WE CELEBRATE THE GREATNESS OF THE FATHER'S EVERLASTING GIFT FOUND IN THE LORD'S SUPPER

"Celebration" is a key word in our vocabularies because it expresses from Christians a "shouting forth" of what has been done in the Incarnation. God came to us in flesh and blood. In the person of the Man of Galilee He was born among us; lived among us; ministered among us; died among us; arose among us; and ascended among us. His sacrifice on the Cross was truly among human beings who were seemingly hopelessly divided among themselves as to who He was and why He had come to be treated so brutally. In what sense could there be anything remotely resembling a celebration except for those who saw it as a victory in a power struggle? Little by little it became obvious you could kill a man like that but you really couldn't destroy Him. It also became more and more evident at the time of the Resurrection that His teaching would live beyond anyone's life who had witnessed such events. His sacrificial death would become a celebration!

The bread that came down *from heaven* would not only serve to exonerate Him in the eyes of some but provide a celebrative atmosphere for the ancient Body of Christ or the Church. For still others disappointment and even despair would set in because the crucified One was not dead at all. In the secrecy of homes and other places He would even come much alive through the celebration of His Supper! Heaven would touch earth and earth would touch heaven. It is known that some disciples simply seemed to live from one of His Suppers to the next. There was an urgency and a frequency that pervaded them. How can I go on living without my Savior and Lord? When can I partake of His precious Body and Blood again? They were unfamiliar with our theories and eroded basic meanings of "the" Sacrament. At face value they celebrated the Father's everlasting gift!

So, *we celebrate the greatness of the Father's everlasting gift found in the Lord's Supper.* With the Holy Spirit's prodding we need to celebrate more often!

## WE MAINTAIN THE LOVE OF JESUS COMES MOST PERFECTLY IN "THE" SACRAMENT

My guess is there are many professing His name who would argue with this affirmation. In fact, I know there are! Nevertheless, let us help them to jog their memories. Can the Resurrection have any serious validity apart from the Crucifixion? Dare we ever separate these two events in our appreciation of the Faith? Isn't laying down your life for your friends (and enemies) the apex of the manifestation of love? Jesus gave totally and completely of Himself in a humbling event before people who mocked and scorned Him. What else could He have given? He evaded and avoided worldly adulation to hang upon the Cross, even refusing to call upon legions of His Father's helpers to save Him. What else could He have done? He was perfectly obedient—even unto the Cross—because that was the will of the Father. What else could be expected of the Son who came from the heavens to live an earthly life not at all befitting of One sharing in the Holy Trinity. The love found in His Body and Blood calls us forever to a love that refuses to be limited in how far it will go for us.

This perfect love finds its expression in a simple and yet sublime act of worship. It came *from heaven.* It is profoundly personal in the sense each professing person partakes with his/her own agenda and presuppositions. It is powerfully communal as groups—regardless of numbers—receive His holy Body and Blood that binds them together in the loving energy of the Holy Spirit. How can we possibly know Him and have deep appreciation for His Resurrection unless we die with Him? For you and me this bread *from heaven* that lives forever is "the" Sacrament that has no equals. We must not eat the old manna and die in our sins. It comes in many forms—even in our churches—and is inevitably beguiling!

So, *we maintain the love of Jesus comes most perfectly in "the" Sacrament.* I plead with you not to deny or belittle it!

## WE BELIEVE THERE IS REALITY—NOT MERE IDEALISM—IN HIS BODY AND BLOOD

I suspect most of us have heard, "Christianity is a fine thing but just won't work" or variations. Likewise we have heard the retort in one form or another: "But have you tried it!" The problem of dealing with the "ideal" or "what should be" and the "real" or "what is" is ever with us. Our task is to be honest but never underestimate or blur the revelation to us. You and I can promise many things based on Holy Scripture. What we cannot do is tell God what He can or cannot do! This is an ongoing spiritual phenomenon and means our faith in the Lord Jesus simply has to see us through. Can the "ideal" become the "real" in given situations? I believe it can. I also believe this is particularly true of the Lord's Supper. Some of our quandary is reduced to two questions: Are we prepared to take Holy Communion by coming to His table expectantly and openly? Are we aware that we are as privileged as the early disciples and saints? If we can give an unconditional affirmation to both, I firmly believe His Body and Blood become for us bread *from heaven.*

In our day and time it has become too easy to push the ideal understanding as witnessed to by the Ancient Church into a corner of irrelevancy. Our Lord did not institute "the" Sacrament for a given period of time or tell us we would eventually outgrow it! Yes, there is reality here and now for those who need His Body and Blood. Here is a "leap of faith" for all of us, at the same time the "one, holy, catholic, and apostolic" Church and the Gospels—plus Saint Paul's writing—convey to us what must never be pigeonholed in the miscellaneous section of our religious consciousness. Don't deny the efficacy of "the" Sacrament by shrugging it off as so much idealism.

So, *we believe there is reality—not mere idealism—in the Body and Blood.* What comes from heaven is practically intended for our spiritual nurture and power!

## WE CONFESS OUR ONGOING NEED TO GROW IN THE UNDER-STANDING WE RECEIVE BREAD FROM HEAVEN

I know of no single act of worship that radiates more blessed mystery than His Supper. Of course, this is why traditional Catholicism practices prayer before "the" Sacrament reserved in a tabernacle; there is the adoration of Christ's presence in the elements. However, I suggest to you, this is no reason for liberal Catholics and Protestants of many names to write off the need to be ever learning about such an exquisitely thrilling gift. I confess to you it takes lengthy meditation and even discouragement to break through a prevalent attitude of routine and complacency. How many television, radio and print media images imprint your brain every day? Probably this runs into the hundreds and thousands. How many images of a chalice and bread or cups and wafers or the Crucified One on the Cross imprint your brain on any given day? A culture that once aided and assisted Judeo-Christian values—for the most part—no longer does. In fact, quite the reverse is true and has been so now perhaps for two generations.

Read and reread the key passages in the Gospels especially John 6:53–58, as well as Saint Paul's passages in First Corinthians. Read various translations and revisions. Memorize them and take them into your heart with gratitude. Prior to every service of Holy Communion call upon the Holy Spirit for guidance. Remember always to do so humbly and sincerely. One of the most helpful prayers of all is: "O Holy Spirit of God, take me as your disciple. Guide me, illuminate me, sanctify me." Use Saturday night or early Sunday morning or both as a preparation time. Books like *The Imitation of Christ* by Thomas à Kempis are very helpful. In the section entitled "About the Blessed Sacrament" we read: "O Jesus, sweetest, kindest, what great worship and thanksgiving we ought to show you, what never-ending praise, in return for your holy body! There is not a man to be found able to unfold in words its wonderful power."

So, *we confess our ongoing need to grow in the understanding we receive bread from heaven.* We plead with you, dear God, to teach us more!

## WE EMBRACE WITH ALL OUR MIGHT THE EUCHARIST THAT GIVES US CHRIST HIMSELF

We are called "to become" people of the Eucharist and then called "to be" people of the Eucharist! Let us eat His flesh and drink His blood! Let us become full of Him! Indeed, they are strange words for a society bloated with immoral and sacrilegious excesses. In a way they are even more strange for many professing His holy name who count "the" Sacrament of such little worth they would reduce to a bit of bread and a touch of grape juice the splendor of a heavenly banquet. May the Father forgive His children for treating the Eucharist slightly above an afternoon coffee break of pastry and coffee. Where is our greatness? It is found in the Christ. Where do we discover the Christ fully and completely giving Himself for us? In the Eucharist.

We are not starving sons and daughters with no bread *from heaven*. We are not children languishing in thirst because the chalice is empty. We must embrace with all our might that His Body and Blood are for those who truly believe that He is the Son of the Father who came to die for their sins. Can we not once again in droves around the world come repentently before His altar and receive "the" Sacrament? Can we not once again in droves leave His altar with tears of joy streaming down our cheeks? Can we not only do this weekly but daily in a world that daily seeks to take our Faith from us? We must hold Him tightly in love, gratitude, and obedience. That is possible! The Apostles, saints, martyrs, and disciples of the ages witness to that truth.

So, *we embrace with all our might the Eucharist that gives to us Christ Himself.* May our arms never grow tired of holding Him near and dear!

## Conclusion

As we seek to pull into unity our visit together, we also are inspired to provide summary and substance to the words found in 6:53–58 of John's Gospel. They all seem to fit together in a perfect symphony, don't they? Whatever we have said in preceding sermons, in time they all communicate to us we Christians have bread *from heaven*. It is always more than we can scrutinize, analyze, or even finalize. Our affirmations can continue, spoken or unspoken. They will guide and direct us. They will help us always groping in a kind of heavenly painful joy, thrilling us forever to move onward and upward by the grace of almighty God! The Father calls through the eucharistic Body and Blood of His Son. The Holy Spirit in celestial sweetness and firm whispers says in love: "This *is* My Body; this *is* My Blood." Amen.

## Exploration

1. Do you know Holy Communion is a celebration?
2. Have you ever tried to measure Christ's love?
3. Why do we refuse the powerful reality of His Supper?

4. How can we keep growing as people of "the" Sacrament?
5. What hope do we have without our Lord, especially without His Body and His Blood?

# ❧POSTLUDE❧

PILGRIM: YOU ARE so good to me! I yearn for "deeper things" and struggle away to achieve more knowledge. Then, you speak to me about grace and tell me that's all I need because Your power is made perfect in weakness. Lord, You are truly a miracle worker! Now, You have opened many doors for me. Now, I am beginning to learn something profound from the ages about John 6:53–58. I am so very grateful! Have I really come a long way or is my prideful self deceiving me again?

**Jesus**: In your own limited way you have put in print a beginning understanding of the Holy Sacrament. Being deceived by pride is very important. Place that in your memory.

**Pilgrim**: There is a certain ecstasy to Your agony during those final days, Lord. No creative genius can really depict them. The unique power of Your Body and Blood given for us causes me to shout for joy. But it also causes me to tremble. Just to be lost in such power and boundless love is at times all I desire. Forgive me, Lord, but there is a sadness that enters my heart and mind. It makes me so sad many in our churches just don't seem to understand—even to small degree—this gift that is allowed to be trapped in various kinds of wrappers. Please, I plead, enlighten me.

**Jesus**: My son, human sin and its depths are always with us. Do not lose heart. I call upon you to share with others the tiny truth I have enabled you to see. Remember to give away what you have been given.

**Pilgrim**: My Lord and my God, why is it You always have just the right words? I already know the answer. It is because You are fully God and fully man. It is because no one in all history is Your equal. It is because in You and only You we find our salvation. How privileged we are to have Saint John's message, breathed by the Holy Spirit of the living God! Just a few verses bring to us more joy, strength, and goodness than all the trillions of words spoken by countless famous people. I am humbled by having access to the Sacrament. I am even more humbled by being in a position to celebrate "for and among" Your needy children. Please help me to be worthy.

**Jesus**: Your thoughts come from the soul of one on the verge of serious spiritual growth in My will and ways. I will continue to guide you but stay close. The Devil is not pleased with your progress.

**Pilgrim**: Strange as it may seem, Lord, I feel at peace with myself. Yes, the Devil will visit me again. I pray the Holy Spirit will sustain me and I can be victorious. It will not happen in my own strength and I have to learn that again and again . . . painfully! Please allow me to experience such interior peace more often. The tensions and frustrations of life deplete my energy all too often. Oh, Your Body and Your Blood, Lord, how stupendously wonderful they are! Such love and mercy are embodied in simple elements. Truly, when the Sacrament is celebrated and we receive it, all the demons in hell must cringe in horror. Words fail me, Lord. My thoughts and feelings have moved beyond saying what I experience.

**Jesus**: Be assured I know what you think and feel. Be assured of my ever-lasting love. I remind you: stay close. The Devil despises My Body and My Blood.

**Pilgrim**: Lord, I am spiritually exhausted for the first time in my life. Perhaps I have now lost my life and have now found it. Perhaps I know at last that to obey Your teaching is really to be Your disciple. Perhaps I know what it means to go in through the narrow gate. I repay You the only way I know how. I offer myself as a living sacrifice, trusting in Your Body and Your Blood.

**Jesus**: My Father and I are in perfect unity. Eternity belongs to us, along with the Holy Spirit. Be faithful.

**Pilgrim**: I believe that if I had only the verses from John 6:53–58 the rest of my life would be meaningful and fruitful. Of course, I know, dear

Lord, there is much more to learn from these verses. Please make me a blessing to every life that I touch. Please continue to teach me. Please empower me at all times and all places to be Your person, speaking the truth in love. Please keep me in harmony with the Holy Spirit. It is true, Lord, that whether I live or die I belong to You and Your Supper provides ongoing spiritual strength. I pray You will satisfy my hunger and thirst, now and for evermore.

**Jesus**: Do not worry or fret, only cling tenaciously to Me.

# CHAPTER 10

# Other Writings

## ❧AN ATTITUDE OF GRATITUDE❧

*1 Corinthians 1:4*

LET ME TELL you about an interesting man. He was a Jew of great and profound learning. Tradition says that he was below average in height and nearly bald. Many predicted that he would become the leader of his people against the hated Romans. Since he was a Roman citizen, this would have been a very shrewd political stratagem. He could not believe in the significance of a certain religious sect. Therefore, outright persecution and persistent intolerance were the ways in which he related to it. His heart, mind, and soul worked with magnificent dedication for any cause he thought was right.

Many of his contemporaries visualized a special place in history for him—until it happened! He became sidetracked. Another Jew's spirit caught hold of him. Many said it was a shame he had to become part of a minority group that really stood no chance against either the Jewish religious elite or the Romans.

What amazed his former religious and political colleagues the most was the fact that he now gave thanks all the time for the people and things about him. It seemed that a teasing phobia had seized him. Everything he wrote had to have an expression of gratitude in it. He was often in prison and his life was continually in danger. He never knew when his next breath would be the last one.

Some place in every book of the New Testament written by Saint Paul, you will find expressions of gratitude. He was a man who literally lived in a thankful mood. His attitude of gratitude produced a certain very uplifting spiritual fragrance.

The fourth verse of the first chapter of First Corinthians begins: "Always, I thank my God. . . ." Many of us say: "When I get my way, I thank my God," or "When I have my ego inflated, I thank my God," or "When the company gives me a promotion, I thank my God." Saint Paul says: "*Always,* I thank my God."

Here is an attitude of gratitude that both opens the windows of heaven and promises the spiritually good life here and now. It ushers certain treasures into our lives.

In the first place, there is *respect for life and death.*

When a baby is born, give thanks! Here—in very miniature size—is the image of God. He did not ask to come into the world. He did not select his parents. He has nothing to do with the clothes he wears, the food he eats, or the place he lives. Yet, in a few pounds is a human being with all sorts of potentialities.

Will he be President of the United States? Ask his mother. She knows perfectly well that the chances that he will attain this office are almost like putting him in a canoe and telling him to paddle across the Pacific Ocean. Yet, don't you dare tell her that he can't make the grade. Her son is capable of anything.

Fathers, do you love that little slobbering and burping bundle of joy? He is putting a rather sizable dent in your pocketbook, isn't he? He cries as though he, not you, were the head of the house.

Is the child more than an additional member of the family? Is there genuine respect for the new life that may seem to be a competitor? All babies, male or female, wanted or unwanted, big or little, wet or dry, normal or abnormal, fat or skinny, pretty or ugly, deserve to be treated with thankfulness.

When a human being draws his last breath, give thanks! A man's eyelids are pressed shut. This life is over.

A wife shrieks in horror: "He wasn't ready! Oh, he is lost forever!" How does she know he isn't ready? Justice is in the hands of God. Human souls can communicate; they cannot trade places with one another.

A lovely lady, active in the church and in other organizations, dies suddenly at the apparent peak of her productivity. A civic leader remarks: "What a shame to lose the efforts of such a woman. Her death is surely premature." How does he know her work isn't finished? The work of eternity goes on. There may be some indispensable people, but only for a moment.

"Always, I thank my God"; therefore, I have respect for every life and every death.

Let us look at another treasure: there is *reverence for God as Creator.* God is the source of all that "was, is, and shall be."

When one approaches this truth in a receptive mood, it is stunning. We become so small and insignificant that we want to squirm, until we remember Jesus Christ. He entered history to become our Savior and Lord. This one great act takes the sting out of our helplessness and shows us we worship a God who refuses to forsake his children.

If your God is a magnificent Heavenly Father who cares so much for you and me that He sent His only begotten Son to die upon a Cross and to rise from a tomb, give thanks!

When you view the stars in the heavens, give thanks!

When you see the sun shine, give thanks!

When the rains come, give thanks!

When the snow falls, give thanks!

When there is a stale scrap of food on the table, give thanks!

When you see great factories produce a bountiful supply of goods, give thanks!

Christians are not called upon to worship God through nature or any other aspect of creation. Nevertheless, they are to hold Him in reverence as Creator.

Always give thanks for the special place of human beings. It could be that there are superior beings on Planet X. Of what relevance is this to your understanding and worship of God, or your duties to Him, His Son, and His Son's Church? If those superior beings are out there, undoubtedly our discovery of them will affect us. However, you and I must live one day at a time. The Sermon on the Mount that we have had for two thousand years contains principles we have not yet practiced or even fully believed.

Thanksgiving must never be confined to the fourth Thursday of November. I can think of no more humanly devastating crime.

It is in the attitude, "Always, I thank my God," that a final treasure comes into our midst. It is *the responsibility for coworkers in the community.*

Give thanks that there are others to help your spiritual growth.

There are two extremes in the religious life that cause the Church to suffer.

One says: "God and I can work out anything. I don't need anyone else." Jesus didn't even attempt this long, tortuous road. Perhaps God and you can solve your problems. Be careful it isn't a simple case of you asking you and you telling you what you should do. Fellow Christians and non-Christians belong. Enjoy them!

The other extreme maintains: "I can't do anything alone. I need help from every dedicated Christian all the time to make it through the pearly gates." While this may sound like a very religious stance, it is frequently a mask for what has many names. It is best understood by the word "para-site"; that is, one who feeds from the labors or assets of another without giving anything in return. A human being does not grow spiritually by having others continually cater to his whims. Always thank God for those saints who will walk the second and third mile with you, but never expect a free ride. No sincere person devoted to Christ and His Church desires to be a religious freeloader.

Saint Paul understood and practiced the art of positive thinking head and shoulders above any of our modern-day exponents. What is more positive in our total approach to life than to breathe the air of *"Always,* I thank my God?"

On your graduation day, I sincerely commend to you this frame of mind and temperament of heart. It is a "spiritually complete" philosophy of life.

———

*Pulpit Digest May 1970*

# ❊A PLEA FOR CHRISTIAN UNITY❊

*John 17:20–26*

OUR BLESSED Lord calls us to be One. In the world that we currently live this both intrigues and provokes. How do we even begin to talk about this call given to us from Saint John's Gospel?

As a dedicated ecumenist for many years, I have often marveled at the scholarly work that has been done and continues to be done. However, I believe we have reached a time in our ecumenical pilgrimage as God's people that we must become *humbly simple.*

Therefore, I ask us this day to look at six basic areas of belief—ancient and yet ever new—to provide a beginning place for us simply and humbly to visit about Christian unity.

## *Trinity*

In the first place God has seen fit to reveal Himself to us as Father, Son, and Holy Spirit. To speak of the Father is to speak of an eternal Person. The same is true of the other two Persons. They are not mere names, images, or titles. They are—in fact—*three eternal Persons,* always having existed and forever existing. The revelation of the New Testament and the Church Fathers is clear; not to believe this is to place us in jeopardy before One who has unmistakably revealed Himself to us.

We are well aware of the forces that seek to destroy the way God has chosen to come to us. Such proponents often do little more than parade names for God by us that suit their viewpoints and agendas. Of course, God creates, redeems, and sustains. However, our blessed Lord, Jesus the Christ, does not relate to God as "Creator"; He relates to Him as the "Father." Perhaps God is sometimes other than these three Persons but that only clouds the pressing truth of His *certain revelation* as Father, Son and Holy Spirit.

## Holy Scriptures

In the second place a very rich Judaism, the Church, and the Holy Spirit have given to us writings that proclaim the Word of God. Such written authority, when taken lightly, always leads Christ's people astray. To nitpick over this translation and that translation is almost like having access to a basket of perfectly ripened fruit and tossing out a pear or orange and keeping an apple or grapefruit. To be sure, there must be an uncompromising loyalty to the ancient manuscripts and where deviation occurs we are called to be blatantly honest.

The precious and Holy Word of God is a gift to you and me. It is to be loved, appreciated, studied, followed, and memorized. It is our *priority piece of literature from the living God!* We are to be taught from it. We are not to superimpose our agendas and viewpoints upon it. It would appear some would go so far as to maintain God agrees with them and proceed to tell us God is "their" cooperative instrument to enlighten the Christian religion that has never really had it right! The Church gave us "The Book" but "The Book" provides the ongoing format for the integrity of the Church.

## Blessed Virgin Mary

In the third place how much trouble we seem to have with the greatest feminine power among Christians! She has a uniqueness all her own because the Father chose her to be the Mother of our Lord. From the very earliest centuries of Church history she has had a *uniquely singular* place in the Faith. Except for her Son, no other being has had the impact upon you and me that she has had. Only those who disbelieve the Holy Scriptures would call her just another virtuous Jewish woman who happened to be in the right place at the right time!

Our blessed Mother Mary has much to show us. Not only does she provide a magnificent model of poverty, chastity, and obedience; she evidences the life of a hurting mother trying to come to terms with a controversial son. Indeed, modern women can relate to her! They must relate to her in order for the Faith to regain its ideal of virginity and faithfulness in marriage with sexual relations and human birth accepted as sacred. The dark and painful road that *radical* feminism would have us choose must be seen for what it is: hell, now and forever.

## *Holy Communion*

In the fourth place, in those early days after the Lord's Ascension and Pentecost, our spiritual ancestors gathered to receive "His Body and His Blood." They did this generations before the *New Testament* became a unified reality under the guidance of the Holy Spirit. To receive this Sacrament was to receive Christ and be nourished by His sacrifice. The power generated from this simple meal of bread and wine caused an ancient world order to be shaken to the core. You and I are recipients of the Sacrament that dares to dispense *the very life of Jesus the Christ.*

For far too long far too many have professed the Lord but denied the way He has chosen to give us *spiritual stamina.* Indeed, how shall we escape if we refuse that intended to give us the grace for the victorious living of these difficult days? Must we be starving and emaciated children before the Father whose Son continually offers His Body and Blood? The means to be spiritual giants is there for the taking. Why must we be invariably concerned with programs and organizations that promise only to attain goals that are secondary to the holiness and wholeness promised by the Eucharist?

## *Ordained Ministry*

In the fifth place the ordering of ministry today is *probably the most crucial* of all of the tasks facing the visible Church. Those who do not have an ordained ministry based upon apostolic succession frequently blur the lines established by the ancient Catholic and Orthodox Churches. It appears to be a matter not of invalidity but incompleteness. All who profess Christ are in ministry. Yet, there are those set aside, especially in the priestly and sacramental ministry. Our Savior and Lord along with His Apostles set the pattern. Until proven otherwise by Holy Scripture and sacred Tradition with the guidance of the Holy Spirit, only those of the male gender can be so set apart.

Is the constant pressure of women to be ordained priests a reason to capitulate for the sake of peace in the Church? There are many who are very positive about such a step and speak loudly—even in rage—about inequity. Yet, the *Catholic and Orthodox wellsprings* from which we all drink maintain this cannot be done. Who are we to believe? What voice are we to obey? It seems to me the answer is clear-cut. If we desire to abandon the consistent teaching of the Church—both Catholic and Orthodox—across the centuries and believe "apostasy" and "heresy" are only words soon best forgotten, let us as men seek to cancel the authority and responsibility of the Church originally given to us. Then, let us be cast into hell whimpering with Adam, "She made me do it!!"

## The Church

In the sixth place we really only have *one creed that is universal.* Throughout the world it is said by Anglicans, Roman Catholics, Orthodox, and Protestants. It is the ever-powerful and relevant statement the Nicene Creed. In direct language it says the Church is "one, holy, catholic, and apostolic." It was formulated centuries before the eastern and western division of the Church. The authenticity and truth it conveys in those four adjectives continue to point to the work of the Holy Spirit among us. I have serious doubts that we can improve upon it. There is a cohesive quality and eternal ring imperative for today.

To be "one" is to say, regardless of the expressions given by the true disciples of the Christ, there is a unity of time and space and yet transcending both. Our Lord did not spawn an infinite number of Churches, dependent on human temperament and cultural dictates. He established "one." To be "holy" is to take special note it is *not just another organization among organizations* that we join like a service club, fraternity, or sorority. Our Lord says "even the gates of hell shall not prevail against it." We are to imitate the "spotless, unblemished Lamb of God." To be "catholic" calls us to accept the universality and pervasiveness of our Faith. To be "apostolic" reminds us Jesus chose twelve men to launch and give direction to His organization, militant and triumphant.

So, as our Lord calls us to be one, is what has been said just too simple? I humbly hope and pray that is not the case. Only as we become like children, teachable and obedient, can we really be one with our Lord and one another. A host of witnesses has given us the Holy Scriptures and sacred Tradition; the Holy Spirit abides and provides. So much has been and is entrusted to us. We are much aware of the onslaughts of Satan that would mutilate and annihilate. They come from many directions, expected and unexpected. May God be merciful to those who would not merely alter the Faith but subvert it to the point of giving the world another religion, apostate and hell-bent.

This sermon was preached from the pulpit of the Parish of All Saints (Ashmont) in Boston, Massachusetts by the Rev. Dr. Donald Charles Lacy on Sunday, September 20, 1992. He preached the sermon also over LESEA TV Broadcasting (Indianapolis and South Bend) in the Fall of 1994.

————

*Evangel Press, 1992*

# ❀SAYING A WORD TO SINNERS❀

EVEN THOUGH I walk through the valley of the shadow of death, I will fear no evil, for you are with me; your rod and your staff, they comfort me (Ps. 23:4 [NIV]).

Today in very brief span of time we can travel about a large city and see more sin and death than some of our grandparents ever saw in their lifetimes. To prove our point I invite you to take a tour, both fiction and fact, but bearing a full gift of truth.

1.

The scene is a room in a rundown hotel. There are holes in the rug. There are large gaping voids in the plastering. Dust and dirt cover everything in the room. In the bed is an alcoholic dying of bad liquor. His thin unshaven face is enough to make many shriek in horror. He doesn't have very long to live, perhaps seconds. He is alone. He weeps as he counts the lost opportunities. He grew up on an Iowa farm. His parents were good, hardworking Protestants. They are both gone to their eternal reward. He remembers with blinding remorse how he never sobered up until his mother had been in her grave two days. His parents had sacrificed for his college education. He had abused one opportunity after another. He had deliberately followed the line of least resistance, thinking all would be well anyway. What stings the most deeply are those challenging moments he knowingly throws away. Apparently, he can blame no one but himself. Soon it will all be over.

Now our scene shifts to a hospital room.

There we discover a harlot dying of a massive brain tumor. There are no get-well cards. There are a few flowers but the names of the senders are conspicuously missing. Only a doctor and three nurses visit her. She is barely old enough to have grandchildren. In her keen moments her father's business place in New England comes to mind. She, as a girl, worked as a clerk in his department store. Everybody seemed to like her and continually commented about her beauty. She had several opportunities to marry intelligent, hard-working young men. Eventually she marries . . . marries . . . marries . . . marries. The continual rejections and increasing sense of inadequacy are just more than she can handle. She refuses to have children, recognizing the burdens but not the joys of having them. In place of getting off the merry-go-around of parties she bolsters her self-esteem by a last desperate try; she becomes a member of the oldest profession in the world. Now, as she slobbers and groans, the opportunities of yesterday make her sane moments hell. She recalls dozens upon dozens of situations where she brazenly trampled on God's mercies. She had mocked at those who counted religion anything more than scented conscience salve. Had she made fun of God too long? When the last breath comes, would she be sane? Is there any hope for someone who has gone out of her way to defame some of the ideals in life which are mandatory for stability? Maybe the end will come tonight.

Again the scene changes.

The sun is beginning to rise. In a gutter is a man lying face down. The dirty water is reddened by his blood. He is a gambler dying of bullet wounds. He is conscious but unable to move. A delivery man sees the body from across the street. He thinks this must simply be another one of the city's drunks. Interestingly, this dying man was prominent in civic affairs and was known far and wide as a very capable individual. But . . . he couldn't control his gambling. It was a disease with him. Of course, there were those many times he could have avoided the temptation. He deliberately tested his powers of refusal and lost again and again. He remembers the sleepless nights following his decision to go into the rackets. A voice kept saying "No." Through some clever maneuvering he managed to get his conscience to believe as long as he was going to gamble, he might as well do it with the big boys. He remembers a vivid sermon preached on the evils and problems connected with gambling. He also remembers his reaction to it. He lowered his Church pledge. The increased money in his pocket actually meant more money for his gambling escapades. He joked that "After all, God isn't a sore loser." He need not be lying in the gutter dying, but he is and the awful truth is he has put himself there.

Our scene turns now to a busy intersection.

An auto has hit the side of a truck at a terrific rate of speed. The auto has flipped over and over. Beneath it is a teenage boy dying of injuries.

Sirens are screaming. It's too late, and anyone close by can sense the always awful scent of premature death. There are several witnesses. All agree the boy is clearly at fault. His mind goes back to the policeman in his home neighborhood who told him in a nice way to slow down. He laughed at them. One of his teachers pleaded with him to take it easy. He was unimpressed. After all, what did this teacher know except a little classroom subject matter. Even his girlfriend talked to him every time he took her out about his criminal driving manners. Yet, the world was his. Whatever he wanted to do, he did it. He did it deliberately and with an almost morbid sort of satisfaction. He was dying. He was not a big enough man to stop this. He wished a few of those who loved him would come by. All at once, he had learned how to say "Thank you." The sun was rapidly setting. Months—yes, years—of opportunities were about to be wiped off the slate. There was no one to blame but himself.

There is a fifth scene.

The house is old and well kept. It is in a respectable neighborhood. Next to a large picture window is an old lady sitting in a wheelchair. Her despondency saturates everything about her. One look at her face and you immediately know there is something drastically wrong. She is dying of a broken heart. You see, the story goes like this: She never had time for her children as they were growing up. There were hundreds of other things more important than they. Of course, she loved them. Mothers were expected to love their children. All four of them now lived out of the city and rarely stopped by. Occasionally she received a birthday card. To make a long story short: When they needed her, she wasn't available. Now she needed them. They somehow couldn't feature her ever needing anyone. Alone and severely depressed she gazed out of the window. Her bleeding heart pumps faster as though it is racing to a destination. Her shriveled soul is gasping even to keep immortality a certainty. Occasionally a smile tinged with sadness comes upon her face, as she visualizes those many, many instances when they needed her. The children didn't need her money. They were starving for a little genuine affection and unhurried concern. They didn't care about her loneliness and bitterness. How could they? It wasn't that they disliked her. It wasn't that they wanted to withhold due honor. They just did not have any feelings on her behalf. Death from a broken heart is weirdly painful.

In all scenes death and the conditions surrounding it seem highly deserved. When people continually and deliberately sin, how can you and I have mercy on them? Indeed, why feel sorry for them? God did everything but force them to right pathways. How can we excuse them? We believe in forgiveness, but how far can we go with it? If we trample on God's mercy enough, we rightly deserve the states in which each of our friends finds himself or herself. Common sense tells us there has to be limits. If there are people in the world who adamantly refuse the dictates of their consciences and the pleading of the Holy Spirit; what can you and I do, except let them die in their wretchedness?

2.

What could you and I say to such people—*as followers of the Christ?*

Isn't it one thing to be wrong and yet quite another to be wrong deliberately, even arrogantly? When people refuse to do what is right and they know it; what can they expect other than loneliness, despair, guilt, and hopelessness? Surely all five of our friends are getting what they justly deserve. "What a man sows he reaps"; it's that simple—*or is it?* Indeed, what can we say to our errant friends?

First, there is the alcoholic dying of bad liquor. "Put pressure on the state and federal govermnents to get better laws passed" or "What a shame! Let us give more money to our home missionary projects" or "Amend the Constitution again! Prohibition should never have been repealed" or "Poor fellow. Let's get more social workers into the field" or "It's just one of those things." "Here is a real honest-to-goodness deliberate sinner who is getting what is coming to him" or "If I had lived the same way, I would expect nothing better."

Oh, this man does not want to hear about our proposed humanitarian reforms and listen to our jumbled and jaded justice! He wants to *hear* and *believe* more than anything else the fourth verse of the twenty-third Psalm: "Even though I walk through the valley of the shadow of death, I will fear no evil, for you are with me; your rod and your staff, they comfort me." This is a word to all of humanity, even those who have tried to spit in the face of God and even those who have cursed the lowly Galilean, Jesus. Sometime today let's stop and count the opportunities we have had to become better followers of the Christ.

What can we say to another of our friends?

Second, there is the harlot dying of a massive brain tumor. "Poor woman. Let's get some wealthy person to endow a research grant to study this condition" or "It is a shame, but what can you expect. God's justice must be done" or "Surely our hospital chaplaincy can be doubled to deal with such patients who must have special care" or "Even Jesus was lenient with her kind. Let's not be too quick to judge. Of course, her agony is self-inflicted" or "Anyone who stoops to such things deserves the wrath of God."

Oh, this lady does not want to hear words coughed up from an arid social awareness or listen to our silly attempts to be God! She wants to *hear* and *believe* more than anything that blessed forth verse: "Even though I walk through the valley of the shadow of death, I will fear no evil, for you are with me; your rod and your staff, they comfort me." Would you and I walk through that valley with her holding her trembling hand? She had opportunities to be decent, to be moral, to be good. Did she laugh at decency, morality, and goodness? Yes, and without shame. Let him or her who has not already had a chance to be a better follower of Jesus the Christ this day be the first to cast the stone.

Again, what can we say to another of our friends?

Third, there is the gambler dying of bullet wounds. "Stamp out organized crime! Put everyone behind bars who is in the rackets" or "Make gambling illegal. This will curtail the appetite" or "I feel sorry for him, but anyone with that small amount of brain power is bound to get into trouble." or "Why didn't he go to another city where he wasn't known" or "The wages of sin is death."

Oh, this man is dying, and he doesn't want to listen to our subpar moral blubbering! He wants to hear and believe more than anything else that word give to all sinners—even you and me: "Even though I walk through the valley of the shadow of death, I will fear no evil, for you are with me; your rod and your staff, they comfort me." Think of all the times our little bad traits may have become one big bad habit which brought our downfall. When you and I are offered a chance to see the face of Christ more clearly, do we take it? Even now our own thought processes and soul sensitivities are shifting, sorting, and searching.

Now what can we say to our young friend?

Fourth, there is the teenage boy dying of auto injuries. "There ought to be a law against letting them get their license so young" or "I feel so sorry for him. I am sure God will not punish him very much" or "Well, maybe he can be an example for some of those other show-offs" or "Anyone who was cautioned as often as he was probably got what was coming to him."

Oh, this lad does not care to hear subtle adult judgment or moral lessons on how this accident will prevent others! Death is close and something or someone that transcends the here and now is urgently needed. Some of our correctives in the "religious life" make about as much sense as handing a drowning man a cup of water. How many of us are meek and mild on the sidewalks but a Brahma bull at a rodeo in our moving automobiles, especially if another driver irritates us? He, too, wants to hear and believe that most blissful portion of the Twenty-third Psalm.

We must not leave out our last friend.

Fifth, there is an old lady dying of a broken heart. "She got just what was coming to her" or "Her children ought to pay her some attention" or "Maybe we ought to form a cheer committee in her neighborhood" or "Maybe if she gets some of her just reward now it won't go so rough with her in the hereafter" or "She sowed selfishness and indifference to need and now she is collecting the horrible dividends."

Oh, this broken heart needs mending and not a bunch of self-appointed heart surgeons standing around playing "do gooder" and "moral pillar!" She longs to hear and believe that special word from the Psalmist. By the way, how many hearts have you and I broken deliberately with no thought given to the mending procedure?

3.

Our friends are what some of us might have been under the proper conditions. May you and I remember the many roads we have traveled and be given the high honor of repeating this fourth verse of the twenty-third Psalm to our five friends and thereby be an instrument causing them to believe this promise tied to eternity.

Our real conclusion is a type of holy provocation in three questions. What do any of us actually deserve? If the Lord's presence at our death were dependent upon making use of our opportunities to serve Him, how many of us would qualify? What are we now doing with this immediate opportunity to become a better disciple of the Christ?

My, how God loves us. Yet, He sees us as we really are!

*Great Preaching 2001*

PART 2

GENERAL SELECTIONS

# CHAPTER 11

# Mary, Mother of Jesus

## ✤ A MOTHER'S QUESTIONS ✤

AT THIS TIME of year you and I are saturated by the spirit of Christmas. The music of Christmas carols makes us feel better. Our blood seems to tingle even more than the little bells of the Salvation Army. We choke up a little now and then at the sight of a beautiful and inspiring Nativity scene. Our worries seem to subside and our joys seem to gain the upper hand. We feel the need to be a little more friendly. Even the most introverted individual manages a smile and a "hello" now and then. Poems and inspiring speeches that are repeated year after year evoke glad tidings. These feelings are expected. There is nothing unusual about them. They too are good and right and proper.

There is a story that remains untold until this very hour. It must be made known to all who cherish the Christmas season, especially the world's mothers. That awesome and wondrous land of make-believe frequently can convey more truth than a whole catalogue of statistics. Turn the clock back, back, and back to just a few days after the birth of a Jewish baby boy.

Let us celebrate this blessed season by looking at it from a highly unusual, but I am certain good and right and proper angle. Saint Luke records: "But Mary kept all these things, *pondering* them in her heart." This is Mary's state of mind shortly after the birth of Jesus. A series of three questions work their way through her mind. She *ponders* each of them.

*The first inquiry is:* "Is my baby really the Christ?" Mary begins talking to herself:

> Is it possible that here in my very arms is the Anointed One of God? I recall Gabriel said to me: "Hail, O favored one, the Lord is with you!" He spoke others which were comforting and so very complimentary. He even explained to me that the Holy Spirit would be responsible for my conceiving His Son. Yet, I wonder? Why was I chosen? There are other virtuous women in the land.
>
> Joseph is certainly not the only one who can trace his ancestry back to David. Jesus, you don't look any different from any of the many other babies I have seen. It is true you are quite good-looking

by comparison. Some day you will be a fine Jewish man, respected and valuable, who takes his rightful place in the community.

My son, tell me, are you the Christ? Others think so, I think I want to think so, but it is so difficult. The shepherds were led to us by God. They marvelled at you. Joseph has been a man of the finest and most considerate actions. Poor man. He has been under a great strain. He will want you, my son, to work in his carpenter's shop.

I wonder, oh, I wonder, are all these happenings real! Are those signs which point to you being the Son of God real or have I selfishly imagined God chose me?

Oh, see how He smiles and jerks His tiny head! He is quite a specimen. God, forgive me; but it is so hard for me to believe that this sweet, lovable, and handsome baby is really the Messiah. Oh Mary, stop thinking of yourself like some half-green girl with a doll in her arms. Your son has become bored with your facial expressions and has gone to sleep. Somehow, I must face up to the facts. By some strange stroke of the Almighty, Jesus is the Messiah and I—simple, poor, and virtuous Mary—am his mother. Let me touch your forehead again, my son. He is such a good baby.

You and I are forced to ask—at least—once in our lives: "Is Jesus really the Christ?" It is neither heresy nor blasphemy to ask such a question. In fact, it is a privilege and a "must" to ask it. The question is an invitation. Despite our appearance of Christianity, human nature in inclined to say: "It is highly improbable that almighty and everlasting God would utilize a young Jewish woman to give birth to Jesus, His Son." There is one outstanding fact in the Gospels: God chose a particular time in history to send His Son to live and die among wayward human beings. Whether or not we believe, this is decisive in our lives. One can be religious and not be a Christian. One can be a Christian only because of Jesus Christ.

Again we turn back the clock and see a dedicated mother. The baby is awake and wants Mary to hold him. She picks him up, forgets about her work, and begins to *ponder*.

*Her second inquiry is:* "If Jesus is really the Christ, how costly will this be for him?"

Again Mary speaks to herself:

Gabriel says that you will be great. Greatness often has meant real sacrifice. It frequently has been spelled out in many and various hardships.

Jesus, will you ever be cold? Jesus, will you ever be hungry? Jesus, will you ever be insulted? Oh, my little one, how costly will it be to be the Christ? Life can be cruel. People can greet you with a kiss and then stone you without mercy. Circumstances can be such that even if you suffer in excruciating pain, hardly anyone will care. Jesus, if I could protect you through all your years . . . if I could suffer for you. Now, things seem so beautiful, lovely, and promising. I am holding you in my arms and nothing else matters. Could it be that way forever? Mary, how silly can you be. The child has to grow up.

The cost may break all of our hearts. Oh God, what if some who do not know Him as I do kill Him? There are those who hang others upon crosses. Oh God, how costly will it be?

Jesus, let me touch your rosy cheeks again. They are perfect. Let me hold those delicate hands. They are precious. Let me touch your feet. They are pretty.

Your mission will be costly. Perhaps some day you will pray this little prayer: "Eternal God, may Thy will be done on earth as it is in heaven." Ah, just think, I am the mother of the Messiah. He will pay dearly because of this.

My, how his mother bores Him! He has fallen into another pleasant slumber.

You and I are forced to ask at least once in our lives "If He is the Christ, how costly is it to follow Him?" We can speak penitently about giving up certain things. What did Jesus ask His disciples to give up? We can speak enthusiastically about particular things we are going to begin doing. What did Jesus tell His disciples to be doing? It is at a deeper level that a system of "do's and don'ts" that we perceive how costly it is to be a Christian. The actual cost is perceived only in terms of living in a climate Saint Paul calls: "in Christ." The winds of obedience to God and sincerity with men blow freely in this climate. Out of it nearly all rightful "affirmatives and negatives" naturally emerge. Our relationships are far more significant than our pronunciations and denunciations. Of course, the cost is great to follow Christ.

For the final time we turn the clock back and see a dedicated mother. The baby cries in hopes of gaining a little extra attention. Mary picks Him up and rocks Him in her arms gently. He is pleased and cries no more. Her brow becomes wrinkled and her thoughts more sobering.

*Her third and last inquiry is:* "If Jesus is really the Christ and this will be costly, will it be worth it?"

Mary *ponders*:

Gabriel says: "of your Kingdom there will be no end." How difficult is it for a mother to see why her son has to be a Savior for others! Why should this innocent fellow have to pay any price for the sins of those He doesn't even know? Are others worth it? What if vast multitudes are ungrateful for the price He must surely pay? There are so many, many who do not deserve my son as Savior.

Jesus, you sweet and delightful bundle of joy. You have brought to your mother feelings that she could experience only after you were born. I will never be able to describe to you and for you the happiness and sense of fulfillment you have given to me.

Your mother's heart turns to sadness each time she visualizes what shall surely come upon you. She can't understand why anyone so harmless and so pure and so kind. . . . They aren't worth it! You can grow into a fine man, die for them, and they still won't care! I won't let it happen! Oh, Father in Heaven, it is just not worth it!

I am sorry, son. The protective love in a mother's heart had to express itself. I must leave these things in God's hands. Oh God, may the son. You have given to me drink from every bitter cup You have selected, but I plead that none of this will be in vain.

Jesus, your mother thinks in spoken words too often. What do you know about that. He's fast asleep.

So you and I are forced to ask at least once in our lives: "If He is the Christ and it will be costly to follow Him, will it be worth it?" Regardless of the pathway we select, we shall pay a price. The most pathetic and disturbing sight in all of life is to watch someone experience the depths of hell and then refuse the attitude of Christlike compassion which is a natural product of such experience. We must not miss these opportunities. Of course, Jesus is the Christ. Of course, it is costly to follow Him. Of course, it is worth it. The voice of God determines the true worth of anything. God has spoken through His Son, Jesus Christ, and has proclaimed His Way "the" Way.

Christmas, 1969
Dear Mother of Jesus,
   We apologize for the way we have treated your son. Oh Mary, we repent for the way we have treated Him! Oh Mary, may God forgive us for our cowardly Christianity! Despite our indifference, we know your

Son is the Christ. We know there are times when the cost runs high. What really appalls us and makes us bitterly ashamed is when we ask: "Is it worth it?"

It is Christmas time in our land. We have seen little things here and there which lead us to believe there is hope. Mary, we are certain there is hope. Even now, we hear hearts beating to an inspiring tune:

*Jesus Christ, the Savior is born*
*Glory to God!*
*Jesus Christ, the Savior is born*
*Glory to God!*

We do care for your son. We genuinely love Him. Mother of Mothers, we kneel in adoration before Him. Quiet your fears and rest assured that His birth and death are not in vain.

*Affectionately and Appreciatively yours,*
*Those Who Care*
*P.S.: Right now some are promising to follow Him . . . . Wherever He leads.*

––––––––

*Queen of All Hearts* November–December, 1969
CSS 1982 [A Mother and Her Infant Son]. Used by permission from CSS Publishing
Company, Inc., 517 S. Main Street, P.O. Box 4503, Lima, Ohio 45802–4503.
*Indianapolis Star* (abbreviated) December 25, 1982
*Mary's People* November 25, 1990
*South Bend Sunday Tribune* December 25, 1994

# ❋DEVOTION TO MARY SHOULD TRANSCEND❋ DENOMINATIONS

## *Local Methodist pastor sees Blessed Mother as the key to authentic ecumenism*

RECENTLY, A sincere person of the Protestant fundamentalist persuasion accosted me and said with firmness and a tinge of dogmatism, "The trouble with you mainline Protestants is that you don't believe in the deity of Jesus." I responded in this fashion: "Oh, but many of us do believe Jesus was God and, of course, that makes His mother, Mary, the Mother of God."

There was pain in the bewildered reaction, but it was hopefully redemptive pain born out of the work of the Holy Spirit.

Devotion to the Blessed Mother transcends the limited understanding of Protestant fundamentalism, a movement that has probably issued more encyclicals of its own than all of the popes. It is indeed an intriguing phenomenon of religious experience that some of the most dedicated Christian persons have completely overlooked the imperative significance of Mary. She has been placed again and again in the position of having little importance even in the face of biblical facts which point to a lofty place in God's scheme of salvation.

Furthermore, the Blessed Mother can and does transcend the current pettiness of both radical feminists and rigid chauvinists. She is a peacemaker. A woman was chosen to give birth to God. Is there something more significant and influential for women than that? I doubt it. She brings to the Faith the most sublime forms of maternity and femininity! Try to match such power! To believe in the omnipotence, omnipresence, and omniscience of God is to assume God could have come to us in any way, at any time, and under any conditions.

The fact is that God chose to come to us through a woman. No man dares consider the Faith in its full dimension ignoring the truth that even the Apostles did not and could not perform Mary's function in the economy of salvation.

It is devotion to the Blessed Mother that helps unite us as Christians. When Protestants lose their widespread hang-up that Roman Catholics have worshipped and do worship her, they can perceive by the power of the Holy Spirit an authentic ecumenism that calls us "to be one." When many Roman Catholics stop apologizing for their emphasis on her in order not to offend the Protestant community, they can put her back where she rightfully belongs.

Who can be better accepted and appreciated in a practical sense than a fully caring and totally pure mother that is obedient to God? Indeed, is there something more profound than that God directly and specifically chose a woman to give birth to the Son?

By most measurements we live in a time that says chastity is outdated and purity is an ideal best avoided. The increase in premarital sexual intercourse is a colossal disgrace and it is happening among Christians regardless of church affiliation. Extra-marital relationships and divorce have so pervaded our society and even God's people that we seem to be at the point of declaring the commandment on adultery null and void!

Who can speak to such a spiritually nauseating and morally debilitating situation? Mary, the chaste and pure mother of God. What can pave the way for precious persons to reverse their plunge towards hell? Mary, as the model of chastity and purity.

Jesus is our Savior and Lord. However, Mary by God's decree is always a part of that relationship to a greater or lesser degree. Jesus was and is God, perfectly human and perfectly divine. Mary, by never being divine or even having been considered a deity, lends her person to being human in the same sense as you and I.

Therefore she chose to be chaste and pure. Through her example you and I can choose to be chaste and pure. This does not detract from Jesus; it simply points to another dimension of the salvation that has been given to us to receive or reject. If we have any difficulty with this, we simply should jog our memories that God existed as the Trinity before Mary and that God, in fact, did not need Mary in order to continue being God. Her entire being and essential significance are dependent on God's action.

Ecumenically, the Blessed Mother of God provides the means for us to value again with joy and confidence chastity and purity. While there may be hesitancy on the part of many Protestants to deal with—let alone understand and accept—the Immaculate Conception and Assumption into Heaven, they have no excuse to avoid the spiritual means to bring again to the highest priority these twin holy attributes. Roman Catholics (and Orthodox for that matter) do not hold a monopoly on her! She belongs to all of us who profess her Son as Savior and Lord.

The ongoing opposition to the Blessed Mother's rightful place of honor which includes devotion, is centered around the widespread belief among many conservative Protestants with little sense of the "ecumenical" that she is considered a savior in her own right and Roman Catholics worship her in place of Christ. Vatican II is slowly but surely eroding that demonic insistence. Pope John Paul II in time should greatly aid in dispelling such misinformation and prejudice. For example, in a homily on December 8, 1982, on the Feast of the Immaculate Conception at the Basilica of Saint Mary Major, he said: "Mary's role is to make her Son shine, to lead Him, and to help welcome Him."

What is often missed by some well-meaning, pietistic Protestants is that they value highly the intercessory prayers of those they consider strong and stalwart in the Faith; Mary never enters their minds. Who has not heard some deacon, elder, pastor or lay leader praised for prayers on behalf of so-and-so. Surely we can pray to the Blessed Mother, asking her intercession on our behalf and others. Dare we ask for her credentials!

It is very important that the words of Vatican II—specifically under "The Church" where the role of Mary is discussed—be conveyed again and again. For example, we find: "Therefore the Blessed Virgin is invoked by the Church under the titles of Advocate, Auxiliatrix, Adjutrix, and Mediatrix. These, however, are to be so understood that they neither take away from nor add anything to the dignity and efficacy of Christ the one Mediator." Further, it says, "For no creature could ever be classed with the Incarnate Word and Redeemer." Still further, we discover the capstone, "The Church does not hesitate to profess this subordinate role of Mary."

Another very crucial document to come out of Vatican II, "Decree on Ecumenism," is a brilliant basis for underscoring the centrality of Christ. The opening lines tell us, "The restoration of unity among all Christians is one of the principal concerns of the Second Vatican Council. Christ the Lord founded one Church and one Church only." This certainly says nothing about the Blessed Mother heading the Church or replacing Christ or—for that matter—acting as an equal to Him.

To get a balanced and necessary viewpoint one needs to return to the document "The Church" and its discussion of devotion to the Blessed Virgin in the Church. There we find, "Mary was involved in the mysteries of Christ. As the most holy Mother of God she was, after her Son, exalted by divine grace above all angels and men. Hence the Church appropriately honors her with special reverence." Can anyone who is serious about the Faith find fault with this? I really don't think so, regardless of what label he/she wears.

Is the "Hail, Mary" meant for all Christians?

My answer is a resounding affirmation! It is majestically simple and filled with ongoing insight. Is it biblical? Yes. It meets the spiritual needs of praise and petition. It shows God's pleasure with Mary and His work in her. Yet, with all of this praise of her, we—in reflection—discover she points to her Son and in reality find homage paid to her is dependent on Him.

Will we some day find the "Hail Mary" in hymnals and books of worship throughout the Faith? I fully expect this to happen. Why? Because the Blessed Mother is the key to authentic ecumenism in our day and time.

---

*The Criterion* (official newspaper of the Archdiocese of Indianapolis) July 22, 1983

*Our Sunday Visitor* August 16, 1987

*International Christian Digest* October 1987

*Marion Helpers Bulletin* (edited) October–December 1987

*The Light of Christ* (Military Council of Catholic Women—Rome, Italy)
February–March 1988

*Mary's People* June 23, 1991

# �֍WILL MARY BECOME A SYMBOL�֍ OF CHRISTIAN UNITY?

### *Christians of all denominations are showing a new appreciation for the Blessed Mother*

IS ONE OF the most divisive forces in the Christian faith now becoming the most uniting?

The Mother of Christ, Mary, has for centuries been the cause of many severe disruptions in the Universal Church. For generations, some Protestants have been taught that Roman Catholics and the Orthodox worship Mary. The resulting division in the Church has affected millions who have called her Son "Savior" and "Lord."

However, I believe that a new day has dawned for Christians when it comes to appreciating the role of the Mother of Christ.

Certainly a key contribution is the direct way Vatican II documents treat the subject. Mary is seen as one who gains her great significance and place in salvation history by pointing to her Son. In Him is found the ultimate power of redemption. He chose to dwell in her womb and humanly enter history by being her Son. Whatever excesses have occurred in Marian piety in centuries past should no longer be a point of contention.

Also, Protestants are rereading their Bibles, especially the first two chapters of both the Gospels of Matthew and Luke. For those who believe solely in the Holy Scriptures as the imperative to know Jesus Christ, some amazing perceptions are leaping from the pages. How could we have missed this? There, for all to see, is the magnificence of the Mother of Christ.

Both clergy and laity are doing a better job of studying the history of the Faith. Mary as the Theotokos or Mother (Bearer) of God is at least as old as the Council of Ephesus (431).

When we review the Reformation, we discover Martin Luther calling her "the tender Mother of God." None other than Billy Graham has admitted that many Protestants have neglected her in recent times.

Another modern development influencing a new appreciation of Mary is the need for a powerful and legitimate femininity that finds an answer in Mary. Men will kneel before her purity. Women can relate to someone whose life seemed to be filled with frustration.

The appeal of the devout and dedicated mother is also attractive in an era of sexual promiscuity and the abandonment of parental roles. There was only one mother of the man Christians call "Savior" and

"Lord." Her name was Mary. At one precious time in history He was, in fact, her little boy.

The late Archbishop Fulton J. Sheen captured the feeling for much of the world: "Lovely Lady, dressed in blue/Teach me how to pray!/God was just your little boy/And you know the way!"

Finally, non-Catholics are even coming to appreciate the significance of praying the Rosary. All these beads really do mean something! Indeed, some have learned it is a means of continually summarizing and lifting up the Gospel story.

These positive ecumenical developments in the appreciation of Mary do not mean that all interreligious problems have been miraculously solved. But it does underline the emergence of a new awareness among those willing to test the validity of their stereotypes.

Can a lovely woman who epitomizes poverty, chastity, and obedience be a cause of disunity among Christians? The wisdom of the Universal Church is teaching some of us that the answer will eventually be a resounding "no."

As a sign of this movement of reconciliation, how can all Christians do something positive? By turning to the Holy Scriptures, of course, and repeating together in shared joy Luke 1:28: "Rejoice, O highly favored daughter! The Lord is with you. Blessed are you among women."

---

*Our Sunday Visitor* October 1991

# ❧ CHRISTIAN UNITY AND ❧ INTERRELIGIOUS CONCERNS ❧

ADVENT AND Christmas offer an excellent opportunity for the United Methodists to share in the special significance of the Mother of Jesus, the Blessed Virgin Mary.

Biblical passages in the early chapters of Matthew and Luke offer ideas for reflection on why the Roman Catholics, Orthodox and many Anglicans give Mary a prominent place in their faiths.

The reverence for Mary can be seen as both a gift of Scripture and tradition. It has provided solace and inspiration for millions of people throughout the centuries.

Methodist heritage is closely connected to the Church of England, which continues to honor Mary in such organizations as the Society of Mary and the Ecumenical Society of the Blessed Virgin Mary. While the Wesleys seem to have said very little about her, Article II in our Doctrinal Standards and General Rules indicated Jesus "took man's nature in the womb of the blessed Virgin."

Among the literature by Protestant writers about our Lord's Mother is Martin Luther's commentary on the Magnificat. In his introductory section he refers to her as "the tender Mother of God." Furthermore, he requests in closing that God give a right understanding of this portion of Holy Scripture "through the intercession and the sake of His dear Mother Mary!"

As we celebrate the birth of Jesus, let us also remember Mary, for it was through her that salvation came to humankind in the form of a baby.

———

*Interpreter* November–December 1993

# ✳IMAGINE ALL CHRISTIANS PRAYING✳ THE 'HAIL MARY'

THE RECENT Catholic–Lutheran agreement on justification was called "a milestone along the not easy road of the reestablishment of full unity among Christians" by Pope John Paul II. Many of us neither Catholic nor Lutheran gave thanks with some emotion.

Having been a part of the statewide Methodist–Lutheran Dialogue over a period of years, it was especially heartwarming for me. One of my discoveries during the dialogue was magnificent writing by Martin Luther that provided joy and optimism for the Advent/Christmas seasons. Indeed, Luther was a son of the Catholic Church!

His commentary of "The Magnificat" (Luke 1:46–55) runs some 25,000 words. It is addressed "to his Serene Highness, Prince John Frederick, Duke of Saxony, Landgrave of Thuringia, Margrave of Meissen, My Gracious Lord and Patron." He calls it his "little exposition." It is dated Wittenberg, March 19, 1521.

He begins by calling the passage a "sacred hymn of most blessed Mother of God." His prayer is that "the tender Mother of God herself procure for me the spirit of wisdom profitably and thoroughly to expound this song of hers." Some Lutherans might argue with this, but I suspect not many Catholics would.

When speaking of Mary's background of being "a poor and plain citizen's daughter," he reflects on the "Jerusalem daughters of the chief priests and counselors who were rich, comely, youthful, cultural, and held in high renown by all people."

"Mary confesses that the foremost work God did for her was that he regarded her," according to Luther. He follows by saying, "which is indeed the greatest of his works, on which all the rest depend and from which they derive." This means "grace and salvation" and "all gifts and works must follow." Sound familiar?

Especially of significance is his inquiry, "How ought one to address her?" He answers by saying, "O Blessed Virgin, Mother of God, you were nothing and all despised; yet God in his grace regarded you and worked such great things in you." Can this be anything more or less than ancient Catholic dogma?

His title "Mother of God," so prevalent throughout the work, was used consistently by Luther. It was officially ascribed to her at the Council of Ephesus in 431. It would appear he never deviated from this title throughout his life and theological development. Are Lutherans listening?

He reports that "she concluded the Magnificat by mentioning the very greatest of all God's works—the Incarnation of the Son of God." She is seen as a person who "freely acknowledges herself as the handmaiden and servant of all the world." Who can argue with this, especially Catholics and Lutherans?

Luther concludes, "We pray God to give us a right understanding of the Magnificat, an understanding that consists not merely in brilliant words but in glowing life in body and soul. Then, his last sentence is, "May Christ grant us this through the intercession and for the sake of his dear Mother, Mary! Amen."

I am no authority on either Lutheran or Catholic theology but it seems to me both have a unique gift, following their agreement on justification. Martin Luther provides a bridge of understanding at once powerful in its sign of unity and realizable in the hearts/minds of those so long divided.

Perhaps Lutherans and Catholics even now might pray together the "Ave Maria": "Hail Mary, full of grace, the Lord is with you. Blessed are you among women and blessed is the fruit of your womb, Jesus. Holy Mary Mother of God, pray for us sinners, now and at the hour of our death."

I do not believe Martin Luther would have any problem with that. Hopefully, no Catholic would. In fact, why not bring all who profess the name of Christ into the act? Can you imagine all Christians throughout the world praying the "Hail Mary" on Christmas Eve? What do we have to lose?

———

*The Catholic Moment* December 19, 1999
*South Bend Tribune* December 31, 1999

# ❧VIEWS OF MARY SHOULD UNITE CHRISTIANS❧

EVERY TIME I am at the University of Notre Dame, or even in the vicinity, I reflect upon a beautiful and holy lady. Some say she is the biggest source of division among Christians. How can this be? Really, next to her Son, she is the greatest sign of unity.

In reflection and with a bit of mystical vision, I invite you to Holy Scripture and then a hopeful response.

Saint Luke 1:26–38 (New American Bible) aids us to launch into a spirit of unity:

*In the sixth month, the angel Gabriel was sent from God to a town of Galilee named Nazareth, to a virgin betrothed to a man named Joseph, of the house of David. The virgin's name was Mary.*

And all the Baptists confidently affirmed, "We are hearing the Word of God."

*Upon arriving, the angel said to her: "Rejoice, O highly favored daughter! The Lord is with you. Blessed are you among women."*

And all the Roman Catholics shouted for joy and proclaimed, "Indeed, that is the way it is!"

*She was deeply troubled by his words, and wondered what his greeting meant.*

And all the Methodists were socially concerned and sought sincerely to help her.

The angel went on to say to her: "*Do not fear, Mary. You have found favor with God. You shall conceive and bear a son and give him the name Jesus. Great will be his dignity and he will be called Son of the Most High. The Lord will give him the throne of David his father. He will rule over the house of Jacob forever and his reign will be without end.*"

And all the Lutherans boldly confessed. "There is one Christ, true God and true man."

*Mary said to the angel, "How can this be since I do not know man?" The angel answered her: "The Holy Spirit will come upon you and the power of the Most High will overshadow you; hence, the holy offspring to be born will be called Son of God. Know that Elizabeth your kinswoman has conceived a son in her old age; she who was thought to be sterile is now in her sixth month, for nothing is impossible with God."*

And all the Orthodox chanted in glorious tones, "Truly it is worthy to bless thee, the theotokos, ever blessed and pure, and the Mother of our God."

*Mary said: "I am the servant of the Lord. Let it be done to me as you say." With that the angel left her.*

And all of the Congregationalists were quick to point out her freedom of acceptance or rejection.

Furthermore, Saint Luke 1:46–55 assists us in our pilgrimage towards unity:

*Then Mary said: "My being proclaims the greatness of the Lord, my spirit finds joy in God my savior, for he has looked upon his servant in her lowliness; all ages to come shall call me blessed."*

And all the Amish thought to themselves, "God has given us a perfect blend of humility, sincerity, and sweetness."

*"God who is might has done great things for me, holy is his name; his mercy is from age to age on those who fear him."*

And those in the Christian Churches concede, "If we believed in formal creeds, we would really like the message in these words."

*"He has shown might with his arm; he has confused the proud in their inmost thought."*

And the entire evangelical community called out, "Put aside all that heavy theology and simply be born again."

*"He has deposed the mighty from their thrones and raised the lowly to high places."*

And all the Anglicans agreed God's purpose was at work and meditated on our Lady of Walsingham.

*"The hungry he has given every good thing, while the rich he has sent empty away."*

And the Presbyterians and Reformed knelt in awe of their sovereign Creator.

*"He has upheld Israel his servant, ever mindful of his mercy; even as he promised our fathers, promised Abraham and his descendants forever."*

And all those precious Christians who defy labels and come in a myriad of flavors said, "Amen. Amen. Amen."

So, you see, Our Lady is a sign of unity and not division. She belongs to all who call her son Savior and Lord. All who call her Son Savior and Lord belong to her. She is truly "Our Lady for all Seasons."

————

*South Bend Tribune* December 21, 1998

*The Catholic Answer* May–June 1999

*The Catholic Answer Book of Mary, Our Sunday Visitor* 2000

# CHAPTER 12

# Founding Fathers

## ✸TRILOGY✸

### Thank You, Ben Franklin and George Washington

THE BICENTENNIAL Celebration marks the two hundredth birthday of the United States of America.

In 1776 the Founding Fathers were giving you and me the foundation of a great nation. As we look to those inspired men of glorious bygone days, Ben Franklin and George Washington immediately come to mind. Who has not read parts of or all of *Poor Richard's Almanac* and his *Autobiography*? The earliest history any of us learned was the name of our first president. Little is ever said about their religious attitudes and beliefs. Even less is mentioned about the gratitude and appreciation due them for their religious sensitivity.

Ben Franklin was a citizen of the world who made no attempt to hide his religion. He was such a serious student of the Bible he left us his own version of the Lord's Prayer. Listen to the beauty and accuracy of it: "Heavenly Father, May all revere thee, and become thy dutiful children and faithful subjects. May thy laws be obeyed on earth, as perfectly as they are in heaven. Provide for us this day as thou hast hitherto daily done. Forgive us our trespasses, and enable us to forgive those who offend us. Keep us out of temptation and deliver us from evil." Ben took the time to list what he considered the outstanding and essential virtues of this life. Not being superstitious, the listing contains thirteen. Here they are: (1) Temperance, (2) Silence, (3) Order, (4) Resolution, (5) Frugality, (6) Industry, (7) Sincerity, (8) Justice, (9) Moderation, (10) Cleanliness, (11) Tranquility, (12) Chastity, and (13) Humility. Franklin said, "As to Jesus of Nazareth, I think the system of morals and his religion as he left them to us, the best the world ever saw or is likely to see."

George Washington was a strong-willed, paternal type. For him there was never any question as to the existence or non-existence of a Supreme Being. There simply had to be One in order for the creation to have taken place at all. There may be a tendency on the part of some to exaggerate in picture form his prayers at Valley Forge or elsewhere. Yet, this is a known quality that certainly helped to produce his greatness. He was the type Christian who built this religion on a broad base. A narrow sectarian approach just wasn't a part of his religious orientation. Washington believed strongly in the God who made him and his fellow pilgrims. He was the most outspoken at the point that rights of conscience in religious matters were to be protected.

Many in our day are critical of an emotional patriotism and firm allegiance to a particular nation. To be sure, we do not live in the eighteenth and nineteenth centuries. World conditions are radically different from those just a "few, short" years ago. However, gratitude and appreciation are never out of date. Indeed, you and I are summoned on our national birthday to say "Thank you" to two towering giants of a great religious faith.

### Thank You, Tom Jefferson and John Adams

The Bicentennial celebration should bring all of us in a spirit of gratitude a little closer to two Founding Fathers who contributed so very much to the foundation of our nation. They felt deeply that the United States of America had a unique destiny. They believed so strongly in this that personal sacrifice was not of major consequence.

Thomas Jefferson, the third president, and John Adams, the second president, were imbued with religious perspectives. This should cause every one of us to offer a special prayer of thanksgiving. One of the most strange and yet fitting facts is they both died on exactly the same day. Even more unusual and yet marvelously appropriate is that the day was July 4, 1826!

Jefferson's brilliant mind has inspired the world for two centuries. The moral and spiritual splendor of Christianity at its best always held a special place in his thinking. In his own right he was a gifted religious thinker. He read the New Testament in the original Greek! Unknown to most Americans is the amazing fact he wrote his own version of the New Testament. It's called *The Life and Morals of Jesus of Nazareth*. Actually what he did was to take the Gospels in Greek, Latin, French, and English; place them side by side; and produce Jesus in the eyes of Thomas Jefferson. His concern was to discover and exalt the Gospel *of* Jesus as distinct from the Gospel *about* Jesus. He leaned heavily on Matthew and Luke. Mark and John were used sparingly. It was started while he was president in 1804 and finished in 1819. Jefferson called himself a Christian.

John Adams claimed he had been a church-going animal for seventy-six years. He was given to rather long and complicated sentences. His own definition of Christianity is an excellent example. Here it is: "The brightness of the glory and the express portrait of the character of the eternal self-existent, independent, benevolent, all powerful and all merciful creator, preserver and father of the universe, the first good, first first, and first fair." John Adams believed there were good men in all nations. Even more important, he attempted to act on that principle.

The Declaration of Independence, written by Jefferson, closes with these words: "with a firm reliance on the protection of Divine Providence, we mutually pledge to each other our Lives, our Fortunes, and our Sacred Honor." May God once again give to us two inspired national leaders so dedicated to religious ideas and ideals. May you, I and our descendants be worthy—at least—partially to deserve such extraordinary leadership in these times that "try men's souls."

## *Thank You, Five Fathers of Faith*

One of the most powerful influences in molding our national character is the many and divergent religious ideas. For this we are called to be especially thankful as we mark two centuries of growth and progress. Five of the Founding Fathers speak to us anew.

Sam Adams proclaimed "Revelation assures us that righteousness exalts a nation." The history books tell us he was not always the most tolerant man in the world. He believed strongly—if not always charitably—in his convictions. His religion was traditional and Puritanical. He lived out his life departing little from his stern Calvinistic family background. In his later years he wrote these inspiring words to his daughter: "If you carefully fulfill the various duties of life, from a principle of obedience to your heavenly Father, you shall enjoy that peace which the world cannot give nor take away."

James Madison was a learned gentleman who studied for the ministry at Princeton University. With his precise, analytical mind we discover a natural and beneficial wedding of the political scientist and the theologian. He is called by many "Father of the Constitution." Isn't it intriguing that a man once deeply involved in theological studies became the chief engineer of the document which has held us together as a nation for two centuries! He believed a person's relationship to his Creator was an extremely sacred matter. If necessary, government was to see to it that religious freedom was preserved.

Thomas Paine was perhaps the most individualistic and unconventional of the Founding Fathers. Oftentimes, he was misunderstood and accused of being an atheist. His methods were frequently unorthodox, and his lack of diplomacy in dealing with religious subjects is legend.

However, in his own unusual way he loved God and mankind. A short time before this death, he wrote: "I consider myself in the hands of my Creator, and that He will dispose of me after this life consistently with His justice and goodness."

Alexander Hamilton is not usually portrayed as being deeply religious. Regardless of this image, the record shows the sacred rights of man were foremost in his mind from the time he was a teenager. Just before his death he wrote the following in a letter to his wife: "The consolations of religion, my beloved, can alone support you; and these you have a right to enjoy. Fly to the bosom of your God, and be comforted."

John Jay was a regular churchgoer. He accepted the literal truth of the Bible and worshipped accordingly. Yet, he was one of the most tolerant men of the time as witnessed by his sincere concern for the religious liberties of all. In one of this letters, he wrote: "The moral or natural law was given by the Sovereign of the universe to all mankind."

Some would label these men "lesser lights" behind Franklin, Washington, Jefferson, and John Adams; but no one can deny their permanent place in our religious heritage. Thank you, gentlemen, for your versatile brilliance!

---

*Prepared in 1976 for churches, newspapers, clergy, and laity in the South Indiana Conference of the United Methodist Church and the Indiana Area Bicentennial Committee.*

## ❋FOUNDING FATHERS RELIGIOUS QUIZ❋

THE FATHERS OF our nation were not only intellectually brilliant men. They were very religious. Match the author to the statement. If you score seven or more right answers, consider yourself above average. If you score six or less, better brush up on something very significant to you or your loved ones.

1. Ben Franklin
2. George Washington

3. Thomas Jefferson
4. John Adams
5. Sam Adams
6. James Madison
7. Alexander Hamilton
8. John Jay
9. Thomas Paine
10. Patrick Henry

A.   In his farewell address he said, "Of all the dispositions and habits which lead to political prosperity, Religion and Morality are indispensable supports."

B.   Wrote his own version of the New Testament and called it *The Life and Morals of Jesus.*

C.   Defined Christianity in this manner: "brightness of the glory and the express portrait of the character of the eternal, self-existent, independent, benevolent, all powerful and merciful creator, preserver and father of the universe, the first good, first first, and first fair."

D.   Wrote his own version of the Lord's Prayer.

E.   In a letter to his daughter said: "If you carefully fulfill the various duties of life, from a principle of obedience to your heavenly Father, you shall enjoy that peace which the world cannot give or take away."

F.   One of the first presidents of the American Bible Society.

G.   In a letter to his wife wrote: "The consolations of religion, my beloved, can alone support you; and these you have a right to enjoy."

H.   Studied for the ministry at the College of New Jersey (now Princeton University).

I.   In his book, *The Age of Reason,* said: "I believe in one God, and no more; and I hope for happiness beyond this life."

J.   In a well-known speech said: "Is life so dear or peace so sweet as to be purchased at the price of chains of slavery? Forbid it, Almighty God!"

Key to the quiz:
   1. D
   2. A
   3. B
   4. C
   5. E

6. H
7. G
8. F
9. I
10. J

---

*Indianapolis News* July 4, 1981

*CSS* 1982. Used by permission from CSS Publishing Company, Inc.,
517 S. Main Street, P.O. Box 4503, Lima, Ohio 45802–4503.

*Gary Post-Tribune* July 5, 1986

# ❋RELIGIOUS FAITH OF OUR FOUNDING FATHERS❋

IN MANY SECTORS of society today, the term "Founding Fathers" is
not only avoided but labeled inappropriate for consideration. Yet, surely we
cannot allow revisionists to destroy appreciation and gratitude for ten men.
I know no one who would call them saints or even saintly. Even in light
of Watergate and all the other "gates," can we refuse to say "thank you" to
those who gave us so much?

In tribute, hear the roll call of a few great men.

Ben Franklin: He was a first-rate statesman, diplomat, editor, scientist,
and philosopher. Rarely, in all of history has anyone been so talented in so
many of life's endeavors. Some of us have read parts of or all of *Poor
Richard's Almanac* and his autobiography.

George Washington: About the first history any of us ever learned was
that he was our first President. He was a brilliant leader of men on the
battlefield and in the government.

Thomas Jefferson: Like Franklin, he was a versatile brilliant man. Our
third president is one of the world's best examples of a philosopher-statesman.

John Adams: In 1797 he became our second president. One of the most
strange and yet fitting facts is that he and Jefferson died on exactly the same
day. Even more unusual and yet marvelously appropriate is that the day was
July 4, 1826!

Sam Adams: This man was a revolutionary patriot. When the fires for
independence died down, he kindled them anew.

James Madison: Our fourth chief executive was physically the smallest ever to occupy the White House. He and John Wesley, the founder of Methodism, tipped the scales at just over one hundred pounds.

Alexander Hamilton: Here was a financial wizard who became the first secretary of the Treasury. In the day when some men settled their differences by duels, he was killed by Aaron Burr.

John Jay: He was the first chief justice of the Supreme Court. His influence in foreign affairs was seldom matched.

Thomas Paine: At the beginning of the Revolution, with prophetic zeal and insight, he wrote, "these are the times that try men's souls." His pamphlet *Common Sense* has been read around the world.

Patrick Henry: First governor of Virginia. His "give me liberty or death" speech used to reverberate throughout the nation's classrooms.

These are the ones especially to whom I owe a debt of immeasurable gratitude.

In prayerful joy we are called to look at their religious attitudes.

Ben Franklin was a citizen of the world who made no attempt to hide his religion. He was such a serious student of the Bible he left us his own version of the Lord's Prayer. Listen to the beauty an accuracy of it: "Heavenly Father, May all revere thee, and become thy dutiful children and faithful subjects. May thy laws be obeyed on earth, as perfectly as they are in heaven. Provide for us this day as thou hast hitherto daily done. Forgive us our trespasses, and enable us to forgive those who offend us. Keep us out of temptation and deliver us form evil." Ben took the time to list what he considered the outstanding and essential virtues of this life. Not being superstitious, the listing contains thirteen. The last one he nearly forgot. When it is given, you will see why. Here they are: (1) Temperance (eating and drinking), (2) Silence, (3) Order (organization), (4) Resolution (do what you resolve to do), (5) Frugality (waste nothing), (6) Industry (lose no time), (7) Sincerity (think innocently and justly), (8) Justice, (9) Moderation (avoid extremes), (10) Cleanliness, (11) Tranquillity (be not disturbed at trifles), (12) Chastity, and (13) Humility (Imitate Jesus and Socrates). Franklin said, "As to Jesus of Nazareth, I think the systems of morals and his religion as he left them to us, the best the world ever saw or is likely to see."

Now, let us take a moment with the one labeled "father of his country." Washington was a strong-willed, paternal type. He was deeply religious in his own unique way. For him there was never any question as to the existence or non-existence of a Supreme Being. There simply had to be One in order for the creation to have taken place at all. There may be a tendency on the part of some to exaggerate in picture form his prayers at Valley Forge or elsewhere. Yet, this is a known quality that certainly helped to produce his greatness. He was not the type Christian who built his religion on a narrow sectarian base. Washington believed strongly in the God who made him and his fellow pilgrims. He was probably the most outspoken at the point that rights of conscience in a religious matter were to be protected.

Jefferson's brilliant mind has inspired, not only our country, but many others as well, for well over two centuries. The moral and spiritual splendor of Christianity at its best always held a special place in his thinking. In his own right he was a gifted religious thinker. He read the *New Testament* in the original Greek! Unknown to many Americans is the amazing fact that he wrote his own version of the *New Testament*. It's called *The Life and Morals of Jesus of Nazareth*. Actually what he did was to take the Gospels in Greek, Latin, French, and English; place them side by side; and produce Jesus in the eyes of Thomas Jefferson. His concern was to discover and exalt the Gospel *of* Jesus and distinct from the Gospel *about* Jesus. He leaned heavily on Matthew and Luke. Mark and John were used sparingly. It was started while he was President in 1804 and finished in 1819. It might be interesting to know the number of presidents in this century who have written their own version of any part of the Bible! Jefferson called himself a Christian.

John Adams claimed he had been a church-going animal for seventy-six years. He was given to rather long and complicated sentences. His own definition of Christianity is an excellent example. Here it is: "the brightness of the glory and the express portrait of the character of the eternal self-existent, father of the universe, the first good, first first, and first fair." John Adams believed there were good men in all nations. Even more important, he attempted to act on that principle.

Sam Adams proclaimed "Revelation assures us that righteousness exalts a nation." The history books tell us he was not always the most tolerant man in the world. He believed strongly—if not always charitably—in his convictions. His religion was traditional and Puritanical. He lived out his life departing little from his stern Calvinistic family background. In his later years he wrote these inspiring words to his daughter: "If you carefully fulfill the various duties of life, from a principle of obedience to your heavenly Father, you shall enjoy that peace which the world cannot give nor take away."

James Madison was a learned gentleman who studied for the ministry at Princeton University. With his precise, analytical mind we discover a natural and beneficial wedding of the political scientist and the theologian. He is called by many "Father of the Constitution." Isn't it intriguing that a man once deeply involved in theological studies became the chief engineer of the document which has held us together as a nation for more than two centuries! He believed a person's relationship to his Creator was an extremely sacred matter. If necessary, government was to see to it that religious freedom was preserved.

Alexander Hamilton is not portrayed as being deeply religious. Regardless of this image, the record shows the sacred rights of man were foremost in his mind from the time he was a teenager. Tragically, at the age of forty-seven he was killed in a duel with Aaron Burr. Just before his death he wrote the following in a letter to his wife: "The consolations of religion, my beloved, can alone support you; and these you have a right to enjoy. Fly to the bosom of your God, and be comforted."

John Jay was a regular churchgoer. He accepted the literal truth of the Bible and worshiped accordingly. Yet, he was one of the most tolerant men of the time as witnessed by his sincere concern for the religious liberties of all. In one of his letters he wrote: "The moral or natural law was given by the Sovereign of the universe to all mankind."

Thomas Paine was perhaps the most individualistic and unconventional of the founding fathers. Often times, he was misunderstood and even accused of being an atheist. Is it possible he was labeled an atheist by some because he differed openly and vociferously with their beliefs? In his own unusual way he loved God and humankind. A short time before his death he wrote: "I consider myself in the hands of my Creator, and that He will dispose of me after this life consistently with His Justice and goodness."

Patrick Henry was deeply concerned about the preservation of morality and virtue in society. In fact, he advocated state-supported religion as a necessary expedient. His emphasis was on a "virtuous" clergy that would lead by example. The record showed that as a lawyer he defended some sects that were dwarfed by the established church. As a sensitive enemy of slavery, he said "I am drawn along by general inconveniences of living without them, I will not, I cannot justify it."

Thus, we come to the end of an inspiring parade of fallible—but obviously great—men who helped to build the foundation of a powerful nation. They helped to found the United States of America on ideas and ideals in which they firmly believed. Their religious sensitivity is not only a marvel but something of a miracle of the entire world to look upon.

We are heavily in debt to them. We are continually called upon to repay this magnificent heritage by sharpening our religious sensitivities.

Many in our day are critical of an emotional patriotism and allegiance to a particular nation. To be sure, we do not live in the latter part of the eighteenth and the early part of the nineteenth centuries. World conditions are radically different from those just a "few, short" years ago. However, *gratitude and appreciation are never out of date.*

The Declaration of Independence closes with these words: "with a firm reliance on the protection of divine Providence, we mutually pledge to each other our Lives, our Fortunes, and our Sacred Honor." May God once again give to us a group of "founding fathers" so dedicated to religious and political ideals. May you, I, and our descendants be worthy enough in God's sight to deserve such extraordinary leadership in these times that "try men's souls." Why? So, this nation, under God, shall have a new birth of freedom with morality as a priority.

————

*Evansville Press* (edited) June 29, 1974
*Muncie Sunday Star Press* (abbreviated) July 6, 1997
*Evangel Press* 1998
*South Bend Sunday Tribune* July 5, 1998
*New Castle Courier Times* July 4, 2000

CHAPTER 13

# *Ecumenism*

# ❋ECUMENICALLY SPEAKING: NATIONAL❋ WORKSHOP ON CHRISTIAN UNITY

FOR NEARLY TWO decades the National Workshop on Christian Unity has been a major ecumenical event. It began in 1963 at the National Council of Catholic Men in Atlantic City. From the start Protestant participation was a key factor. It's an annual event for all "involved in" or "concerned with" Christian Unity.

Nearly four hundred of us gathered in Grand Rapids, Michigan, April 19–22 to appreciate and understand the cause of unity among those professing the name of Christ.

Dr. Elizabeth Bettenhausen (Lutheran Church of America), who teaches at Boston University School of Theology, was our first major speaker, with theme "May *All* Find Their Home, in You, O God."

Each morning two worship services were held. One was a Roman Catholic Mass and the other was a COCU Liturgy/Eucharist. Some felt the pain of a divided Church as Roman Catholics gathered in one room and Protestants in another. Yet, a spirit of optimism and praise was evident as we emerged to begin a busy day.

Nine different seminars were offered, with top persons in their respective fields. Dr. Paul Crow, president of the Council of Christian Unity, led "Introduction to Ecumenism" and Dr. M. William Howard, former president of the National Council of Churches, "Institutional Racism: An Inherent Threat to Ecumenism."

The seminar catching the most attention was entitled, "What Does It Mean to be Evangelical and Ecumenical?" It was led by Dr. Richard Mouw, a professor at Calvin College and Dr. Robert Middleton, senior pastor, First Baptist Church Birmingham, Michigan. In recent years, they noted, hopeful signs were manifest among evangelicals as they moved more into the mainstream of church life. Reputable seminaries, the movement toward social concerns and the breaking-down of barriers with persons such as Billy Graham and Pope John XXIII were mentioned. The consensus was that "the world is too strong for a divided church."

Bible study was led with sincerity, brilliance, and humility by Dr. Philip A. Potter, general secretary, World Council of Churches. "The deep malaise of our time is mistrust," he said.

United Methodists were treated to a luncheon and study session at Trinity UMC. Dr. Robert Huston gave us a report on the United Methodist/Roman Catholic Theological Consultation (1977–1981); specifically, a paper, "Eucharistic Celebration: Converging Theology— Divergent Practice." Jean Caffey Lyles of the "Christian Century" presented observations on how we relate to ecumenical concerns as United Methodists. Perhaps most notable is our pragmatic approach and lack of priority to ecumenism, she said.

The workshop orator was Dr. Howard Hageman, president of New Brunswick Seminary (Reformed Church of America). In a style old and yet refreshing he preached a thrilling sermon in St. Andrews Cathedral. We also were inspired by Liturgical Dancers from Aquinas College, the chancel choir of LaGrave Christian Reformed Church and a cordial welcome by the Most Rev. Joseph M. Breitenback, Roman Catholic bishop, Diocese of Grand Rapids.

Dr. Avery Post, president of the United Church of Christ, closed the workshop with words which seemed to sum up how everyone felt. He said, "full unity is a gift" and in the history of the ecumenical movement "something has run its course."

Indeed, we're on the threshold of something new. Amen. Amen. Amen.

————

*Hoosier United Methodist* May 1982

# ✤DECALOGUE FOR ECUMENICAL DISCIPLESHIP:✤ A CALL TO DAILY COMMITMENT

*I pray not only for them, but also for those who believe in me because of their message. I pray that they may all be one. Father! May they be in us, just as you are in me and I am in you. May they be one, so that the world will believe that you sent me. I gave them the same glory you gave me, so that they may be one, just as you and I are one: I in them and you in me, so that they may be*

*completely one, in order that the world may know that you sent me*
*and that you love them as you love me.*
*—John 17:20–23—*

IN A WORLD that seems to be shrinking on daily basis we are being led by the Holy Spirit into exciting and challenging areas and arenas. As disciples of Jesus the Christ we are no longer just witnessing in more or less carefully defined communities. Most of us discover ourselves in daily contact with persons seeking to be more than they are under the banner of Christ. In many cases our option is not the decision whether to relate to this one or that one. It is the option of helping to determine the quality of the relationships that by the sheer force of today's living has brought them into being. Therefore, our ecumenism must be intentional and have the hallmarks of a practical discipline.

Dare we suggest a "decalogue?" Yes.

*1. Daily affirmation that Jesus calls His followers to be one.*

An early morning prayer time or a regular devotional period can be enriched by recalling and/or reading John 17:20–30 along with whatever else may be on the agenda. Just don't put it in some secluded spot and give it the last thirty seconds! The memorization of this passage so that it can in fact be a part of our thinking and feeling processes should not be overlooked. We seem to place in our memories many other less significant ideas that may be a part of personal systems already overloaded with questionable items.

It is this daily affirmation of Christ's call to be one that brings to the conscious level a sobering and magnificent acknowledgement: the Holy Spirit is at work in ways pointing to our Lord's call being fulfilled. In short, He will no longer be denied a positive answer to His prayer. "Oneness" is not any longer one of the lesser lights on earth, merely shining brightly in the faraway heavens. It is a light ever-increasing in brightness in the here and now, which shines in and through people, places, and things with or without their permission.

*2. Daily praise for the infinite variety of religious expression evidenced in the Universal Church.*

Too long we have sifted and sorted in order to be loyal to a narrow denominational and/or doctrinal image. Praise God for the infinite smorgasbord placed in our midst! Too long we have been bound by categories that have inevitably tended to bring us out of range of insights coming from traditions other than our own. How shall we escape in our time if we neglect a salvation coming to us in unlimited expressions and yet lifting up one Savior and Lord? The Holy Spirit enables us through all senses to share in the greatness of the Universal Church.

Such praise, while it ought to be part of our personal worship and study should never be limited to that. At a gathering of clergy and/or laity, or even in a largely secular gathering, praise God openly and forth-rightly for the cornucopia always there but especially open to view in our time. The sheer hope and joy coming from such an orientation to life (and death) has a way of lighting candles in some of the darkest dungeons constructed by Satan to prevent Christ's people from being united.

*3. Daily study of the beliefs and/or organizational life found in denomination(s) other than our own.*

Most of us have found our religious pilgrimage to be with one or just a few denominational groupings. Even clergy deeply involved in the ecumenical movement are ordained by this or that segment of Christ's Body. While they may hold standing in more than one, we are not speaking of several. It becomes imperative, therefore, to look beyond such seemingly necessary confinements to others that are different and yet the same. Gone is the day of being impoverished by straightjackets that can neither contain nor embody the fullness of the Christ and His Church.

We are blessed with numerous teaching and learning tools that can bring us, at least, in an informational way what fellow pilgrims believe and how they understand polity. Such a worthy endeavor cannot be done in a haphazard way. The significance of it requires purposeful study every day. Hopefully, one positive result will be to challenge us to understand why we are what we are in a denominational sense. There is no cause to fear contamination because—after all—we all belong to Him!

*4. Daily prayer for those within and outside our denomination that all might appreciate and be enriched by the diversity found in the Universal Church.*

The freedom found in spontaneous prayer is a delightful delicacy. How could we possibly continue our journey without it? Having made that admission, our prayer life can be weakened and severely limited if this is our singular mode of visiting with God. We can also find ourselves in strictures by interceding solely for those who serve with us in a local church setting and/or in a denominational framework, even if we do so with punctuality. Our prayers should reflect spiritual growth and who dares to thwart appreciation and enrichment found in rich diversity?

Holy Scripture as it speaks to us in Ephesians 4:1–16 provides the background and fertile soil out of which such prayers naturally emerge. Yet, there is more involved than this recognition. Firm commitment is needed. We are called to discipline ourselves each day to pray for those "within and outside" in order that the indispensable ministry of the Holy Spirit may work wonders in the Body, ultimately adhering only to the perimeters set by the Lord of the Church.

*5. Daily practice of intentionally conversing with a person(s) in another denomination(s) about the Christian Faith.*

Christians can and do tell fascinating stories about themselves and their Faith. We miss much by not entering into conversation and even dialogue with others wearing different labels. We are brothers and sisters; this can become apparent in the openness of sharing what makes sense in our religious lives. The learning experience alone can make for greater empowerment of the Gospel. It is important we not argue to the extent we contradict and work against the unity already present. It is likewise important, however, we be honest and forthright with minds wide open.

Some of the best conversations can come about in an informal way under the guidance of the Holy Spirit. The "chance" meeting of someone who just happens to have curiosity about your tradition and wants to meet for coffee each morning is the kind of experience that enhances you and him/her. Our "intentionality" can take us into seemingly unplanned but marvelously helpful encounters that the Holy Spirit makes possible because of readiness.

*6. Daily meditation on what it means to be a part of the Body of Christ.*

Especially important for our nourishment are the twelfth and thirteenth chapters of 1 Corinthians. At least a weekly reading of them enables us to have the words, phrases, and verses at our ready disposal during whatever portion of the day (or night) we elect to meditate upon

His Body. While the twelfth chapter delineates for us the working of the one Spirit and the one Body with many parts, the thirteenth sends the holy rays of an undergirding and abiding love upon us as instruments of reconciliation.

We need not be apprehensive about whether this idea or that idea fits into a denominational mold or mentality. We certainly need not enter into meditation threatened by what this person or that person will think of our discoveries. Granted, we live in an age of intimidation and manipulation. Yet, doesn't the Lord of the church promise the Spirit to His people and that it will lead them into all truth? Furthermore, Saint Paul reminded a young seeker that disciples of the Christ were not given a spirit of timidity but one of power, love and self-control.

*7. Daily acknowledgement of our roots found in the rich heritage of Judaism.*
This seems to be an easy one to forget or avoid! Yet, in our day and time it is necessary in order for us to get a full picture of salvation history. We are blessed with every-increasing workshops, publications, etc., that reveal the closeness of those adhering to the Star of David and those claiming the Cross from the very beginning of our Faith. The Jewishness of Jesus and the sect status of Christianity in the early years are not to be forgotten. In fact, they are to be celebrated and built upon. While we kneel before Jesus as Savior and Lord, we also—along with our Jewish friends—call Abraham our father.

The growing trust among Jews and Christians is cause for joy and hope. Triumphalism that has blighted our witness for centuries deserves exposing and fortunately this is occurring to the benefit of both Jews and Christians. The Hebrew Scriptures were an everpresent force in the lives of Jesus, Mary, Peter, James, John, and Paul. Does not the Christ quote Deuteronomy 6:4 as He speaks of the great commandment? Stereotypes that are largely negative do not fade easily. To come to terms on a day-to-day basis with the verities out of which we Christians (to an extent) evolved is indeed an exemplary habit.

*8. Daily openness to the continually emerging opportunities for worship and understanding among Christians.*
The Holy Spirit is at work! The separation felt and actually experienced among His disciples is melting away. While there is still pain in Christ's Body that comes from some exclusions at our Lord's Table, there are more and more other types of worship that are fully open to all. Yes,

Roman Catholics are singing hymns by Martin Luther and Charles Wesley. Yes, Protestants are taking more seriously the real presence of their Savior and Lord as they receive "His body and blood." The creative mixing of liturgies and the rewriting of many forms of worship are enabling us to come to grips with more uniting us than dividing us.

Insights and wisdom are coming to us out of the ancient Church(es) with the Orthodox often leading the way. Anglicans are building bridges as they often provide a middle ground to which all Christians can relate. Yes, and who can deny the healing relevance of the "Decree on Ecumenism" and the momentous Lima Document? To be open to receive such a magnificent outpouring of the Holy Spirit is nothing more than claiming what is rightfully ours. As a "royal priesthood" we were never intended to hobble along like crippled and starving children. We were and are meant to grow in understanding. The King's Castle has many rooms for his subjects to explore, all of them providing wholeness and holiness.

*9. Daily admission that it was and is scandalous for Christians to be divided.*

To recount the horrendous deeds of those who claimed to know and follow the Christ, especially as they related to one another, provides a stench singularly painful and humiliating. To own such a disgrace, however, grants us the humility and sincerity to move to better days. Our forefathers and foremothers (much like us) were not so despicably evil as they were incomplete and limited. Perhaps our most insidious problem is to gloss over our differences. Yet, an even more destructive tendency may be to disown a scandal that dates, at least, from the time the Corinthians were trying to decide to whom they belonged. We do well to pose Saint Paul's inquiry, "Is Christ divided?"

There is creative tension that comes from admitting our dividedness each day. In our depths we call forth the Crucifixion of the Lord, remembering the countless crucifixions we continue to inflict. Then, we are brought face to face with our special task which is to make scandal a thing of the past by obeying the call to be one "so that the world may know." During those moments we also discover the power to go on until we hear Him say, "Well done, good and faithful servant."

*10. Daily consecration of our entire being to the cause of Christian unity.*

"To consecrate" has an irrevocable and eternal ring to it. It is appropriate because of the holy joy and enduring solemnity it brings. We cannot as disciples of the Christ play at union, merger, consolidation, assimilation, etc., any longer. Ours is an inspirational but serious undertaking. It may very well mean an invitation to die, what some would call an untimely death, or to carry crosses a flabby and sometimes flippant Church(es) would consider far beyond the call of duty. Yes, and as substantial strides are being made we may learn to appreciate as never before the Son's cry, "Father, forgive them."

Our day calls for an undivided allegiance to the cause of Christian unity. It is not merely one seeking conversion(s) to a way of life in which we can be caught up in a myriad of deeds and thoughts, allowing us to escape from the blessed work culminating in both a visible and invisible church. With minds fully open but determined, hearts not only warmed but aflame, and spirits willing but guided by "the Spirit" we are girded for warfare. While we do not presume to know the final shape of the unity we seek, by the grace of God we shall be victorious.

———

*CSS* 1986. Used by permission from CSS Publishing Company, Inc., 517 S. Main Street, P.O. Box 4503, Lima, Ohio 45802–4503.
*Pulpit Digest* September–October 1987
*Touchstone Winter* 1988
*South Bend Sunday Tribune* (edited) July 4, 1999

# ❀DISCIPLINE IS REQUIRED TO BE❀ TRULY ECUMENICAL

SOME YEARS AGO, after being chairman of the Ecumenical Concerns Department of the former Indiana Council of Churches, something became crystal clear to me: Ecumenically minded people needed a practical discipline. So, I sat down and began to write. Shortly, birth was given to a "decalogue for ecumenical discipleship." Over the years it has become ten action steps for this unique and much-needed ministry. It is a call to daily commitment.

1. Daily affirmation that Jesus calls his followers to be one. An early morning prayer or a regular devotional period can be enriched by

recalling and reading John 17:20–23, along with whatever also may be on the agenda.

2. Daily praise for the infinite variety of religious expression evidenced in the Universal Church. Too long we have sifted and sorted in order to be loyal to a narrow denominational and/or doctrinal image.

3. Daily study of the beliefs and/or organizational life found in denominations other than our own. Gone is the day of being impoverished by straitjackets that can neither contain nor embody the fullness of Christ and his church.

4. Daily prayer for those within and outside our denomination that all might appreciate and be enriched by the diversity found in the Universal Church. How could we possibly continue our journey without it?

5. Daily practice of intentionally conversing with a person in another denomination about the Christian faith. We miss much by not entering into conversation and even dialogue with others wearing different labels.

6. Daily meditation on what it means to be a part of the Body of Christ. Especially important for our nourishment are the twelfth and thirteenth chapters of 1 Corinthians, which should be read at least once weekly.

7. Daily acknowledgement of our roots found in the rich heritage of Judaism. While we kneel before Jesus as Savior and Lord, we also—along with our Jewish friends—call Abraham our father.

8. Daily openness to the continually emerging opportunities for worship and understanding among Christians. The separation felt and actually experienced among His disciples is melting away.

9. Daily admission that it was and is scandalous for Christians to be divided. To own such a disgrace grants us the humility and sincerity to move to better days.

10. Daily consecration of our entire being to the cause of Christian unity. This has an irrevocable and eternal ring to it. It is appropriate because of the holy joy and enduring solemnity it brings.

Our day calls for undivided allegiance to the cause of Christian unity. With minds fully open but determined, hearts not only warmed but aflame, and spirits willing but guided by "the Spirit" we are girded for warfare. While we do not presume to know the final shape of the unity we seek, by the grace of God we shall be victorious!

———

*Indianapolis Star* March 18, 2000

# ❋NOW IS THE TIME TO ANSWER THE CALL❋

THE BOOK OF *Discipline* (1988) says Christian unity is "alive and well" in the United Methodists. Under "Our Theological Task," specifically "Ecumenical Commitment," two statements leap from the page.

The first maintains, "Christian unity is not an option; it is a gift to be received and expressed." The second relates: "United Methodists respond to the theological, biblical and practical mandates for Christian unity by firmly committing ourselves to the cause of Christian unity at local, national and world levels."

These are statements of great strength. Both call our attentions to the imperative nature of the ecumenical enterprise and all that involves.

Of course, the crux of the matter is, "Have we said what we mean and do we mean what we have said?" If we probe a bit further, we uncover an area of "risk taking" that has too often given us a split personality. Our vested interests can immobilize the best of ecumenical ventures.

The time has come for us as United Methodists to live out the mandates of ecumenical discipleship. This means more than "tipping our hats" to the Consultation on Church Union and the Baptism-Eucharist-Ministry (BEM) document!

The time has also come for us to stop grieving the Holy Spirit and lead the way into vital resiliency, sacrificial giving, and holy commitment.

How many of us have ever read and studied the "decree on Ecumenism" coming out of Vatican II? It is a document that should be required reading for all United Methodist clergy and laity. In a profound way it is the Roman Catholic Church reaching out to us in ways that are unprecedented. For example, it says, "We should therefore pray to the Holy Spirit for the grace to be genuinely self-denying, humble, gentle in the service of other, and to have an attitude of brotherly generosity towards them." We are referred to as "separated brethren" and not as heretics on our way to hell! While many clergy may be aware of this far-reaching change, do they have the courage at all administrative levels to act on it? We are being called by the Holy Spirit to recover the eucharistic appreciation and understanding that the Wesleys bequeathed us. Our own Dr. James F. White in *Introduction to Christian Worship* tells us, "The eucharist is the most characteristic structure of Christian worship. It is also the most widely used form of worship among Christians, being celebrated daily and weekly in millions of congregations and communities all over the world."

John Wesley received Holy Communion weekly and sometimes daily. He lived and died an Anglican priest. The celebration of this sacrament on a weekly basis with the seriousness and joy that is intended brings us into a pattern with the vast majority of Christians. Indeed, our worship can be more than a service club's levity and a fraternal order's rigidity!

Of all the articulations of what we believe, only one stands out as a full doctrinal statement from the undivided Church. The Nicene Creed, (381), gives us key adjectives to aid in delineating the Universal Church: "one, holy, catholic, apostolic." If we truly believe Christian unity is not an option, our course of action is obvious. This creed is to be said many times during the year and pondered in groups. Furthermore, it offers a specific preaching-teaching opportunity for every United Methodist minister. It does not address particular contemporary issues; it is regarded as the most sufficient formulation of the faith we currently have.

In a pragmatic sense, what are United Methodists doing about sharing their facilities and clergy with those of other denominations? How much money can be saved and redirected into worthy missions projects to a hurting world by utilizing the same sanctuaries and/or educational units every Sunday? Why not share clergy across denominational lines on a regular basis?

This need not lead to lack of accountability. After all, if we are all in this together surely we can all be winners. United Methodism is considered the most practical of all denominations. With our firm and inspired position on Christian unity we can show all who profess Christ as Savior and Lord that we are in fact, not just in theory, fully committed. We can do this most tangibly through our facilities and clergy.

Much of what we accomplish depends upon middle-management of the district superintendency. If there is a fear and an unwillingness to venture into what *Discipline* most assuredly maintains, we shall be frustrated, compromised and defeated. To be faithful to our enlightened and truly heartwarming stance is to bring Christian unity up from a miscellaneous item on the district superintendent's agenda and place it near the top. Surely the apportionments will still get paid!

Pastors are reminded *Discipline* indicates they are "to participate in community and ecumenical concerns and to lead the congregations to become so involved." Indeed, the time has come for United Methodists in key leadership roles to act with confidence upon the lofty and crucial call of our Lord "to be one."

So, our momentous opportunity is given birth by the book which we agree "reflects our understanding of the Church and of what is expected of its ministers and members as they seek to be effective witnesses in the world as a part of the whole Body of Christ!"

———

*Hoosier United Methodist* December 1989

## ❧A LETTER TO A ROMAN CATHOLIC❧

AT DUBLIN, Ireland, on July 18, 1749 an Anglican Priest and the founder of Methodism wrote "A Letter to a Roman Catholic." The man's name was John Wesley. It seems only fitting that another one be written by one of his spiritual sons.

Dear Roman Catholic Friend in Christ,

Greetings in the Name of our Savior and Lord, Jesus the Christ!

I have wanted to write to you for sometime, and now the Holy Spirit has provided that opportunity. Always I give thanks for you as I continue to work out my salvation in fear and trembling.

My relationships with you have been, are, and will be positive and very helpful. While centuries of division and human sin have sought to drive us apart, you have been so generous to me in so many ways. My letter seeks to share with you a beginning list. I do so in humility, sincerity, and gratitude.

In terms of history and its significance I have discovered over and over again that you share in an unbroken chain the Faith once revealed. We Protestants tend to see history, especially Christianity, as broken in periods of time. Perhaps the extreme view is that of charting our Faith from the first century to the fourth century and then believing very little happened that was important until the fifteenth century and the birth of Martin Luther. Please forgive us! Deep down we know there were great Christians for that thousand years but we find it so hard to admit. Continue to befriend us that we may see and appreciate the continuous splendor of Christ's followers from the very beginning until this moment. Of course, we read of human sin that existed in those years we tend to overlook. Your own historians do not deny such situations and, in fact, sometimes highlight them. Thank you. But when was any time ever free from sin? We Protestants tend to commit the very sins we accuse you of committing. It is far past time for us to admit such a narrow view of history. In particular, I am so sorry that the Knights Templars to whom Saint Bernard of Clairvaux gave energy and strength fell by the wayside among Roman Catholics in the fourteenth century.

You have kept before the world a lovely lady. Indeed, the Blessed Virgin Mary was the Mother of our Savior and Lord. We repent for the misunderstandings of her singular place in the Faith. Surely Satan has had a good time provoking and perpetuating the stereotype among Protestants that you worship her, elevating her above her Son. Vatican II has been helpful in showing us that her ongoing power and greatness are tied to her Son. She is great because of Him. Her real purpose has always been to draw others to Him. Oh, dear friend, the model of chastity and purity she has continually evidenced is so needed in today's world! Please don't dethrone her and try to explain away the virtues she gives to all of us. I humbly pray that women of today will look to her. I fear that if they don't *soon*, the disrespect among people will reach astronomical proportions. Men want to look upon women in respect. The Blessed Virgin Mary and what she represents is the key to move us away from the hellish chasm that threatens to make women far less than what they were intended to be. Our dear Mother Mary is so beautiful and winsome. I beg of you to imitate her virtues, especially women that motherhood and marriage may be given priority claims.

The priesthood is such a fascinating topic. I freely admit that not one of all the many priests I have known over the years has been a bad one! My early mentor was Fulton John Sheen, the Archbishop. As a communicator and man of wisdom, I have never seen his equal. In fact, would you believe some of my earliest sermons were really summations from his books? I don't believe my Protestant congregations knew that. I willingly and openly confess! It wounds me almost daily the way your priests are oppressed by the Evil One. The issue of ordaining women to the priesthood has created conflict most often at the point of cultural values as opposed to spiritual values. The Holy Father, Pope John II, has spoken with authority and responsibility on the matter. I hope and pray you will follow his decision. The world, especially the Roman Catholic Church, cannot afford a schism. Many of us look to you for stability on such an issue and trust you will accept the direction of the Holy Spirit. It was in the intimacy of Christ and the Apostles that our precious Faith was born. The Pope in his manliness and maternal-like nurturing qualities shows all who profess Christ's Name what must surely have been the style of the Saints Peter and Paul. Trust and obey!

Thank you for an understanding of the Church that I firmly believe Christ and the Apostles intended. It seems we Protestants so often just can't separate the church from the local Lions or Rotary clubs! Bless you for this wonderful way for coming to terms with the institution, ever new and yet ever old, that is both militant and triumphant. We have spawned so many churches and have fought among ourselves. Often we have called you bad names and have arrogantly assumed the role of "one, holy, catholic, apostolic" Church in ways that were truly reprehensible. Your sense of catholicity in terms of universality and wholeness is something I believe we are slowly but surely learning. Bold and dominant Peter was and is the Rock. It wasn't and never has been enlightened fellows like John Calvin, Martin Luther, and Ulrich Zwingli. My direct spiritual mentor, John Wesley, very reluctantly formed my church. My colleagues often have to be reminded he lived and died a priest in the Church of England. You see, dear Roman Catholic friend, there are many connecting lengths that take both of us back to the ancient Catholic Church for whom Christ and His Apostles gave their lives.

How shall we survive these turbulent times without sound teaching? You are so fortunate in having a magisterium that can speak with responsibility and authority on a universal level. Protestants often long for sound doctrine, biblically-grounded, and in touch with needs of the times that comes from an authoritative source. You have been so charitable in giving to us the *Decree on Ecumenism* that speaks of "separated brethren" and not "outcasts" waiting for the fires of hell! Thank you. The Holy Father's Encyclical Letter *That All May Be One* is cause for unbounded hope. You are the leader in the cause for Christian Unity and such teaching, even among Orthodox, is making its mark. Again, thank you, my brother. Please help us to appreciate the depths of the Eucharist. Please help us to begin to understand the loving power of the Papacy. Maybe we can eventually find full unity in our unique relationships to the Holy Father, much as your various orders have found. We both known that truth has never been popular but let us pray and fast for that day when all professing Christ's Name can do so in harmony "that the world might believe." Dear friend, I have forgiven you for the hurt you may have caused. Humbly and sincerely I implore you to forgive me.

So, my brother in Christ, let us forgive and be open to the Holy Spirit. I love you and respect you. In fact, I look up to you to lead us into the twenty-first century. With God all things are possible.

I choose to close the same way John Wesley did in 1749.

I am, Your affectionate servant, for Christ's sake,

Donald Charles Lacy
South Bend
29 February, 1996

---

*Evangel Press* 1996
*The Catholic Answer* July/August 1996
*South Bend Sunday Tribune* September 15, 1996

# ✤METHODISTS, CATHOLICS FIND TIES✤ THAT BOND

THE ANNUAL National Workshop on Christian Unity, meeting in Louisville, Kentucky, is now history. Major representation across the country came from the Roman Catholics, United Methodists, Episcopalians, Lutherans, and Presbyterians.

Early in the workshop, Roman Catholics and United Methodists met together in a mini-historical event. We shared a paper titled "Methodist-Catholic Dialogues: 30 years of Mission and Witness." I was thrilled by the work that had been done both nationally and internationally. The generous spirit that pervaded the meeting was cause for optimism and hope.

In a realistic and honest way we acknowledged that our internal tensions intrude into ecumenical settings. However, we recognized our baptism, our confession of the Christian faith as attested in the Scriptures, and our common calling to mission bind us together.

Catholics and Methodists never really divided from one another. Roman Catholics tend to look to the theology and ecclesiology of John Wesley. John and his brother, Charles, lived and died Anglican priests. There is no indication they ever wanted it any other way. Their thought shows a strong patristic and sacramental base. This has provided an excellent common basis for moving forward. John's "Letter to a Roman Catholic" gives a special look into his thinking.

Among the results of these dialogues is a vision of what is necessary for a united Church. Such a vision was articulated in 1991. If full communion is achieved, specific elements need resolution.

The unity of the church to which we are called is a "koinonia" or communion given and expressed, at least, in five areas. They are: common confession of the apostolic faith; common sacramental life entered by one baptism and celebrated in Eucharist fellowship; common life in which members and ministries are mutually recognized and reconciled; common mission witnessing to the gospel of God's grace to all people and serving the whole creation, and expressed on the local level and universal levels through conciliar forms of life and action. The goal of the search for full communion is realized when all the churches are able to recognize in one another one, holy, catholic and apostolic church in its fullness.

It is to be recognized that Methodist understandings of the church emerge from a commitment and enthusiasm for mission. Certainly one reason for the separation from the Anglican Church came from a willingness to adapt pragmatically. This meant minimal theological resources and maximum openness to the needs of the newly emerging American culture. This was very successful evangelistically and Methodism for a time became the largest Protestant community in America.

Catholics have similar feelings about the importance of mission. However, they regard the sacramental, confessional, and esslesiological issues as central. These are also considered at the source of the unity the churches seek together. Therefore, even agreements reached by officially appointed theologians will carry different weight and interest for the Methodist-Catholic communities.

From the very first of the international reports there has been the suggestion that Catholic dioceses and Methodist conferences set up joint commissions to evaluate such agreements. Beyond that, it is suggested reporting be passed on to appropriate authorities. Then, findings would be communicated to congregations.

In his Encyclical Letter "Ut Unum Sint" or "on commitment to ecumenism," John Paul II says, "In our ecumenical age, marked by the Second Vatican Council, the mission of the Bishop of Rome is particularly directed to recalling the need for full communion among Christ's disciples." The Pope's "Litany for Christian Unity" in the United Methodist Hymnal is one indication of how far we have come. Another is the inclusion of some of Charles Wesley's hymns in Catholic worship. Perhaps Saint Paul has the final word when he says, "Love does not rejoice in what is wrong but rejoices with the truth" 1 Corinthians 13:6 (NAB).

---

*South Bend Tribune* Wednesday June 28, 2000

# CHAPTER 14

# *Features*

## ❋JOHN WESLEY—AN INTERPRETATION OF A❋ PAINTING BY FRANK O. SALISBURY

JOHN WESLEY, the founder of Methodism, did not possess the physique of a large man. He was only five feet six inches tall and probably never topped one hundred and twenty pounds. In his outdoor preaching, he was often beset by mobs wild enough to frighten the most ardent Christian. Yet his self-control was such that he never gave a sign of fear and soon had the violent mob under his influence. It is difficult to imagine what would have happened to him had he not exercised such superb self-mastery.

The spirit of the man shone from his steadfast eyes. His self-control was obvious in them, more than in any other feature of his face or part of his body. He knew that in order to tame wild animals one must look directly into the eyes of the beasts, and when he appeared before a mob he would gaze squarely into the eyes of his hecklers. This must have been a major reason for his control of them; perhaps this characteristic exerted a sort of hypnotic power. In any case, it must have been quite confusing to the rowdies to have someone look at them with a Godlike compassion. Wesley had a message to give to those unruly rustics who needed something to fill their spiritual void.

The methodical habits of John Wesley are well known. The firm jaw, the determined lip, the strong nose, the high forehead reflect his strength of purpose and resoluteness of character. The celebrated modern portraitist, Frank O. Salisbury, has caught not only Wesley's features, but also his spirit. Here is a man whose whole bearing seems to say, "I must fulfill my destiny," a man who by his steadfast purpose and methodical means turned a considerable portion of the world upside down.

A natural question is, "How did he get that way?" Much of his determination and his methodical temperament can be attributed to his early training. His mother was a major force in his life, and Susanna Wesley was the personification of system. How else could she have accomplished all that she did? Great mothers produce great sons, and she was one of the world's greatest mothers. John's father also was a man of orderliness.

Samuel Wesley brought devotion and careful procedure to his tasks as a clergyman.

John Wesley became an organizer of the first caliber. His skill in organizing and guiding persons in the Christian life was at the very heart of his success as a great Christian leader. "Scriptural holiness" was his objective, but he knew that unless efficient methods were used, the objective would remain no more than an ideal.

It is true that he could be dictatorial, as men in high and responsible positions have sometimes been. Wesley was determined to keep the authority over his preachers and his societies firmly in his grasp. We can see the firmness in practically every feature of this magnificent painting. Yet it is important for us to remember Wesley's viewpoint. He was not the head of an established church, nor could he think of himself in such a capacity. He headed a religious and reforming society. Such a task required tenacity of purpose on the part of the leader and discipline among the members. His society has grown into an efficient and well-organized branch of the church.

For all Wesley's gifts as an organizer, one flow in his leadership showed itself near the end of his career. His own autocratic direction of the societies would be terminated by his death, and he knew it; yet he had no one prepared to take his place as their leader. He seemed to lack the quality of inspiring a strong man to serve as his lieutenant for any length of time; even his brother Charles was no exception. As a last resort a group of one hundred preachers was selected to take the place of John Wesley. Yet from their labors has risen the mighty Methodist Church, marked by Wesley's own righteous zeal.

In Wesley we also note the God-given qualities of compassion and simplicity. His God was a God of compassion; in the fateful prayer meeting at Aldersgate, Wesley's heart was "strangely warmed" by the realization of His grace. Thereafter this Methodist of Methodists often implored Him for the love that grows from such a realization. If the Aldersgate experience had never occurred, we should probably be viewing a man who evidenced only a steely, military firmness. Instead we see in John Wesley the attitude of the believer who says, "I determined not to know anything, save Jesus Christ and Him crucified."

One of the best examples of both his simplicity and compassion is found in a letter to William Wilberforce. At about the time of Wesley's death (1791), Wilberforce was fighting almost single-handedly in England the war against slavery. The preacher encouraged the great statesman:

Unless the divine Power had raised you up to be as Athanasius *"contra mundum"* [against the world], I do not see how you can go through your glorious enterprise, in opposing that execrable villainy, which is the scandal of religion, of England, and of human nature. Unless God has raised you up for this very thing, you will be worn out by the opposition of men and of devils; but if God be for you, who can be against you? Are all of them together stronger than God? O! Be not weary in well-doing. Go on in the name of God, and in the power of His might, till even American slavery, the vilest that ever saw the sun, shall vanish before it.

He did not present an essay on the evils of slavery. He did state succinctly and compassionately a need for the eradication of that horrendous evil.

Discipline, leadership, compassion, simplicity—these were the jewels that John Wesley possessed.

———————

*The Church and the Fine Arts* 1960 Cynthia Pearl Maus, editor

# ❧COMPLIMENTARY RESOLUTIONS❧

DONALD C. LACY, Convenor of the Committee on Complimentary Resolutions, read the following statement:

"It was with ardent expectations that all of us approached this Annual Conference. The union of two bodies of Christian Churchmen and women had been proclaimed at Dallas. The United Methodist Church promised to be more effectual, efficient, and effervescent. The redrawing of conference lines teased our curiosity. We could perceive new potentialities through improved structures. As we went about our work in an objective manner, one could detect a certain feeling tone. It was a mixture of sadness and thankfulness. From time to time what was in the depths of our souls came to the surface. Yes, Robert F. Kennedy had been brutally assassinated and we were naturally troubled; but our emotions were stirred more so about someone closer to us. State it however we please, it always came out more or less this way: Our Bishop is retiring.

Soon—very soon—twenty years of unparalleled guidance will come to an end.

"Bishop Raines, your departure is causing us no small amount of insecurity. We speak again and again about the security the connectional system offers both clergy and laity. However, everyone of us knows that this system is 'never, never, never' any better than the episcopal leadership given to it. Any expression of the appreciation in our hearts is woefully weak. For many of us you are the only Bishop we have served. The general church tells us in unmistakable language how splendidly and enviably fortunate we have been.

"During these trying times of unmitigated upheaval and unprecedented revolution, each of us searches for something of an absolute quality to be our guiding star. Forms throughout the church are undergoing change and impressive institutional structures are being given birth. Our guiding star has not been an 'it' but a 'him.' Through these two decades we have looked to you as the epitome of episcopal leadership at its very best. When we observe the attainments of the conference, the area, and even world Methodism, we discover the phrase 'Born to be a Bishop' very apropos indeed.

"Out of antiquity and the Christian gifts to the world have come seven virtues: prudence, justice, temperance, fortitude, faith, hope, and love. Your practical wisdom has kept the conference with its feet solidly on the ground. Your sense of justice is best depicted by a member of the present Cabinet: 'He is the most democratic bishop I have ever known.' Temperance in thought and deed has restrained us from going off deep ends that beckoned to us. Fortitude understood as 'firm courage' has injected a righteous persistency and consistent concern which we shall always cherish. Your faith has taken us to devotional heights lesser men could not have even visualized. Your hope shows us the face of our Blessed Lord and Savior with greater clarity and meaning. Thank you for loving us as individuals and as a conference.

"Several years ago a general upon retirement told the entire nation, 'Old soldiers never die; they just fade away.' There were those who thought this was a rather awkward attempt to be dramatic. We trust that we as an annual conference are being neither awkward nor dramatic when from the inner-most parts of our beings we simply and sincerely say with intense feeling, 'Great Bishops never die; they just continue to inspire us.'"

It was supported by the Conference.

———

*Official Journal of the North Indiana Conference* June 9, 1968

## ❋REVEREND, THE SPEAKER DIDN'T SHOW UP!❋

EVERY PASTOR HAS had or will have that unenviable invitation to speak on the spur of a moment to a service club. It seems to me this is like anything else in the countless opportunities we have in the parish ministry. It is far better to be prepared for that inevitable moment ahead of time than it is to try to start from scratch to prepare something of interest and inspiration to a group of men. As immediate past president of our Lions Club, I offer the following "pep talk" to brother pastors. It can be presented—with adaptation—to any service club. It is easy to tuck away in your mind simply by remembering the words "using . . . refusing . . . abusing."

Fellow Lions: Three things have impressed me about the people in your community. They are (1) a plenteous supply of human energy, (2) economic resources well above the average, and (3) talents galore.

I would like to focus on the third of these in that it indicates to me the most pressing problem in your community.

For some reasons or reason, your talents are just not getting used in the churches of the community.

Have you ever thought about the possibility that whenever we do not *use* these God given blessings we have—in fact—elected to *refuse* or *abuse* them?

To *refuse* a talent demands no direction on your part at all.

The very best way to show God and your fellowmen you are refusing your talents is to do nothing. If God has blessed you with an inspiring singing voice, be careful never to do any church choral work or sing out during the hymns. If the Creator has given to you the powers of organizing group activities, always stay silent and appear bored in your church committee meetings. If you have the talent of standing before a group and speaking, never allow your name to be approved even for substitute teaching in the Sunday School. Of course, what we think is direction and beneficial action may be no direction at all.

I am reminded of a church board that thought it was going to build a new house of worship by exerting enough energy to pass certain resolutions in four successive months. They decided (a) We agree to erect a new sanctuary, (b) The new one shall be located on the site of the present sanctuary, (c) All material in the present building shall be utilized in the new sanctuary, and (d) Our congregation shall continue to worship in the old sanctuary until the new one is finished.

In a more serious vein, you and I just don't realize how often we say "No" to our talents, especially in our Church.

Now to *abuse* one's talents requires misdirection.

Strangely, it takes as much or more energy to misdirect a talent as it does to direct it. The decision to apply business ability in illegitimate commerce does not of necessity mean less time and effort. The sharp mind that oversees an international narcotics ring has to be cultivated. The political chieftain whose voice rings with persuasive prejudices did not develop his style in a few minutes.

Our tastes may not be conducive to seeing some of our actions as abuse. How about the fellow who is called to preach and ends up giving his talents to the advertising field? How about the fellow who is called to be a medical missionary and ends up giving his talents to a lucrative practice here in the states? How about the charming, handsome singer whose Saturday night engagements make participation in the church choir an impossibility? How about the church committee which needed your skill in publicity, but you never showed up because it met on your regular poker night?

Our churches can and have survived open hostility and gigantic doses of adversity. A pressing and most relevant question in my mind, gentlemen, is: "Can they survive the subtle onslaughts of well-meaning, talented laymen?"

As pastor in the community and as a fellow Lion I urge you to *use* your talents in your churches. *Refusing* and *abusing* them is just not keeping our community on the lofty plain on which it can and ought to dwell. Thank you.

———

*The Clergy Journal* June 1970

# ❀TODAY'S PROBLEM❀

I KNOW OF no one who seriously doubts the truth of Paul's advice to the Romans when he said: "For by the grace given to me I bid every one

among you not to think of himself more highly than he ought to think. . . ."
Conceited persons seldom make headway in any area which requires human
relationships. Indeed, Paul knew what he was talking about.

At the same time, there is something I'd like to say to Paul. Perhaps as
you read the Scriptures you, too have felt like saying, "Yes, that's so, but—"
"What a marvelous insight, except—"

So, I would say to Paul, "Sir, we must roll this over in our minds a
while before we apply it to our situation in the latter half of this twentieth century. It may come as some surprise to you, Paul, but what you
said isn't really our problem."

Today's problem is that man is *not* thinking highly enough of
himself. The self-confident man of the world largely has disappeared.
Insecurity is felt in every form of human endeavor. The oceans and
mountains which used to provide natural barriers and boundaries have
long since been surmounted. Brute physical force to insure one's independence has seen its day. The finest underground shelters could be
made into a shambles.

Man's inventions seem to have pushed him individually into insignif-
icance. There are no earthly powers which can restore his importance.
His superior intellect has sought to work apart from an inner wisdom,
and thereby he has become greatly frustrated. The dominant theme is
that mankind has about had it! This is spoken of in many loud and
various ways.

We don't think *highly enough* of ourselves! Because of this, three
"demons" or complexes infect and afflict us. We give them all sorts of high-
sounding and technically-approved names. However, they all boil down to
words of not more than two syllables.

*The first is the* I'm-so-little complex.

In this case an odd sort of helplessness settles over us. It isn't quite the
plague of feeling useless. It isn't the misfortune of being unable to spot
abilities within ourselves and others. It isn't that one considers himself a
nuisance in God's creation. It isn't the calamity of believing human nature
cannot be converted. It isn't the scourge of living under the pressures of a
dictatorial system.

It *is* fumbling around in the fog of despair. It is causing our God-
given dignity to be defined in uncomplimentary terms. It *is* much like
the fly caught in the spider's web. For a time it will remain a fly, alive and
kicking. It still has a few fleeting moments to remember its secure and
productive days.

For those of us caught in the I'm-so-little complex, there is still life and shreds of meaning. Even certain purposes have places in our plans. For some of us it is alarmingly true that we are only a minute segment of any vocation we enter. Gratitude is difficult, because uniqueness is highly improbable and creative endeavors well-nigh impossible.

Those burdened with this complex admit that they can't seem to get anyplace, and yet they don't know what is wrong. They take their state of helplessness in stride. They breathe its air. It is true they can't seem to get anyplace; they have no place to go. It is also true they don't know what is wrong, and they have no deep desire to know what is wrong. They feel like monkeys in a jungle. The jungle is neither good nor evil. It is just a jungle, and they must bear whatever it has to offer. If there is a giant fruit tree upon which to feast, all well and good. If there is a lion's paw knocking them unconscious, all well and good.

They feel so engulfed by it all that defensiveness isn't even necessary. They move with hardly a whimper from tasteless *toleration*, to parasitic *relaxation*, to an unobtrusive *abomination*. The recurring theme of their lives is: "We only have one life to live, and soon it will be past. Anything we may have done will not last."

"Oh, great theologian and philosopher, do you not see that our problem is one of not thinking highly enough of ourselves? The I'm-so-little complex is not even a decent form of humility."

*The second lethal little demon is the* I-can't *complex.*
Here a deep-seated inferiority feeling thwarts our effectiveness. Granted, we need the serenity to accept what cannot be changed. Granted, we need the courage to change what should be changed. Above all, however, we need to know one from the other.

The individual weakened by the I-can't complex finds this a foreign field of thinking. Serenity is an ideal characteristic which has little relationship to his world. Courage is for those who know they can attain certain goals; not for the one who is unconcerned by either the changeable or the nonchangeable. Frequently he feels too inferior even to attempt to make the differentiation.

In the all-important area of religious experiences, how many times has each of us said, "I can't?" Is this response due to an inferiority feeling? Do we say "I can't" as frequently in the other aspects of our lives? Could it be that this complex is reserved solely for this crucial area? Is it possible that "I can't" is merely an expression more accurately phrased "I won't?" Is it fair to allow a potentially dynamic communion with God to go undeveloped because we have either consciously or subconsciously made "I can't" and "I won't" synonymous? "I can't" is a human excuse, but "I won't" indicates deep ignorance of our Divine nature and all its potentialities in us.

This complex puts a severe limitation on the most worthy of our ventures. If Jesus did nothing else for His followers, He certainly released them from the futility of inferiority. His ranks are composed of dedicated people who are not defeated before they start.

"Oh, wise man who was driven to your knees on the way to Damascus, do you see that our problem is simply not thinking highly enough of ourselves?"

*The third ailment does not need a fancy name. It is the* wishy-washy complex.

An attitude of indecision dampens and damns our lives. We can't make up our minds whether or not we want to be the best persons we know how to be. A clergyman says something we just can't go along with. A respected community leader hurts our feelings and this cuts to a trickle our spring of enthusiasm for some moral principles. The choice of being good or bad in a world of three billion human beings seems like an impertinence. So, we can't be bothered now.

The delay to do something of major benefit or cease doing something of great detriment succumbs to time. A year later no action has been taken. This does not seem very long until we break it down into 8,760 hours, or 525,600 minutes, or 31,536,000 seconds. Those precious moments have gone forever. Father Time refuses to wait for us, our wishy-washy complex triumphs again. Many just don't trust themselves to make such decisions. The reason is clear: They really don't think much of themselves.

An intriguing story has come out of the distant past about one of the Devil's conferences with his evil spirits. He asked, "Who will travel to Earth and persuade men and women to ruin their souls?"

One ambitious spirit quickly said that he would go. "How will you do it?" asked the Devil.

The Spirit replied, "I will tell them there is no punishment after death." The Devil laughed and said, "Sorry, that won't do."

A second loyal spirit volunteered, and stated that he would accomplish the task by telling them there are no rewards after death.

The Devil frowned and said, "Oh, that won't get the job done either. We need something that will appeal to all classes, ages, and dispositions."

Just then a very evil-looking spirit came forward and said, "I will tell them there is plenty of time to decide for doing good."

The Devil broke into a victorious smile and sent him on his way.

Candor demands to be heard. Most of the successes and excesses of all immorality can be laid at the door of religious procrastination.

The wishy-washy complex operates in only one field of education: The School of Impractical Inertia and Applied Stagnation.

Some Jewish religious leaders approached Jesus one day. One asked, "Teacher, which is the great commandment in the law?"

Jesus replied, "You shall love the Lord your God with all your heart, and with all your soul, and with all your mind. This is the great and first commandment. And a second like it, you shall love your neighbor as yourself."

It is not conceit or vanity or self-righteousness to love ourselves as children of God and our neighbors for the same reason. The kingdom of God is within us; here is our source of wisdom and strength—"the universal nature which gives worth to particular men and things."

How else shall today's problems be resolved?

———

*Science of Mind* October 1970

## ✳PASTORAL VISITATION SEEN AS✳ OUTREACH TOOL

AT UNION CHAPEL [Indianapolis] over a two-year period we have experienced an adult membership increase from 624 to 750, a 30 percent increase in worship attendance, and more than 40 percent increase in financial giving. Some persons attempt to relate our growth to geographical location, but this is dubious because new housing additions are several blocks and even miles away. The major reason from a pragmatic viewpoint is very simple: the resident membership responds very favorably to the generous use of pastoral shoe leather.

It all started when we moved into the parsonage and I immediately notified the membership I would be calling on all of them in their homes over a thirteen-week period. This was handled administratively by simply running their names with dates in advance through the church's weekly newsletter, so that families would know when to expect me. This has now been done three times. Some do not want the pastor to call, but this is less than 5 percent.

There are, at least, ten basic reasons in defense of regular pastoral visitation to all resident members. These hold true, regardless of the size of the church. In short, it may take two or three or even four pastors to get the job done; but the abiding benefits are the same.

In the first place it builds pastoral-lay rapport at a one-on-one human relations level. It is significant that we communicate in our people's homes with them in an unhurried manner, sipping coffee or iced tea. The pastor in fact becomes a known friend, and the layperson becomes a specific human being to the degree that the pastor can immediately say, "I know who he is and where he lives."

In the second place it keeps the pastor ever familiar with the thoughts and emotions of his people. Really, this prevents the pastor from speaking continually about subjects and topics which his people find irrelevant. It also gives him insights at points of special needs within family units.

Third, it makes the pastor a man among his people. He is seen "close-up" without clerical robe and the need to relate to them in a corporate worship experience. It affords him the opportunity to be less of an image and more of a human being who has given himself to the professional ministry.

In the fourth place it provides the context from which the pastor will do much of his preaching. Theological, sociological, and psychological texts become thoroughly submerged as tools to minister to people's needs. Abstractions are given flesh and blood connotations.

Fifth, it strengthens the pastor's health. The pulpit and desk are put into the background. Physically, ten walking calls might be worth as much as an afternoon on the golf course. Mentally, the pastor grows at points of encounter whether they be verbal or nonverbal, positive or negative. Spiritually, the pastor is more healthy because "those lazy laity become real persons and he realizes how much they are already doing for him."

In the sixth place it gives him much needed potential member names. Who moved in next door? This sensitizes his people to their responsibility for the growth of their church. Of course, he is careful to check out all names given to him. He then gives credit where credit is due, and oftentimes that's directly back to the layperson.

Seventh, it communicates "pastoral care" in a way our laity understands and appreciates. There is nothing quite like a thirty or forty minute visit from the pastor to tell the Smith family that the "Reverend" cares. In all probability they will appreciate this more than the finest sermon he will ever preach and will remember it far longer.

In the eighth place it opens psychological doors that can be opened no other way. When a layperson is sitting in his own kitchen or living room, there is a unique freedom of expression forthcoming. In a way the pastor has taken the risk of meeting him on his own ground.

Ninth, it sells and resells the connectional system. Who is interested in conference apportionments and programs? The pastor. Who best communicates the necessity of such United Methodist workings? The pastor. Our people will accept their obligations and will give their cooperation as the pastor proves to them again and again the validity of our system by working closely with them.

In the tenth place it increases the respect for the pastoral office. He becomes more than the competent professional who knows how to use the language and administer the latest Council on Ministries project. He is in fact the shepherd or pastor who is first of all sensitive to human beings and their needs.

It seems to me pastoral visitation within this context is a kind of "vanishing pastoral discipline" which has been placed on an optional basis with some real loss to Jesus Christ and His Church. As an instrument it has more to do indirectly with the key areas of evangelism, worship, and stewardship than many other things a pastor can do.

---

*Street'n Steeple* Board of Discipleship (UMC) 2nd quarter, 1973

# ✤THE THREE Rs✤

IN THE EARLY part of his ministry Jesus used a parable to describe the Christian religion. It involved a grain of mustard seed. The mustard seed was often used by Jesus and others to illustrate something small and powerful. "If you have faith as a grain of mustard seed . . . nothing will be impossible to you." (Matthew 17:20–21 [RSV]).

When we ponder a bit, there emerges a definition of our faith. There are three guideposts—relationship, redemption, and realization.

Our religion is basically a living *relationship* between us and God.

The heart of Christianity is seen in the words "when it is sown." Jesus emphasized the small size of the seed. He also emphasized its dependence on the soil for its growth. By itself the seed was of no great value. It was when it was related to its natural source of life that it had power to grow. Christianity is not a human philosophy with no roots in eternity. It is not a simple matter of human kindness and good will. It is not a system of social legislation and human well-being. It is not an abstract idea of the nature of existence. To be sure, all these things are aspects, but if you permit yourself to stop there, you never truly view the relationship. The roots of Christianity are far deeper and more vital than all of these aspects put together. The deeper meaning of Christianity is crystallized in the sentence: "It is the life of man rooted in the life of God." Our relationship to God is set up in and through Jesus Christ who is the revelation of God and the Savior of mankind. God is the source and soil of all Christian qualities. When we detach ourselves from the Christ who has made this truth known, we sever the cord that makes it possible for us to be Christians.

The position of Jesus differentiates our religion from all others. Both the Jews and the Moslems have very similar faiths. However, in both cases Jesus is not elevated to the supreme place of importance as He is in Christianity. For most Jews, Jesus was an enlightened prophet. For most Moslems, He was an exceptionally good man who was very intelligent. The Christian says that he finds God in Christ.

Flowing from this is a whole series of divine blessings. In some strange, wondrous, and inexplicable way God was and is in Christ reconciling persons to Himself. Forgiveness of sins is no longer a matter of sacrificial gifts to pacify an angry God. Peace of mind becomes far more than idealistic contemplation. Fears are diminished in proportion to our trust in him. Unspeakable joy is a natural product. All in all, the transformation of human life enters the realm of that which is possible. The simple but enduring fact that Jesus Christ is the source of the Christian religion needs to be relearned. The relearning process must take place in both mind and heart. We can see the fruits or results of Christianity, but back of these is the majestic figure of our Lord. Without a thorough acquaintance with the Source, the translation of the Christian message into visible results becomes an impossible task.

From relationship we go to *redemption*.

Christianity makes it possible for us to be redeemed.

In the story of the mustard seed Jesus plays up the contrast of size. It is our contact with Jesus that makes redemption a reality. The seemingly insignificant relationship to a man called Jesus the Christ is the beginning of all significance.

The life of Jesus himself is an excellent illustration. His birth was a small event in a big world dominated by Roman power. Although there were signs and wonders at Jesus' birth, the majority of the people in Bethlehem were concerned about bigger things than the birth of a baby. The majority of the people would have sneered and laughed at the idea that a baby would become the Savior of the world. The least becomes the greatest. The servant becomes the master. The weak becomes the strong.

Relationship, redemption, and now *realization*.

To realize means to make real. Christians make real their faith by continued service to others.

The parable tells us that when the mustard seed matured it became an object of usefulness. "When it is sown it grows up and becomes the greatest of all shrubs, and puts forth large branches, so that the birds of the air can make nests in its shade." The Christian religion continually fulfills itself in service to humanity. Its continuous flexibility to meet and serve in all situations is the secret of its amazing vitality. As we serve others, Christianity multiplies itself and becomes morally effective in helping to mold human beings into what they were originally intended to be. As we give ourselves, we grow. As churches give themselves, they grow. When Christianity is weighted down by self-satisfaction and is satisfied with what has already been accomplished, slow but persistent strangulation has set in.

Frank Laubach's teaching illiterates to read is an international achievement. Back of his inspiring attainment is a powerful principle: "No illiterate is taught to read who will not first of all agree to teach, at least, one other." Herein lies the key to a growing church. When you learn of Christ and accept him, promise that you will be responsible, at least, for one more besides yourself. Communities have potentialities with regard to religion. I have never seen one yet that has exhausted its supply of people to be won for Christ and His church. If you are unable to contact someone who is non-Christian, then approach someone who professes Christianity but needs counsel and encouragement to become rooted and grounded in the faith.

*Tidings* (Tract-of-the-Month) 1975

## ❧GARFIELD'S INAUGURAL ADDRESS❧

SURELY THESE YEARS in the mid-1970s and beyond are going to go down in historical records as a time the Bicentennial was given over to millions of words and literally tons of published materials. Perhaps no nation will have been drenched so artfully and righteously. While no one seriously doubts the importance of such a celebration, it does tend to make society generally and writers in particular overlook other inspiring aspects of history.

In place of turning the clock back two hundred years, it might be well to focus on a document nearly one-hundred years old. It is one of genuine pride for Disciples of Christ. March 4, 1881, James A. Garfield gave a masterful Inaugural Address. It is all the more remarkable in view of the fact professional writers for presidents were not commonplace. General Jim poured himself spiritually, intellectually, and psychologically into it. While he was President considerably less than a year, the work stands as a monument to his powers.

By design it divides into ten categories of crucial importance.

The nation's past is elevated with a majestic beauty. The statement "We cannot overestimate the fervent love of liberty, the intelligent courage, and the sum of common sense with which our fathers made the great experiment of self-government" beams brightly from the initial lines.

The Constitution is seen and fully accepted as an instrument under which a people desirous of freedom want to move forward within the bounds of organized government. In reference to the Civil War and the danger it posed to the Constitution in subdued simplicity he says, "the supremacy of the nation and its laws should be no longer a subject of debate."

The Negroes are treated in a context of joyous and necessary emancipation coupled with compassion for the disturbances caused in the Southern communities. With a flair of literary genius and political sagacity he points out: "There can be no permanent disfranchised peasantry in the United States."

Then, the President deals with the economic realm, speaking specifically to the areas of prosperity and finances. Certainly one of the most interesting and forthright statements is: "The chief duty of the National Government in connection with the currency of the country is to coin money and declare its value." This statement is illustrative of the exemplary positive approach he utilizes throughout the address.

Agriculture is given a brief but uplifting treatment. He visualizes the wave of the future by saying, "As the Government lights our coasts for the protection of mariners and the benefit of commerce, so it should give to the tillers of the soil the best lights of practical science and experience."

Manufacturing is also treated with brevity but in words sparkling with meaning. "Our manufacturers are rapidly making us industrially independent . . ." is the keynote.

World commerce is viewed as a major opportunity area. The " . . . shortening of the great sea voyage around Cape Horn by constructing ship canals or railways across the isthmus which unites the continents" sounds the trumpet for the marvel occurring in Panama decades later.

The President again is very positive and forthright in the area of religious freedom. In just six words there is no doubt about the emphasis. He maintains, "The Constitution guarantees absolute religious freedom." Ecclesiastical organizations have their sphere. They must not in any way be allowed to usurp the functions and powers of the National Government.

A special care and concern seems to be that of civil service. The President speaks with authority: "The civil service can never be placed on a satisfactory basis until it is regulated by law." As is so typical, he sees the solution to problem and proceeds to point the direction for constructive action.

Finally, he bolsters the ethos of the country by dealing with the authority of the nation. The task is one of working "within the authority and limitations of the Constitution." This he convincingly proclaims he is willing to do and with despatch.

President Garfield at no point preaches or theologizes, as some might expect. In fact, it is only through the closing words that he even mentions God: " . . . I reverently invoke the support and blessings of Almighty God."

His Inaugural Address is a tribute to the Disciples of Christ that nourished and enriched his life, public and private. As the American people are continually bombarded with Bicentennial materials, why not set the clock back just a hundred years and thank God for the legacy given in President Garfield's masterly document?

---

*Discipliana* Winter, 1975

## ❧ON MEETING THE NEW ARCHBISHOP❧

AT THE INVITATION of a friend, I went to the Cathedral Church of Saint James in South Bend recently to hear and meet the Archbishop Designate of Canterbury—Bishop George Carey.

He will become the leader of 70 million Anglicans throughout the world next month.

To say the least, it was a rare—but deeply appreciated—opportunity for a United Methodist clergyman. After being welcomed by the Right Reverend Francis C. Gray, Bishop of the Northern Diocese of Indiana, the "soon to be enthroned" Archbishop spoke on "A View of the Church."

He shared with us that, as a lad, he learned that even though people may be far from the Church as an institution, we should never write them off.

He saw much damage during World War II and inquired: "Is there a God?" But in time, as a teenager, he came to the quiet but profound conclusion that "God is; and He is in Jesus Christ."

His parish priests assigned him the first three chapters of the Gospel of John to memorize, which he did. Then he was assigned Romans 5, 6, 7, and 8! These became a part of his spiritual bloodstream.

In his early ecumenical journey, Vatican II was quite influential.

He reminded us that the most precious of all ministries is the parish ministry, and that we should never be afraid of raising money!

His spiritual journey has made him an eclectic in that he has incorporated a number of theological viewpoints into his thinking. He sees himself as a "bishop in mission" and not just one doing maintenance. He said that he firmly believes that "if God calls, He equips."

He emphasized the 1990s as a decade of "evangelism." Imbedded in the emphasis are three key words: communion, witness (martyr), and service. The local church is always one of "feeding the flock and fostering the fringes," he said.

We are never to underestimate church buildings for their iconic value. They are always saying something to the world.

Already knocking at his door is the question of the ordination of women to the priesthood. It may very well be the thorniest and most divisive issue to confront him, and there will be no avoiding it.

As I shook his hand, I told him that I often reminded those about me that John Wesley lived and died at Anglican priest. He indicated the truth of the matter and spoke with sadness about the Methodists leaving the Church of England.

————

*Lafayette Journal-Courier* March 17, 1991

# ✸BEATITUDES FROM THE BATTLEFIELD✸

HAVING RECENTLY returned from the twenty-eighth National Workshop on Christian Unity in St. Louis, I was again reminded of the problem of unity—sometimes like a battlefield—in the life of churches.

Since the days of the first-century letters of St. Paul to the Galatians and Corinthians, there has been some discord among those professing the name of Him who calls His followers to love one another.

The workshop sought to bring together for dialogue in an ecumenical setting Roman Catholics, United Methodists, Presbyterians, Orthodox, Baptists, Episcopalians, Disciples of Christ, United Church of Christ, and many others. It had its beginning during the 1963 convention in Atlantic City of the national Council of Catholic Men in direct response to Vatican II. I have been a participant in fourteen of the twenty-eight, and believe that they have had an important influence on my life and ministry.

The theme this year was "Come Holy Spirit—Renew the Whole Creation."

The opening worship was held in the Basilica of Saint Louis (Old Cathedral) with the Rev. Herbert W. Chilstrom, Bishop of the Evangelical Lutheran Church in America preaching. One of the lessons was read by the Rev. Dr. Clarence Carr, pastor of the Washington Metropolitan African Methodist Episcopal Church of St. Louis. It was a standing-room-only event. *Blessed are those who will not allow denominational labels to get in the way of coming together to worship the Lord.*

The keynote address was delivered by the Rev. Vinton Anderson, Bishop of the fifth district of the African Methodist Episcopal Church. *Blessed are those who will stand before us and witness to the Lord of the universal church.*

Dr. Constance Tarasar of the Orthodox faith led a seminar on "The Holy Spirit in Ecumenical Conversation." *Blessed are the scholars who explain to us their understanding of our theological underpinnings.*

A social event with fun, food, and fellowship found most of us in The Cedars, across from St. Raymon's Maronite Church, a church having its origin in ancient Syria. *Blessed are those who will share food and drink together as one people belonging to Jesus the Christ.*

In the closing address, the Most Rev. Edward I. Cassidy, president of the Pontifical Council for Promoting Christian Unity, spoke of the advances being made in Catholic-Orthodox relationships in liberated but strife-torn Eastern Europe. *Blessed are those who have suffered with the Lord for the faith, especially the countless precious persons being martyred.*

*Lafayette Journal-Courier* May 5, 1991

# ❋WHAT ISSUE SHOULD BE THE FOCUS OF THE❋ PRESIDENTIAL CAMPAIGNS?

THIS WEEK, AS state primaries wind down and preconvention campaigns heat up, President Clinton and Sen. Bob Dole have faced off over welfare reform. That follows a week of campaigning on the gasoline tax and its repeal. *USA Today* asked readers what issues should be the focus of the campaign for president.

*The focus must be unity for the United States of America in the context of a world community. That must be done in the sense of religious values, not parochial or denominational values, but eternal values that humankind has found valuable, workable, and necessary.*
—Donald Charles Lacy, 63, clergyman, Walkerton, Ind.

*USA Today* May 23, 1996

# ❋"FATHER" IS INESCAPABLE TERM IN BIBLE USE❋

IS GOD SUFFERING from an identity crisis? If He is in some quarters, that really is nothing new. The names for God would fill many pages. Here are just a few: "First Principle," "Process of Integration," "Cosmic Organism,"

"Life Essence," "Fundamental Substance," "Principle of Concretion," "Divine Architect," "Sum Total of Accumulated Idealism," "Elan Vital," "Life Force," "Supreme Intelligence," "Stream of Tendency," "Cosmic Essence," "Impersonal It," "Allah," "Great Spirit," "Mother." The list seems unlimited.

Today there is a very persistent attempt on the part of some either to substitute or negate God as "Father." It is sinister and subtle. It seems to spring from those who have looked upon the Bible as far less than the Word of God. Is this something totally unexpected and out of step with their bias? I think not. Those of us who find our roots in an evangelical and catholic orientation have seen it coming for a long time.

We are summoned as Christians, regardless of denominational label or lack of it, to look at our Lord's way of relating to God. Jesus does not say: "Process of Integration, hallowed by Its name"; "In my First Principle's house there are many rooms"; "Sum Total of Accumulated Idealism, forgive them"; "No one comes to the Cosmic Essence, but by me"; or "Mother, into thy hands I commit my spirit."

Jesus calls God "Father." The entire New Testament in fact calls God "Father." The word is utilized nearly three hundred times.

In the Gospels Jesus calls God "Father." In Matthew there are forty-two references. In Mark there are only five instances, but who can forget such verses as: "And whenever you stand praying forgive, if you have anything against anyone; so that your Father also who is in heaven may forgive you your trespasses. But if you do not forgive, neither will your Father who is in heaven forgive your trespasses." Luke gives to us the word eighteen times. As we look to John we are caught in a time-consuming count because Jesus refers to God as "Father" 111 times. So for Jesus, God is "Father." It is as though He wants there to be no doubts.

All of the Apostle Paul's letters call God "Father." Whether we are reading in the first chapter of Romans ("Grace to you and peace from God our Father and the Lord Jesus Christ") or the second chapter of Philippians ("and every tongue confess that Jesus Christ is Lord, to the glory of God the Father") in every one of his letters there is no doubt. It is like the unrelenting clanging of an eternal bell.

The Letter of James provides examples in the first chapter. This one especially catches our eye: "Religion that is pure and undefiled before God and the Father is this: to visit orphans and widows in their affliction, and to keep oneself unstained from the world."

In both of Peter's Letters we find the same story. Who can forget the exclamation, "Blessed be the God and Father of our Lord Jesus Christ!"

The often overlooked letter of Jude begins with these words: "Jude, a servant of Jesus Christ and brother of James, to those who are called, beloved in God the Father and kept for Jesus Christ, may mercy, peace, and love be multiplied to you."

The Letters of John refer to God the Father with the exception of the third one, which was written to an individual.

The Book of Hebrews offers this mystical but practical challenge: "Besides this, we have had earthly fathers to discipline us and we respected them. Shall we not much more be subject to the Father of spirits and live?"

A reading of the first chapter of the books of Acts brings these hope-filled words: "He said to them, 'It is not for you to know times or reasons which the Father has fixed by his own authority. But you shall receive power when the Holy Spirit has come upon you; and you shall be my witnesses in Jerusalem and in all Judea and Samaria and to the end of the earth.'"

In that sometimes awesomely intriguing closing book of the New Testament, The Revelation to John, we discover: "We who conquer, I will grant him to sit with me on my throne, as I myself conquered and sat down with my Father on his throne."

Some things do not change. Whoever and whatever else God is, He most assuredly is your Father, my Father, and our Father. The large liberal segments especially found in mainline denominations who would neutralize or even remove God as "Father," have their own identity crisis. At best, we may call their efforts "questionable theological gymnastics" and at worst "emerging apostasy."

There are two imperative inquiries. In the first place, isn't the Word of God today telling our liberal friends more than they want to know about man's relationship to God? In the second place, if the New Testament—especially our Savior and Lord in the Gospels—calls God "Father," are you and I in any position to improve upon that?

———

*South Bend Sunday* Tribune June 15, 1997
*The Catholic Answer* January/February 1998

# ✼"TONY, THE BISHOP OF WALKERTON" LIVED✼ AND SHARED HIS FAITH

THE RECENT passing of the Rev. Anthony L. Letko has caused many of us to continue to reflect in deep appreciation of him. For more than four decades this unique man served unselfishly the people of four counties. In his own way he was a man of genius, who was a gifted general practitioner among Catholics and non-Catholics alike.

When I went with him to a special service in St. Matthew Cathedral, I knew my friend was one of a kind. Bishop John D'Arcy spoke to him as "Tony, the Bishop of Walkerton." Father Letko and I received Communion that day together. Why? Because when he said, "You can receive Communion, if you believe in the real presence," I told him I did and so did John Wesley.

The numerous times we went to lunch together at the Notre Dame University Club lingers like a fragrance of ecumenical brotherhood. His conversational skills, even in his late eighties, were a thrill to experience. His tips that were usually $2 bills always brought smiles and "Thank yous." I often wondered, "Can it be this much fun to be in the presence of a holy man?"

The reading material he assigned to some of us was indeed enormous, even for those who spend much of their lives in reading. "Conservative" and "traditional" were the periodicals and books. Yes, they reflected the man, but don't ever believe his mind was closed. Those big twinkles in his eyes seemed invariably to say, "I respect what you have to say that here is a better way."

His knowledge of the parish and areas surrounding was mind boggling. At one time he must have known thousands of persons by name. Every business, home, and farm between South Bend and Walkerton had meaning for him. The truly amazing thing was that he was always positive and never condemning. People were people to him. Of course, I got the idea he would rather I be a Catholic than a Methodist!

His life and ministry are a magnificent affirmation of the priesthood. Maybe we will never again see the likes of Father Letko. That wouldn't bother him. The priesthood was what was important. When he said "Keep the faith," that meant Catholicism and the Christians who shared in the essential ancient revelation. It did not mean the faith according to Tony's rendition.

"The Holiness of the Priesthood" by Joseph Staudinger, S.J., speaks of a priestly mentality by saying, "For him the great mystery of the altar is enacted in a manner privileged and sublime beyond description." Furthermore, he states, "He is, along with Christ, priest and victim at once owing to the fact that he is included in and with Christ in the sacred action that takes place under his hands." I love the way the author relates the words that especially depict Father Letko: " . . . he must be priest and only priest, every inch of him!"

Saint John of Kronstadt, in "Counsels of the Christian Priesthood," says, "A true shepherd of his flock, a true father of his people, will live on in their grateful memory even after his death." Indeed, generations yet unborn will benefit from one man who obeyed Christ and His church. Father Letko was a perfect blend of the idealist and realist. His head was in the clouds but his feet were planted squarely on the ground.

In "A Letter to a Roman Catholic," John Wesley says, "Let us resolve, God being our helper, to speak nothing harsh or unkind of each other." Father Letko continues to teach us a very important lesson: even though much of his ministry was pre-Vatican II, he was able to live with no harshness or unkindness. His priesthood would never be compromised but his Lord was welcome to remold His Bishop of Walkerton.

So, "Hallelujah" from a single priest pervades the countryside and continues to warm our hearts. Yes, and "Keep the faith" is an ever-present reminder of a command that must never be allowed to be lost in the debris of a mundane and fickle society. His gentle but firm spirit shows us a "priest for all seasons" who will always have something to say to all of us.

---

*South Bend Tribune* April 23, 1999

# "BIBLE CHARACTERS IN FREEMASONRY" PROVES USEFUL

I HAVE A book that has a favored place on my bookshelves. It's entitled, *Bible Characters in Freemasonry,* and the author is John H. Van Gorden.

Mr. Van Gorden's book is a great reference tool, and over the years I have used it many times.

The introduction begins with "Ye are the light of the world. . . ." Then the author says, "That awesome commission and responsibility, with which Jesus Christ challenged His followers two thousand years ago, still challenge us today. Jesus' disciples, inspired and enlightened by God through the Holy Spirit, brought the light of the Gospel to the world's darkness."

I learned early on everything is very carefully done in the book. Section 1 is "Major Characters (In Freemasonry)." It is very helpful, for example, to know Abraham of the Old Testament (Hebrew Scriptures) is mentioned in the Symbolic Lodge Degrees; York Rite (Royal Arch and Knights Templar Degrees); Scottish Rite (19th, 24th, 25th, 26th and 29th Degrees).

Then, we look up Jesus Christ and discover He is mentioned in Scottish Rite (12th, 18th, 19th, 27th, 29th and 31st Degrees). Of course, there are numerous others listed with similar references.

The remainder of the book is composed of Section 2 "Minor Characters (In Freemasonry)" with some very helpful appendixes. Among the minor characters mentioned are Azariah (Scottish Rite: 4th and 14th Degrees), Gareb (Scottish Rite: 24th Degree), and Simon of Cyrene (Scottish Rite: 18th Degree).

Appendix B, "Historical Characters in Freemasonry," is unusually helpful. It gives not only the Scottish Rite Degree and occasionally a York Rite reference but a brief biographical note and life span. For example, Philo Judaeus, Jewish philosopher of Alexandria, lived from ca. B.C. 30 to A.D. 50 and is in the Scottish Rite 19th Degree.

Need I say more? Well, yes! The index itself is comprehensive and an excellent aid in utilizing the book. I have lost track of the numerous times I have called up this brilliant work for basic information and in defense of Freemasonry.

———

*The Double Eagle* Spring 1999

**METHODIST MASS**

DONALD CHARLES LACY

*What others have said about* Methodist Mass:

*"A most significant liturgical effort."*

Dr. Don E. Saliers
Candler School of Theology

*"Your adaptation of the Roman Catholic liturgy and your own Methodist service was, to me, very powerful and beautiful."*

Sr. Agnes Louise
Marian College of Fond du Lac

*"It is ecumenical in the finest sense, profoundly historical, and thoroughly Christian."*

Dr. Mark Noll
Wheaton College

CHAPTER 15

# *Worship Materials*

## ❋METHODIST MASS❋

### *United Methodist Mass—The Idea*

THE REV. Donald C. Lacy of Union Chapel Church, Indianapolis, Indiana, describes a worship form that worked for that suburban Indianapolis congregation.

Friends and members of the Union Chapel Church in Indianapolis are being treated to a creative, ecumenical worship service that began in July 1971. It is called a "Methodist Mass."

Worshipers enter the sanctuary during the organ prelude. Lay participation is at a maximum with pastor and laity sharing in fifteen of the twenty-four parts of the service. No attempt is made to differentiate between what is strictly "United Methodist" or "Roman Catholic." The service is interwoven as a unified worship experience, a total act of corporate worship.

The high point of the service is when worshipers kneel at the Communion railing. I distribute wafers bearing the crucifix in the paten, which are held for a few moments. I then pass by each one with the chalice containing grape juice. Each worshiper touches the wafer in the juice and places both contents into his mouth.

As I move from worshiper to worshiper, I simply say, "The Body and Blood of Jesus Christ." Occasionally, I reverse the procedure and ask each one partaking to say the words quietly to himself.

The entire service from beginning to end is one of celebrating the Good News found in the birth, life, death and Resurrection of Jesus Christ. The most consistent feeling tone is "eucharistic" with the comingling and expression of human divine gratitude at both the mystical and practical levels.

In accordance with the *Companion to the Book of Worship*, edited for the Commission on Worship, the mass is divided into five major movements with a grand total of twenty-four parts. Twelve parts of the service are from United Methodist Liturgy and twelve are from "The New Order of Mass" in the Roman Catholic Church.

The initial movement, *Remembrance*, includes sentences from the United Methodist service, a Roman Catholic greeting, the United Methodist "Collect for Purity," and the Roman Catholic "Kyrie" and "Gloria."

227

The next movement, *Proclamation*, is composed of the first reading with response, second reading with response, and the "Homily." All are taken from the Roman Catholic service.

*Offertory* is the most lengthy movement. It involves the United Methodist "Invitation," "General Confession," "Prayer for Pardon," "Comfortable Words," "Sursum Corda" and "Vere Dignum." They are followed by the Roman Catholic "Sanctus." The "Prayer of Consecration" and "Prayer of Humble Access" are both United Methodist.

The fourth movement, *Participation*, includes the Roman Catholic "Receiving and Presenting the Gifts," "The Lord's Prayer," and the "Agnus Dei." The "Distribution of the Elements" is United Methodist.

*Thanksgiving* is the final movement of the service. "The Prayer of Thanksgiving" is United Methodist. "The Blessing" and "Dismissal" are Roman Catholic. An organ postlude then allows worshipers to depart.

The idea dates back to my work as an assistant to a Roman Catholic chaplain several years ago. It came to be a part of my conscious thinking nearly two years ago when my article, "A Mother's Questions" was accepted and published in the Monfort Father's magazine, *Queen of All Hearts*.

When the summer of 1971 came at Union Chapel and the need to interest and inspire parishioners at an early service became imperative, I announced a series of forty-minute worship services called "Methodist Mass" would begin on July 4 and last through Labor Day weekend. It was extended on into October, and now is a regular first Sunday of the month experience in the contemporary worship service.

New possibilities are continually opening to relate to the basic movements and parts of the worship. For example, the youth choir sings various parts from time to time.

The response has been positive with many ministers and laymen alike inquiring to see what "Methodist Mass" is all about. Attendance has varied from sixteen to more than fifty. Some visitors have come to the service from far outside of the Indianapolis area to take their reactions back to their churches.

When a worshiper comes for the first time, he is usually surprised. The most consistent reaction among laymen is: "It's different and impressive" or words to that effect. From a more professional perspective I hope, with acceptance from the laity, that the Methodist Mass will eventually become a legitimate tool under the guidance of the Holy Spirit for "ecumenism" in the highest and best sense of the word especially among United Methodists and Roman Catholics.

---

*The Interpreter* January 1973

## THE ORGAN PRELUDE

## *I. Remembrance*

### SENTENCES

Behold, I stand at the door and knock, if any one hears my voice and opens the door, I will come in to him and eat with him, and he with me.

Beloved, let us love one another; for love is of God, and he who loves is born of God and knows God. In this the love of God was made manifest among us, that God sent his only Son into the world, so that we might live through him.

### GREETING

Pastor:   The grace and peace of God our Father and the Lord Jesus Christ be with you.

**People:   Blessed be God, the Father of our Lord Jesus Christ.**

### COLLECT FOR PURITY

**Pastor and People: Almighty God** unto whom all hearts are open, all desires known, and from whom no secrets are hid: cleanse the thoughts of our hearts by the inspiration of Thy Holy Spirit, that we may perfectly love Thee, and worthily magnify Thy holy name; through Christ our Lord. Amen.

### KYRIE

Pastor:   Lord, have mercy.

**People:   Lord, have mercy.**

Pastor:   Christ, have mercy.

**People:   Christ, have mercy.**

Pastor:   Lord, have mercy.

**People:   Lord, have mercy.**

### GLORIA

**Pastor and People: Glory to God** in the highest, and peace to his people on earth. Lord God, Heavenly King, almighty God and Father, we worship you, we give you thanks, we praise you for your glory. Lord Jesus Christ, only Son of the Father, Lord God, Lamb of God, you take away the sins of the world: have mercy on us; you are seated at the right hand of the Father: receive our prayer. For you alone are the Holy One, you alone are the Lord, you alone are the Most High, Jesus Christ, with the Holy Spirit, in the glory of God the Father.

## II. Proclamation

FIRST READING                                                                 Pastor

> Pastor:     This is the Word of the Lord.
> **People:    Thanks be to God.**

SECOND READING                                                                Pastor

> Pastor:     This is the Word of the Lord.
> **People:    Thanks be to God.**

HOMILY                                                                        Pastor


## III. Offertory

INVITATION

Pastor: Ye that do truly and earnestly repent of your sins, and are in love and charity with your neighbors, and intend to lead a new life, following the commandments of God, and walking from henceforth in his holy ways: draw near with faith, and take this holy Sacrament to your comfort, and make your humble confession to almighty God.

GENERAL CONFESSION

**Pastor and People: Almighty God**, Father of our Lord Jesus Christ, maker of all things, judge of all men:

We acknowledge and bewail our manifold sins and wickedness, which we from time to time most grievously have committed, by thought, word, and deed, against thy divine majesty. We do earnestly repent, and are heartily sorry for these our misdoings; the remembrance of them is grievous unto us. Have mercy upon us, most merciful Father. For Thy Son our Lord Jesus Christ's sake, forgive us all that is past; and grant that we may ever hereafter serve and please Thee in newness in life, to the honor and glory of Thy name; through Jesus Christ our Lord. Amen.

PRAYER FOR PARDON

Pastor: Almighty God, our heavenly Father, who of Thy great mercy hast promised forgiveness of sins to all them that with hearty repentance and true faith turn to Thee: Have mercy upon us; pardon and deliver us from all our sins; confirm and strengthen us in all goodness; and bring us to everlasting life; through Jesus Christ our Lord. Amen.

## COMFORTABLE WORDS

Pastor: God so loved the world that he gave his only Son, that whoever believes in him should not perish but have eternal life.

If we confess our sins, he is faithful and just, and will forgive our sins and cleanse us from all unrighteousness.

If any one sins, we have an advocate with the Father, Jesus Christ the righteous; and he is the expiation for our sins, and not for ours only but also for the sins of the whole world.

## SURSUM CORDA

Pastor: Lift up your hearts.

**People: We lift them up unto the Lord.**

Pastor Let us give thanks unto the Lord.

**People: It is meet and right so to do.**

## VERE DIGNUM

Pastor: It is very meet, right, and our bounden duty that we should at all times and in all places give thanks unto Thee, O Lord, holy Father, almighty everlasting God.

## SANCTUS

**Pastor and People:** Holy, holy, holy Lord, God of power and might, heaven and earth are full of Your glory. Hosanna in the highest. Blessed is he who comes in the name of the Lord. Hosanna in the highest.

## PRAYER OF CONSECRATION

Pastor: Almighty God, our heavenly Father, who of Thy tender mercy didst give Thine only Son Jesus Christ to suffer death upon the cross for our redemption; who made there, by the one offering of himself, a full, perfect, and sufficient sacrifice for the sins of the whole world, and did institute, and in his holy gospel command us to continue a perpetual memory of his precious death until his coming again: Hear us, O merciful Father, we most humbly beseech Thee, and grant that we, receiving these Thy creatures of bread and wine, according to They Son our Savior Jesus Christ's holy institution, in remembrance of his passion, death, and resurrection, may be partakers of the divine nature through him: who in the same night that he was betrayed, took bread and when he had given thanks, he broke it, and give it to his disciples saying, 'Take, eat; this is my body which is given for you; do this in remembrance of me.' Likewise after supper he took the cup; and when he had given thanks, he gave it to them, saying, 'Drink ye all of this; for this is my blood of the New Covenant, which is shed for you and for many, for the forgiveness of sins; do this, as oft as ye shall drink it, in remembrance of me.' Amen.

## PRAYER OF HUMBLE ACCESS

Pastor: We do not presume to come to this Thy table, O merciful Lord, trusting in our own righteousness, but in Thy manifold and great mercies. We are not worthy so much as to gather up the crumbs under Thy table. But Thou are the same Lord, whose property is always to have mercy. Grant us therefore, gracious Lord, so to partake of this Sacrament of Thy Son Jesus Christ, that we may walk in newness of life, may grow into his likeness, and may evermore dwell in Him, and He in us. Amen.

## *IV. Participation*

### RECEIVING AND PRESENTING THE GIFTS
### PASTOR AND PEOPLE

### LORD'S PRAYER

Pastor: Let us pray with confidence to the Father in the words our Savior gave us:

**Pastor and People: Our Father,** who art in heaven hallowed be Thy name, Thy kingdom come; Thy will be done on earth as it is in heaven. Give us this day our daily bread; and forgive us our trespasses as we forgive those who trespass against us; and lead us not into temptation, but deliver us from evil.

Pastor: Deliver us, Lord, from every evil, and grant us peace in our day. In your mercy keep us free from sin and protect us from all anxiety as we wait in joyful hope for the coming of our Savior, Jesus Christ.

**People: For the kingdom, the power, and the glory are Yours, now and forever.**

### AGNUS DEI

**Pastor and People: Lamb of God**, you take away the sins of the world: have mercy on us. Lamb of God, you take away the sins of the world: have mercy on us. Lamb of God, you take the sins of the world; grant us peace.

### DISTRIBUTION OF THE ELEMENTS

## *V. Thanksgiving*

PRAYER OF THANKSGIVING

**Pastor and People: O Lord,** our heavenly Father, we, Thy humble servants, desire Thy fatherly goodness mercifully to accept this our sacrifice of praise and thanksgiving; most humbly beseeching Thee to grant, that, by the merits and death of Thy Son Jesus Christ, and through faith in his blood, we and Thy whole Church may obtain forgiveness of our sins, and all other benefits of this passion. And here we offer and present unto Thee, O Lord, ourselves, our souls and bodies to be a reasonable, holy and lively sacrifice unto Thee; humbly beseeching Thee that all we who are partakers of this Holy Communion may be filled with Thy grace and heavenly benediction. And although we be unworthy, through our manifold sins, to offer unto Thee any sacrifice, yet we beseech Thee to accept this our bounden duty and service, not weighing our merits, but pardoning our offenses; Through Jesus Christ our Lord, by whom, and with whom, in the unity of the Holy Spirit, all honor and glory be unto Thee, O Father Almighty, world without end. Amen.

BLESSING

Pastor:     The Lord be with you.

**People:**     **And also with you.**

Pastor:     May almighty God bless you, the Father and the Son and the Holy Spirit.

**People:**     **Thanks be to God.**

THE ORGAN POSTLUDE

––––––––

# ❋TAMING DEMONS: A LITANY OF HEALING❋

THE MINISTER BEGINS by reading the Scripture and offering the Invitation.

*There are six things which the Lord hates, seven which are an abomination to him: haughty eyes, a lying tongue, and hands that shed innocent blood, a heart that devises wicked plans, feet that make haste to run to evil, a false witness who breathes out lies, and a man who sows discord among brothers—Proverbs 6:16–19 RSV.*

A gracious invitation is given to you to join me with a prayer on your lips and a mind wide open to the spiritual life. Seven demons are loose in each of us. They play no favorites. They gleefully upset us and place us in anguish that oftentimes is difficult to describe. How shall you and I tame them? We are called to pray and think seriously together.

## *1. Praying Together:*

Haughty eyes are an abomination in Your sight, O God. Bring to our attention the times we are arrogant. Cause us to be sensitive to the reaction our disdain produces in others. Forgive us for feeling superior to other brothers and sisters about us. Teach us again that all human beings are equally precious in Your sight. Keep us humble to the essential duty of being examples of the Christian Faith before others. Hear our insolent ways, O Father, and cause genuine respect to filter into our attitudes. In the name of Jesus Christ our Lord and Savior. Amen.

REFLECTING IN SILENCE:

In our quest for deliverance let us ask some basic questions. Am I willing to be *one* of the children of God? Should I go to a certain person with whom I recently was overbearing and ask for forgiveness? Was my Lord and Savior ever scornful of anyone? Will I be ready for the opportunities of tomorrow which will provide a chance to be a better person? What ability do I have which I would like for others to notice and appreciate? Who do I know that I can help out of the rut of a haughty attitude? Am I really ready to face up to the consequences of any action I may take?

Pastor: Let us invoke the Holy Spirit:
**Pastor and People: Come Holy Spirit** of God with Your healing powers.

## *2. Praying Together:*

A lying tongue is an abomination in Your sight, O God. Forgive our little deceits and our blatant lies. Forgive, too, those countless times we have been hurtfully deceptive. We acknowledge our frailty and state of being human, but may we never use this as an excuse. We are sorry for those times, O Lord God, too many times when we allowed our tongues to wag until the truth was no longer in them. Call upon us again this day for truthful answers and we shall be faithful. May our falsehoods of the future be at a minimum as we walk with the Holy Spirit as Guide. In the name of Jesus Christ, our Lord and Savior. Amen.

REFLECTING IN SILENCE:
  In our search for improvement let us ask some deeply personal questions. How often do I call dishonesty by another more approved and less harsh name? Do I always feel it is wrong when I am lying? Do I fall into the routine of revealing facts in such a way as to "aid and abet" gossiping? Is the unspoken truth a better solution where certain critical human relationships are involved? Am I willing to be abused and maligned for standing by what I feel to be the highest and best? Am I willing to be accountable for lying not only to others but to myself as well? Will I go where the truth leads me?

  Pastor: Let us invoke the Holy Spirit:
  **Pastor and People: Come Holy Spirit** of God with Your healing powers.

## 3. Praying Together:
  Hands that shed innocent blood are an abomination in Your sight, O God. Wars are all about us, and we are bewildered. Give us the perspectives which enable us to see what is and is not innocent blood we implore You, great God of the Universe. We ask for forgiveness for those executioners who have killed many human beings with no justifications, except that they were just in the way. Sometimes those of us who profess the Christian Faith are shocked by the innocent blood on our hands. We wish it were not there. We ask that you wash our hands that they may be as pure as undriven snow on our vast farmlands in winter. In the name of Jesus Christ, our Lord and Savior. Amen.

REFLECTING IN SILENCE:
  As we probe for healing let us ask some pointed questions. Is it my concern that innocent blood is being shed here and abroad? How important are other persons that I do not need to help me be a respectable person in the community? Would I be willing to stick my neck out for someone I don't know and have never seen? How much bloodletting in a figurative sense is being done in my own community? How do I go about applying the scriptural injunction to be "my brother's keeper?" Would I willingly shed some of my own blood for the cause of Christ?

Pastor: Let us invoke the Holy Spirit:
**Pastor and People: Come Holy Spirit** of God with Your healing powers.

## 4. Praying Together:

A heart that devises wicked plans is an abomination in Your sight, O God. We do plot against others. We do so in hopes they will fall into evil times and ways. O Redeemer of Mankind, we are sorry and humbly offer our repentance. Sometimes it is jealousy, sometimes it is pure selfishness, and sometimes other causes are glaringly evident. We are not in any way proud of our hearts that do have those terrifying places in them calling for the downfall of someone. The hardness of our hearts surprises even us. Hear our ardent prayers, O Giver of Mercy. In the name of Jesus Christ, our Lord and Savior. Amen.

REFLECTING IN SILENCE:

In our yearning to be someone better let us ask some probing questions. Will I admit to my God what I really feel in my heart which shows itself to be in critical need of major repairs? How many other names do I give to my plans which are geared directly or indirectly to destroy or hurt a brother/sister on the same pilgrimage? Do I "contrive" and call it "constructive" when I know better? Is "wicked" a word that carries no important meaning for me? Would I be willing to take as much time revising my life as devising schemes to try to win the race for fame and fortune?

Pastor: Let us invoke the Holy Spirit:
**Pastor and People: Come Holy Spirit** of God with Your healing powers.

## 5. Praying Together:

Feet that make haste to run to evil are an abomination in Your sight, O God. Why is it we make great efforts "to go to or be controlled by" those things or people who can injure us? Heavenly Father, this is so difficult for us to understand. We know we are going in wrong directions, and yet we speedily move on our ways. We see others pursuing a course that can eventually only lead to crippling someone. Grant Your rays of Therapy to shine upon us and make us whole in both body and soul. Right now some are caught in the web of contradictory ideas and emotions. Help us, O Creator, to move in right pathways that lead to right destinations. In the name of Jesus Christ, our Lord and Savior. Amen.

REFLECTING IN SILENCE:

As we cry out for understanding let us ask some highly significant questions. Why don't I exercise my free will in rejecting those chances to sin? Am I willing to admit to both God and myself at what point I most frequently succumb to evil? Why do I sometimes confuse even myself by calling into question some elementary moral principles men and women have held sacred for as far back as humankind can remember? Since I have the powers to run a spiritual race, why don't I set my eyes at this very instant on an eternal crown?

Pastor: Let us invoke the Holy Spirit:
**Pastor and People: Come Holy Spirit** of God with Your healing powers.

## 6. Praying Together:

A false witness who breathes out lies is an abomination in Your sight, O God. We are made to remember the ninth commandment given to Your servant, Moses. We bow before the hard fact that in human relations this is a common problem. Lift us above this quagmire which leaves us sinking in body and spirit, O God of Love. Sensitize us to the rigid requirements of adult Christian behavior. Forgive us for the shades of falsehoods we have presented in a deliberate attempt to cause others discomfort and harm. We shun away for the term "bearing witness," but we realize all too well its connotation. We earnestly pray it will not need to be applied to us ever again in the days ahead. In the name of Jesus Christ, our Lord and Savior. Amen.

REFLECTING IN SILENCE:

As we take a solemn look at ourselves with hope and trust let us ask some revealing questions. Under what guises do I sometimes bear false witness? Do I intentionally lead others down this thorny but inviting road? If I am presently guilty, am I willing to stop right now? Should I go about trying to correct bad relationships among persons for which I am partly responsible? How can I know my own motives better?

Pastor: Let us invoke the Holy Spirit:
**Pastor and People: Come Holy Spirit** of God with Your healing powers.

## 7. Praying Together:

A man who sows discord among brothers is an abomination in Your sight, O God. There are enough barriers to good human relations in our world without planting seeds of strife. There is enough "brother against brother" in our world without scattering wild and even devastating seeds of dissensions. O Father of all brothers and sisters help us to see once and for all what we are really doing at home and abroad. We are guilty and do earnestly seek our restoration to the Great Shepherd's fold. Grant us the spirit of forgiveness one towards the other. Then prod us to be faithful. In the name of Jesus Christ, our Lord and Savior. Amen.

### REFLECTING IN SILENCE:

In our pain of giving birth to the holy and healing attitudes let us ask some crucial questions. Do I relish the disruptive rivalry I create among persons who have little or no control over me? Why do I enjoy watching some people suffer both in private and public contentions? What do I lack which makes me fall short of wanting others to be free of turmoil? Am I able to distinguish between spiritual unity and religious conformity? Why do I wish the downfall of some members of Christ's Church? Will I do any better in thought and deed after reading this? Why haven't I called upon God sooner?

Pastor: Let us invoke the Holy Spirit:

**Pastor and People: Come Holy Spirit** of God with Your healing powers.

## 5. The Minister Offers the Conclusion:

With firmness this series of verses from Proverbs reteaches lessons of practical wisdom with indisputable worth. Each of the seven demons is real—at times shockingly real—as we experience human existence in its unlimited forms. Each demon is to be met with a sincere and honest prayer in our hearts and an ongoing inquiry into every facet of our beings, leading to times of joy and healing.

**Everyone Praying Together: We love You** Father, we love Your Son, and we love Your Holy Spirit. Amen.

———

*Sharing* February 1989

# ✿DAILY FOOD FOR THE JOURNEY✿
## PASTOR'S MORNING WORSHIP

IN THE NAME *of the Father, the Son, and the Holy Spirit Lord Jesus, I begin this day in need of Your love, forgiveness, and mercy. (3 times)*

Holy Spirit of God continue Your work in, through, for, and with me. Remind me of the "cloud of witnesses" that provide inspiration for today's journey. Teach me what is needed for the day. Empower me, like Jesus, to do the will of the Father. Sustain me through the joys, sorrows, victories, defeats, and indifferences of the day.

## *Brief Reading(s) from Holy Scripture*
### *Creed (Apostles or Nicene)*

Lord Jesus, forgive me for my sins of omission and commission. Now I earnestly offer my prayers to You . . .

Lord Jesus, the Gospel of John gives us Your *indispensable Word*: "I am telling you the truth: if you do not eat the flesh of the Son of Man and drink his blood, you will not have life in yourselves." You also say in the Gospel of John: "Whoever eats my flesh and drinks my blood lives in me and I live in him." This blessed mystery of today and eternity is with us.

Lord Jesus, as Your disciple, I pray that these elements of which I am about to partake shall embody *by the power of the Holy Spirit* Your "real presence."

Lord Jesus, I receive Your body for my congregation.
Lord Jesus, I receive Your body for myself.
I do this in remembrance of You.
Lord Jesus, I receive Your blood for my congregation.
Lord Jesus, I receive Your blood for myself.
I do this in remembrance of You.

Thank You, Lord Jesus. (3 times)

I lovingly and steadfastly believe my body is Your body and Your body is my body.

### *DAILY FOOD FOR THE JOURNEY*
#### *— Pastor's Morning Worship —*

I lovingly and steadfastly believe my blood is Your blood and Your blood is my blood.

Lord Jesus, May holiness abound!

Praises be to You, Oh God, Your Son's
body and blood have nourished my congregation.
Praises be to You, Oh God, Your Son's
body and blood have nourished me.

The Lord's Prayer

Lord Jesus, let come what will; *in the power of the Holy Spirit* I shall renounce the Evil One and proclaim Your Name by thought, word, and deed.

And now with thanksgiving may the fruit of the Holy Spirit—love, joy, peace, patience, kindness, goodness, faithfulness, humility, and self-control—be in evidence as I seek to fulfill my calling this day.

In the Name of the Father, the Son, and the Holy Spirit. Amen.

> When morning gilds the skies,
> My heart awaking cries,
> May Jesus Christ be praised!
> Remind me each morning of your
> constant love, for I put my trust
> in you. My prayers go up to
> you; show me the way I should go.

*Evangel Press* 1998

# ❊NOURISHMENT FOR THE DAY: MORNING❊ WORSHIP FOR LAITY

IN THE NAME *of the Father, the Son, and the Holy Spirit*
*Jesus, You are my Savior and Lord. (3 times)*

Holy Spirit of God continue Your work in, through, for, and with me. Please forgive me for those good thoughts, words, and deeds that I fail to bring about; I am insensitive to Your pleas. Please forgive me the wrongs I knowingly inflict on others. My life truly longs for spiritual growth; I yield myself this day to those wonderful possibilities for holy living. May my life be immersed in Your healing and reconciling powers.

Reading(s) from the Psalms
Creed (Apostles or Nicene)

Lord Jesus, I sincerely and humbly offer my prayers to you . . .

Lord Jesus, You continually speak to me in Your *Holy Word* about Discipleship:

In the Gospel of Matthew You say: "Go in through the narrow gate, because the gate to hell is wide and the road that leads to it is easy, and there are many who travel it."

In the Gospel of Mark You say: "Does a person gain anything if he wins the whole world but loses his life? Of course not!"

In the Gospel of Luke You say: "Do not judge others, and God will not judge you; do not condemn others, and God will not condemn you; forgive others, and God will forgive you."

In the Gospel of John You say: "If you obey my teaching, you are really my disciples; you will know the truth, and the truth will set you free."

In the Acts of the Apostles You say: "But when the Holy Spirit comes upon you, you will be filled with power, and you will be witnesses for me in Jerusalem, in all of Judea and Samaria, and to the ends of the earth."

Lord Jesus, in the inspired writing of Your servant, Paul, he says: "Offer yourselves as a living sacrifice to God, dedicated to his service and pleasing to him. This is the true worship that you should offer."

## *NOURISHMENT FOR THE DAY*
### *— Morning Worship For Laity —*

Lord Jesus, in the inspired writing of Your servant, Peter, he says: "Humble yourselves, then, under God's mighty hand, so that he will lift you up in his own good time."

I lovingly and steadfastly believe Your *Holy Word*.
I lovingly and steadfastly seek *by the power of the Holy Spirit*
to live Your *Holy Word*.

Praises be to You, oh God, for another day to *serve* and *share* your Son, Jesus, my Savior and Lord (3 times).

Lord Jesus, a precious new day is at hand; *in the power of the Holy Spirit* I shall renounce the Evil One and proclaim Your Name by thought, word, and deed.

Come, Holy Spirit, fill my life this day with Your Fruit: love, joy, peace, patience, kindness, goodness, faithfulness, humility, and self-control. With thanksgiving I totally surrender myself to You!

In the name of the Father, the Son, and the Holy Spirit. Amen.

Holy, holy, holy!
Lord God Almighty!
Early in the morning
Our song shall rise to thee.

The Lord's unfailing love and mercy
still continue, fresh as the morning,
as sure as the sunrise.
The Lord is all I have, and so in Him I put my Hope.

————

*Evangel Press* 1989

# ❋COME, HOLY SPIRIT❋

## *Service of Worship*
"PROCLAIMING AND Celebrating the Power of the
Holy Spirit in Our Day and Time"
O Holy Spirit of God, take me as your disciple.
Guide me, illuminate me, sanctify me.

## The Introduction

PRELUDE

*CALL TO WORSHIP

> Enter into God's special presence with praise. Come and bow down to the Holy One who made heaven and earth. Praises be to the God who comes to us as Father, Son, and Holy Spirit. Holy Spirit of God by wind and fire, open us to Your healing power and lead us to be receptive.

*ADMISSION OF SIN AND NEED OF FORGIVENESS

> God of mercy and compassion, our sins are before us. We have committed wrongful acts and we have omitted rightful deeds. Our entire beings cry out for forgiveness. Come, Holy Spirit of God.

*HYMN OF ADORATION

> "Oh for a Thousand Tongues to Sing"
> "We Gather Together"
> "Now Thank We All Our God"
> "How Great Thou Art"
> "Praise to the Lord, The Almighty"
> "Holy, Holy, Holy! Lord God Almighty"
> "Love Divine, All Loves Excelling"

## The Liturgy of the Word

OPENING PRAYER (UNISON)

> **Holy Spirit of God, You are our powerful comforter and guide. Our weaknesses and failure to experience the fruit promised to us are an ever-present cause of sorrow. Our hopes of today and tomorrow are built upon Your continual working in us, for us, through us, with us, and among us. Saturate us with your healing and bring to our remembrance the ministry of Jesus and the Apostles. Amen.**

FIRST LESSON

> Readings from the Old Testament, Acts, or Revelation

ACT OF PRAISE

> Selections from the Psalms or other suitable passages of Holy Scripture

SECOND LESSON

> Readings from the Epistles of the New Testament

*GLORIA PATRI OR ALLELUIA

*GOSPEL

HOMILY

REFLECTION

Your Word, O God, is eternal. Holy Spirit of God, fashion us after Jesus Christ and the Apostles.

CREED

**We believe in one God, Creator of all that was, is, and shall be. We believe the one God manifests Himself to the creation, especially humankind, as Father, Son, and Holy Spirit.**

**We believe in Jesus, the only eternal Son of God who was with the Father from the beginning. He was conceived by the power of the Holy Spirit and born of the Blessed Virgin Mary. He lived among us and ministered to us primarily in a threefold ministry of preaching, teaching, and healing. Through the gift of His birth, life, crucifixion, resurrection, and ascension we accept Him as our Savior and Lord. He will come again to judge the living and the dead. His kingdom is everlasting.**

**We believe in the Holy Spirit, the giver of life who guides, comforts, empowers, and sustains. In unity with the Father and the Son He is worshiped and glorified. We yield ourselves daily to the Holy Spirit's leading to holiness for the victorious living of these days.**

**We believe in one holy catholic and apostolic Church, ever moving towards visible unity so that the world might believe. We believe in life after death, judgment, and eternal abode for all faithful disciples of Jesus Christ in communion with Him and the saints of all ages. Amen.**

HYMN OF PREPARATION

"Breathe on Me, Breath of God"
"Come, Holy Spirit, Heavenly Dove"
"O Spirit of the Living God"
"Spirit of God, Descend Upon My Heart"
"Come Down, O Love Divine"
"Holy Spirit, Ever Dwelling"
"Come, Holy Ghost, Our Souls Inspire"

## *The Liturgy of the Sacrament*

PRAYERS OF PEOPLE AND PASTOR

Let the people humbly with sincerity intercede for their brothers/sisters and petition their God as the Holy Spirit gives guidance. Let the pastor, as the shepherd of the sheep, pray for the state of the universal Church and other matters as the Holy Spirit gives guidance.

## THE LORD'S PRAYER

Pastor: Let us pray confidently to the Father as our Savior and Lord taught us.

**Pastor and People: Our Father** who dwells in heaven, with great reverence we proclaim Your name. Your kingdom come, Your will be done on earth as it is in heaven. Give us today everything we need. Forgive our sins as we forgive those who sin against us. Lead us away from temptation and keep us safe from evil.

Pastor: Grant us deliverance, dear Lord, from all evil and grant us peace for our time. With the healing strength of the Holy Spirit grant Your protective love.

**People: For the kingdom, the power, and the glory are always Yours. Amen.**

## PASSING OF THE PEACE

Pastor: Lord Jesus, You promised and gave to the apostles Your peace that the world cannot take away.

**People: Praise God!**

Pastor: May the peace of the Lord be with you.

**People: And also with you.**

Pastor: May the sign of peace be offered among us.

## PREPARATION OF ALTAR AND RECEIVING OF GIFTS

Let the elements be brought to the altar and/or let them be prepared for distribution. Let offerings for the ministry of the Church and the upbuilding of the Name of Jesus Christ be received.

## *PRAYER OF CONFESSION (UNISON)

**Almighty God, loving and just, we seek Your forgiveness. We acknowledge and are deeply sorry for our sins. Our thoughts, words, and actions are a cause of great pain and sorrow. We have done those things we should not have done and we have refused to do those things we know we should have done. We have erred and strayed from Your revelation to us. We humbly confess our failures, especially the resisting of the Holy Spirit.**

**Please forgive us, restore us to newness of life, and lead us to that holiness intended for us.**

**In the blessed and holy Name of Jesus Christ. Amen.**

\*PRAYER FOR PARDON AND FORGIVENESS

    Lord Jesus, pardon Your people of their sins and forgive us our wayward ways. In the power of the Holy Spirit heal us for the sake of Christ and His Church. **Amen**.

\*GREAT THANKSGIVING

    Pastor: The Lord be with you.

    **People: And also with you.**

    Pastor: Lift us your hearts.

    **People: We lift them to the Lord.**

    Pastor: Let us give thanks to the Lord our God.

    **People: It is right to give Him thanks and praise.**

    Pastor: Praise be to You, our God, Your creation and providence are manifest. You created us only a little lower than the angels and in Your image. We have all sinned and remain less than what we are intended to be. Yet, You loved us so much that You gave Jesus, your Son, to be our Savior. By the mouths of the prophets we were told of His coming from the lineage of Abraham, Isaac, and Jacob. By the power of the Holy Spirit He was conceived and born of the Blessed Virgin Mary. His threefold ministry of teaching, preaching, and healing has provided hope for an otherwise degenerate world. We give thanks this ministry through the Holy Spirit was extended to the apostles and continues among us. In His suffering on the Cross, triumphant Resurrection, and memorable Ascension we call forth our own place in salvation history. Therefore, with Your people of every age, the Church militant and triumphant, and all of creation we jubilantly join together in praises that know no boundaries:

    **People: Holy, holy, holy Lord, God, of power and might, heaven and earth are full of Your glory. Hosanna in the highest. Blessed is He who comes in the Name of the Lord. Hosanna in the highest.**

    Pastor: In the Name of the Father, Son, and Holy Spirit we gratefully receive what has been ratified both on earth and in heaven. On the night He offered Himself up for us He took bread and gave thanks to His Father. Then He broke the bread and gave it to His disciples saying, "Take and eat; this is My Body which is given for you. This is done to remember Me."

    When the supper was over He took the cup, shared it with His disciples, and gave thanks saying, "Everyone of you drink from it for this is My Blood shed for you and humankind for the forgive-ness of sins. This likewise is done to remember Me."

After the institution of the Holy Communion, our Savior and Lord was arrested, abandoned by His followers, beaten and humili-ated. He was obedient to death on the Cross and arose as He said He would as a full and perfect sacrifice for our sins.

Our Father, as we remember all Your mighty acts in Your son, we accept in thanksgiving and celebrate with joy this gift above all others.

We offer ourselves as a living sacrifice, holy and acceptable to You, that we may proclaim to the world, as well as our brothers and sisters in Christ, the magnificence and mystery of the Faith.

Holy Father, send the power of Your Holy Spirit on us and these gifts of bread and wine that they may become the body and blood of our Savior and Lord. We are reminded, "Whoever eats my flesh and drinks my blood lives in me, and I live in him." Holy Spirit make the living Christ truly present among us that we may be one body united by one spirit. Guide us to serve Him in a lost and unregenerate world, faithfully allowing this worship to point to final victory.

And now Holy Spirit, in unity with the Son, we glorify Your pres-ence and praise the Father as You work in us, through us, for us, with us, and among us, now and forevermore. **Amen.**

HOLY COMMUNION

Pastor: The blessed and holy Body of Jesus Christ.

**People: The body of our Savior and Lord.**

Pastor: The blessed and holy Blood of Jesus Christ.

**People: The blood of our Savior and Lord.**

PRAYER AFTER COMMUNION (UNISON)

**Thank You Father, through the merits of Your Son we have been refreshed by the receiving of His precious Body and Blood. In Your everlasting mercy You have fed us and given us drink. In love, joy, and peace we celebrate the work of the Holy Spirit; in the Name of Jesus Christ. Amen.**

*HYMN OF DEDICATION

"Amazing Grace"

"I Love to Tell the Story"

"O Master, Let Me Walk with You"

"Jesus Calls Us; O'er the Tumult"

"He Leadeth Me; Oh, Blessed Thought"

"Take My Life, That I May Be"
"Shackled by a Heavy Burden"

## The Conclusion

*APOSTOLIC BENEDICTION

> Now may the peace and promise of God the Father, the Son, and the Holy Spirit be among you and abide with you always; may you look to the Holy Spirit as your guide in anticipation of service to a needy Church and sinful world; and may that Spirit through testing and trials bring you safely to heaven's gates. **Amen**.

*CONGREGATIONAL RESPONSE

> **Thanks be to God for the Son, our Savior and Lord, and for the Holy Spirit among us.**

*DISMISSAL

> Pastor: Our worship together is ended.
> **People: Thanks be to God.**
> Pastor: By the power of the Holy Spirit we look forward to worshiping again.
> **People: Amen.**

POSTLUDE

———

*Evangel Press,* 1989

# ❋LAKESIDE DEVOTIONS❋

## Invitation

JESUS WALKED along the shore and saw two brothers who were fishermen, Simon Peter and Andrew. Jesus invited them to follow Him so they could catch men. They left their nets and followed. Jesus went on and saw two other brothers, James and John; He also invited them to follow Him and they did.

Lord Jesus, You have invited me to follow You. I accept Your invitation. I accept the responsibility of telling others of Your gracious love. No greater invitation can be given and I thank You from the bottom of my heart. You are My Savior and Lord.

# LAKESIDE DEVOTIONS

## *Abundance*

Jesus got out of the boat and saw a large crowd. His heart was filled with pity and He healed their sick. That evening His disciples urged Him to send them away to buy food. Jesus refused; then He took five loaves and two fish from His disciples and gave thanks to God. Everyone ate enough and there were leftovers.

Lord Jesus, how often we are spiritually starving people! You are able to supply our every need and to do so abundantly. Thank You. May each of us seek always to be given food and drink from Your storehouse that is never empty. Only You can really satisfy us.

## *Security*

His disciples got into a boat and started across the lake but midway they were caught in a storm. Jesus was on land praying. He saw their plight and walked on the water out to them. They were terrified but He calmed them and the wind. They were greatly amazed.

Lord Jesus, our weaknesses and fears are painfully obvious. We can never be secure within ourselves and with others, unless You enter our beings. Storms in our lives are always manageable as You calm them and enable us to be victorious. Grant that the world at large might humbly receive the only real security there is.

## *Teaching*

Jesus went to the lakeside, where He sat down to teach. The crowd gathered around Him was so large He had to get into a boat, while they stood on the shore. He taught them by parable. He concluded by telling them if they had ears, then to listen!

Lord Jesus, Your teaching thrills us and prods us to heights of living that truly inspire. We are aware that many know of Your teaching and study it. Our continual prayer is that having heard it, they seek wholeheartedly to live by it. We kneel before You for further instruction.

## *Opportunity*

Simon Peter and other disciples of Jesus went out in a boat. They fished all night but caught nothing. At sunrise Jesus stood at the water's edge and told them to throw their net on the right side of the boat. They did and caught many big fish.

Lord Jesus, when You are at our side, we can sense the opportunities for growth and service. It is as we try to "go it alone" that we get into difficulty and accomplish nothing worthwhile. Grant that our every thought, word, and deed will reflect harmony with You and Your ways. Then, we shall surely be a success!

---

*Evangel Press* 1990

CHAPTER 16

# Book Reviews

## ✽"BIBLICAL PREACHING" BY✽ HADDON W. ROBINSON

HADDON W. ROBINSON has written a very readable book for preachers and seminarians. He shares the knowledge gleaned over the years from his own studies both in and out of the classroom. While his apparent purpose is to write a textbook for evangelicals on preaching, he has done more than that. He has given us a balanced approach not only homiletically but also theologically. However, he does make a compelling case for the expository style of Biblical preaching.

This book will teach excellent principles to those aspiring to the pulpit and will serve as a delightful old/new course in Biblical preaching for the veteran preacher. Dr. Robinson is careful to be specific without being simplistic; he is skilled at presenting fundamentals without being negative and arrogant. His style is continually inviting and generally remains free from awkwardness in phrasing and hackneyed expressions.

The book is a natural for every seminary library and pastor's study. For those who practice the fine art of preaching, the book's usefulness promises to be evident for a long, long time.

———

*Biblical Preaching by Haddon W. Robinson. Baker Book House, Grand Rapids, Michigan, 1980. $9.95, hardcover, 230 pages. Reviewed by Donald Charles Lacy, UM Pastor/Author, Indianapolis, Indiana.*
*Good News January/February, 1983*


## ✽"TALES OF CHRISTIAN UNITY" BY✽ THOMAS RYAN

FOR ANY PERSON interested in Christian unity this work is both exciting and profound. Father Ryan is a deeply committed ecumenist who is at the Centre for Ecumenism in Montreal.

It tells of a year's journey in Europe and the Middle East. It is divided into three major sections: An Oriental Tale; A Geneva Tale; and A Canterbury Tale. Each is well-written and a personal dimension persists which adds to the flavor of the book.

Father Ryan especially writes for parishioners and busy pastors. It is his conviction: "There is a great gap between what goes on among the theologians who are representing our churches in the official dialogues for unity, and what is communicated to and understood by the majority of people who make up no matter what parish." If such persons will read carefully this work, such a gap should become a delightful challenge and not an ominous chasm.

The only weakness is its failure to move into tales of Lutherans, Methodists, and Baptists; the author is well aware of this and hopes for another time of travel that will add to his tales.

It is highly recommended for those laity and pastors who want to learn about a faith that spreads before us an enormous smorgasbord. Roman Catholic laity in particular with find this book very rewarding.

———

*Tales of Christian Unity.* Thomas Ryan. Paulist, 1983. 281 p. $9.95 pb.
*Church and Synagogue Libraries* July/August 1985

# ✸"STUDIES AND COMMENTARIES: 1984"✸ (SOCIETY OF MARY)

THIS PAMPHLET collecting various articles on the Blessed Virgin Mary and produced by the (Anglican-oriented) American Region of the Society of Mary is characterized by theological profundity, intellectual integrity and ecumenical sensitivity. Consider some of the contributions:

"The Annunciation" by Geoffrey Rowell was originally delivered as a sermon in New College Chapel, Oxford, and was inspired by a great painting by Fra Angelico. The author's recurring emphasis is on Mary's willing response and receptivity. With an apt and winsome terseness he proclaims, "Devotion to Mary as Mother of our Lord and Savior is never a turning aside from Christ, but our acknowledgment and recognition of

God's first choosing of her, and of her embodiment of humanity's responsive reaching out to God's saving grace."

Harry Reynolds Smythe begins his contribution with this straightforward statement: "The Blessed Virgin Mary is understood and reverenced . . . in Anglican tradition in relation to her son Jesus Christ our Lord." He finds a balanced position between those Protestants who kneel before *sola Scriptura* and excesses of popular devotion found among some Roman Catholics. He views "Theotokos" as the most relevant title for Mary, and is very helpful to those who tend to dismiss her because of the paucity of references in Scripture. Smythe is a brilliant ecumenical bridge builder.

Louis Weil, a professor at Nashotah House in Wisconsin, brings us valuable insights into the Virgin Mary as related to the Collects of the *Book of Common Prayer*. He focuses on specific Collects with Marian emphasis and reminds us that they are a "significant theological source for our understanding of the role of the Blessed Virgin in Christian piety."

The concluding work is a sermon preached by Arthur MacDonald Allchin, Canon of the Metropolitical Cathedral Church of the Christ in Canterbury, on the occasion of the Society's official Oxford Movement celebration. We are alerted to the truth that the devotion to Mary growing out of the Oxford Movement was not "some optional extra, some devotional extravagance," not a mere afterthought.

The significance of this pamphlet far outweighs its size. From beginning to end it is an instrument of ecumenical reconciliation. If one is seriously interested in the place of the Blessed Mother in the Faith, as am I, a Methodist minister, then it becomes virtually "must" reading.

------

*Studies and Commentaries: 1984. By Various Authors.* The Society of Mary (c/o Wallace H. Spaulding, 1206 Buchanan St., McLean, Va. 22101). 44 pages. $3.
*New Oxford Review* April 1986

# ✱ "UNITY OF THE CHURCHES: AN ACTUAL POSSIBILITY" ✱ BY HEINRICH FRIES AND KARL RAHNER

THIS BOOK IS a gift of magnificence to ecumenism and the Church Universal. It contains nine theses "directed toward and assisting in the uniting of the churches." Each thesis is carefully developed with brilliant theological and ecumenical scholarship. Heinrich Fries has written five of the commentaries and Karl Rahner four. However, both assume responsibility for all of them, which is an ecumenical happening itself with major import!

Both men are noted and universally-acclaimed ecumenists. They are exact and thorough without giving the impression their work is definitive.

It is a book that is not only informative but provocative, especially among those serious-minded clergy and laity that give a priority to Christian unity. It is a "must" addition to any library that seeks to offer up-to-date thinking in ecumenical theology. Few will read it with rapidity and quick digestion. Most will want to read and ponder, perhaps over a significant period of time. It would be a noteworthy addition to the personal libraries of ecumenically-oriented professors, executives, pastors, priests, and rabbis.

Perhaps the greatest compliment that can be paid to the authors is that they offer a skeletal framework for the unity of the churches that translates into "an actual possibility."

———

*Unity of the Churches: An Actual Possibility.* Heinrich Fries and Karl Rahner. Paulist/Fortress, 1985. 146 p. $6.95 pb.
*Church and Synagogue Libraries* November/December, 1986

# ❋"HOW TO UNDERSTAND THE CREED" BY❋ JEAN-NOEL BEZANCON AND OTHERS

THIS VOLUME IS a sensitive, scholarly approach to what is popularly known as the "Nicene Creed." More accurately, the authors are careful to point out the full story of its development and indicate its final form was ratified at Chalcedon in 451 and became the most universally used creed.

All aspects of the creed are discussed in a spirit of ecumenicity. Many imperative definitions and pertinent quotations are given along the way. While the authors are Roman Catholic, they are generous to include materials that should interest and affirm the entire Church. For example, early in the work a "Confession of faith of the Reformed Church of France based on Martin Luther" is given a full page.

The information presented should have special appeal to adult classes in religion among Roman Catholics. It is much in the spirit of Vatican II. Roman Catholic clergy, religious, and laity will especially find the content valuable. However, Protestant clergy would also be enriched greatly not only from reading it but studying it. As resource material, all congregational libraries will find it valuable.

The Catholic richness and respect for the Hebrew Scriptures that the authors have instilled into the volume may make for slow reading among those not theologically trained. One cannot read this like a favorite newspaper and/or magazine. Be assured the extra time, energy, and concentration are well worth it for any serious-minded Christian.

---

*How to Understand the Creed.* Jean-Noel Bezancon and others.
Crossroad, 1988. 150 p. $11.95.
*Church and Synagogue Libraries* November/December,1988

# ✤ "ONE BREAD AND CUP: SOURCE OF ✤ COMMUNION" BY ERNEST FALARDEAU

THE KEYNOTE OF Father Falardeau's book is clearly stated: "As the source and center of the Christian life, the Eucharist is of special interest for those who study and live the life of Christ." He discusses the Eucharist ecumenically and provides continual reference to pertinent Vatican II documents. In addition to that he brings into his discourse not only the views of other Christians but does so in a positive and helpful way.

A brilliant scholar, the author holds a Doctorate in Sacred Theology from Gregorian University and a Masters degree in Library Science from (Case) Western Reserve University. He is a nationally known ecumenist and a member of the Congregation of the Blessed Sacrament.

The book is carefully and distinctly organized under seven chapter headings. It also presents helpful material in the preface, introduction, conclusion, and bibliographic references.

The work is especially informative for those who appreciate and understand the great significance of the Eucharist as it pertains to Christian unity. All persons, regardless of denominational affiliation, would discover benefit from reading it because it is on the "cutting edge" of ecumenical spirituality. It tends to be more pastoral than academic. Since this continues to be an ecumenical age and the meaning of the Eucharist is an increasingly serious topic of discussion across the Church(s), virtually all libraries should benefit from having copies.

————

*One Bread and Cup: Source of Communion* Ernest Falardeau.
Michael Glazier, 1987. $6.95 pb. 134
*Church and Synagogue Libraries* January/February, 1989

# ✻"EVANGELICAL CATHOLICS"✻ BY KEITH A. FOURNIER

## *Introduction*

THE BOOK'S GENIUS is in the fact it seeks to bring together in a meaningful synthesis various understandings and labels found in the Christian Faith. It succeeds in a marvelous way and offers pastors, in particular, a new way of experiencing the current ecumenical scene. The style is down-to-earth and quickly becomes interesting and helpful at the same time. The pages exude energy and strength in the drive towards a unity for which Christ prayed near the time of the Crucifixion.

The author is both an attorney and a college teacher. As the Dean of Evangelism and the legal counsel at the Franciscan University of Ohio he has been in a unique position to observe and participate in some of the great movements influencing and shaping the Universal Church. He was a part of the renewal movement at the University, which has sent waves of concern and reform throughout the Roman Catholic Church. His approach is very personal and invites readers into a realm free from the divisions that have plagued the Universal Church from the beginning. He does a great service for religious leaders, lay and clergy, by weaving together strands that have often been in opposition; this is especially true for those on the "Firing Line," namely pastors and priests in parishes.

## Capsule

There are four major parts with a total of thirteen chapters. There are also many designated subdivisions that make for easy and quick reading. The overall outline is clear and distinct, providing the practicality of reading the book at several settings.

The first major part is simply called "Evangelical Moments." The author understands himself as an "evangelical Catholic Christian." Some experience those three claims as either contradictory or standing together in certain limited configurations. His contention and experience is that not only can he be all three, but they are necessary to define his relationship with Jesus Christ and His Church. This is true as well with his role in the church's ongoing mission to bring all men and women to salvation in Jesus Christ. The evangelical wave is sweeping across Christian churches of all traditions. He makes a case for "evangelical" being an adjective. Injustice and divisiveness have been spawned in the church, at least to some extent, because of the misuse of this grand term.

The second major part is called "Evangelical Family Living." Catholic Christians really do not see good works as a means to justification. The great medieval theologian Thomas Aquinas taught that we are born on the natural level; nothing we do can merit eternal life. The only thing that can merit salvation is the sacrifice of Christ. When we become justified at the point of inner conversion, we are raised from the natural to the supernatural level. When we are raised to a new height, our actions on the natural level are redeemed and transformed. The contrast many experience between faith and works may simply be caused by our inability to integrate Christian principles and morals into the secular marketplace. There are genuine efforts among Catholics and Protestants to integrate faith and works as they rediscover a biblically sound approach to social action. We should not see a contradiction between faith and works. When we genuinely love, we integrate faith and works. We are members of the Family of families, the family of God or the Church.

The third major part is titled "Our Evangelical Heritage." It is the briefest of the parts but essential reading! There is a long and impressive line of evangelical preachers. Probably the greatest was the Apostle Paul. He is a prime example of a transformed life, one that became a powerful tool for the kingdom. Christ's death and resurrection permeated his teaching and preaching. John Chrysostom, one of the Eastern Fathers of the Church, was most famous for his forceful and prophetic preaching. Dominic converted many souls to the Savior. The Wesley brothers' ministry was fired by their own experience of saving grace. Other names that can quickly be added were Protestants Charles Finney and D. L. Moody as well as Clarence Walworth, a nineteenth-century Catholic priest. There are many wonderful missionary preachers in our own time, Billy Graham in particular. Divisions seem to occur in our heritage because of serious, unresolved relational struggles that often take place between key leaders. The pain of the struggle is so great that it is never properly resolved. The opportunity for such healing, however, has never been greater!

The fourth and final part is "Restoring Our Evangelical Family." For too long we have failed to see one another as members of "the Family" of families. Mistakes have been made on all sides. In the documents of Vatican II and subsequent ones, Roman Catholic leaders have acknowledged participation in the rifts. John Paul II has sought to pave the way for Christians once again to experience full unity for which we were intended. Satan is our common enemy; he wants us divorced and fragmented. Must we continue to fall prey to Satan's efforts to keep us divided? Ecumenical efforts and ministries are messy, frustrating, and risky. Yet, they are also wonderful! To be Catholic is to be ecumenical. In fact, to be Christian is to be ecumenical. We must acknowledge it was never our Lord's intention for His people to be divided. God will bring the church back together again; we can only cooperate. The greatest impediments to true Christian evangelism are usually Christians. We need to move ahead, especially in prayer and divine power, to restore "the Family." This means a commitment to "true" ecumenism. John Wesley's "letter to a Catholic friend" shows the heart of a man on fire for the Gospel and true ecumenism.

## Some Major Points

*"Catholic" means universal or all-inclusive.*

An early bishop, Ignatius of Antioch, wrote a letter to Christians in Smyrna just before his martyrdom in A.D. 110. He wrote, "Where the bishop is present, there let the congregation gather, just as where Jesus Christ is, there is the Catholic Church."

Many similar texts to that of Ignatius demonstrate an early Episcopal form of church government. In addition, the term "Catholic" was used when referring to all Christian people. The church is intended to be Catholic and include all believers under one umbrella. It is a critical fact and seems all too often forgotten.

By the second century, errant doctrines began to infiltrate the church. Splits began over vital issues such as the divinity of Christ. The bishops of the early united Christian church began to use the word "Catholic" to distinguish the church of Christians who held to the true Gospel from groups like the Montanists and Arians. So, in the very early centuries "Catholic" was being used like a first name. Saint Augustine, Bishop of Hippo, recalls his mother praying, "I did have one reason for wanting to live a little longer: to see you become a Catholic Christian before I died."

*Christianity has a wealth of tradition, and "tradition" is not a bad word.*

It is not a matter of tradition binding and Jesus setting one free. It is discovering Jesus and freedom in one's tradition.

The reformers and medieval theologians take us back to the early church fathers. These include Ignatius, Polycarp, Tertullian, and numerous others. They are wellsprings from which to drink. The Didache is the earliest compilation of post-New Testament writings. It shows that very early the Christians gathered together for liturgy. Unearthing the church's past is to point out the incredible wealth of worship, wisdom, and biblical understanding.

To dig into the life of Saint Francis of Assisi is to discover a man filled with the Holy Spirit and an evangelical fervor. To study the renewal movement he inspired is to discover that all of Europe had been set aflame by one little man. He was so in love with Jesus and the church that—despite the inconsistencies with her—he refused to abandon her. This is another great evangelical moment in tradition that evidences the Good News of the church.

The elements of a classical revival and its perpetuation of spiritual renewal are fivefold: prayer, repentance, conversion, the power of the Holy Spirit, and mission.

A prevailing hunger for depth of prayer and an understanding of the power of intercession and spiritual warfare are paramount. Eucharistic chapels or informal gatherings are appropriate. Prayer is to be proclaimed, taught, demonstrated, and expected. The pressure can be one toward heaven and away from worldliness.

A penitential lifestyle does not have to mean heaviness or despair; it can mean true joy. The word "penitential" has been used throughout Christian history to denote those men and women who have grasped that repentance is not a one-time affair. It is a call to continual conversion, one acknowledging our sin and God's greatness.

Conversion is not a matter of what we do but what God does. We must allow Him to penetrate our lives. We can refuse to let Him enter. When we do open the soul's door, He touches us with the tenderness of His love. Conversion is the continual call of the Christian to become fully complete and mature in Christ.

It is normal to evidence the power of the Holy Spirit. "Normal" is a word we need to recapture. The secularization prevalent in our contemporary age is "abnormal." It does not bring freedom, joy, and peace. Only the power of the Spirit breaking forth into human experience can do that.

Every Christian is called to the work of the Master and that is "evangelism." We are called, to penetrate this age with the Good News of salvation in Christ. We are to advance with this message and its transforming power. We can regain lost ground and advance the cause of Christ.

*The love of Jesus is profoundly personal.*

He is the One who loves emotionally and tenderly. The Man of Galilee loves with His entire self and holds nothing back.

One of the most beautiful passages in Mark's Gospel is a prime example of His unconditional love. He is approached by a leper. The social norm in His day was to turn away in fear or disgust. The Scriptures tell us Jesus was moved with pity and He stretched out His compassionate hand.

To love as Jesus loved is to love with deep and heartfelt compassion. It means loving with a heroism that enables us to stand against our contemporary age and embrace those it has rejected. Such unconditional love brings about healing. Furthermore, it touches our interior wounds or the brokenness nobody is permitted to see.

*A little gray-haired lady, Mother Teresa, is a contemporary saint.*

She is a faithful messenger of the Gospel. She is also a source of salvation and hope to untold millions.

Christ shines through her life as through few others we will ever encounter. Her character radiates the grace, mercy, and power of God. Her words and works continually proclaim Jesus and His Gospel. The Lord is so preeminent in her life that she has become Jesus. This is true not only to those to whom she ministers, but also to thousands who have never met her; they have only heard her speak, read about her, or watched her work from afar.

For her there is no conflict between the interior life and external acts of charity. She integrates an intimate relationship with Jesus with genuine piety and social action. This is the full family life or the true union of faith and works. It is the hunger that lies at the heart of much of today's evangelical Christianity. Its Roman Catholic expression is often misunderstood by Protestant brothers and sisters.

*It is time to rediscover the evangelical counsels as the normative vehicle for both interior change and external action.*

These counsels are poverty, chastity, and obedience.

The spiritual discipline of poverty involves two aspects: what we possess and what possesses us. It is not against our having what we need to live. It is against our being had by our attitude toward what we have! Everyone cannot practice poverty in the same manner.

Chastity—even voluntary celibacy—has a basis in Scripture (Matthew 19:12). Saint Paul saw voluntary celibacy as a tremendous opportunity to be more available to the Lord and His people. Chastity includes two major concepts: the sacredness of reproductive creativity and sexuality as a way to show our love for God.

Obedience is the greatest antidote to our self-centered age. Our practice must begin with the Source of all authority, the Lord of the universe. Even God's Son submitted His will to the Father. Therefore, Jesus was free to live a truly counter-cultural life.

*All families, to some extent, are dysfunctional and the family of God is no exception. We suffer from the sins of our fathers.*

The problem emerged with catastrophic impact in the eleventh century. Some disputes over political, ecclesiastical, theological, and even liturgical issues finally led to a split between Western and Eastern Christians. It was known as the Great Schism of 1054. The Roman Catholic Church and Greek Orthodox Church went different ways. In a great show of reconciliation and healing between Catholics and Orthodox, Pope Paul VI and Athenagoras revoked the mutual excommunication decrees that have blocked reunification efforts for almost a thousand years.

However, the scars left by the Great Schism did not lead to the depth of hurt, anger, and divisiveness we now experience throughout the church. Such a legacy falls on the shoulders of the Reformation. At the outset was a call within Catholicism to correct abuses in the church. It ended with Catholics leaving the church and beginning new movements outside the church's umbrella. This was a radical divorce and we are children of it.

*True ecumenism is rooted in the following:*

Acknowledgment of the whole family and our membership in it; an ability to grieve over our family's separation and long for its full unity; a recognition of the challenge we face in the contemporary mission field; a willingness to embrace our own traditions with confidence and humility; the humility to learn from one another and allow one another to operate freely in our respective part of the family; and the desire to work together for the sake of the Gospel.

Firm adherence to these will allow Catholic believers to rejoice at the sight of a thriving Romanian Baptist church. It will also allow Protestant believers to rejoice at the swelling crowds present in a Polish cathedral. Both are meeting our common Father, being saved through the merits of our common Savior, and being led by the same Spirit. We need to be flexible about culture and respectful of disagreements within the family. Our need is to empty ourselves of pride.

*Cursillo has dramatically affected thousands of people.*

The focus is personal evangelism. Precious human beings have been able to come into a deeper relationship with Jesus Christ.

Cursillo had its origin in Spain in 1949. It is "a movement of the church with its own method that makes it possible to live what is fundamental for being a Christian in order to create small groups of Christians who would evangelize their environment with the gospel and help structure Christianity." The complete title of the movement means "the little course in living Christianity."

It is best known for its special ministry weekends, a community experience. Participants listen to talks, discuss them and make practical applications. They also celebrate the Eucharistic liturgy. One of the most interesting and sustaining things is the follow-up program that involves small weekly reunions. The long-range goal is that Christ become the preeminent influence in society.

## Tidbits

We must build together on a solid foundation, building on a truly common heritage so as to achieve, in God's strength and wisdom, a true ecumenism—a true respect for the whole church family and a true desire to see evangelical gospel live and flourish within all Christian churches and transform nations. (p. 65)

I challenge you to fall in love with the Scriptures because of their richness and power and because of what they are: the words of Christ, the words of the living Word, the love letters of Love Incarnate to a love-starved world. (p. 79)

Through the ages, our Christian family has been blessed with many profoundly faith-filled intellectuals. The early church Fathers were some of the finest scholars and apologists the church has ever had. (p. 138)

One day we will see the true family unity all of us should desire—the unity Wesley so much wanted with his Catholic brother in Christ. Until then, we can together cry out the ancient prayer of our ancestors recorded in the last verses of our family album: "Amen. Come, Lord Jesus. The grace of the Lord Jesus be with God's people. Amen."—Revelation 22:20–21, NIV (p. 218).

---

*Evangelical Catholics.* Keith A. Fournier. Thomas Nelson Publishers, 1990 Nashville, TN. *Logos Productions,* 1991. Used by permission.

# ❈"VAN GOGH AND GOD" BY CLIFF EDWARDS❈

## Introduction

DR. EDWARDS' book is one that has a precious aroma about it, largely because one wonders if there is such a study and is delighted to learn there is! We learn of a dimension of van Gogh that we suspected was there but weren't sure. The author shows the artist as philosopher of life, unorthodox theologian, and determined seeker of a global spirituality. Vincent's life and work are seen as a rich source for all those who search for a deeper knowledge of God. This enables the reader to move away from the frequent presupposition that he was lost in religious fanaticism until he found his true vocation as a painter. Every religious professional will be stretched and enriched by the careful reading of it. Parish ministers will discover sermonic material that promises to fascinate serious worshipers.

Professor Cliff Edwards' education is virtually a study within itself! His Ph.D. comes from Northwestern in biblical studies and world religions. He has studied at the University of Strasbourg in France and the University of Neuchatel in Switzerland. Furthermore, he has done work at Hebrew Union School of Bible and Archaeology in Israel and the Daitokuji Zen Buddhist Temple and Monastery in Kyoto, Japan. He is currently professor of philosophy and religion at Virginia Commonwealth University. However, the potential reader should not be so awestruck that he or she is frightened away. The author does a superb job of being scholarly, readable, and sometimes spellbinding.

## *Capsule*

The initial pages are the foreword by Henri J. M. Nouwen, the author's preface, a chronological guide of van Gogh's life, and a chronology of the letters. All are worth the reader's time to ponder. The remainder of the book is divided into six chapters, illustrations, notes, works cited, index to the letters, and name index. It is a welcome—even clever—organization of the material.

Chapter One is "A Pilgrim's Progress." Vincent found deep, personal meaning in the biblical description of life as a pilgrimage; in fact, he devoted the first sermon he ever preached to that theme. It was in November of 1876 that he mounted the pulpit of a small Methodist church in Richmond, England. There, he affirmed life as a pilgrim's progress. At the age of twenty-three he was convinced that he would follow in his father's footsteps as pastor, missionary, or teacher of the Bible. This one sermon seemed to mark out directions his spiritual quest would take during the remaining fourteen years of his life.

Chapter Two is "Religious Transformation." Although Vincent apparently had boyhood dreams of becoming a pastor, following in the footsteps of his father and grandfather, two wealthy uncles in the art trade seemed to have convinced their less affluent pastor and brother otherwise. So, Vincent was apprenticed as clerk in the famous art establishment of Goupin and Company in The Hague. There he became an obedient and dedicated worker. Four years later he was promoted to the London branch. During his second summer there he went through a time of crisis. It was a decisive turning point in his life.

Chapter Three is "From Book to Books." His spiritual development is nowhere more dramatically revealed than in his transformation from a man of one book, the Bible, to a man of many books or the literature of his age. It is also true no other change in his perspective is so clearly demonstrated in his paintings as is this transformation. Vincent moves from a devoted student of the Bible to an avid reader of novels by Zola, Hugo, Dickens, Eliot, and others. It is as though he moves from a Bible-centered pietist to a radical evangelist for contemporary literature.

Chapter Four is "The Vulnerability of God." Van Gogh lived his brief life at the juncture of two ages. One was the age of religious certainty, which was dying and defensive, and the other was the age of scientific certainty, which was young and aggressive. Belief in God was under devastating attack by some and considered irrelevant by many. It was also undergoing radical reformulation by a few. Friedrich Nietzsche was placed in an asylum the very year that Vincent voluntarily entered the asylum at Saint-Remy.

Chapter Five is "The Oriental Connection." His enthusiasm for Japanese prints and his willingness to learn from Japanese artists led him to experiment. The Ryksmuseum Vincent van Gogh in Amsterdam displays three of his oil paintings which are his careful copies of Japanese prints. He was convinced that nature, along with the lessons he had learned from Japanese prints and the sun-drenched Japanese atmosphere of Provence, would heal and liberate him and his painting. Vincent not only saw himself as a monk worshiping Buddha, he saw his Yellow House as a Buddhist monastery under the direction of an abbot. His deepest insight might well have been written by a Zen Master.

Chapter Six is "Symbolism." This was for him not a clever code created by artists; it was a dynamic "gift" from a deeper or a higher source which opened itself to that artist who lived in love and simplicity, persisting in daily labor within nature. To come into communication with that profound level where symbolism occurs, the artist must give up the ego self and its cautious, conventional ways—venturing everything on an act of feeling and faith. The quest for the day's tasks and persistence in the work itself were for Vincent a source of revelation; it was a way to the hidden aspect of reality which is also symbolic.

The section on "Illustrations" is a special delight with careful data presented. Excerpts from letters to different persons, especially Theo, are quoted with each one. These pages alone make the book worth reading. With his "Self-Portrait" we discover this quotation in a letter from Theo:

"My dear friend, if you had spent rainy nights in the streets of London or cold nights in the Borinage—hungry, homeless, feverish—you would also have such ugly lines in your face and perhaps a grating voice too."

## *Some Major Points*

*The Esau-Jacob narratives of Genesis (chapters 25–27) are both poignant and revealing when applied to Vincent; they focus upon external appearance as revelatory of internal character.*

Though we must resist pushing the details of the biblical narrative too far, it is a strong likelihood that this imagery suggested by Pastor van Gogh and remembered vividly by Vincent years later influenced the artist. Upon his father's death, Vincent renounced his part in the inheritance and sent his father's most precious possession, a Bible, to Theo. Then, he moved out of the parsonage forever.

At the heart of the story of Esau's loss of his father's blessing, is a deception in which hairy animal skins are placed on Jacob's hands. This is done so that the blind father Isaac might feel them and believe "the hands are the hands of Esau," coarse and hairy, and so bestow the blessing intended for Esau on Jacob. Vincent, as a struggling artist, believed that others saw him as a coarse animal. In 1883 he wrote to his brother, Theo: "In the daytime, in ordinary life, I may sometimes look as thick-skinned as a wild boar, and I can understand perfectly well that people think me coarse."

*In September of 1876, in his early twenties Vincent quoted Jesus' words from the Sermon on the Mount about the "narrow path." This comes from one of his letters while deeply engrossed in Bible study.*

Struggle and suffering accompany the biblical depiction of such a path. Vincent sought to understand the implications. His own major pleasures were nature, art, and literature. He was also forced to examine the possibility that the narrow path required elimination of those joys from his life. *The Imitation of Christ,* considered by Vincent a companion to the Bible, preached a world-denying discipline; it distinctly called upon him to despise the world. How was he to interpret this call to a single-minded devotion to the things of salvation?

His transformative journey focused on the issue of the nature of religion in personal life. Crucial questions emerged. Does religion make a claim that is exclusive? Can it include the paths of nature, art, and literature? Does a serious spiritual quest enhance or rule out other pathways of meaning? There was no rapid or easy solution. This issue would remain contested and the battle line would shift first in one direction and then in another.

*Vincent's continual search for unification of his life and the variety of ways to meaning led to a constant attempt to discover equations which might unify the words of nature, art, and literature.*

His transformation to a man of many books allowed him a more critical stance toward the Bible of old. In letters to Emile Beenard, the young painter who was struggling with his deep feelings for Roman Catholic tradition and piety, Vincent was most willing to discuss the Holy Scriptures. Vincent began to have a scathing criticism of the Old Testament. His own search for unity and inclusiveness seems offended by the Old Testament or Hebrew Scriptures' exclusivity.

An enormous issue arising at the point where Bible and art intersect soon became the focus of discussion for Vincent and Emile. One was a Dutch Calvinist in search of a deeper unity and the other was attempting to rediscover his heritage of Catholic piety. The critical problem focuses upon the problem of doing "religious art" in the modern age. How do we distinguish Christian religious art from any other art? What should the churches commission and utilize?

*God, Bible, parents, and clergy had been closely related in Vincent's mind. "Did his new critical stance include criticism of God, even the God beyond that of the clergy?"*

Vincent does not simply ascribe to God's human attributes, perceiving God as some giant human being. He sees God specifically in his own innermost experience of frustration, failure, and striving as an artist. He also experiences God in the concreteness of his own most intense and significant personal history.

His approach to God emerges more clearly as he expresses his regard for God's "study that has gone wrong." His own new creed, practicing the high-spirited path which is free to risk mistakes, reveals the manner of God's own artistry. It is an artistry whose daring makes possible such a blunder as the creation of this flawed world. For Vincent's mistakes, blunders, and imperfections are the location of hope. Blunders are the assurance that God acts with a self-forgetfulness that attempts more than can be reasonably expected or accomplished during the present. He insisted throughout his artistic career that people cannot be justified or speak in good faith when they judge his work otherwise than as a whole and in a broader way, taking into account his purpose and endeavor.

*Experience led Vincent to deepen and simplify his understanding of the unifying power of love. He shared with the painter Rappard a creed that made clear love beyond language and beyond conceptualization.*

Love is creative and life-giving for him. He says what the germinating force is in a grain of wheat, love is in us. The intimacy and simplicity of love give it a seriousness and holiness beyond abstract ideas. He believes the more one loves, the more one will act; love that is only a feeling would never be recognized as love.

"God" is the name we might use for the mystery of love's presence in life. Acts of love are the concreteness of the presence of God in life. Vincent understands both "God" and "love" as locating themselves not primarily in religions, which pass away, or even in works of literature and art, which can lose their relevance over time. He finds them locating themselves in the simplicity of life and in the germinating power of the family, the cradle. This is the home of every peasant and laborer. New life at its simplest, without power or pretense, is a visual and experiential proof of life, love, and therefore of God's presence. He quoted approvingly from Victor Hugo that "religions pass away, God remains."

*It was Vincent's personal experience that led him to select the child in a cradle as best evidence for God. Too little attention has been given to the months he spent beside a cradle.*

Ordered out of the parsonage at Etten in December of 1881, he rented a simple studio in The Hague. There he took in a seriously ill and pregnant prostitute with her young daughter. Influenced by stories of women in distress in Dickens, Eliot, and the Bible, he sought to save the life of "Sien." Hospitalization and a difficult birth were successful. Vincent then cared for the mother, her daughter, and a new baby boy in his cradle. Theo objected to this action on the part of Vincent. Vincent responded by asking a question: "Which is the more delicate, refined, manly—to desert a woman or to stand by a forsaken woman?"

If there is room for black theologies and feminist theologies, Vincent would have added a theology of the child, a theology of the family cradle. It is in the cradle that the God who is located directly in our most profound experiences is present. God's presence in the cradle is presence as the germinating force of humanity as love. In the child, interdependence and transformation intersect. The cradle is the meeting place of Divine and human; it is a place of vulnerability and love.

*One of the unresolved struggles in Vincent's life was his concern for the oppressed of the newly Industrialized cities; yet, there was his love and need for the rural countryside of his childhood memories.*

Would he choose the new city or would it be the old countryside? Would he paint the cities of Dickens and the Goncourt brothers or become a peasant painter like Jean-Francois Millet? Perhaps his life was too brief to reach a solution. However, he most often had a suspicion of the city as an environment unsuited for profound thought and chose the countryside for recuperation and labor. He advised Theo that in order to grow, one must be rooted in the earth.

Specifically, Vincent heard the desolate moors tell him to try persuading Theo to leave the art trade in Paris and join him as a painter in the country. He did this in spite of the financial disaster a move might cause both of them. Generally, he felt on the moors the absolute claim of God. He used a powerful image found in Victor Hugo's novel *Ninety-Three* which depicts merciful goodness and self-righteous goodness.

*Vincent was nearly correct when he reminded Theo that all the Impressionists had felt the positive influence of Japanese art; indeed, for the most part, they had.*

It was Claude Monet and Van Gogh who sought a profound liberation through a unity of nature and the Japanese perspective. Monet was successful enough in selling his work that he could retire from the intrigues of Paris to a country home in the rolling hills of Giverny; there, he could have gardeners construct flower beds, a lotus pond, and even a Japanese humpback bridge. Monet could afford both the time and money to build his own corner of Japan.

Van Gogh had little time and money. To find a Japanese landscape he was required to become a stranger and a pilgrim once more. He traveled to the only Japan he could afford, sunny Provence. It was there he spent his days in the fields and orchards; he hiked far into the hills. During rain and winter storms he painted in homes, cafes, or in his studio that was hung with Japanese prints. Vincent described the Impressionists as the "Japanese of France" and counted himself among their number.

*Vincent's western religious heritage had taught him that egocentricity was sin. It had also taught him that he was called to join humanity in the Body of Christ and become a servant of human need.*

Can one truly break the bonds of egocentricity while languishing in the anthropocentrism of the Judeo-Christian tradition? Is hyperreflection upon the self any different, qualitatively, than the West's hyperreflection upon humanity? Can one find liberation from self while maintaining the narrow privilege which sees humanity's mission as subduing the earth and even enforcing dominion over the non-anthropomorphic universe?

He had transcended one narrowing barrier after another. He seemed to move from worldly acceptance and success, to religious institutionalism and authority, to a suffering servant's task for humanity. In Provence his lifelong love for nature was rekindled and intensified by a search for the secret of the Japanese artist; the most subtle form of egocentricity, anthropocentrism, gave way in a surrender to nature. Even being shut away for weeks in his asylum room did not shake his deepening sense of companionship with nature. When he fired the borrowed pistol into his side, it was in the very shadow of the wheat sheaves of a harvested field.

*Wheatfield with Crows is often viewed as his final masterpiece. The artist or viewer stands at the convergence of three dirt paths; one moves to the right, one to the left, and one directly ahead.*

What are his own feelings in regard to this masterpiece? Vincent preferred storms for their restorative power, their beauty, and their revealing of the Divine. Thunderstorms symbolized the better times of pure air and the rejuvenation of all society. Inhabitants of the Belgian village where he served as evangelist remembered a "thunderstorm episode"; it was cited to characterize the strange preacher from Holland. In what sense are his crows "sinister?" According to his sister, Vincent was enchanted by birds and birds' nests from his youth.

The primary focus is on the wheat itself. Two-thirds of the canvas is ripe wheat disappearing beyond the edges of the painting to right and left, stretched across the entire horizon. The viewer looks directly into the stand of windswept wheat. In the painting one is called upon to take the trouble of looking at wheat, a sea of twisted and golden stalks. The impermanence of humanity and wheat is freedom and creativity; it is also the Eternal.

## *Tidbits*

"Vincent's religious transformation occurred at the very moment he gave up the family sponsored academic route toward Christian service and opened his search to include the domains of nature, literature, and art." (p. 66)

"The contrasting directions of Vincent's belief in God, concrete personal experience and vague mystery, are the very directions he could describe as nourishing or inspiring his art." (p. 76)

"I believe that Vincent counted his leaving Sien the greatest of his failings and the deepest of his disappointments, even if Sien herself did not favor the continuing of the relationship. I believe he grieved for that strange family for the remaining eight years of his life." (p.81)

"It is remarkable that of the more than 2,000 paintings and drawings Vincent produced in Holland, Belgium, Paris, Aries, Saint-Remy and Auvers, it is specifically the works done on his trip to the 'equivalent of Japan' that have continued to grow in popularity with people of many cultures around the globe." (p. 99)

————

*Van Gogh and God.* Cliff Edwards. Loyola University Press, 1989 Chicago, Ill.
*Logos Productions,* 1992. Used by permission.

# CHAPTER 17

# Study Materials

## ❋LOCAL CHURCH HELPS❋

CERTAINLY ONE OF the key changes in the 1972 *Discipline* as compared to the one in 1968 is the totally new second subparagraph under Section XV (The Local Church and Parish Councils on Ministries), Paragraph 153, which says:

> The Council on Ministries shall elect teachers, counselors, and officers for the church school other than those subject to election by the Charge Conference. They shall be nominated, by the work area chairperson of education after consultation with the age-level coordinators and pastor or such other groups or persons as the Council on Ministries may designate. It is recommended that the Committee on Nominations and Personnel be a resource in this process.

The language is strong. "They shall be nominated by the work area chairperson of education" are words we dare not take lightly. When we want to put teeth into something, how do we word it? At some point that commanding verb *shall* makes an appearance. Even though we discover the chairperson is to consult with others, there is no mistaking the emphasis. Likewise, the committee on nominations and personnel is in the background because it is simply a recommended resource.

Those granting such powers are to be commended. This is another grand illustration of placing our laity in positions of decision making. We are, in fact, moving toward a *shared ministry* among clergy and laity in terms of both responsibility and authority.

Why should the pastor and/or the professional staff have the last word in deciding who does most of the teaching, counseling, and administering in the church school? To come at it a little differently and perhaps more realistically: why should the present pastor have all the headaches that go along with what in many churches were formerly unilateral pastoral decisions?

This gives rise to the thoughts of who and/or what this person should be. With the exception of the council chairperson, potential power, within the council centers around the use of the education leader's *Discipline*-given prerogative to nominate a myriad of teachers, counselors, and officers for the church school. With this in mind, it is only reasonable to do a bit of probing. Here is a beginning list of some basic attitudes.

The chairperson ought to be—

1.  Fair to the members of the council on ministries,
2.  Fearless before pressure groups,
3.  Finite in recognizing mistakes,
4.  Free to state personal feelings,
5.  Friendly to pastoral leadership,
6.  Faithful to United Methodist literature,
7.  Familiar with the membership of the local church,
8.  Flexible enough to handle an unsympathetic council and/or board,
9.  Forceful with age-level coordinators,
10. Fruitful in producing a steady flow of new ideas.

The committee on nominations and personnel will, we hope, do a thorough job of selecting persons for places of leadership. Our new *Discipline* tells us, in effect, to do our homework especially well in placing before the officiary of the local church a person worthy of being the work area chairperson of education. It isn't too early to look toward your fall charge conference.

———

*The Church School* January 1974. Used by permission.

## ❧A PILGRIMAGE THROUGH THE❧ EPISTLE OF JAMES

IT IS NOT crucial to this study of the Epistle that we debate the particular James who is responsible for it. However, we should mention there is more than one possibility. Three prominent New Testament figures bear the name James; James the son of Zebedee, James the son of Alphaeus, and James the brother of Jesus. Tradition has said the latter of the three is the author. With his prominence in the church at Jerusalem and his understanding of the Christian faith and the orthodox Jewish Law it is difficult to make a case against tradition.

The Letter easily divides itself into five sections with each section containing gems of the Judeo-Christian faith that can and do make a difference in our lives.

## *Section One: Chapter 1:1–25*

The salutation in the first verse is simply a way of saying the letter is written to all of Christ's followers throughout the world. This is why we call it a general or catholic epistle.

The author then leads us into a series of general exhortations (verses 2–18). These verses tell of how the church endured trials which tested their faithfulness and the persons who lacked faith cut themselves off from God. Riches were seen as a real burden to the faith. God was not a tempter. Christians were seen as God's first fruits.

The entire first section provides us with countless "spinoffs" in a practical sense. The first section shows that to be tested by various trials is to purge us of all impurities and leave us cleansed. Wisdom is seen as more than philosophical speculation and intellectual knowledge. It is wisdom for dynamic living here and now. In the early church there were no class distinctions. All were precious human beings seeking to worship the God of Jesus Christ. Every person has the problem of being pulled by good and evil tendencies and seems to be a walking civil war. While God is creative, He is unchangeable. It is imperative to have a teachable spirit. In essence this is enough humility to learn. Those inspirations and instructions received in houses of worship are to be put to work in the hour by hour joy and sorrow, love and hate of every day. In Christianity is found an ethical demand.

Verses 1:13–15 and 1:19–20 lend themselves brilliantly to sermonic application. The first is a "route of ruin." Temptation comes when a person is lured and enticed by his own desire. Then there is the movement from temptation to sin. Finally, we go from sin to death. The second calls upon us to accept the truth of a great workable principle: be quick to hear, be slow to speak, and be slow to anger. We might say, "Don't get mad about it!"

Self-control is the main theme in verses 19, 20, and 21. We may read them in a Christian sense and yet they would be just as appropriate to Judaism.

Verses 22, 23, 24, and 25 have to do with the whole area of hearing and doing. It is never enough simply to receive the word. We are called upon to obey the word by doing what it commands.

### Section Two: Chapter 1:26 through 2:26

In this second section the down-to-earth living of the faith leaves little doubt as to what is expected of us. We have all seen religion made something majestic and marvelous "within" the church at the expense of neglecting it "outside" the church. Snobbery in the church was a potential problem then, even though the master and the slave might be sitting side by side. The gospel seems to offer so much more to the poor than the rich. The royal law is one of total obedience. In fact, it is said to break a portion of God's law is to become a law breaker. The orthodox Jew conformed by external pressure. The Christian was governed by internal pressure.

While there are those who try to make a case for major disagreements between Paul and James in regard to faith and works, this appears unsubstantiated. We are to remember Paul, in his letters, is speaking to the conversion experience at its inception. James is speaking to those already professing to be within the faith. For James it is not "faith or works." It is "faith and works." In the authentic religious experience the two are inseparable.

Verse 26 stands alone and deals with the control of the tongue. "To bridle one's tongue" is a common figure of speech among Greek writers of that period. True religion is then concisely defined in verse 27. In 1:27 "religion without blemish" is found in the creative tension of "reaching out" to visit orphans and widows and by keeping oneself unstained from the world.

The first thirteen verses of the second chapter speak of the problem of deference toward rich people. Partiality toward the rich is seen as supremely obnoxious. The author, in effect, assumes that there are no rich Christians. No special privileges are to be shown to the rich whatsoever. Any privileges are to be reserved for the poor. The identification with the "rich" as being blasphemers and the poor as being heirs of the kingdom seems rigid. The total religious life is obedience to the commandments specifically and collectively.

Now we confront three separate and parallel arguments in 2:14–26. The author is seen as an earnest, common-sense moralist throughout this passage. He is directly and totally concerned with everyday conduct. In the initial argument it is seen that people who praise virtue don't always practice it (14–17). In the second, James attacks the weakness of faith as pure intellectual orthodoxy (18–19). In the third he combines a Greek literary style with a rabbinical appeal to proof texts (20–26). Read also Genesis 22:1–14 which shows Abraham's faith manifesting itself in "work."

### Section Three: Chapter 3:1–18

Section three presents us with a common sense understanding of teaching and teachers. In the early church teachers worked within a congregation. Others, especially the apostles, moved from locality to locality. Therefore, teachers were in the position to greatly influence an individual church or group. Remember that to enter into the tradition of the rabbis was to enter holy ground. A rabbi was a very powerful figure. His opportunities for good or bad were enormous. Apparently, some degenerated into being spiritual tyrants concerned only with status. Too many preachers and teachers tell people rather than *listen* to them! In fact, the "agenda anxiety"—getting across a given amount of material regardless of the state of the pupils—seems to be a common mistake.

Verses 1 through 5 speak of believers who pose as teachers, yet are not qualified for the responsibility of the office. This reflects the democracy of the early church. Being a teacher is a grave responsibility to be avoided by most. The first verse gives rise to the theme of "teaching and power." Teaching at its best gives us competence in a trade, shows us our need for repentance, causes us to acknowledge our impotence, and reveals God's omnipotence.

Verses 6 through 8 emphasize the seriousness of the wrong use of the tongue by the phrase "set on fire by hell." The tongue never rests. Its poison is deadly. The sixth verse describes a body, mind, and soul disease which exalts only oneself, is infatuated with self-seeking influence, and seeks the degradation of everyone else.

Verses 9 through 12 point to the admission that good may come from evil.

The author discusses true wisdom in the passage running from 13 through 18. Intellectual ability, when used rightly by a humble and devout soul, is a heaven-sent blessing. It can also be destructive when used wrongly by a selfish egotist. The listing of eight terms depicting wisdom is common to Hellenistic Judaism and the New Testament. Each has its place in the definition. Righteousness is used in an Old Testament understanding; that is, a quality persons attain by works and which God rewards.

### Section Four: Chapter 4:1 through 5:11

The fourth section is an area of ideas giving birth to necessary understandings of the life we live today. The overpowering desire for pleasure with an ensuing feverish search for it, creates situations that continually harm. Real humility has a certain glory about it. Pride that always seeks its own selfish fulfillment really "shuts out" the needs of others and thereby "shuts itself in" creating immeasurable spiritual ignorance. We must not assume James is denying the joy of Christian life; real joy is known through repentance (and forgiveness). To judge others is a fascinating activity, especially if it involves distinguished persons. We are reminded that only God is Judge. The final verses in chapter 4 lift up for us the truth that self-confidence must always be seen in relation to God's sovereignty. As we enter chapter 5, there is an obvious thrust of social concerns. It is done vividly by seizing upon the frantic terror that is or will come upon the rich with no sensitivity for the poor. The selfish rich are like cattle being fattened for the slaughter. The coming of our Lord calls attention to the need for Christians to be forever on the watch and to be found in fellowship with one another at his coming. There is a patience which triumphs and Christians of all the ages have known this firsthand.

Chapter 4 verses 1–2 indicate a quick transition from a mere stoical stance to a Judeo-Christian point of view.

Verses 3 and 4 do not say pleasure is wrong yet we see two separate spheres of influence: the world versus God's people.

Verses 5 and 6 are difficult. There is obscurity and a possibility of textual corruption. However, we should not miss what seems to be the point: God especially helps those who are humble.

Verse 7 is a simple statement that God is stronger than the devil.

What can a preacher say through the God-given instrument of the sermon? What will the laity help him say? In this kind of context where partnership is understood let's look at the first part of 4:8. It gives rise to "that first step." We might ask, "What are the barriers that keep us from drawing near to God?" Then, we might inquire, "What are the bulldozers that are able to destroy those things which get in the way of our drawing near to God?"

Verses 8, 9, and 10 basically contain an admonition to move toward God spiritually and He will do likewise. "Cleanse your hands" is symbolic and figurative.

Verses 11 and 12 is one of several passages which is an entity within itself. There are interesting comparisons with Leviticus 19:16–18 and Matthew 7:1–5.

Verses 13 through 16 is another series complete within itself. There is nothing that leads one to believe it is strictly a Christian point of view. In fact, "Lord" is God separate and distinct from Christ.

Verse 17 is in a way a terse statement of truth which stands alone. It is a "decisive definition" of sin. Sin may be defined as personal and subjective, impersonal and objective, and inclusive and conclusive. It could point to any serious ethical teacher in various religions, except for the usage of the word sin which gives it a definite Judeo-Christian flavor.

We now enter the fifth chapter and look into the first six verses. Apparently all rich men are regarded as sinners. In a sense "the last days" have already begun. Defrauding workmen of their pay is a serious crime in Judaism. The rich prepare their own doom by their own acts. It is important to recognize in these verses that a Palestinian background is presupposed; only in Palestine were workmen hired: in the rest of the Roman Empire, fields were worked by slaves.

## *Section Five: 5:12–20*

It is significant to remember that in the times of Jesus and His disciples many evil practices had grown up. Certainly one of them was the use of oaths. The taking of them was so commonplace that even the smallest business transactions had difficulty being consummated without an oath. The person simply wanting to be truthful was often hurt by not knowing the intricate rules of the game. We see a praying, singing, and healing early church. The religious application of oil was standard practice among faithful Jews. Whenever a man became ill, a rabbi anointed him and prayed over him. There was no question our spiritual ancestors were men and women of prayer. The truth is something which is being done day-in and day-out. To be instrumental in bringing a sinner into the fold is the surest way for us to save our own.

How can pastor and people share this passage most beneficially? Verse 12 lifts high the truth of "keeping your promise." As a Christian I am expected to make a promise without enforcing it with an oath and to be clear about any promise I make. As a Christian I do not play the part of a hypocrite by promising something I do not intend to fulfill and I do not utilize an oath as an evil method to promise retaliation.

In the second half of verse 16 we might spend some time "rating our prayers." There are the constructive and helpful ones, and there are destructive and hurtful ones. Such an inventory is most uplifting and enlightening for pastor and people alike.

We begin here with swearing being forbidden in verse 12. A person's swearing to tell the truth is undesirable. An attitude of always attempting to tell the truth is far superior. Matthew 5:34–37 seems to ooze from James's lines.

Verse 13 speaks of the consecration of all our emotions and is not connected at all with the preceding verse.

Verses 14 and 15 show us the official organization of the Christian community was under the rule of elders. Such elders were believed to have unique powers as they applied oil while saying prayers. The "Lord" giving the healing is Christ. It is to be understood that the great strength of prayer is conditioned by whatever is God's will.

Verses 16, 17 and 18 are, to some extent, a continuation of 15. The sick person is to confess his sins. James emphasizes what Elijah achieved was not by some bizarre, magical performance. Elijah was a dedicated person who utilized prayer as many others can.

Verses 19 and 20 are a complete thought. Both Proverbs 24:24–25 and 1 Peter 4:8 provide interesting references. A key topic of discussion over the years deals with whose sins are being covered, the one being converted or the one doing the converting. The most wise answer seems to be that it is not a case of "either/or" but one of "both/and."

The Epistle terminates uniquely with no indication the end has been reached. There is neither an attempt to provide a climax nor bid farewell to the readers. James keeps the door wide open to further inspiration and instruction.

The Letter of James is a brilliant wedding of Jewish thought and Christian perspectives. Where else in the entire Bible can you and I be taught by the shrewdness of the Proverbs and the saving power of the Sermon on the Mount at the same moment?

READ THE LETTER OF JAMES.

The amount of material in this article is more than can be dealt with in one session. The class could plan a two or three session study. However should the class elect to study the Epistle of James in one session, divide the class into five groups (even if a group consists of only 2 persons). Each group will take a section and read the Scripture in their section followed by the corresponding section in the article. The groups will report back on what they learned about what it means to be a Christian according to James. How might we live the Christian life today?

---

*Cross Talk* June/July/August, 1976 (Vol. 5, No. 2). Used by permission.

## TEACH AND LEARN EVERY DAY

HOW MANY OF us take the time to list or even recognize the countless teaching and learning opportunities that come our way in just a few days' time? What happens to us in terms of Christian education between church school(s) and worship service(s) on a week-to-week basis?

Taking a brief inventory, I discovered some marvelous opportunities under my very nose:

- I was attending a service club meeting. This happens to be the group that makes a great deal out of the "four-way test" in the business world. The thought occurred to me, "What about the four-way test in the religious and moral realm?"

 After hearing much about the practicality of the club's test, I made a suggestion. "Fellows, it seems to me there is a foursome that helps us weigh the direction of our lives." Since I was the Protestant clergyman in the group, they gave me a listening ear.

 I continued: "We are a worldwide, outstanding service organization, but let's try this inquiring foursome on for size: Will what I am thinking and/or doing harm someone else, myself, my family, or a larger group of which I am a part?"

 Then a local bank president said, "I think Jesus has been trying to get this written on our hearts for centuries."

- Take a recent bean supper where several thousand fraternal brothers joined together for fun, food, and fellowship. Most of us at our table had never met before. The fellow sitting next to me began to talk about his long experience in the insurance business. Not telling him I was a pastor, I began to reminisce a little about teaching in the public schools of Indiana and some insurance courses I had taken.

 He said, "You know, one of the most difficult groups to deal with is preachers."

 I responded rather dryly, "Is that so? Well, how do you mean that?"

 He said half cynically, "Those guys just don't pay their bills too well, and they always seem so self-serving with their memberships and budgets."

 The temptation was to set him right verbally without delay. Instead, I took his bowl, filled it with another delicious helping of beans, and delivered to him the last large piece of cornbread. He was delighted. I wanted to tell him how our Lord's men had waited on tables, but it seemed anticlimactic—even preachy—so I didn't.

- The morning coffee break has been a delight to me over the years, regardless of the community in which I am serving. A recent one was especially productive. Sitting around the table were both laypersons and clergy. One layperson was making a speech about how cold, closed, and sophisticated some of our churches were. It was no secret United Methodists were in that category.

After a time, one of the clergy said, "Isn't there going to be an ecumenical Communion service in our community early in October?"

Having remained silent for some time, I replied, "Oh yes, that's true, and our church is hosting it. The administrative board has already given unanimous approval to its being held in our sanctuary and extends a cordial invitation to everyone."

• Pastors in home visitation receive ministry as well as give it. An elderly woman and I were having a lengthy conversation whose consistent theme was her loneliness, poor health, and lack of friends. My tendency in such a situation is to excuse myself after a few minutes, but this time I heard her out. Being drained emotionally and behind in schedule, I "let loose and let God take over."

During the parting prayer, which was largely a paraphrase of the universally repeated one from Saint Francis of Assisi, I asked God to help me stop shutting people out so that I would not "shut myself in." My confession spoke to her need.

Effective ministry, lay or clergy, is one that discovers that the entire universe is a huge classroom. In this context, as we alternate between being teachers and pupils, God's work gets done, the Good News comes alive, and you and I are blessed beyond words.

---

*Church School Magazine* April 1977. Used by permission.

CHAPTER 18

# *Preaching*

## ✥PREACHING IS . . .✥

OUR PROTESTANT heritage carries with it the centrality of preaching in congregational worship as the chief means of elevating Jesus the Christ as Savior and Lord. To emphasize worship is to emphasize preaching, and vice versa.

Our laity can help clergy become better preachers. As comrades in the cause of Christ and His Church, they can aid us who preach in communicating the Word of God to hungry and thirsty souls. However, before they can really give us a helping hand, the professional ministry must recognize in fear and trembling some of the enduring essentials of preaching. I call your attention to a beginning list of twenty characteristics of faithful preaching.

1. Preaching is *sacramental*: it brings people in touch with the grace of God. (I wonder how many preachers believe that in any serious sense!)
2. Preaching is *saving*: it creates opportunities for precious human beings to come to terms with their Redeemer and in fact be made right with Him.
3. Preaching is *satisfying*: both preacher and parishioner have a need to share thoughts and feelings under the guidance and inspiration of the Holy Spirit.
4. Preaching is *scholarly*: every local pastor should be a "theologian in residence." Too long we have attempted to separate the preaching and teaching functions. The pulpit is to be occupied by a preacher who is also a teacher. Today's sensitive and well-educated laity eventually will not settle for anything less.
5. Preaching is *searching*: it does not claim to lay before a congregation pat answers to those mysteries where Scripture does not provide clear answers. Nevertheless, it points to The Answer. And it humbly admits that its value is being a means and not an end in itself.
6. Preaching is *selfless*: it becomes obedient to the work of the Holy Spirit in and through both our intellects and emotions. In short, we do not preach "the" sermon; we preach the Crucified and Resurrected Christ.

7. Preaching is *sensible*: it explicitly or implicitly presents the option of belonging to Christ and spending eternity with Him or belonging to the world and being lost in hell. (We may not especially like the word "hell," but our Lord manages to use it upon several occasions.)

8. Preaching is *sensitive*: it does not seek to dominate and manipulate those whom God loves. (Of course, some will perceive anything other than positive pointers to worldly success as being insensitive.)

9. Preaching is *serious*: it deals with man's whole being, in both the present and ultimate terms. We are not entertainers; we are under orders from the Master . . . and that's serious business.

10. Preaching is *significant*: it really doesn't have any substitutes. In preaching, the Holy Spirit is uniquely at work creating a dialogue between preacher and people.

11. Preaching is *social*: it does not occur in a vacuum. Common kindness, courtesies, and compliments are important to gaining the right to be heard. Most will listen gladly without padded pews and a revolving spotlight on the pulpit. However, few—if any—will tolerate arrogance and disrespect by the preacher.

12. Preaching is *spiritual*: the preacher in the pulpit represents an historical Figure who is now present through the Holy Spirit. Therefore, both a mystical and mysterious quality exist with true preaching, and we must beg God that it be recovered in our churches!

13. Preaching is *stimulating*: it renews moribund congregations and calls to repentance those who hear and thus discover the saving power of the Lord. Let us not write off mass evangelism with integrity. Yet, we are mandated to be on guard against questionable—even enormously hurtful—methodology, which stresses the preacher and not Christ.

14. Preaching is *strong*: it brings the Word of God into meaningful contact with the living needs and concerns of a congregation. Therefore, it is not apologetic; it does not back away from the truth as it is given by God in His Word.

15. Preaching is *subjective*: while the Word comes to and for human beings, it also comes through a preacher who is tainted by original sin and whose perspectives are limited. "Truth through personality" is an accurate depiction.

16. Preaching is *submissive*: we are called to deliver what is given to us and not necessarily what we might like to preach about. We are to die daily to the will of the Master—and that means Sundays in the pulpit.

17. Preaching is *survival*: there is an urgency on the part of the preacher who believes that preaching has to be done. "Woe be unto me if I

preach not the Gospel" was never more valid than today.

18. Preaching is *sustaining*: we nourish our flock and they, likewise, nourish us. The interaction that can and should take place between preacher and people is often a banquet!
19. Preaching is *sweaty*: we are to toil and perspire until the riches of the Faith give forth their life-giving gems. We who preach must probe the Word, study and apply preaching skills, draw wisely upon the unlimited sources that inundate us from the secular world, and make use of various literary forms in our preaching.
20. Preaching is *symphonic*: there is a harmony that results among God's people with convincing clarity when preacher and people agree that to be right with Him is all that ultimately matters. Only the Maestro of marvels, the Master Himself, can conduct such a concert!

In the most elementary sense, we are called to worship God through Christ and to serve one another. We are not apt to do much conscientious and rightly-motivated serving unless we have first worshiped our God in the fellowship of others with expectancy, relevancy, and frequency.

Saint Paul tells us, "So faith comes from what is heard, and what is heard comes by the preaching of Christ" (Rom. 10:17 [RSV]). You and I are not likely to improve upon that as we seek to make worship a keynote in our church. How good it would be if United Methodists everywhere put our official emphasis during the next four years upon worshiping "in Spirit and in Truth!"

---

*Good News* November/December, 1979
*Ministry* July 1980
*The Priest* February 1983
*Pulpit Digest* January/February 1984

## SERMON ILLUSTRATIONS FOR THE HOLY FAMILY

WE ALL REACH peaks in our lives that bring great relief, a strong sense of accomplishment, and even a feeling of being ready for death. For some parents it is at the point a son or daughter graduates from high school or college. For others it is living to see the first grandchild. For a writer it could very well be the instant he or she learns the best-seller list has been reached. The examples can go on indefinitely, depending upon one's values and motivations in life.

An aged rabbi named Simeon was able to hold Jesus in his arms. The baby was the "consolation of Israel." Having seen firsthand the prophecy of the ages come to fruition, he was ready to pass the way of all flesh. His honor was the one surpassing all others . . . or was it?

You and I know the birth, life, death, and resurrection of Jesus. Yes, and we can add to that hundreds of years of church history that have seen Christians lose battles but never the war.

*Emphasis* December 27, 1981 (Luke 2:22–40). Used by permission.


# ❊SERMON ILLUSTRATIONS FOR❊ BAPTISM OF OUR LORD


FROM MY SEMINARY days I can vividly remember the heated debates over the modes of water baptism. There was a vocal segment of students (and professors) who said that immersion or total submergence in the water was the only way it could authentically be done.

As you might expect there were all shades of actions and reactions. A favorite among some of us who had not be immersed was the half-funny and half-serious comment that we pulled a "D" from old Professor So and So because we couldn't do the "backstroke in the baptistry." Some of us didn't take to kindly to those who said, "Well there won't be anything wrong with you fellows . . . as soon as you are covered with water and become Christians."

In some circles the debate rages today, but, thank God, it seems to be only a difference of theological opinion generally and not an issue to launch crusades.

St. Peter learned that the Holy Spirit transcends such argumentation and invites us to drink of such waters.

*Emphasis* January 10, 1982 (Acts 11:4–18). Used by permission.

# ✤SERMON ILLUSTRATIONS FOR SIXTH✤ SUNDAY AFTER EPIPHANY

"LEPROSY" IN THE Old Testament is such a nasty word. It denotes not only a terrible disease with terrifying skin disfigurations but separation and alienation. To be sure, putting lepers away in colonies and caves was a means of keeping a community healthy.

But is this disease the only one that has caused such stark and bitter estrangement from those considered normal? The answer is "no," especially in terms of ailments in soul and mind.

When compared to humankind's massive problems in human relations, leprosy seems almost insignificant by comparison. Such problems have built walls that have haunted us for centuries. What about racism? It just doesn't go away, does it? What about food and clothing for the down-trodden that number in the millions? That doesn't go away either. What about peace? We all recall the prophet's ancient but up-to-date cry, "Peace, peace, when there is no peace."

Feel sorry for the Old Testament lepers—if you will—but come to terms with our own leprous predicaments as we near the year 2000.

———

*Emphasis* February 14, 1982 (Leviticus 13:1–2, 44–46). Used by permission.

# ✤SERMON ILLUSTRATIONS FOR✤ FIRST SUNDAY IN LENT

PROMISES CAN BE made and so easily broken. Sometimes between sunup and sundown a promise can be torn into shreds.

Virtually the same thing can be said about contracts. The court dockets are crowded with suits that were drawn up by persons who either broke contracts or want to break them. Just because it's in print and the pertinent parties have signed doesn't mean an official agreement will go unbroken!

What about a covenant? Fortunately, that is a word with heavy meaning that is coming back into our religious vocabularies. It carries a divine connotation to it. Really, it is more than the Law, as Saint Paul pointed out in his Letter to the Galatians. God's covenant with Abraham preceded the giving of the Ten Commandments to Moses.

Ours is a Covenant-God. He promised a Redeemer to his people and He didn't fail them. What about our side of that covenant?

————

*Emphasis* February 28, 1982 (Genesis 9:8–17). Used by permission.

## ❋SERMON ILLUSTRATIONS FOR FOURTH❋ SUNDAY AFTER PENTECOST

THE "SIGN OF the Cross" is centuries old. In our day and time not only do we see Roman Catholics utilize it as a reminder, we even note the Protestant family has seen the value of it.

I like to think the first one to see it in the distance was the Blessed Mother, Mary. Imagine as she held the tiny baby in her arms the thought of Him hanging on the cross! Yet, I really think and deeply feel that she knew what was going to happen all along. She understood He was to be Savior and Lord; that meant crucifixion and resurrection.

One of the most meaningful dialogues in the ecumenical movement is that of probing the place of Mary—in a sense the Mother of God—in the faith. In my little book, *Mary and Jesus* (C.S.S.), I have built a bridge that hopefully many will use . . . and the traffic should be moving in two directions.

Mary was the first to take up her cross.

————

*Emphasis* June 19, 1983 (Luke 9:18–24). Used by permission.

## ❋SERMON ILLUSTRATIONS FOR SIXTH❋ SUNDAY AFTER PENTECOST

IN THE EDUCATION *of Henry Adams* the author says, "Harvard College was a negative force, and negative forces have value."

In a day that seems never to get its fill of "positive thinking," one would think the slightest indication of negative thoughts would cause an internal upheaval. Our boundless and seemingly ever-increasing insecurities and uncertainties are continually being met by surface answers. As a friend recently said, "You folks are merely putting band-aids on cancers."

Legitimate prophets of God have always understood that "negative forces have value." The "don'ts" in life go into forming spiritual reality just as much as the "dos."

Oh, it may cost you heavily in some circles to insist, "thou shalt not commit adultery" or "thou shall not bear false witness." Yet, prophets are called to do just that . . . and a lot more.

————

*Emphasis* July 3, 1983 (1 Kings 19:14–21). Used by permission.

# *SERMON ILLUSTRATIONS FOR EIGHTH* SUNDAY AFTER PENTECOST

A YOUNG MAN needs money for his college education. The quickest and best summer money is in a factory on an assembly line. There is an opening. The difficulty is that he isn't mechanically-minded. Social Studies and English are his fields. An assembly line with complicated machines producing parts and pieces is scary stuff, but he decides to take the job.

The foreman, a veteran who has run every machine, begins the briefing job. With apprehension and some mental blocks, the lad attempts to watch respectfully. So much of what he sees is so foreign to him and his inclinations. Then the veteran says something to him that makes a big difference. He says, "Now, son, this is your area, and all you have to do is keep putting these pieces on this machines as they come down the line and then take them off at the proper time and put them on this conveyer belt. You don't have to know a thing about what comes before or after."

How like our God as we fit into His scheme of things!

————

*Emphasis* July 17, 1983 (Deut. 30:9–14). Used by permission.

# ❖SERMON ILLUSTRATIONS FOR TENTH❖ SUNDAY AFTER PENTECOST

RELIGIOUS PERSONS tend to get "hung-up" on rites and practices. For those in apostolic times circumcision seemed to be a perpetual topic of discussion and upon occasion the reason for heated debate. Even the most dominant apostles of the times, Peter and Paul, had their exchange of heated words.

What are the "hang-ups" in the world in which you and I live? Institutionally, I suspect we can make a rather lengthy list. What about the Moral Majority? It isn't difficult to get sides quickly, some affirming and some negating. What about the World Council of Churches? Stands are being taken and the rigidity is increasingly noticeable. Well then, what about the National Council of Churches? There are defenders and there are critics, some of them severe. What about the Vatican? Even in an age of ecumenicity and inspiring openness, there are those shouting a "tool of the devil."

Saint Paul relates in Galatians 5:6, "For in Christ Jesus neither circumcision nor uncircumcision is of any avail, but faith working through love." Can't most of our "hang-ups" be handled by simply applying this basic Pauline understanding?

------

*Emphasis* July 31, 1983 (Col. 2:6–15). Used by permission.

# CHAPTER 19
## Newspaper Columns

### ✳SOBER REFLECTION . . . JOHN F. KENNEDY✳

IT TOOK THE sudden, tragic, and terrifying death of a gifted young man to bring out the finest feelings in many, many Americans. There are scenes from those days the brilliance of a host of writers could never have created. Remember a big strapping black teenager sobbing as though his heart was torn asunder? He tries to wipe the tears away with that huge, trembling hand. He mutters the only thing that seems to make sense: "Mister Kennedy was my friend." Remember an aged, partially blind man sitting in a wheelchair? He is in deep thought. He has only a few distant relatives living. Finally, he lifts his head and in a surprisingly clear voice erupts: "Oh God, why wasn't it me! My life has been lived. Oh, why can't I take the young President's place!" Remember a proud, pretentious Protestant in extreme spiritual pain? In loneliness and helplessness he kneels in a church, which is crowded with mourners. He is brought face to face with a humiliating but glorious truth: the nation has not only lost a president; it has lost a Roman Catholic Christian.

Perhaps for the first time since the Second World War large numbers of Americans saw keenly a universal neon sign blazing in the heavens: "All nations are under God. All individuals eventually—perhaps unexpectedly—must give an accounting to Him." The sobering effect was penetrating beyond words.

So, one lovely and promising gift, rudely and cruelly, was snatched from our midst barely three years ago. Most have learned this gift was not intended to be elevated to the point that it might dwell among God's greatest gifts. To do so would make it an unnecessary burden and not a gift.

All events of those few days three years ago are like an enormously heavy package of history—gift wrapped in destiny. Temporarily, you and I acquired a deeper appreciation for the need of a Revitalized Soul, both individually and as a nation under God.

Neither the political scientist nor the theologists could foresee the spiritual healing powers radiating from the death of one man. Martyrdom can be carefully planned and consummated. The coming together of the forces labeled "Caesar" and "God" to produce a sacrificial event of momentous proportions lies just beyond human capability.

To John Fitzgerald Kennedy life was a gift to be received with thanksgiving and lived to the hilt. In his dealings among men he admired courage more than anything else. The ReVitalized Soul like its Master says, "Courage! Victory is mine. I have conquered the world."

*Hagerstown Exponent* November 24, 1966

# ❀GOD LOVES US❀

HOW DO WE deal with tragedy? Much too often we react in bitterness. A sword is gouged into our soft religious flesh and it hurts: An automobile accident has taken the lives of two dear friends. They were good people, but we had never given them a *serious* invitation to our church. Oh, we hinted a few times that their lives would be greatly helped by it. Our words betrayed us. They were interpreted to mean the church is something less than the Body of Christ and a spiritual fellowship of believers. Every time we visualize the crinkled hood, smashed sides, and broken windows of their automobile, the pen of bitterness writes another negative word. Red-hot coals touch a tongue not yet fully dedicated to Christ and His Church: A seminary professor and outstanding preacher once told us without warning, "I don't like God!" Some of us stared in amazement at what we heard. One or two chaps were ready to register a complaint with the Dean or call a psychiatrist. Several minutes later in the class period he said, "I don't like God because several years ago He took away our baby's life that I wanted more than my own." God spoke to him in the only way he would listen. The pastor's point was made and the softness in his face told us the story of tragedy remade into triumph. There is no absolute law that says we have to react in bitterness.

We can respond in love to the God who is an expert in healing broken hearts. Our trouble is in trying to use our own strength in mending our brains and soothing our emotions. We take a little sweetness and patch it on a place worn raw by our internal turmoil. We produce a mask of kind understanding and wear it on suitable occasions. We lift our head higher than they should be for proper posture and pretend our injuries don't show. We talk ourselves into becoming interested in some new fad in hopes it will make us forget. We can save much time and energy by going directly to God. A great deal of shoe leather can be saved simply by falling upon our knees. Many sentences can be omitted simply by articulating with sincerity the words, "God help me!" *God is master of creating. He is also master of re-creating.*

Tragedy may or may not be a manifestation of God's wrath. It is a means to quicken and perfect our religious lives.

Prayer: Father of Jesus Christ, forgive us for the ways we have reacted negatively against unusual opportunities placed before us. Amen.

---

*Hagerstown Exponent* August 10, 1967

# ❉GOD LOVES US❉

WHAT PART DOES prayer play in your life? Is it best described as "routine" and "words"?

The Christian Church Member cries out daily: *Oh God, I shall put away these things hindering my communication with Thee!*

Old hatreds are buried and new ones are chased away. As we are getting ready to lift names and faces up to God, we must not allow incidents that occurred years ago or minutes ago prohibit this elevation. Nothing, absolutely nothing, eats away and rots our prayer life more disastrously than a regiment of hatreds parading across our mental horizons to the tune of "an eye for an eye and a tooth for a tooth." One dreg of hate can stop up the most beautifully constructed pipeline to Heaven.

We cannot reasonably be enemies of the progress being made in the space age. Nevertheless, something about the strides that are being taken do not ring true. Perhaps it is because the human family has not learned to live together in peaceful brotherhood. Millions upon millions of men have been destroyed by their faulty relationships with one another. To be a reactionary in the eyes of many is to be a sinner. To fail to react in favor of men becoming brothers is surely to be a bigger sinner.

Pleasure items should be given their proper places and times. Why should a catchy new television program cause us to postpone our afternoon prayers? God deserves prime time. Why should our neighbor's new sports automobile cause us to question God in our nighttime prayers about unearned prosperity? No place in the Scriptures do we read God promising any of His Son's followers flashy cars. Why should the new swimming pool at a friend's home cause us to reschedule our evening talk with God? The oceans are God's and all that dwell therein. Does that new filter tip have to be given a part of the regular time set aside for morning prayers? God has more to offer than a few inhalations.

Our Heavenly Father genuinely cares for you and me. His Son bled, suffered, and died for us. He continues to bleed, suffer, and die for us. Indeed, God does not disappoint. He loves us. How else could He put up with you and me?

Our minds and hearts return to the First Century Church. In the fourth chapter of the Book of Acts we read: "And when they had prayed, the place in which they were gathered together was shaken." Dare you and I ask for anything less than this?

Prayer: Oh Savior of the World, cause those hindrances to a power-filled prayer life to be taken from our midst. Amen.

———

*Hagerstown Exponent* March 28, 1968

## ❧GOD LOVES US❧

WELLING UP IN the springs of man's consciousness is a story, old and magnificent.

Many years ago—too many to count—God looked upon one of His creations. It was called "The Planet Earth." God remembered how he had fashioned it into the shape of a ball and tossed it out in space. It was His special project because of the creatures who would inhabit it. On this massive and gigantic ball was placed a being who bore the image of God. This creature would have everything at his fingertips including the Creator's hand. God's "pride and joy" was obedient. His great and tender heart was shattered and began to throb in pain. After rendering proper punishment, He gave His attention to other matters in His universe. He had to do something in an attempt to forget man's disobedience and thanklessness. As the centuries passed, God could contain His feelings no longer. He must turn His eyes once again upon "The Planet Earth" and see what His thankless children were doing. By now there were thousands upon thousands of them wandering to and fro. All had heard and seem evidence of the supreme forces in the universe. Some believed all forces were really one and called Him "Father." God wept as He viewed their lost condition, their confusion, and their sins. Oh, how they needed a savior and a right relationship to Him! As He wiped His tear-filled eyes, He cried out, "I can stand it no longer! I love them! I shall send My Son as Savior to show them the Way." The blazing suns trembled, the silent moons shook, the sparkling stars quivered, and every planet knew God had spoken.

However you and I paint such a picture, a glorious fact shines brilliantly: God is very generous with human beings. Perhaps the earth is a sphere. Perhaps God spent millions of years creating it. Perhaps God is not as much like us as we like to think. Perhaps . . . perhaps . . . perhaps. When we say "God is very generous with human beings," the word "perhaps" is awkward and offensive. Try to place monetary value on God's generosity. Try to estimate in dollars and cents how much the birth, life, death, and resurrection of Jesus Christ are worth.

God gives His all. When pondering the value of Jesus Christ, Saint Paul exclaims, "Thanks be to God for His inexpressible gift!" In one of those rare moments the Apostle could find no accurate words. Indeed, God's gift of Jesus Christ is an example of generosity that defies dictionaries and vocabularies.

Prayer: Father God too long we have received Thy Son, Jesus Christ, in a manner of fact way: forgive Thy ungrateful children. Amen.

---

*Hagerstown Exponent* July 18, 1968

# ❊GOD LOVES US❊

WISE MEN AND women never undervalue what goes unspoken.

This is the difference between success and failure in the business world. After he makes an unpopular decision involving one of his men, the plant foreman watches for seething resentment. When an executive has to command one of his lieutenants to carry out an odious order, he watches for signs indicating ego injury. The most logical action by the front office may be taken with extreme caution because of secret conclaves in the hearts of its employees. At the conference tables where equals are supposedly meeting with equals the unrehearsed sneer and rehearsed cough are a definite part of the proceedings. When a large order is being contracted by a company, both parties not only sound out one another in words but in actions that speak as well.

Deciphering the unverbalized is the difference between mediocrity and greatness in the professions. How about your medical doctor? When you go to him to be treated for an inherited liver ailment which you bemoan as a sure killer, can he quickly see you have a little acid indigestion and not much else? Does he probe further and see your upset stomach is probably due to worry over your acute sickness which doesn't exist . . . yet? Does he probe still further and determine other non-physical factors which are blowing your "sure-death disease" into an oversized balloon? Does he slowly let the air out, slowly make you aware of your real condition, and slowly perform a healing operation on the personality? A great attorney at law studies his client's every move. If you are lying every step of the way, he will let you know he can spot your treachery. Then he may bluntly tell you he can do nothing for you, until your inadequacies and failures are stripped of all fancy pleats and trimmings . . . those false ruffles just won't do. The two of you launder your dirty linen, or he sends you elsewhere. Of course, all of us have to come clean before Jesus Christ can really plead our case before God.

Oftentimes what remains unspoken is more important than what is spoken. Let's take a quick look at the international level of politics. Few diplomats were ever primarily interested in the rotund Mr. Khrushchev's printed and spoken speeches. It was the dialogue within his own mind which American statesmen had to hear. They studiously labored over his antics such as table pounding, unorthodox toasts, sudden winces, and unexpected smiles. To know only a person's words is never to know him at a depth level. Every foreign embassy in the world has learned this. Some have had to relearn it in order to survive.

Let's spend a moment on the local community level. All of us have heard the expression "Oh, I can read him like a book." This begins to be true insofar as we have more than the printed page and spoken word to go by. Those who consider themselves close friends for years frequently discover there is a whole area of one's personality which the other knows almost nothing about. The squirming, dodging, fabricating, laughing, and crying were not watched closely enough. Had the signs been observed closely, tragedy might very well have been averted.

You and I always say what we mean . . . frequently in unspoken words.

Prayer: God of boundless love, teach us to be more mindful of what precious human beings are really trying to say to us. Amen.

———

*Hagerstown Exponent* September 12, 1968

# ❋DO POLITICS, RELIGION MIX?❋

THE NUMEROUS prominent Protestant preachers across the country entering into the political arena provide an intriguing phenomenon. Their directness and finesse in public relations that utilizes all of the media has become almost an all-pervasive force. Their promotional abilities in many cases seem even superior to those "regular politicians." Who is to say whether this is good or bad, constructive or destructive?

Of course, this is not the first time pulpiteers have voiced their political preferences in American history.

In the last century there arose a personality whose oratorical abilities were national and even international in scope. He had neither radio nor television. Yet, his magnetic voice and popular pulpit prose made him a masterful political figure.

But wait, we are getting ahead of our story.

Henry Ward Beecher, the son of Lyman Beecher and brother of Harriet Beecher Stowe, began his ministry at the First Presbyterian Church in Lawrenceburgh, Indiana, in 1837. In 1839 he moved to the Second Presbyterian Church in Indianapolis. It was not then the magnificent cathedral it is today. In fact, the young preacher found a membership of exactly thirty-two persons. The Hoosier capitol could not hold him.

In 1847 Henry Ward, his wife, and their children made their way to Plymouth Congregational Church in Brooklyn. For the next forty years the great orator would hold forth, sometimes preaching to thousands at one service.

During those four decades, it is safe to say no preacher on the American scene spoke more eloquently on so many different political issues. He was the recognized king and his kingdom included countless officeholders and others involved in politics. Henry Ward Beecher was a promoter par excellence. He knew presidents. He liked to think they took his advice. There is even some indication he aspired to the presidency. Just how serious a run for the White House was, we shall leave up to the historians. It was often said the great preacher allowed his emotions to control his intellect; therefore, he assumed his high profile that evoked tears and laughter were indicative of real power.

Volumes of his writings remain to be studied and—for the most part—appreciated. They illustrate again and again his sensitivity to American life, especially in the political sphere.

But there is a certain sadness about this winsome preacher and capable politician. There seemed to be a flaw in his character that eventually surfaced at the very pinnacle of his career. His flamboyance, political dexterity, and oratorical magnificence were never able to silence a single sinister fact. He was officially charged with adultery and was tried in a public trial.

*Rushville Daily Republican* September 20, 1980

## ❖WORLD WATCHES TENSIONS BUILD❖

THE WORLD WATCHES as tensions build in and around Poland, a gallant nation.

In this century Poland has been caught in the middle of two world wars. The death, destruction and despair have been astronomical. Both Germany and Russia have taken turns humiliating a very brave country.

Now Soviet Russia weighs the pros and cons of bringing the Poles in line more fully with socialism or "the socialist path." Of course, there are options. Whatever one(s) the Soviets decide to utilize, something looms with lethal clarity arid persistence: at whatever cost Poland will remain a part of satellite system in eastern Europe protecting the USSR. A renegade Yugoslavia headed by an almost arrogantly independent Tito cannot be tolerated. For one thing, Poland's border touches that of Russia's. An independent Poland? Unthinkable!

Let's suppose the Soviets decide an all-out, crushing invasion is a necessity. What would be the response of the Poles and, in particular, the military forces? Widespread thinking seems to be that the Polish army would defect in large numbers and carry on guerrilla warfare. Would this be an example of pride and courage blinding the inevitable? That's a most difficult question to answer, largely because we do not know exactly what the USA, France, and England would do under such circumstances. As one ponders such a frightening situation, the moral reality of dying in vain refuses to go unheard. Our theorizing could go on and on, following much the same line of reasoning. But there is another factor, indeed a very important person, pundits seem reluctant to mention.

Did you ever hear of Pope John Paul II? Well, who hasn't. The Holy Father comes from Poland. His story of tenacity during some of his country's darkest days has been told often. He survived triumphantly. Just when everyone, including many Roman Catholic prelates, said it was not possible for him to be elected the Bishop of Rome, he was. He is a most interesting blend of conservatism, tradition, orthodoxy, and liberation. Did his emergency and consequent victorious journeys to the four corners of the world give many in Poland a false sense of hope that at last Soviet Russia would both back down and back away? Perhaps. Would the Holy Father die for his countrymen? I think so. In fact, if called upon to do so, I strongly suspect he would give his life as the Vicar of Christ for all of us. Soviet Russia could grow insanely frustrated trying to deal with such a foe!

To say we hope and pray the Russian Bear behaves itself is a bit hackneyed. Of course, we "hope and pray" for such a result. What we Americans seem never to be skilled at is watchful patience. Our historical, political, and even theological perspectives can be so very limited. You and I know nothing of the severe pressures under which generations of Poles have lived. God in His infinite wisdom has spared us.

So, as we wrestle with our economic morass, crisis in basic morality, and sagging morale, what about Poland?

Ponder these haunting words from Svetlana Alilluyeva, the daughter of Joseph Stalin, at the time of the Soviet Dictator's death: "My father died a difficult and terrible death. God grants an easy death only to the just."

---

*Rushville Daily Republican* December 16, 1980

# ✤AN INSPIRATIONAL BOOK✤

WE ALL HAVE our favorite books. Those who have substantial libraries have several favorites. I have one that sits in my reference section. It is bound in a serene blue. The lettering is in a striking gold on the end facing those pursuing that group of books. The title? Well, it's *Alcoholics Anonymous* (Third Edition—New and Revised). It is more than a favorite. It is a special volume with a value beyond anyone's checkbook. The opening page contains several heartfelt words from the man who gave it to me. Among those words you will find this: "Look back over your life. Honestly, now, can't you see how the loving Hand of God has brought a happy ending to many events that seemed to be unmitigated tragedies at the time?" The signature at the bottom of the page is simply "Joe." What about the contents?

Really, the reader should begin near the end. There—in brief—we discover six Appendices. Each deserves comment.

"The A.A. Tradition" is really "Twelve Traditions." In essence it is a mini-constitution that enables the movement to survive and endure. Without being totally exact, here is a look-see. The common welfare is to come first; there is only one ultimate authority (a loving God) and A.A. leaders are just trusted servants; the only requirement for membership is a desire to stop drinking; each group is—for the most part—autonomous; there is one primary purpose and that is to carry its message to the alcoholic still suffering; a group should never endorse, finance, or lend its name to any related facility or outside enterprise, lest it be diverted from its primary purpose; each group should be fully self-supporting; A.A. should remain nonprofessional, but may employ special workers; A.A. should never be organized, except for boards or committees directly responsible to those they serve; A.A. has no opinion on outside issues and hopefully will not be drawn into public controversy; public relations is based on attraction in place of promotion with personal anonymity maintained; and anonymity enables principles to be placed before personalities.

"Spiritual Experience" specifically refers to personality change sufficient to bring about recovery from alcoholism. With boldness and absoluteness we discover: "Most emphatically we wish to say that any alcoholic capable of honestly facing his problems in the light of our experience can recover, provided he does not close his mind to all spiritual concepts. He can only be defeated by an attitude of intolerance or belligerent denial."

"The Medical View on A.A." contains quotations from a number of prominent professionals, especially psychiatrists, who heartily endorse it. Perhaps the most profound and succinct statement was said nearly thirty-five years ago by Dr. W. W. Bauer. In effect, he said A.A. is neither a bunch of crusaders nor a temperance society; they just know that they must never drink.

"The Lasker Award" was given to A.A. in l951 by the American Public Health Association. A part of the citation reads: "In emphasizing alcoholism as an illness, the social stigma associated with this condition is being blotted out."

"The Religious View on A.A." indicates there is a widespread blessing given to it by clergy in nearly every denomination. Father Edward Dowling, S.J. and Harry Emerson Fosdick are quoted.

"How to Get in Touch With A.A." says a group can be located through the local telephone directory, newspaper office, or police station. Contacts can also be made through local priests or ministers. If one cannot be found in your locality, then a letter should be addressed to: Alcoholics Anonymous, Box 459, Grand Central Station, New York, New York, 10163.

The great bulk of the book is personal stories. All are worth the time of any thoughtful and caring person.

Who is "Joe"? He is my very talented brother. His address? Well, he lives on the West Coast . . . in sobriety. He was born January 30. Happy birthday, my brother . . . and victor!

———

*Rushville Daily Republican* February 28, 1981

# ❋PRESIDENT PHYLLIS SCHLAFLY?❋

A RECENT BIOGRAPHY has caused increased interest in Phyllis Schlafly that vivacious and brilliant lady from Illinois.

For a number of years she has vehemently and expertly opposed the Equal Rights Amendment. In fact, she is probably the greatest single influence such an amendment has not been approved by enough states to become the law of the land.

Sadly (and inaccurately) Phyllis has been depicted as something of a tool of far right-wingers who seem short on logic and long on demagoguery. Let's take a look at the facts.

My first contact with her was at the International Platform Convention in Washington, D.C., during the summer of 1976. She debated an officer of the NOW organization; she was so superior in debating skills and intellect it seemed to me there was little contest. The imperial demeanor about her and the way she could righteously strike at the jugular were much in evidence. I dare say there was no man alive that day who could have conquered Phyllis! She was excitingly mean without being vulgar. She moved with respect upon her opponent but never left any doubt about who was going to leave the platform with head high awaiting a new opponent. Really, anyone who could not have appreciated her performance on that day I have to believe was either very prejudiced or irretrievably stupid. So much for a personal experience. What does her resume say?

Phyllis received the B.A. from Washington University in Saint Louis; the M. A. from Harvard University; and the Doctor of Jurisprudence from Washington University Law School. She is a member of the Illinois Bar Association. Among her many honors are: Phi Beta Kappa, LL.D. from Niagara University, Pi Sigma Alpha (Political Science Honorary), nine honor medals from Freedom Foundation at Valley Forge, Woman of Achievement (*Globe Democrat*), and Brotherhood Award (National Conference of Christians and Jews). She is the author of nine books and a syndicated newspaper column. The International Society of Girlwatchers calls her "the world's most watchable mother" (she has six children). She has lectured or debated on the campus of more colleges and universities than this column can list (nearly a hundred).

Isn't it ironic a lady with so much professional equipment and personal charisma has given herself so totally and completely to stopping ERA? One would expect her to be doing quite the opposite. Had the proponents of this controversial amendment had her services, would it have already passed? I think so. Of course, Phyllis would have it no other way. She knew her case, was dedicated to it, and is very likely the one most influential in preventing its passage. But that isn't the biggest piece of irony.

Who, among today's women is better qualified in time, to become our first president from the weaker (you have to be kidding!) sex? She is a leader with integrity and that highly unusual ability of being able to put together what traditionalists call the ideals of motherhood and what liberationists label feminine competence. She is a mother superior whose submissiveness is a work of art.

Will we someday call her Madame President? Perhaps. In light of past and current issues, she just might put a lot of men, women, and families back together.

———

*Rushville Daily Republican* February 28, 1981

# ❉WHEN WE FORGET TO WATCH THE CLOCK❉

HAVE YOU AND I ever really confronted the religious implications of this truth: "Time waits for no one?" Have we come to terms with the awesome fact that we only have one life to live here and now? With all of our scientific advancements we cannot prolong it much and often-times not at all.

There is a certain rich man. He amasses more and more of this world's goods. Then he channels them into the most tax-favorable areas. Soon he has to purchase another safe into which he can pile more insurance policies, stocks, and bonds. His health begins to break. It grows steadily worse; but, ah, there is still time to eat, drink and be merry. He has the best medical specialists that money can buy. They keep him alive to enjoy his possessions. Finally, the body is completely worn out. No medical or philosophical genius can keep him breathing for more than a few days. Time is rapidly running out. His entire life is best described as "routine rationalizations." His final act is the king of all rationalizations. He buys the best section of a mausoleum in hope that he can cheat Father Time by proclaiming earthly immortality. If we prevent a nuclear war, even the mausoleum will have crumbled in a thousand years. The Old Testament is correct when it says a thousand years are as one day with God.

Most of us are not wealthy and are likely to get a certain consolation from such a tragic approach to life. Our minds begin to tell us how little of this world's goods we have and how unlikely this is to happen to us. Let us remember that the devils are not ordered out of heaven because of their wealth. It was their disobedience that made them unacceptable to God. Regardless of our economical status, there are deadly rationalizations at work in our lives. The road to hell is not paved so much with good intentions as it is with lethal rationalizations.

Time is on nobody's side. The astute executive knows neither he nor his firm can produce more time. He also knows it is of crucial importance that all available time be well-spent. With this perspective in mind, how are we using this day? How will we use our tomorrows? Are we teaching our children the wise use of their moments on the stage of history?

Prayer: Dear God, Creator and Sustainer, let Your love so overpower us that all our future days may become successful and victorious in Your sight. Amen.

Basic Affirmation: I promise to use my time to the best advantage under the guidance of a just God.

*Senior Times* October 25, 1991

# ❋WHEN ENTERING A NEW YEAR❋

HOW DOES ONE profitably enter a new and promising year?

The key word is responsibility. There is never any meaning in life apart from this noble and yet challenging idea. Serious-minded Christians around the world believe that each of us is intended to grow spiritually. There are certain areas, in particular, where expectations run the highest.

We are held responsible by a just God for regular Sunday attendance in our churches. In place of using a thousand and one devices to get people into our churches, why don't Christian church members stick by this principle?

Surely it is not wrong or even inappropriate to expect those who have united with the Body of Christ to be in His church with exacting regularity. How can you and I anticipate any meaning in life, unless we give God .006 of the week on Sunday morning?

We are held responsible by a patient God to sell our churches to others. There is a certain awesome power in evangelistic salesmanship that we seldom tap. It is obviously through some attempt to abuse this part of the lay and ministerial obligation. This, of course, is no acceptable reason for you and me to ignore evangelism as just so much emotional trivia.

We are held responsible by a merciful God for all of life. It is total and complete stewardship that Jesus talks about. Talents and time are just as important in their own way as in money. You and I are to take care of and utilize everything God has given to us, even life itself. On that Great Day of Truth, our Lord may very well ask us if we taught a Sunday School class, sang in the church choir, and served as an effective member of the evangelism committee before He ever mentions money.

We are held responsible by a personal God for private worshipful sessions with Him. However great or small human freedom may be, each of us needs to admit there are times when everyone of us can know our Maker more fully and talk with Him more in detail, if we will! Jesus Christ is not a robot or a computer. He was human flesh and blood who walked and talked among people He loved. In the twentieth century He asks us to walk and talk with Him.

Prayer: Dear Father of Mankind, in Your boundless love forgive our shortcomings and inspire us with firmness to responsible living. Amen.

Basic Affirmation: I promise to uphold my church by congregational worship, reaching out to the unchurched, dedicating my time and talents anew, and holding private sessions with God.

*Senior Times* January 3, 1992

# ❀WHEN CARING SEEMS OUTDATED❀

THE HUMAN BEING is precious. The old man who takes the name of God in vain so often, doesn't realize what he is doing . . . the old woman finds sadistic enjoyment in depicting the younger generation as "a bunch of desperados going to hell on a push-cart." . . the disturbed man who chronically complains everybody is against him, including the Man upstairs . . . the vain woman who visualizes every community organization as a private weapon . . . the young fellow who accepts God solely as Creator and ignores His Son, the Savior . . . the young lady whose every wish is geared to catching any man who shows promise of rising socially and economically . . . the little boy who cheats at basketball . . . the little girl who steals her friend's doll. All are precious to God and to you and me.

There are others. Those who give an angry "no" to our every invitation to the services of the Church . . . those who try again and again to justify themselves apart from Christ and His Church . . . those who feel membership in a particular church and social status are inseparably tied together . . . those who refuse to see the lay and professional ministry as a continuous undertaking through the centuries . . . those who offer infantile excuses for never attending the House of the Lord. Jesus Christ has died for all of these personality types.

The glorious resurrection of Christ is never seen clearly apart from the shadow of the Cross on our Blessed Lord's tomb. Great spiritual victories are wrung out of turmoil, turbulence, and travail. From time to time we all search in the spiritual realm for something for nothing. Sometimes we find it and learn it costs us nothing. It goes under many labels. It is best described as "sweetened by indifference and served up in jiggers of spiritual doodling." A generous financial contribution will not put your arm around the shoulders of a friend. It will not tell him how much you want him to come to terms with Christ and His Church. Serving on a committee is not the same as falling on your knees and praying for one who in countless ways has spurned the love of Christ and His Church.

Prayer: Gracious and merciful God, grant us the courage and bravery to love every precious human being; In Your Son's Name. Amen.

Basic Affirmation: I promise with God's help to care for all human beings under all circumstances.

———

*Senior Times* August 7, 1992

# ❈WHEN PUTTING IT OFF SEEMS THE❈ RIGHT THING TO DO

ONCE A MAN saw a vision in which the Devil was presiding over his evil spirits. Soon he came to the main business of the meeting and said, "Who will go to the earth and persuade men to ruin their souls?" One ambitious spirit rose and said he would go. The Devil asked, "How will you do it?" "By persuading them there is no heaven," was the answer. The Devil growled, "That will not get the job done." A second loyal spirit volunteered. "And how will you do it?" inquired the Devil. "By persuading them there is no hell," was the reply. The Devil grumbled, "That will not attain my goal. We must have something that will appeal to all classes, ages, and dispositions." Immediately, a sinister-looking spirit came forward and said, "I shall go." "And how do you propose to do it?" demanded the Devil. "I will tell them there is no hurry," he responded. The Devil jumped with glee and sent him on his mission. Most of the successes and excesses of evil can be laid at the door of religious procrastination.

Many receive into their lives the habit of putting off until tomorrow their religious impulses. Sometimes we attempt to tell ourselves this is an inborn trait; but back there someplace, wasn't it learned? Some wrap their arms around the habit of religious procrastination and hug it like a child with a teddy bear. Perhaps both are in need of a little human and Divine attention.

Countless numbers conceive of this life as being an end in itself. Of course, if this existence that you and I are now passing through is all there is and ever shall be, it makes sense to do things the way most of us do them. The most blaring of all characteristics of society today is the utter unconcern of life beyond the grave. We laugh and joke about "not being able to take our material possessions with us." What strikes at my religious barometer is this: "It is neither a laughing or joking matter. We absolutely cannot take them with us." All we really have is our individual nakedness before God. Our ways offer damaging evidence that we want to believe and in some cases, I fear, do believe there is not such a thing as a deathless soul. Unless this life is a grooming chamber for the next, we are left with an unarisen Jesus Christ. He is still dead. If this is the case, our religion terminates with Good Friday. The motto of "get all you can while the getting is good because you're going to be dead a long time" makes the face of God grow scarlet with anger.

Prayer: Eternal God, show us Your boundless love again that we may repent of our damnable religious negligence and indifference; through Jesus Christ our Lord and Savior. Amen.

Basic Affirmation: I promise to see my procrastinations in the religious life for what they are: attempts to squelch the truth of an immortal soul.

---

*Senior Times* January 29, 1993

## ❊DON'T LET YOUR AMBITIONS TURN❊
## INTO GREEDY MISSIONS

"I AM GOING to have that!" There is something or perhaps even someone we are going to possess. If you are like I am, there are a number of times in my life that was very real.

If it is a worthy goal that will benefit others, most likely we are onto something good. If it is the kind of possessing that calls into question ethics, then what? We do have a quandary!

Just maybe greed is the real issue at hand. We don't care much who gets hurt; we are going to have it! Ambition is a powerful force but it can be deadly.

So, how can we think through the consequences of our actions? Well, of course, only a novice in human relations pretends to be an expert here! But don't we have to be careful?

Someone has said, "If we are too careful about our actions, we never do anything." That's true and yet it isn't. Simply "to be" is to have actions and that's life!

Maybe you are considering a course of action that will impact others right now. You are on the verge of moving greedily to possess something you have wanted for a long time. Is it worth it?

Once in awhile we really get involved in heavy rationalizations, don't we? "I have thought it through and that's mine. Get out of the way or I will run over you." Ouch!

Pure and unadulterated greed has a habit of justifying itself. Money may not be the issue at all. It may be someone else's wife or someone else's husband!

Is greed in the eye of the beholder? Sometimes that can really be a clever way out of our dilemma. "You may think I am greedy but that's just your uninformed opinion!"

Well, people can be very cruel and plan to discredit our worthy motives. So let them be that way! Whoever said we are to police other people's viewpoints?

Sometimes a significant goal is within our grasp. We grab for it and it eludes us. What went wrong and whose fault is it we have failed?

Those of us who have lived some years know to fail may be to succeed. Rudyard Kipling helps us here: ". . . meet with triumph and disaster and treat those impostors just the same."

Did we bring anything into the world? Will we take anything out of the world? We know the answers to those questions and consequently have a basic insight into greed.

———

*New Castle Courier-Times* December 12, 1998

# ✱HOORAY FOR GRANDPARENTS✱

A VERY SERIOUS lady said to me, "Isn't it terrible children have to be raised by grandparents today?" Well, I don't know. My grandparents spoiled me and I loved it.

As I reflected, my mind (and heart) took a short trip. I drove out of New Castle on Brown Road and found my way to the Mooreland Cemetery. As usual, it was well kept.

There, I quickly found the tombstone of my maternal grandparents. They were Glade and Grace (Gibson) Walradth. I shed a tear or two and began to remember some great times.

He was a livestock dealer and farmer. Often, as a boy, he would take me to the sale barns and some days I can still hear the auctioneers. Boy, was that fun!

She always had a sacrificial way about her I have never forgotten. She was a woman who did hard physical work but was also cultured, quoting poetry. She was such a caring lady.

Then my mind (and heart) went on up the road to the Blountsville Cemetery. There, like a little rock of Gibraltar, I spotted another tombstone. Yes, there was another tear or two.

This was where my paternal grandparents were laid to rest. They were Guy and Christie (McCall) Lacy. They were such precious hardworking and strong people.

He was a plasterer and applied his trade across east central Indiana. He took his grandson at the ripe old age of fourteen and told him its time to carry the hod. He was a kind man.

She made the best prune cakes and always saved things for me. She used to kid her grandson about his girlfriends, even before he had one. She was special and never flashy.

As difficult as it was, I had to return to the remark about grandparents raising children. Indeed, it is a different day and time for many across our land. Family brokenness is obvious.

What's happened to us? Why is it necessary for many today to raise both their children and grandchildren? Those questions have bothered me for years and they still do.

There's always enough blame to go around for everyone. So, why not appreciate who and what we can? I was very privileged and shall forever be grateful, even sentimental.

Humanity sooner or later passes through times (and obligations) that just don't seem right. Remember, every potential tragedy is also a potential triumph. Hooray for grandparents!

---

*New Castle Courier-Times* February 6, 1999

# ❋TAKE TIME TO KNOW OUR TEACHERS❋

"THERE AREN'T ANY good teachers anymore," said Mr. Crabby of Complainsville, U.S.A. That's about the most preposterous thing I have heard in a long time. Of course, there are good teachers today.

My first recollection of a teacher was Mrs. Marie Buell in the first grade at Blountsville. Would you believe she always prayed before we ate at noon? I can't recall the words, only the respect.

Many years later it dawned on me what she gave me in the classroom. She was the epitome of stability and security. We were in safe hands and she was a permanent fixture.

Are there women and men much like her today in the early years of school? Yes. Yes. Yes. I'll also bet there is a lot more prayer done in those classrooms than some suspect.

I must confess my favorite teacher was a relative. Her name was Aunt Marjorie (Lacy) Luellen. Her husband, a former trustee of Stoney Creek Township, died quite unexpectedly.

What did she do? Well she started to college and eventually did a graduate degree. She used to laugh about getting all done before she had to retire to a rocking chair.

Marjorie was a sweet and very intelligent woman. She was a pillar in the Blountsville Christian Church and a former postmaster. Yes, and she was a Democrat and I mean a Democrat.

Her teaching career lasted twenty-two years, all in the Union School Corporation of Randolph County. She especially distinguished herself as a sponsor of Little Hoosiers. Bless her heart.

A log house literally was brought to the school in her memory and restored. You think there aren't any good teachers anymore? Well, she taught all of her years after 1970.

I always wanted to see her have a doctor's degree but that didn't happen. Some of us tried but couldn't get that done. But it doesn't matter because Saint Peter probably calls her "Doc" in heaven.

You see, flesh and blood, dedicated to education in the broadest sense makes for good teachers. They are all around us. We do have to take the time to know them.

Take your child's teacher(s) aside and tell him or her you appreciate their work. Isn't teaching a ministry? It is and there are no easy positions in the school systems today.

I loved the three years I taught history and English in Jay County. Maybe it was because I got a really good grounding in practice teaching. That was done in the old New Castle High School.

---

*New Castle Courier-Times* March 13, 1999

## ❋MUSIC SPEAKS TO EVERYONE❋

I HAVE OFTEN pondered the saying, "Music is the only universal language." It intrigues me because there is an abiding truth in the statement. Music speaks like nothing else.

Even though I am not a musician, it has spoken to me uniquely above virtually everything. The only exception would be the Holy Scriptures. Then, I enjoy the lyrical quality of the Psalms.

It seems there is nothing on the face of this earth that moves so many people. Those of us who are dunces in this field, nevertheless, immerse our heads and hearts. What a gift from God!

Music for centuries has motivated men to battle bravely for their nations. In our nation soldiers, sailors, and marines sang the "National Anthem," determined to give their lives.

History books tell us of the superhuman bravery of the soldiers, who surrounded Napoleon Bonaparte. His charisma was supported by music. With an emotional splendor they died for him.

Brahms, Beethoven, Mozart, and Bach all conjure up feasts of emotional, mental, and spiritual involvement. Such genius takes us into pure ecstasy. Heaven is near!

Gospel music with such gifted people as Bill and Gloria Gaither can cause torrents of tears. Our feelings receive an injection of love. Try to count the smiles.

The whole field is so enormous we probe and discover only a smattering of what has been given to us. Who is to say what is better than another? Highbrow or lowbrow—who cares?

Take country music. Try to name all of the performers and you can get a very large headache. Willie Nelson, Dolly Parton, and Garth Brooks are only a beginning.

I am reminded of my Grandfather Guy Lacy, who never made it into high school. That didn't matter. He had his own musical tastes and his oldest grandson loved them.

One hot summer day we were sent to the old Princess theater in New Castle on a work detail. We were to patch the outside walls. We were a good team.

On a late afternoon I heard singing and clapping inside the Princess. Grandfather had disappeared. Finally I found him at the rear of the building with his ear to the wall.

Little Jimmy Dickens was on stage belting out "Take an Old Cold Tater and Wait" and "May the Bird of Paradise Fly Up Your Nose." The dear man had an angelic smile. Don't argue with that!

_____

*New Castle Courier-Times* June 12, 1999


# ❉YOU'RE A MINISTER? I'LL BUY YOUR❉ COFFEE ANYWAY


"BOY, IS THAT a good place to eat!" the truck driver exclaimed. On most trips he managed to stop there and fill up a big tummy. He looked forward to it and loved to see it on the horizon.

My experience is truck drivers always know the best places to eat. It may be fast food or an expensive diner. Nevertheless, they always know where to go.

It seems to be a built-in piece of information that is infallible. Trust them and they will not fail you. When in doubt in a strange area, just ask one.

By the way, have you ever noticed how intelligent they are? My education has been enhanced immensely by some to them. They are not merely doers; they are also thinkers.

Some of my most enlightening conversations have been with them. I have learned not to let them know I am a preacher at first. That has to come later, much later.

I recall this fellow a few weeks ago who expounded on theology. He had insights galore and I listened intently. He really said some powerful things.

Once again this illustrated for me that God is everyplace. Some of our best preachers are never ordained. In fact, they seldom go to any church.

Dirt and grime, some profanity, and wild T-shirts are only the trimmings. What counts is something else. These guys really do some heavy thinking!

Of course, some are openly religious and have lighted crosses on their cabs. That's a breath of fresh air at night on lonely interstates. It's like a beacon.

Perhaps my favorite visit was with a fellow who was cynical of churches and preachers. He told me they were all a bunch of hypocrites. I just listened.

Then, he told me he bet I was some sort of a good counselor and he appreciated my listening to him. Then he swore, burped loudly, and prepared to leave.

He said I want to buy your coffee, sir. I said that's a great idea. So he reached for another dollar before paying. Then, he said you ain't a preacher are you?

I pleaded guilty and tried to smile. He said that he just knew it some place along the line. Then, he smiled and said I am going to buy your coffee anyway.

———

*New Castle Courier-Times* September 18, 1999

# ✸A LOOK BACK . . . MEMORIES OF THE✸ GREAT ONES

"SHE WAS A queen" the man said, as he looked upon his mother's face in death. He remembered so many good things about her. Yet, for some reason he forgot to tell her while she was living.

Really, he was a dutiful and grateful son. He just hadn't recognized and thanked her enough. She was unquestionably a queen in his eyes and some others as well.

Have you ever had similar feelings? Well, I have and sometimes it makes me feel sad. More could have been said and more thoughtful recognition given.

I especially remember Grandmother Grace (Gibson) Walradth, who rests triumphantly in the Mooreland Cemetery. Her parents named her well. She was both graceful and gracious.

That lady was a real prize. She is the only woman I have ever known who could do hard farm work gracefully. This was true whether she milked cows or fried chicken.

It seemed to me she more or less glided through her work. Only after she was gone did I learn her secret. She didn't really know she was a queen but others did.

She had two daughters and three sons. She cared for them with class. Her oldest grandson marveled at her with little appreciation at the time. What a lady!

It was not the work she did that impressed nearly as much as her style. That lady could be gracious around farm animals and piles of you know what. My friends, try doing that!

She was a part of nobility that no one could confer upon her. God gave her that special gift of being "grace" in ways I still get emotional about. She has been at rest more than thirty years.

So, do you know someone with so much rustic royalty? Better tell her today that she is a queen. There are women struggling in the contemporary world in their private and professional lives.

But I'll bet under today's circumstances there is a queen in your life somewhere. Look around and look carefully. Is she graceful and gracious in trying circumstances?

Ah yes, they are among us, aren't they? Their finesse carries the day and those about them are nurtured. Why wait to pass along the accolades?

Well, Grandmother Grace that's it for now. Enjoy your queenship. I can think of only one other woman who ranks ahead of you and that's our Lord's Mother, Mary.

---

*New Castle Courier-Times* November 27, 1999

# ✺A HUMBLE MAN IS A PRECIOUS TREASURE✺

"ALL HE EVER wanted to do was throw his weight around," the man said. For those listening the message was quite clear. Here was a man who valued power and influence over others.

We have all seen them. It seems they are usually ambitious men but sometimes we perceive women the same way. It is a fact of life and adjustment is often necessary.

From a different viewpoint, have you known those who could throw their weight around but who didn't? In fact, they were even expected to do so. Yet, for some reason they didn't.

I remember a man very well, who fit into that category. Not only did he have power and influence, he was handsome. Had he spoken, others would virtually have gotten on their knees.

This fellow was a member of my parish some years ago in Seymour. He came to worship often with his wife and family. You couldn't miss him and his demeanor was that of a statesman.

He was the former governor of the State of Indiana, Edgar D. Whitcomb. He was "class" in the traditional sense. He looked like a governor, senator, or even a President.

Not once in the nearly five years I was in that pastorate did I ever see him throw his weight around. In a way, he even seemed to work at not doing it! I really appreciated him.

Well, how about you and me in our little worlds of power and influence? Is it important we show others we can put people in their places! Let's be honest, dear friends.

A tyrant or overly dominant person can be anyplace, even at the smallest committee meeting. I suppose the reasons are many. Sometimes such a person poisons the entire setting.

Whenever I am tempted to throw my weight around, a few words enter my consciousness. They are crucial. Sometimes they cause my brain to go reeling for a moment.

They come from First Corinthians and go like this: "Love is patient and kind; love is not jealous or boastful; it is not arrogant or rude." That's a wake-up call! It is necessary.

I strongly suspect the best way we exercise our power and influence is with those words burnt into our beings. Then, we can do the work of the Master. Then, our weight becomes positive, even therapeutic.

So, why don't you and I, regardless of our perceived importance, flee from the temptation of being Mr. Big or Ms. Big? Ben Franklin once said, "Imitate Jesus and Socrates." Splendid advice.

———

*New Castle Courier-Times* February 5, 2000

## ✤RESPECT NOT THE PROBLEM✤

"HE WAS A difficult man but I loved him," the son said in regard to his father. Respect was not the problem. A difference in personalities and generations was.

How many people have you known who were difficult but you loved them? Just maybe you and I are among those considered difficult! Hopefully people love us.

My memory takes me back to a man that I thought, as a little boy, was a giant. He must have been ten feet tall in those days. He could do anything and everything.

He was my grandfather Glade Walradth. As the oldest grandson, I seemed to rate a special privilege or two. In retrospect I believe others noticed this long before I did.

When he took me along to the various livestock sale barns in east central Indiana, I thought I was in heaven. When he gave me a fifty-cent piece, I knew I was. Goodness, what good times!

As I walked along with him among the farmers and dealers, I could sense a certain aura. Papaw was somebody. Even in silence they moved so he and I had plenty of room.

As the years passed, I learned he was very successful. He owned hundreds of acres of farmland and was a very skilled businessman. He was a proud man who relished his place.

Well, yes, people said he was a difficult man but I loved him. Papaw Walradth was a man among men in a day and time of rugged individualism and all that entails.

Sometimes he just simply outfoxed his competitors. He always walked with his head and shoulders thrown back. His kingdom was there to see and that didn't help some people very much.

He was a sports fan par excellence. He had two sons who put little Center High School on the map. I believe he fought as hard as they did at some of those games.

Only recently a man told me that in his high-school basketball days, he had helped rough-up one of the Walradth boys. Well, this was about 1940 and things were some different. Basketball was war.

It seems the fellow helping with the roughing-up moved quietly away from the incident. Then, at midcourt he turned to look in another direction and was met with a right to the jaw. Grandfather decided to defend his son's honor!

Was he really a difficult man? It's hard to admit but I guess he must have been. But I loved him and Papaw resides in the Mooreland Cemetery as competitive as ever.

––––––––

*New Castle Courier-Times* March 4, 2000

## ❋A MOTHER'S SPECIAL LOVE❋

"ONLY HIS MOTHER could find him handsome," the old gentleman laughed. Well, there were people poking fun at the little guy. Define good looks and he didn't seem to have any.

There were those who tried to hold back their snickers. For the most part, everyone—regardless of age—just smiled or frowned quickly and moved on. His playmates were not very kind.

Well, God bless them, as far as I know, mothers have always found their daughters beautiful and sons handsome. Giving birth is special, regardless. I strongly suspect there is nothing quite like it.

But there is a bigger—much bigger—picture and that has to do with all children. As far as I know, none of them ever asked to come into this world. Maybe you know something I don't.

I sometimes get the distinct impression children are to fit into our plans. Do they know when they are unwanted? Sooner or later, I am confident they do.

I remember so well when our first daughter, Anne Marie, was born. I remember even more so my feelings at the time. I had become a father and there she was precious and lovely.

To be honest, I didn't know what to do. Do you pass out cigars and brag beyond believability? Of course, it was a fact she was gorgeous and looked most of all like her father.

In some sort of crazy, even mysterious way she was really wanted. Seriously, I didn't have the slightest idea what fatherhood meant. But, boy, I never felt that way before!

Do you want your children? Are they mostly in the way? I pray to God they are received and affirmed in ways that are sometimes big and sometimes small. Enjoy them.

There are no ugly children. Oh, some might be better looking than others but there are no ugly ones. Love them in visible and invisible ways, noting their positive response.

Am I trying to make too big of a case for the love and care of children? After all we are civilized people and will do what is necessary. But often the facts are not with us.

Why do people get married? In my mind certainly one of the top reasons is to have children. From the beginning God decreed husband and wife are to have children. Don't recall that being canceled.

How we treat our children (ours and others) gives a glimpse of the future. So, how does the future look to you? In truth, a whole nation and society in regard to children are struggling to decide.

———

*New Castle Courier-Times* April 1, 2000

# ❧SOFTLY, TENDERLY JESUS IS CALLING❧

"I WANTA GO home," she said in tones at once both longingly and tearfully. She had spent many years away from where she grew up. It was time to make the trip.

Really that is a wistful yearning in the hearts and minds of countless people. They remember those early years and want to return to them. It is both emotion and geography.

There is a strong sentimental strain in me that wants to go home. Be honest now, there is also in you, isn't there? Life was different then and truly beautiful, nearly perfect.

Sometimes the expression is very eloquently spoken in a play. Mrs. Carrie Watts played by Joanne Rains in *The Trip to Bountiful* is almost breathtaking. She wanted to go home.

Those of you who missed that play in the Guyer Opera House in Lewisville, Indiana, missed a real gem. Those who attended gave thanks to God. What a masterful performance!

It was brilliantly directed by Darrell Hughes and Susie Phillips. It reminded me of the superiority of a great play over that of television mediocrity. Hollywood comes in a distant second!

So, across this country there are people wanting to go home. The depth of feeling is distinctly human and points to basic, even primal need. Yes, I choke with emotion, too.

As you might guess, I wonder about yet another home. It is spiritual and comes from our need to be right with God. I have heard the stories since I was old enough to know anything.

Some of us grew up on songs like "Softly and Tenderly Jesus is Calling." Remember how the refrain goes? "Come home, come home; you who are weary, come home . . ." it begins.

Then, we are immersed in a flood of love as it says, "earnestly, tenderly, Jesus is calling, calling, O sinner, come home!" Will L. Thompson wrote that in 1880. Such greatness!

This is perhaps the most moving of all hymns that comes from revivalist days that are so much a part of our heritage. This is especially true of east central Indiana. Praise God!

So, to go home has a lot to do with calling it quits here and now. It means going to our real home, near to the heart of God. Our real home is with Him.

Conversion is many different things for many different people. Yet, they all, sooner or later, seem to meet at one point. Each of us desperately needs to come to God, our real home.

―――――

*New Castle Courier-Times* April 8, 2000

# ❧JUST GOING TO CHURCH DOESN'T CUT IT❧

"OH, HE NEVER gives to church," she said, in disdain. Maybe she felt she was being righteously indignant. Anyway, those about her knew her agenda and thoughts on evaluation.

For her it was necessary to go to church in order to be a good person. My guess is she has more than a few who applaud her stand. Sunday school and/or worship are necessary.

I felt a lot like that until near the time I had finished four beautiful years of pastoring at Hagerstown. With some hesitancy I had to rethink the whole matter. One man caused it.

He was a church member and came once during 208 Sundays and that was for a funeral. But his demeanor of generosity and kindness was inspiring. He was editor of the local newspaper.

The man's name was Eddie O'Neel and he was a man of great wisdom. Can you be a spiritual director and not go to church? Well, that sounds a bit contradictory.

I was a budding journalist of sorts in those days. He always seemed to have time to listen to my struggles towards maturity. Sometimes we visited early in the morning and sometimes late at night.

He was always, at least, one step ahead of me. The truth is on some occasions it was more like five or six. Yes, I spent a great deal more time in his office than he did in church!

He kind of bubbled over with wit and wisdom. He always encouraged me. I never recall a single negative word said against anyone, churchgoers or nonchurchgoers.

What he gave to the community, except for his weekly newspaper, was really intangibles. He bent over backwards to assist and help people. Behind the scenes he gave himself unselfishly.

I suspect he would have published his newspaper and done his good deeds with no pay whatsoever. Probably only his lovely wife kept him from doing just that! He was something.

You may be asking what kind of a person can be a model for others and not go to church? That is a very good question. Frankly, I don't have an answer for that one.

All I know is that little fellow with the big smile was someone I never forgot. Maybe there is an unselfish and generous attitude apart from going to church. Yes, I feel the cold stares!

But think about it. Think about the good people—men in particular—you have known who seldom or never went to church. Maybe all of this says more about the churches than it does about them.

---

*New Castle Courier-Times* June 3, 2000

# ❦TELL YOUR STORY WITH YOUR❦ AUTOBIOGRAPHY

"IT'S A THROWAWAY," the fellow said at the supermarket. That was his job. He was to go through the store daily and determine what was to be thrown out.

Sometimes it was in the fruit section. Other times it was in the vegetable section. Then, there were other areas that he scanned to see what was disposable.

After a time he became known as the "throwaway man." When you saw him, you knew something was about to be tossed. He was a familiar figure around the store.

He didn't mind it for awhile but then it dawned on him how people would remember him. It was important how people remembered him. How about you?

Be honest, now, it is important for each and everyone of us. The fellow mentioned left the store and found another job that paid less money. He was thinking about his grandchildren.

For some years I have urged people to write their autobiographies in their later years. Really, about the best way to remember is to read what they say about themselves. That's true.

My advice if you are beyond sixty is not to put it off. Indeed, everyone can do that. If you need some help in sentence construction, that's available.

You know, we have that right (and duty) to write down who and what we are. Others may disagree, especially if we grossly exaggerate. Even that does not mean we should stop.

How do you want to be known by your grandchildren, great-grandchildren, etc.? Tell them your story because they will want to know. This is neither vanity nor egotism.

I don't want to be known as a "throwaway man," do you? Give some serious thought to all of this. You may even decide to change jobs and get another!

Some intelligent people have said to me over the years no one will care once they have been gone awhile. Not so. There is a built-in yearning to know about ancestors.

I'll bet there are thousands of personal stories waiting to be told "out there." Fess up, now, you haven't done it yet, have you? Today is the best time to begin.

How long is an autobiography? The answer: just as long as you want it to be. Don't leave us impoverished because you didn't take the time to do what you knew you should.

———

*New Castle Courier-Times* June 17, 2000

## ❧A SERVANT IN ALL CIRCUMSTANCES❧

"SHE DOESN'T HAVE an enemy in the world," her grandson marveled. He kept going over in his mind (and heart) her countless good deeds. It was like a beautiful parade.

She just didn't have any enemies. It wasn't that she was high profile and received applause often. It was more like someone being a servant in all circumstances.

His grandmother wasn't widely known at all. In fact, beyond her circle of friends and family she was barely known. That didn't matter and it didn't phase her.

I suppose it takes a fair bit of gall to say someone has no enemies. It does sound unrealistic and even bordering on dishonesty. Yet, that was the case.

I knew such a woman and her name was Christie (McCall) Lacy. Yes, you guessed my secret, she was my grandmother. If she had any enemies, I never knew it.

She was the oldest of eleven children. Her son and my father was the oldest of her eight children. So, she knew what it was to be born into a big family and then have one.

In all the years I knew her I never remember any awards, special recognitions, or even major "thank yous." She simply did her work and lived her life. Duty was enough.

One of her secrets was that she never did any posturing. She was the same lady yesterday, today, and tomorrow. My friends, that is a tremendous gift then and now.

Her own needs were so well sacrificed, I am not certain anyone knew for sure what they were. She met the needs of others, especially her family. What a beautiful person.

Her strength and influence were always present. No one had to tell you Grandmother was pleasantly working behind the scenes. She did so not to hinder but to help.

Sometimes I pray to God to send us more women like her. It seems the world would be such a better place in which to live. They are the modest and skilled humanitarians.

If you have never known such a person, you have missed a great deal. They are the stuff out of which life on this planet is lived at the best. She was a heroine.

Is there some way to honor her today? Certainly a posthumous medal would not be to her liking. However, I do believe she would be thrilled simply if we imitated her.

———

*New Castle Courier-Times* July 8, 2000

## ❋DOING NOTHING IS A WASTE❋

"WHAT DOES IT take to motivate that guy?" the boss said in exasperation. Maybe he is lazy. Maybe his problems are so long-standing there just isn't any improvement.

Well, that sounds hopeless, doesn't it? As long as there is a God in the heavens, nothing is really hopeless. And I don't expect that to change anytime soon!

How do we deal with such everyday problems as laziness, indolence, lethargy, etc.? You may say, "With great difficulty" and, of course, you are right. But there is much more to be said.

Some of our ancestors in this country thought that to be poor meant you were either lazy or sinful. Maybe you hold to that. For me that is a partial truth, needing elaboration.

Yes, there are some people apparently who refuse to work at much of anything. It's as though they are in a kind of stupor and they like it that way. On the surface it looks like illness.

Being a person who expects a lot of himself and others, I have to labor at feeling sorry for those who think getting out of bed in the morning is a waste of time. How about you?

"Freeloader" is a nasty word. However, I must admit I once belonged to a "freeloaders association" while in the Navy. We were sailors who arrived at the YMCA on Sunday evenings for free meals!

Some say as economic systems grow bigger and more complex, sloth has a better environment to survive. Maybe so. But how about great uncle Bill who loafed at the general store every day?

Times do change but does human nature? I don't have a profound answer for that. What I do have is an observation: the so-called "deadbeat" has been with us since time immemorial.

I have great sympathy for those who have been beaten down so often they don't have the will to get up. God understands and so should we! What about the rest of the story?

Life for all of us is sometimes cruel and sooner or later we all know tragedy. There are those who simply refuse to thank their Creator for opportunities. We all have them.

Do we fail in life because of lack of opportunities? I don't think so! Doing nothing and persisting in such behavior is more than waste. It is a terrifying model for our children.

Aren't you ready to do more with your life? I really hope so. Fulfillment comes by "being and doing." Every person is intended "to be" a giant and "to do" good deeds.

————

*Plymouth Pilot News* July 15, 2000

# ❋CONTRADICTIONS OF LIFE HARD❋ TO UNDERSTAND

"I JUST DON'T understand it," she kept repeating. Then she would weep with a heart that was breaking. Her world had fallen apart and there seemed to be no answer.

Her father was such a kind and wonderful man. She had never known him to mistreat her in any way. He was such a pillar of strength for her and others.

Why did he take his own life? Everyone spoke well of him and loved him, she thought. He seemed to have everything to live for and he wasn't old at all, barely fifty.

She prayed intensely and sought God for answers that never came. How could she go on living with such a tremendous burden? Peace of mind kept eluding her.

Sometimes she would fall asleep in the early morning hours on a pillow drenched with her tears. Anger and sadness took their turns. Mostly she just didn't understand.

She kept going back over what she knew of his life. There were no answers. Maybe, in time, as she grew older, all would be clear. The passing of years did help some.

Yet, there were days (and nights) the internal storms of not understanding would come. She had been known to shake her fist in the face of God. That didn't help.

Dear friends, maybe you have been there. Maybe even now there are things in your life experience you are laboring years later to understand. Well, that's most of us, isn't it?

In my more than forty years as a pastor, I believe suicide is probably the most difficult for people to handle. This is especially true if the person is known for his/her goodness.

When truly fine people decide enough is enough of this life, questions emerge for years and years. It is never easy. Hearts break and sometimes continue to break.

The finest man I have ever known took his own life. Oh, there were warning signs and we had begun to wonder. Yet, he was a religious man and very likeable.

I never knew him to be mean or wrongly motivated. It always amazed me how he could turn the other cheek. He was a far better man than I am.

Then, one sultry August night he ended his life. Now more than thirty years later I am still not sure that I understand. He was my father, a very good man, the late Charles William Lacy.

———

*New Castle Courier-Times* September 2, 2000

# ❋DON'T TAKE IT OUT ON THE ROAD❋

"ROAD RAGE IS the guy's problem," she exclaimed. Going down the interstate, his auto took on the appearance of a bucking bronco. Drivers tried to stay several yards away.

Some looked on in amazement and almost disbelief. Others became angry and frankly wanted him off the road, preferably in a ditch. Still others just tried to keep their cool.

You and I know something about this, don't we? Yes, and this sort of rage is new and in a way it isn't. Remember the day you got mad at your wife and drove carelessly?

Sometimes our automobiles are the handy tools to take out our anger. From one point of view that might be a safe and healthy answer. Suppose no one else is on a secondary road.

I suppose it is better to beat up on a vehicle made of steel and plastic than another human being. Yet, what about vehicular homicide? We have a problem.

Most everyone I know who drives a lot of miles experiences some form of road rage. That doesn't mean they set out to kill somebody. It does mean we have our limitations.

What goes on in the home and at work really does influence our driving. A serious argument at home may translate into an unnecessary accident. The boss at work may have been insensitive.

Notice such a rage really is not an isolated emotional explosion with no connections to the rest of one's life. That's true in almost all situations. That helps.

It is something like studying history to know what comes before a key battle may be like a floodlight. All at once we very clearly see who won or lost and why. Revealing stuff.

The next time you get into your vehicle ready to take out your frustration and anger, take a moment to ponder a simple thought. Who or what has the power to make me a fool?

As human as it is, it isn't at all complimentary for us to admit we have allowed others to force us into stupid driving. Who or what made you drive thirty miles over the speed limit? Be honest.

As righteous as it may appear, road rage is truly a demon that may cost your own or someone else's life. Nothing is constructive about running someone off the road. You may have never seen him/her before.

So, cool it, friend, and it never hurts to pray for safe traveling. That doesn't mean only you and your loved ones. It means every precious human being on the roadways.

---

*Plymouth Pilot News* September 2, 2000

# ❧LEARNING TO SURVIVE IN THE WORLD❧

"DON'T MESS WITH me," little Joey would say. He was Mr. Tough Guy. In a way, he had reason to be because his father and mother were seldom at home, in fact often drunk.

He learned that to survive in this world meant first of all taking care of yourself. He was eight years old; dad and mom weren't around much. He had a younger sister to look after.

The streets of the city about the size of New Castle were what he knew best. He mostly slept at home and checked on his sister now and then. He didn't want her hurt.

He had the "street smarts" of a teenager. Making a buck here and there was so easy, even he was surprised. He knew who he could count on and it wasn't his parents.

Only one person made a difference in his life, other than himself. That was his sister, who would soon be six years old. He would protect her at all costs and he did.

Even at his early age he knew how vulnerable she was. No one had better lay a hand on her in a disrespectful way. Some neighbors remarked what a great brother she had.

Of course, in life we always get tested, whether eight or eighty. The little fellow with the tough hide and big heart was no exception. He, too, was vulnerable and others knew it.

Hey, Joey, how would you like that bike for your very own? These were older fellows who had been known to deliver the goods. He had always wanted one, so opportunity was at hand.

Funny thing, there was a catch to the offer. He didn't need to pay even the smallest amount of money. There was one small favor that was asked and it didn't sound right.

He was supposed to enjoy riding around town, while these older fellows "babysat" with his sister. He was supposed to leave her alone in the house for a couple of hours.

God only knew where mom and dad were. Maybe at work, maybe at the tavern, or who knows. But the bike really was a dandy and it looked like a gift easily gotten.

Strangely, something began to click in his mind and it wasn't at all pretty. There was this word "molesting" he had been hearing about. God, that would be awful for his sister to live through.

Then, it dawned on him not only were they messing with him, they were going to do worse things to his sister. No bike is worth that. Sometimes eight-year-old tough guys become men of honor.

———

*New Castle Courier-Times* September 16, 2000

# Features about My Work

## ✣LOCAL MINISTER AUTHORS A BOOK✣

HE LEANED BACK in his chair and thought for a second. "This book has been a part of my thinking for years."

The man is Rev. Donald Charles Lacy, pastor of St. James East United Methodist Church, 1041 Washington and the book on his mind is his own *Gems from James* published by Dorrance & Co., Philadelphia, Pa., $4.95.

"You could say it (the book) crystallized with a series of ten sermons I preached last spring but prior to that I had been writing and even before then, I have always had a deep respect for the Epistle of James."

The book is, in fact, a collection of topical sermons which provide an amplified and commentary-like approach from selected verses in the New Testament letter. According to the publishers, it should appear in Evansville bookstores and dealers later this month.

"My motivations for writing were varied," said the 41-year-old pastor. "Basically I wanted the book to establish an attempt in the restoration of preaching and I think the Letter of James offers a lot of practical advice for living."

"The sermon is a sacrament and an art," he explained. "Unfortunately, it had also been used as one man's vehicle for his grandiose ego, ideally it is a dialog between pastor and congregation—communication."

"My other purpose in writing the book was to show the practical application of James's centuries-old letter to modern Christians."

Explaining the "practical applications" the clergyman who resides at 1040 Washington with his wife Dorothy and his four daughters Anne, Donna, Sharon, and Martha, said that the book of James speaks of "*working* faith."

"Although the letter doesn't have deep theological elements hidden within it, it is rich with down-home advice for every Christian."

Lacy said that his book was written "primarily with Christians in mind" but he quickly added that the "'non-Christians can pipe into the truth which is there."

Although docile and quiet-spoken in his office, Lacy is outspoken and critical of many situations in Protestant America:

"The churches across our land are sluggish giants, wielding little power, spiritual or otherwise.

"The professional ministry has been maimed by 'stained glass pulpiteers' with syrupy clauses and phrases dropping harmlessly about the sanctuaries."

No matter how critical, he offers positive solutions which have come from his long and varied ministerial experience which includes pastorates in Kokomo, Muncie, Hagerstown and Indianapolis.

"The Christian is deeply and sincerely concerned about everything that goes on in the world, moon and elsewhere.

"Even though we did not ask to come into this world, we have been given strength to confront it. This should prevent us from becoming fatalistic and distressingly negative."

Although this is his first book, Lacy is no stranger to publications. He has contributed articles to Christian magazines and periodicals for "about five years."

The marketability of religious books has been on an upward trend with a growing number of prophetic and apocryphal literature but Lacy is concerned about the application of Christianity in day-to-day living.

"Much of the prophetic literature is written just to be sold. Thinking about the future is fine, but the life we live is here and now."

Adding that "the Bible can be used to 'prove' almost anything," he said that he was careful not to proof text.

"I think the book of James is clear enough—it was a source of inspiration for me, I was cautious not to misuse it."

About his own future as a writer, the dark-haired square-set preacher said that he had a number of ideas for forthcoming books.

"I don't call myself a professional writer, for me it is just a way of expanding my present ministry."

George Stuteville, *Evansville Sunday Courier-Press* October 20, 1974

## ⚜PARTNERS IN PREACHING LIKE⚜ CO-OP SERMONS BEST

PARTNERSHIP IN preaching—a lay-clergy enterprise—isn't exactly an everyday occurrence. Nor should it be, says one United Methodist pastor who tried it.

But when a committee of ten laypersons joined forces recently with their pastor at First UMC here to produce a series of eight sermons, results were highly illuminating.

The experience was designed, says the Rev. Donald Charles Lacy, to involve laypersons in the whole process of sermon preparation and evaluation. It was part of his field project for a Doctor of Ministry program at Christian Theological Seminary, Indianapolis.

Here's how the project worked:

A committee of laypersons chosen for their key leadership positions at First Church was recruited and armed with some basic reference materials for a sermon series on the First Epistle of Peter.

Each Monday evening as the committee met to discuss a skeletal outline Dr. Lacy had prepared for the following Sunday's sermon, he took many notes.

As the week proceeded, he wrote a full manuscript of the sermon and provided a copy for each committee member.

Following the Sunday worship service, all interested church members remained for a dialogue with the pastor, under the guidance of committee members.

When the eight-week series ended, the committee studied manuscripts of eight sermons preached before the series and compared them with the eight in the doctoral project. For criteria, they used an abbreviated instrument from "That One Good Sermon" by A. N. Sayre understanding, focus, continuity, relevance, sincerity, truth, and practicality.

The results? They clearly rated the series to which they had contributed input higher than the series in which they had not been involved.

"This sort of thing should happen at least once a year in every church," Dr. Lacy says. The chief danger, he believes, is that sermons could conceivably become a hodgepodge of ideas with little organization. "But this is where the preacher's discipline comes."

Committee members were uniformly pleased. Lay leader Thomas Johnson, who worked closely with the pastor on the project, commented, "Of course I liked the last eight sermons best—most likely because I had a part in them."

*United Methodist Reporter* October 8, 1976

# ❀MARY MAY EMERGE AS SIGNIFICANT❀ MODEL FOR TODAY'S WOMEN

ALTHOUGH CATHOLICS are paying less attention to Mary, the Mother of Jesus, Protestants are beginning to take a new look at her.

She may emerge as the significant model for twentieth-century women, not meek and mild as she has been pictured, but strong and courageous, according to a United Methodist publication.

This recalls to a Hoosier United Methodist pastor an article he wrote about Mary at least ten years ago.

He is Dr. Donald Charles Lacy, pastor of First United Methodist Church at Seymour and a leader in ecumenism.

He recalls that while two United Methodist publications turned down his article about Mary, titled "A Mother's Questions," a Catholic publication, "The Queen of All Hearts," published by the Montfort Fathers at Bayshore, New York, accepted and published it.

Creatively building upon the verse in Luke 2:19 which says: "But Mary kept all these things, pondering them in her heart," Dr. Lacy had portrayed the Blessed Mother pondering three questions.

The questions were, "Is my baby really the Christ?" "If Jesus is really the Christ, how costly will this be for Him?" and "If Jesus is really the Christ and this will be costly, will it be worth it?"

He pointed out in his article that every Christian or would-be Christian at three different stages must likewise inquire if Jesus is the Christ, how costly will it be to follow Him and will it be worth it?

The article closed with a letter to Mary which, while intensely personal, expressed the universal embodiment of religious thought and feeling for Dr. Lacy.

An excerpt from the letter published so many years ago, states:

"We apologize for the way we have treated your Son. Oh, Mary, we repent for the way we have treated Him! Oh Mary, may God forgive us for our cowardly Christianity! Despite our indifference, we know your Son is the Christ. We know there are times when the cost runs high. What really appalls us and makes us bitterly ashamed is when we ask: 'Is it worth it?' . . ."

Thus Dr. Lacy years ago had already taken a new look at Mary, mother of Jesus, that was in tune with the present trend of such prominent leaders as Dr. Ethel R. Johnson of the United Methodist School of Theology at Delaware, Ohio; the Rev. Jeanne Audrey Powers, staff executive for the Board of Global Ministries (Division of Ecumenical and Interreligious Concerns); Dr. Edwin E. Sylvest of Perkins School of Theology at Dallas, Texas, and Dr. Bruce Rahtjen of St. Paul School of Theology at Kansas City, Mo.

Their opinions on the topic were voiced recently in an article by Clyde Chesnutt, associate editor, in the *United Methodist Reporter*, the largest periodical of the denomination with a circulation of more than four hundred thousand people.

Dr. Lacy's article of a decade ago also throws a spotlight on the emergence of ecumenism, for it recently was praised by Monsignor Cornelious Sweeney of St. Ambrose Catholic parish at Seymour, formerly chancellor of the Archdiocese of Indianapolis.

And Dr. Lacy, in turn, had this to say this week: "Monsignor Sweeney's inspiring ecumenical spirit enabled the community (Seymour) Thanksgiving service to be held in St. Ambrose church recently for the first time in anyone's memory, with the mayor, community pastors and the choir of First United Methodist Church participating.

"It was a standing room only occasion with nearly five hundred in attendance," he said. "It was even more ecumenical than Monsignor Sweeney and I had ever dreamed about, due to the Father's laryngitis. As president of the local clergy association I also had to play a part of the role of host pastor."

Dr. Lacy is co-chairman of the division of Ecumenical and Interreligious Concerns of the South Indiana Conference of the United Methodist Church. He also is a member of the Indiana Area Commission of Ecumenical and Interreligious Concerns of the United Methodist Church.

––––––

Isabel Boyer, *Indianapolis Star* December 31, 1977

## ❀DIALOGUE WORKSHOP❀

RABBI JONATHAN STEIN [shown right] and the Rev. Dr. Donald C. Lacy, pastor of Meadowdale United Methodist Church, are coordinators of a workshop on Jewish-Christian dialogue. The session will be the first time [the United] Methodist church in Indiana has brought together Methodist and Jewish leaders to discuss their faiths in an effort to promote better understanding. The workshop will be from 2:30 P.M. to 5:30 P.M. Sunday at the Indianapolis Hebrew Congregation, 6501 Morth Meridian Street, of which Rabbi Stein is spiritual leader.

––––––

*Indianapolis Star* March 24, 1984

## ❀WORLDWIDE CHRISTIAN UNITY❀
## A WORTHY GOAL

DESPITE A CAMPAIGN since the early–twentieth century to unite Christians in the United States, many denominations still resist ecumenism out of fear they will lose their identity, says a local pastor.

The goal of ecumenism—the promotion of worldwide Christian unity—is to bring Christians closer to each other in their actions, worship and thought, said Rev. Donald C. Lacy.

Lacy is the pastor of Salem Community Church in Porter Township about four miles north of Hebron. He and his wife, Dorothy, live in Hebron and have four daughters between the ages eighteen and twenty-five.

He is also the chairperson of the Department of Ecumenical Concerns for the Indiana Council of Churches.

Lacy's department has scheduled a conference for Oct. 29 and 30 in Indianapolis. The topic will be the relationship of the church and government in legislating abortion and gambling.

Although Lacy would not offer an opinion about the relationship before the conference, he did speak about the ecumenical movement throughout the nation.

The United Methodist pastor offered a definition of ecumenism.

"A movement of the Holy Spirit to bring a divided church into unity. I think this is especially expressed in the seventeenth chapter of the gospel of John," said Lacy, who was assigned to Salem Community Church two months ago. He previously worked in Indianapolis.

Lacy, fifty-two, has been active in the ecumenical movement in the state and nation for about thirteen years. He has written three books on the subject.

Although the goal of Christian unity was boosted when the Roman Catholic Church committed itself to ecumenism in the early 1960s, there are some denominations that resist the call to unity, Lacy said.

"Generally speaking, there's a lot of lip service given to Christian unity. There's almost an overbearing tendency for denominations to close ranks and not take the risks."

He said that while orthodox Christian denominations also actively promote ecumenism, some denominations fear they will be gobbled up by the movement.

But ecumenism is not designed to establish a single, worldwide Christian denomination, Lacy said.

"The last thing we want is an organization that would be political; (one) that someone could manipulate."

He said the essence of ecumenism is divine guidance toward a likeness of thought, faith and action for all Christians.

"The Holy Spirit—which is an intangible—is at work in this. Nobody knows what the final shape of the church will look like."

A significant event on the road toward unity occurred three years ago.

All denominations of Christianity gathered in Lima, Peru, to discuss baptism, the eucharist, and ministry. The product of the conference was a document that stated similarities in belief about the three subjects between the denominations.

"It's (the document) a convergence. (It's) not unanimous belief, but a convergence of belief."

The pastor said the Roman Catholic Church has maintained an open attitude toward other denominations. He said some Protestants in America have disliked Catholics and not understood their traditions of rigid organization and an emphasis on liturgy—a series of worship procedures prescribed by the Catholic Church.

"I'm really excited and impressed by the way the Roman Catholic Church has opened itself to everybody. Protestants have the greatest opportunity in five hundred years to get acquainted with their Roman Catholic neighbors and friends.

"There isn't any serious ecumenism if you leave the Roman Catholic Church out."

The direction of immediate future is to get denominations talking to one another, the pastor said.

---

Chuck Knebl, *Valparaiso Vidette-Messenger* August 9, 1985

## PROTESTANT MINISTER CALLS FOR WIDER DEVOTION TO MARY

THE REV. CHARLES Lacy's pulpit extends far beyond the brick walls of Leesburg United Methodist Church in Kosciusko County.

It's now reaching into several corners of the world through publishing.

By the end of the month or so, he figures that more than 1.1 million people will have read his call for believers of all Christian faiths to acknowledge the attributes of Mary, identified in the Bible as the human, virgin mother of Jesus Christ.

An article he's written, "Devotion to Mary Should Transcend Denomination," appears in the October issue of *International Christian Digest,* a new journal of world views on theological issues. It also appeared in the August 16 edition of *Our Sunday Visitor*, a weekly newspaper for American Catholics with a circulation of 225,000, and a recent edition of "Marian Helpers Bulletin," a quarterly booklet for Catholics.

An earlier version of the article was published in 1983 in *The Criterion*, the newspaper of the Archdiocese of Indianapolis.

"When I first read it, I was surprised. . . . One just doesn't expect devotion to Mary from a Protestant man," said Richard Peck, editor of *International Christian Digest*.

"Here you have a Protestant pastor who comes up talking about devotion to Mary being a keynote to ecumenism. We look for that kind of freshness of thought. . . . We were anxious to carry it."

The *Digest* circulates among clergy and laity on each continent, with a total of 13,000 that is growing by about 1,000 a month, according to Peck.

Its board of directors includes the head of the Southern Christian Leadership Conference, a former Catholic University professor now at Cornell, Bishop Desmond Tutu of South Africa, the Anglican archbishop of Australia, a British Broadcasting Corporation correspondent and a Jamaican who is the former general secretary of the World Council of Churches.

Lacy hopes greater exposure of his favorite theme can ease the fragmentation of various religions and help more people find peace of mind. The acceptance of his article by magazines and newspapers encourages him.

"This is a topic that's very near and dear to me. It's a special interest that I can't even rationally explain to you. All I know is somehow, some way, by the grace of God, I feel a special closeness to the Blessed Mother," he said.

It's a feeling he's had for more than twenty years and one he's examined and enlarged upon through several literary projects.

Lacy, fifty-four, ordained in the Methodist Church since 1960, holds degrees in social science, American history and church history. He has served congregations throughout Indiana and been active in numerous interreligious conferences.

He describes himself as an enlightened conservative "who thinks ecumenically, not denominationally."

In his article, he states that devotion to Mary "transcends the limited understanding of Protestant fundamentalism, a movement that has probably issued more encyclicals of its own than all of the popes. . . . Furthermore, the Blessed Mother can and does transcend the current pettiness of both radical feminists and rigid chauvinists."

Mary was chosen to bear and rear one-third of the Holy Trinity, Lacy writes.

"Is there something more significant and influential for women than that?

"It is devotion to the Blessed Mother that helps unite us as Christians. When Protestants lose their widespread hang-up that Roman Catholics have worshiped and do worship her, they can perceive by the power of the

Holy Spirit an authentic ecumenism that calls us to be one.'"

Lacy further writes that Mary, "by never being divine or even having been considered a deity, lends her person to being human in the same sense as you and I."

Mary can be a role model for women and an inspiration to men, he said.

Lacy is aware that his writing and ecumenical work can't overshadow the needs of his congregation in Leesburg. He hopes to keep his obligations balanced. He said only that "the door is open" to evaluate options that result from his work.

"I want to shy away from what the world calls success, because the church is made so impotent by that."

———

Gabriella Jacobs, Ft. Wayne Journal Gazette September 5, 1987

## ❋WORSHIPPING AT THE LAKE❋

WITH A QUIET splash, a Canada goose landed in Lake Tippecanoe just a few feet away from the Rev. Donald C. Lacy's floating pulpit.

He's used to such things.

Lacy brings Sunday services to vacationers each week from a pontoon boat anchored in Patona Bay at Tippecanoe Lake. Both his regular congregation from Leesburg United Methodist Church and vacationers attend the early morning services.

About 8:15 A.M., casually dressed people start drifting to Patona Bay, some carry lawn chairs, other sit at picnic tables scattered around the beach. A few boat across the lake to hear Lacy. The service starts promptly at 8:30 A.M.

"It was beautiful," said Kathy Woodsmall after attending the first outdoor service of the year with her daughters. "The girls need to come, and I like the more casual setting."

She comes to Tippecanoe Lake each weekend from Elkhart and Father's Day was her first visit to the bayside service. She plans to return throughout the summer. Her daughter, Megan, eight, had a different view.

"It was cold," she said, referring to the unseasonably chilly weather. But she kept warm in a teddy-bear print sweatshirt. When pressed, she shyly admitted that she likes the outdoor service better than the indoor one. She added that she watched a fish in the canal during the thirty-minute service.

Lacy passes up the traditional robes to keep the tone of the services loose and easy. This is the fourth year for the outdoor service.

"People are not out (here) for a formal liturgy," Lacy said. It is more of a meditative service, he added.

Although he is an ordained Methodist minister, Lacy makes the service ecumenical. But it keeps the structure of a traditional service with music, a sermon and a few minutes directed to the children attending.

"It's been expanding," said Shirley Polk, a year-round member of the Leesburg congregation. The casual dress and the early hour is part of the attraction, Polk said. Many people have family reunions, stop by the service and have the rest of the day for themselves, she said.

She likes the outdoor service because "it adds another dimension."

Early morning boaters have no doubt what is happening if they happen to cruise by. Two canvas flaps, painted with a religious scene and the words "Lake Tippecanoe Worship," cover the sides of the pontoon. The public address system is clear and powerful, carrying words and music clearly across the quiet bay.

Some boaters pass by, others stop. People wandering in and out of the service don't bother Lacy.

"That's just the way it is," he said with a smile. He likes the casual tone and wouldn't change it. "If it was heavy, it would defeat the purpose of the whole thing."

About one hundred people attended on the shore and by boat on Father's Day. Overcast skies and unseasonably chilly air kept the numbers down, Lacy said. During last summer's heat wave, the service swelled to three hundred participants one Sunday, Lacy recalled.

Lacy goes back to town to conduct a more conventional service at his church each Sunday. The outdoor services will continue, weather permitting, until Sept. 3.

While services on the lake are rare, many churches open their doors to vacationers in Indiana's lakes region during the summer.

Among these is "the little white chapel in the woods," also known as Lake James Lutheran Chapel, which opens its pavilion, beach and facilities to visitors. And Lake George Lutheran Chapel has served vacationers for twenty-three years near the Indiana-Michigan line.

---

Lori Nims, *Ft. Wayne Sunday Journal Gazette* June 25, 1989

## ❀MINISTER CELEBRATES SATISFYING❀ CAREER AS RELIGIOUS WRITER

"I DID NOT realize that my first published article thirty years ago would be the beginning of an extensive and satisfying career," Donald (Don) C. Lacy said.

The Center High School and Ball State Teachers College graduate earned a doctor of ministry degree from Christian Theological Seminary, Indianapolis, in 1976. Marking three decades in religious writing has been a milestone in which the Henry County native has a great deal of pride, he said.

Lacy credits a seminary professor, Ronald E. Osborn, with inviting him to write an article for *The Church and The Fine Arts,* a publication for the religious market.

"And since that time, I have published more than four hundred articles, five books and twelve booklets," Lacy said.

Although he has been a United Methodist pastor in several Indiana churches, his material has appeared in publications of all faiths.

For example, a feature titled "A Mother's Questions" was first published in a Roman Catholic magazine in 1969. The topic was questions that might have been posed by Mary, mother of Jesus, on the night he was born.

The story subsequently has been published in various forms across the nation and in South America. In 1982, *The Indianapolis Star* used an abbreviated version on Christmas Day.

Twenty years ago Lacy accomplished another ecumenical contribution.

He wrote a service first celebrated in the Union Chapel United Methodist Church in Indianapolis, which wove together the Holy Communion of the Methodist liturgy and the new mass of the Roman Catholic Church after Vatican II.

"My intent," he said, "was to provide an ecumenical bridge, especially so Methodists could experience the beauty and profundity of the Roman Catholic mass in English. It was never meant to be anything definite, and Protestants and Roman Catholics alike have praised it."

Lacy's collections of sermons have also attracted attention. He believes his best is "Called to Be." "It is based on the Sermon on the Mount, and has enjoyed some excellent reviews," Lacy said.

While pastoring, he wrote for the *Hagerstown Exponent* and the *Rushville Republican.*

Lacy was active in the initiation of the National Workshop on Christian Unity in Indianapolis in 1989. This attracted protestants, Roman Catholics, and orthodox faiths to church leadership sessions.

Lacy recalls with pride his Delaware and Henry county roots. His mother, Marion Walradth Lacy, lives in Hagerstown. Her parents were Glade and Grace Walradth, residents of Perry Township in Delaware County, and Guy and Christie Lacy of Blountsville. His father, Charles Lacy, was a Congregational Christian minister for twenty years. All are deceased.

If anything is left to fulfill a satisfaction he seeks, his secret ambition is to sit in a church congregation some Sunday morning and hear one of the anonymous sermons he has written for publishers who provide homiletical material for ministers.

Rita Winters, Muncie Sunday Star February 3, 1991

## ❋FORMER HEBRON PASTOR❋
## PENS BOOK ON ACTS

OFTEN, THE QUEST, the chase, proves as exciting as reaching the goal itself.

Dr. Donald Lacy, pastor of Argos United Methodist Church, has spent a lifetime questing after knowledge. *Reactivating Acts: A Preaching, Teaching Program for the Pentecost Season* is the most recent result of the quest by the former pastor of Hebron's Salem Community Church.

Published by Brentwood Christian Press, the book is a guide for clergy in reaching congregations during one of the most significant periods on the Christian calendar.

"Acts is very unique in that it's really the only New Testament church history book," said Lacy. "There's more church history in the Book of Acts than all the other books of the New Testament combined. Without it, we probably wouldn't know a lot about the first century."

Acts relates the history of the inception of the Christian church, the coming of the Holy Spirit and the movement as it spread under the leadership of Peter, James, and Paul. Lacy's book compiles writings from Acts aimed at pastors in particular, but not necessarily limited to them. It serves as a preaching shortcut.

"They can both preach and teach out of the same volume," said Lacy. "In other words, the book is laid out in such a way that you virtually don't have to open the Book of Acts in order to utilize it."

But, while Lacy had clergy in mind when writing his volume, its teachings impact the laity.

"There are large sections that have to do with application, where to take that text and apply it to current living, to laypeople as they live their lives."

So where exactly is the relevancy in a scholarly treatise?

"It enables us to gain the power and the uplifting, the tremendous spiritual uplifting, that comes out of the first century and works as a perpetual dynamo clear into our time."

Lacy might be talking about himself. He's penned almost five hundred articles, books and booklets, and his travels in the pursuit of knowledge have taken him across the nation.

He's the religious equivalent of a Renaissance man. Lacy's professional life has encompassed careers as an author, educator, consultant, humanist and pastor—"all of those things kind of wrapped into one," he said.

Lacy received his bachelor's and master's degrees from Ball State University. Christian Theological Seminary granted him master of divinity and doctor of ministry degrees.

The Muncie native's pastoral assignments include two years, 1985–87, at Salem Community Church, and three years as spiritual head of a Leesburg congregation before taking the Argos assignment.

Even with the pressing responsibilities of a new church, Lacy makes time for his writing.

"I'm always working on things, all my life," he said.

He's just completed a major book review of Raymond Studzinski's *Spiritual Direction and Mid-Life Development*, which will appear in *Synopsis*, a book review service for religion professionals.

"It's a scholarly, well-written book," Lacy noted. "Of course, the theme of spiritual direction is a very prominent theme today."

The review and the Acts book under his belt, Lacy's already searching for new avenues to explore. His questing nature is "a matter of having some idea of what I don't know."

The chase is satisfying, and frustrating, as well.

"It's the pain of never being fully satisfied, too."

Toni Griffith-Byers, *Valparaiso Vidette-Messenger* December 6, 1991

# ❋FORMER LOCAL PASTOR ADDS❋ ANOTHER JEWEL TO HIS LIST

DONALD CHARLES LACY, minister of the gospel and prolific writer (he has penned at least five hundred books, pamphlets and theological treatises), has a strong East Central Indiana background.

He was born in Henry County, graduated from Center High School. and has bachelor's and master's degrees from Ball State University, and master of divinity and doctor of ministry degrees from Christian Theological Seminary, Indianapolis.

Lacy is a veteran United Methodist pastor and has served churches across the state of Indiana. His book, *Jewels From John,* is dedicated to First United Methodist Church, Hagerstown, where he began his professional ministry.

*Jewels From John* was originally preached as part of an all-church Bible Study series. Pastor Lacy divided the gospel into six major sections and each section was preached, week by week.

Lacy said he felt the value to this approach was that an entire church could be focused on an assigned book and sermons are then preached to emphasize a spiritual truth.

The author suggests that *Jewels From John* can be used either as a study book by groups during Lent, a springboard for a pastor to prepare his or her Lenten sermons or as a devotional book for laity who seek spiritual growth.

In commenting on his book, Lacy said, "The Gospel of John is delightfully compelling! This is especially true during the Lenten season as we tend to look for a change of pace in the material used by Matthew, Mark, and Luke.

"This gospel has a way of pushing our homiletical skills to the hilt. Only both a rational and mystical approach can do justice to its magnificence."

In each of his six profiles in *Jewels From John,* Lacy brings out a significant truth in each that would encourage the Christian—and the person *Almost Persuaded*—to seek a closer walk with God.

In summary, Lacy and his sponsoring group, United Methodist Women, point out the following "truths:"

- Philip and Nathaniel—Two Models for Ministry (John 1:43–51).

"Are you and I willing to inspire our friends to move into the hearts and minds of others for their conversion? In a sense, Jesus left the meeting with Nathaniel up to Philip . . . If you and I were to resolve at this moment to touch every life with the intent that life brings another of Christ and His Church, what would happen?"

- Healing at the pool—Lessons for Living (John 5:1–18). In this Scripture, Jesus healed a man who had been ill for thirty-eight years. This angered the Jews who claimed Jesus desecrated their Sabbath (Saturday). In doing the healing, Jesus warned the man to remain free from sin or else a worse illnees might befall him. "Isn't healing an exciting idea?" Lacy asked. "To be broken or diseased and made well is the hope of millions. What a thrilling thing it is when it actually happens! I, for one, believe it does happen."
- Adultery—Forgivable But Not to be Repeated (John 8:1–11). Lacy points out that this is a sin that is age-old. A mob brought a woman taken in adultery to Jesus and requested that she be stoned to death because she had violated the Law of Moses—and they were trying to trap Jesus. Jesus said little, but he kept writing in the sand. Eventually, the male mob turned and left Jesus and the woman alone. "'Where are your accusers?'" Jesus asked the woman. "They have all gone, sir," was the woman's answer. "I do not condemn you either. Go, but do not sin again." Lacy summarizes the discourse with "Adultery is forgivable, but it is not to be repeated."
- Jesus washes feet—An Act of Humility Worth Imitating (John 13:1–20). In this narrative, Peter and Jesus get into a discussion on the matter. Jesus reiterated, "If I do not wash your feet, then I have no part in you." Lacy says the emphasis Jesus made is that the disciples (and Christians today) ought to wash one another's feet. The writer observes that footwashing as an ordinance is not a new idea among denominations. Now, observes Lacy, "does or does not the New Testament make a strong case for footwashing? It seems to me the answer has to be a categorical, yes it does. Our Lord doesn't leave any doubt."
- Pilate—A Man Out of Step With Truth (John 18:28–38). Lacy says Pilate fails to comprehend truth in his midst by three actions: (1) In the first place the charges against Jesus are hazy or missing altogether but (Pilate) proceeds, (2) Pilate tries to determine whether or not Jesus considers himself King of the Jews or a king of any sort, and (3) Even after Jesus tells him that he came to speak about the truth, Pilate still asks, "What is truth?" In asking the question, "Are

you and I out of step with truth?" Lacy answers that "The Pilate in us causes us to be off stride. We are disconnected, disharmonized, disjointed, and just plain disoriented in the spiritual sense."

- The Risen Lord Appears—The Right Way to Fish (John 21:1–14). Fish and fishing are mentioned again and again in the Scriptures. The word "fish" or some form of it appears more that seventy times in the Bible. This particular "fishing experience" has three points, says Lacy. They are: we are to do the correct thing at the correct time; to follow Jesus is to reap a bountiful harvest; and those who follow Jesus have no doubt about his unique existence.

Ed Satterfield, *Muncie Sunday Star* March 7, 1993

# ✻DONALD CHARLES LACY✻

DONALD LACY IS a minister of the United Methodist Church of the USA, and a member of this Society. He has written prolifically and challengingly on Marian themes in the hope of awakening an authentically scriptural devotion to the Mother of God not merely in Methodism but in the other Reformation churches.

The United Methodist Church of the USA is one of the great churches of Christendom with its ten million or so membership. It has in common with the Roman Catholic Church in France the experience of numerical decline alongside considerable spiritual and intellectual vitality. A revival in "re-reception" of its Wesleyan heritage is currently making this church more significant on the total ecumenical scene. The response of this church to the "Baptism, Eucharist, Ministry" project of the World Council of Churches was a model of ecumenical humility in which the church confessed its failure to preserve its Wesleyan and Catholic heritage fully, and its determination to relearn them.

Dr. Lacy is determined to share in this recovery, especially where Marian devotion is concerned. He shows deep humility before the tradition of the Roman Catholic Church. Thus he says, "Many Christians who thought that only they read their Bibles very carefully have discovered that Roman Catholics read it carefully centuries before Luther, Calvin, or Wesley."

Donald Lacy's pamphlets, *Mary and Jesus* and *A Mother and Her Infant Son* are simply and beautifully written. The latter contains several beautiful meditations on Mary and her infant Son as she begins to "ponder these things in her heart." An impressive article, "Devotion to Mary should go beyond denominations" contains this thought: "The Blessed Mother does transcend the current pettiness of both radical feminists and chauvinists. She is a peacemaker."

Dr. Lacy is a true ecumenist. He is prepared to listen to the challenge of the traditions of others, and in turn to call on his own church to enter more fully into the universal Christian heritage. He does so with a conviction and urgency that are unsurpassed on either side of the Atlantic. Our thoughts and prayers should be with him in this task.

—————

*David Carter, Ecumenical Society of the Blessed Virgin Mary* January, 1996

## ❋LACY PUBLISHES WORK ON❋ CONTEMPORARY AUTHORS

DONALD CHARLES LACY, a native of the Blountsville area, holds many titles: author, pastor, ecumenist, educator, and consultant. He has been included in the just published Volume 59 of *Contemporary Authors, New Revision Series*. The series is available in all major libraries in the United States, Canada, and England.

Having strong ties to east central Indiana, he was born near New Castle; went to elementary school in Blountsville; graduated from Center High School; and then graduated from Ball State University in 1954 and 1958. Lacy taught high school in Redkey and Dunkirk before preaching his first sermon to the graduating class of Dunkirk High School in 1957. He was an Associate Pastor of College Avenue United Methodist Church in Muncie and pastored First United Methodist Church of Hagerstown.

When asked who he really is, he simply replies, "that skinny little boy from Blountsville still trying to grow up."

But the highlights of his literary career and ministry testify of the accomplishments of his ministry and life. His legacy and gift of writing covers a time frame from 1960 when he contributed to *The Church and the Fine Arts* (Cynthia Pearl Maus, editor) to 1996 and the publication, *A Letter to a Roman Catholic*, which has appeared in both the Sunday edition of the *South Bend Tribune* and *The Catholic Answer.*

His most-widely circulated work was a feature that appeared in *Our Sunday Visitor* based in Huntington. It was published in 1988 and entitled "Devotion to Mary Should Go Beyond Denominations." It became an internationally-known piece that was republished in numerous publications, including *International Christian Digest* and *Marian Helpers*. It led to major speaking engagements for Lacy.

Dr. Lacy's contributions include a wide variety. Seven books are listed: *Gems From James* (1974 and 1982); *Called to Be* (1978 and 1980); *Mary and Jesus* (1979 and 1993); *John Seventeen* (1983); *Healing Echos: Values for Christian Unity* (1986); *Reactivating Acts* (1990); and *Jewels from John* (1992).

He also authored special worship materials such as: *Methodist Mass* in 1983; *Daily Food for the Journey: Pastor's Morning Worship* in 1988; *Nourishment for the Day: Morning Worship for Laity* in 1989; *Come Holy Spirit* in 1989; and *Lakeside Devotions* in 1990.

He did sixteen major book reviews for *Logos*, published in *Synopsis* in 1988–1994.

A special Christmas greeting, *A Mother and Her Infant Son,* was originally published in 1982 but continues to be republished year after year at Christmastime.

He also has had regular columns in the *Hagerstown Exponent;* the *Rushville Republican; Senior Times;* and *Hoosier United Methodist.*

In his interview with *Contemporary Authors* he provides the following insight for aspiring authors: (1) writing that offers something really significant is born from the wedding of the human and Divine; (2) beware of writing solely for monetary gain and or notoriety; (3) there are no uninteresting people; (4) always be forgiving of your enemies; (5) use computers sparingly; (6) always be humble but never weak; (7) flee from that which is nominal and superficial; (8) affirm and encourage other writers; (9) virtually everything you write will already have been written; and (10) be grateful for every moment of your life.

Lacy, told *Contemporary Authors,* "When you get rejection slip after rejection slip, it is only a driven person that will continue. A fascination in all of this is that if one is convinced he really has something needing to be said, he will find a way to get that done."

---

# ❈METHODIST MINISTER DRAWS❈
# UPON ECUMENISM

GRASSROOTS ECUMENISM runs deep in Rev. Donald Charles Lacy, son of a Congregational Christian minister and self-styled friend of the Blessed Virgin Mary.

Lacy, sixty-five, pastor of Walkerton United Methodist Church and a writer often published in Catholic periodicals, has written more than twenty books or articles, beginning with a contribution to *The Church and the Fine Arts* in 1960.

His most recent book, *Jesus, Our High Priest: A Parish Resource for Studying the Letter to the Hebrews*, is dedicated to the Walkerton parish where he first preached the material.

"Mv parishioners are a group of wonderfully tolerant people," explains Lacy, who prays a half-hour most days on a kneeler that a priest gave him. 'They don't always agree with me, but they respect me. . . . I've I been called a closet Catholic.

"The literary, pastoral, educational, ecumenical strands are all connected in one person."

Lacy, who also was the third generation of plasterers in his family, lists attorney, politician and American history teacher among his early ambitions.

He recognized his literary bent first when he was editor of his high school's monthly newspaper.

"I knew then I was going to be interested in that field," recalls Lacy, who earned bachelor's and master's degrees at Ball State University in the 1950s. He also spent two years in the Navy and taught high school social studies and English.

"I kind of turned a corner when I went into seminary, although I've been involved in numerous other things," says Lacy, earned a master of divinity degree from Christian Theological Seminary, Indianapolis, in 1961 and a doctor of ministry degree in 1976.

Since 1958, he has served churches in two Indiana conferences, including two congregations in Indianapolis where he was chairman of the Jewish-Christian Dialogue for the United Methodist Church at Hebrew University in 1984.

He has also been chairman of the committee for ecumenical concerns for the Indiana Council of Churches and coordinator of a Methodist-Lutheran Dialogue from 1991 to 1995.

"The state of ecumenism, it seems to me, is moving in a lot of different directions under the guidance of the Holy Spirit," he says. "I think the Lord is doing some wonderful and mysterious things."

He is an associate member of the Marian Order of Priests and belongs to the International Order of St. Luke the Physician, the Society of Mary, the National Association of Evangelicals and the Ecumenical Society of the Blessed Virgin Mary.

Lacy has kept up his writing career—and used it to further his ecumenical interests —since the late 1960s, when he published his first magazine feature, "Queen of All Hearts." He published "Decalogue for Ecumenical Discipleship" in 1985 and "Devotion to Mary Should Go Beyond Denominations" in the Catholic *Our Sunday Visitor* periodical in 1987. "The Blessed Virgin Mary has been a remarkably close companion of mine," he explains. "She came to me. I didn't come to her."

"Out of my own experience and my own need and what I thought was the inspiration of the Holy Spirit, I sat down and wrote it. It. was intended to be a bridge."

In 1971, Lacy wrote "Methodist Mass," a ten-page liturgy combining Methodist elements with Roman Catholic materials approved by the Second Vatican Council in the 1960s.

He used the service once a month for three years at Union Chapel United Methodist Church in Indianapolis.

"That too was widely circulated, but it was never meant to be anything definitive," he recalls. "It was so United Methodists could have a feel for the profundity of the Roman Catholic Mass, frankly."

Lacy's latest book, *Jesus, Our High Priest*, grew out of a series of fourteen sermon-teachings he gave at Walkerton United Methodist, which has 320 members and some 150 at worship.

———

Gene Stowe, *South Bend Tribune* April 24, 1998

Photo by Joe Raymond

# ❋A MYSTERY AND A MIRACLE❋

DONALD C. LACY wrote a story thirty years ago, a story of a mother and her son—a story considered a mini-classic by many Protestants.

It is an account of a discussion between Mary and the archangel Gabriel about Mary's newborn son, Jesus.

Lacy, who is pastor of Yorktown United Methodist Church, first began researching the idea for the book—*A Mother and Her Infant Son*—in 1966 for a presentation he was giving at College Avenue United Methodist Church in Muncie.

Three decades later, the piece has been published in dozens of newspapers throughout the United States and Canada, recited in thousands of sermons and performed as a Christmas pageant.

The book was not officially published until 1982, after first being rejected by two Methodist publications. Then it was "snapped up" by a Roman Catholic publishing house, Lacy said.

"It was best seller for CSS Publishing in Lima, Ohio, during the mid-1980s."

Lacy said that it is one of those life experiences that he cannot explain.

"I suppose I couldn't give you a rational explanation—it is both a mystery and a miracle," Lacy said. "It was not really shocking, though, because I learned a long time ago that the Holy Spirit shocks us, and this was not my doing. I was simply a tool."

Lacy was born in Blountsville and graduated from Center High School (now Wapahani) and attended Ball State University. He taught for several years in Jay County before beginning his seminary study at Christian Theological Seminary in Indianapolis.

"It was about that time what I started my writing career," Lacy said. "Since then I've written more than seven hundred pieces, covering a lot of time and going in a lot of different directions."

However, he said none of those articles has touched him the same as *A Mother and Her Infant Son.*

"I sometimes jokingly say that Mary is the other woman in my life, and that is mostly serious, because I feel a very close kinship with her," Lacy said. "She is the central force in bringing Christ to the world.

"One things that continually comes back to me as I read it are the ideals that Mary represents, ideals that our society has played down," Lacy said.

Lacy, who has been in Yorktown six months, says he is always writing something. His next book, his ninth, will be published early next year.

———

Bobbi Walker, *Muncie Star/Press* December 18, 1999
Photo by Stephanie Dowell

## ❋READINGS IN FAITH❋

DONALD LACY'S life was right where he wanted it when he entered the Navy in the 1950s.

According to his carefully formulated plan, he would graduate from school, become a teacher or an attorney and pursue a career in politics.

But God had different plans for Lacy, as he would discover in the Navy.

"We get our own self-interests and work against what God wants," Lacy said. "I guess, looking back, I knew what God wanted me to do in junior high. I just didn't listen."

Serving active duty in the Navy, Lacy was assigned to assist two clergymen—a Roman Catholic priest and an Episcopalian minister.

"Working with them, that is when it began to crystallize with me," Lacy said. "When I got out, I knew I'd be going into the ministry."

Lacy, who had his teaching degree from Ball State, then attended Christian Theology School in Indianapolis where he obtained a doctorate of ministry.

After graduation, Lacy married his wife, Dorothy, and served as a United Methodist minister throughout Indiana.

"I've been to about every area in Indiana except Terre Haute," said Lacy, who currently pastors at the Yorktown United Methodist Church.

But it was at an assignment in north-west Indiana, at a small church in Salem, where Lacy began to look into the link between the Methodist Church and the Roman Catholic Church—a subject that is explored in his latest book, *A Taste of Glory.*

"They celebrated Holy Communion every Sunday, which is very uncommon in Protestant churches," Lacy said of the church in Salem.

Released in May, the book explores John 6:53–58 with an emphasis on the Eucharist.

Although a Methodist pastor for most of his life, Lacy believes that Communion in the past has been misinterpreted by Protestant churches.

"The Catholic Communion is more in the spirit of what Jesus was talking about," said Lacy. "There should be some mystery, some majesty to Communion. Protestants, I think, are not getting the full effect of that."

"Jesus said 'do this in remembrance of me.' Remembrance is more than remember. You remember the scores of ball games. When you do something in remembrance, it takes you right back to the time."

*A Taste of Glory* is the result of twenty years of studying the Gospel of St. John and interpreting its passages. The text is actually taken directly from a set of sermons Lacy delivered years ago exploring the book of John.

"John is my favorite Gospel; it is distinctly separate from the others," he said. "There are parallels between Matthew, Mark and Luke, but John has that mystery, the majesty absent in the other three Gospels."

Although the book has not received any feedback because it is so new on the market, Lacy expects at least some dissension among what he calls "ultra-conservative Protestants" because of the Catholic overtones of the book.

"I have heard some negative comments about my views before," he siad. "And I don't expect the more conservative Protestants will care for the book."

Lacy isn't a stranger to controversy over his beliefs. In the early 1970s, while at the Union Chapel in Indianapolis, Lacy formed what he called the "Methodist Mass" which combined parts of a Catholic Mass including Communion with the verve of a Methodist sermon.

"It was very controversial," Lacy chuckles at the memory. "That was just one of the ways I tried to bridge the gap between Catholics and Methodists."

Lacy's latest book takes up a conversational tone, with some chapters set up as a question and answer session between Jesus and a pilgrim. Each chapter concludes with a series of questions to inspire further thought and a greater understanding.

A prolgoue and epilogue act as conceptual bookends to introduce and wrap up the book's meaning.

"It is meant as a set of mental gymnastics," Lacy said of the book. "To think about the great significance of Holy Communion."

A writer for over forty years, Lacy has explored a multitude of topics and currently writes weekly columns for two area newspapers—the new *Castle Courier Times* and the *Pilot News* in Plymouth.

This summer, a culmination of Lacy's written work from sermons to news articles will be published and released in stores.

Copies of his current book can be ordered through any bookstore or purchased at Danner's Books in Muncie as well as at the Cokesbury chains for $4.95.

---

*The Anderson Herald Bulletin* January, 6, 2001
Author: Keri S. McGrath
Photo by John P. Cleary

## *SENATOR ROBERT F. KENNEDY*
### *December 17, 1966*

---

**ROBERT F. KENNEDY**
NEW YORK

### 𝔘nited 𝔖tates 𝔖enate
**WASHINGTON, D.C.**

December 17, 1966

The Reverend
Donald C. Lacy
200 West Main
Haggerstown, Indiana

Dear Mr. Lacy:

Thank you for your recent letter
and for your thoughtfulness in sending
me your article about President Kennedy.

The respect for President Kennedy
that prompted you to share your article
with us means a great deal to me and
my family. We join in expressing our
deepest thanks and in sending you our
best regards.

Sincerely,

Robert F. Kennedy

# ❖BISHOP RALPH T. ALTON❖
## *July 6, 1984*

THE UNITED METHODIST CHURCH

BISHOP
RALPH T. ALTON

INDIANA AREA
1100 WEST 42ND STREET
INDIANAPOLIS 46208

PHONE
317-924-1321

July 6, 1984

Dr. Donald C. Lacy
Meadowdale United Methodist Church
5701 W. 34th Street
Indianapolis, IN  46224

Dear Don:

This is in comment on your letter of June 12th which awaited my return
from my travel abroad.

I appreciate your comment concerning my involvement in the Indiana
Area these months.  And I particularly support your interest and concern about the ecumenical and interreligious awareness of Indiana
United Methodism.  When I came to Indiana from Wisconsin, I realized
that the strength of United Methodism in Indiana is really a deterrent
to ecumenical involvements.  In Wisconsin, the United Methodist Church
needs the association and fellowship of other Communions that represent a more liberal Protestant view and, hence, the participation of
the United Methodist Church in ecumenical involvements from local
communities to the state level is very high.  In Indiana, that need
for fellowship does not exist, and it is difficult to persuade United
Methodist conferences that their contributions in the field of Christian
unity are important.

Therefore, as far as the possibility of developing an interest in an
Area executive for Christian Unity and Interreligious Concerns is not
very viable.

I haven't had a chance yet to listen to the tape of your sermon which
you preached at Taylor University, but I shall keep it handy so that
at least in my re-retirement I can hear your good word.

Most sincerely yours,

Ralph T. Alton

RTA:kas

## ❋HOYT L. HICKMAN❋
### *Assistant General Secretary, Section on Worship, Board of Discipleship (UMC)*
### *November 1, 1984*

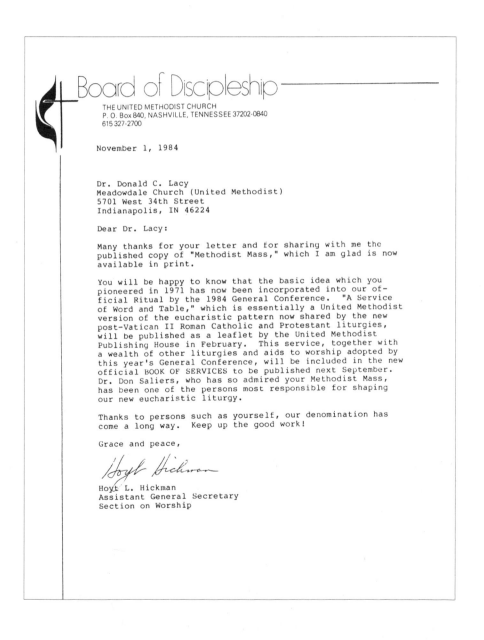

Board of Discipleship ————————————

THE UNITED METHODIST CHURCH
P. O. Box 840, NASHVILLE, TENNESSEE 37202-0840
615 327-2700

November 1, 1984

Dr. Donald C. Lacy
Meadowdale Church (United Methodist)
5701 West 34th Street
Indianapolis, IN 46224

Dear Dr. Lacy:

Many thanks for your letter and for sharing with me the
published copy of "Methodist Mass," which I am glad is now
available in print.

You will be happy to know that the basic idea which you
pioneered in 1971 has now been incorporated into our official Ritual by the 1984 General Conference. "A Service
of Word and Table," which is essentially a United Methodist
version of the eucharistic pattern now shared by the new
post-Vatican II Roman Catholic and Protestant liturgies,
will be published as a leaflet by the United Methodist
Publishing House in February. This service, together with
a wealth of other liturgies and aids to worship adopted by
this year's General Conference, will be included in the new
official BOOK OF SERVICES to be published next September.
Dr. Don Saliers, who has so admired your Methodist Mass,
has been one of the persons most responsible for shaping
our new eucharistic liturgy.

Thanks to persons such as yourself, our denomination has
come a long way. Keep up the good work!

Grace and peace,

Hoyt L. Hickman
Assistant General Secretary
Section on Worship

# INDEX

Henry, Patrick, 179, 181, 183
Hera, 91
Heron, Alasdair I. C., 79
Hickman, H. L., 359
Himalaya Mountains, 17
Homer, 93
*Hoosier United Methodist,* 348
*How Should We Then Live,* 66
Howard, M. William, 185
Hughes, Darrell, 319
Hugo, Victor, 266, 270
Huston, Robert, 186

Ignatius of Antioch, 259–60
*Iliad,* 93
Ilium, 93
Illinois Bar Association, 302
*Imitation of Christ, The,* 77, 141, 267
Indiana Area Commission of Ecumenical and Interreligious Concerns, 334
Indiana Council of Churches, 192, 336, 349
Indianapolis Hebrew Congregation, 334
Indianapolis, Ind., 330
*The Indianapolis Star,* 341
*International Christian Digest,* 337–38, 348
International Order of St. Luke the Physician, 350
International Platform Convention, 302
International Society of Girlwatchers, 302
*Introduction to Christian Worship,* 79, 195
Isaac, 44, 83, 247
Isaiah, 42, 45
Isis, 91

Jacob, 42, 44–45, 83, 247, 267
James (brother of Jesus), 274
James (son of Alphaeus), 274
James (son of Zebedee), 274
James, person, 110, 190, 249, 274, 276, 279–80, 342
James, the letter of, 4–5, 7, 26, 28, 221, 274–75
Jay, John, 178–79, 183
Jay County, 311, 353
Jefferson, Thomas, 73, 176–80, 182
Jeremiah, 39
Jerusalem, 222, 274
*Jesus, Our High Priest,* 349–50

*Jewels from John,* 344, 348
John (book of), 28, 32, 38, 43, 51, 54, 56, 58, 62–63, 65, 102–3, 105, 108, 112, 127, 130–32, 134, 142, 144, 149, 182, 187, 193, 218, 221–22, 239, 242, 345, 354–56
John (person), 66, 79, 92, 110, 190, 249
John Frederick, Prince, 170
John Paul II, 72, 166, 170, 201, 259, 299
John II, 198
*John Seventeen,* 58, 348
John XXIII, 185
Johnson, Ethel R., 333
Johnson, Thomas, 332
Jonah, 100
Joppa, 88
Joseph (Mary's husband), 35–36, 51, 54–55, 59, 160
Joseph (son of Jacob), 42, 83
Joshua, 84
Judah, 72
Judas Iscariot, 71, 108–9, 112
Jude (book of), 221
Julius, 97
Juno, 91
Jupiter, 49, 91

Kempis, Thomas à, 77, 141
Kennedy, John F., 291–92
Kennedy, Robert F., 204, 357
Khrushchev, 296
Kierkegaard, Soren, 22, 68
Kipling, Rudyard, 308
Kokomo, Ind., 330
Kosciusko County, 337
Kremlin, 8

Lacy, Anne Marie, 317, 329
Lacy, Charles William, 325, 342
Lacy, Christie McCall, 309, 322, 342
Lacy, Donna, 329
Lacy, Dorothy, 329, 335, 354
Lacy, Guy, 309, 312, 342
Lacy, Joe, 301
Lacy, Marion Walradth, 342
Lacy, Martha, 329
Lacy, Sharon, 329
Lady of Walsingham, 173
LaGrave Christian Reformed Church, 186
Lake George Lutheran Chapel, 340
Lake James Lutheran Chapel, 340
Lake Tippecanoe, 339–40

*Lakeside Devotions,* 348
Lasea, 97
Lasker Award, 301
Laubach, Frank, 215
Leesburg United Methodist Church, 337, 339–40, 343
Leesburg, Ind., 339
Letko, Father Anthony L., 222–24
*Letter to a Roman Catholic, A,* 348
Leviticus, 103
Lewis, C. S., 66
Lewisville, Ind., 319
*Life and Morals of Jesus of Nazareth, The,* 73, 176, 179, 182
Lima, Ohio, 353
Lima, Peru, 336
Lima Document, 191
Lincoln, Abraham, 19
Lindbergh, Charles, 55
Lions Club, 206
*Logos,* 348
Louisville, Ky., 199
Luellen, Marjorie Lacy, 310–11
Luke (book of), 25, 41, 46–47, 52, 60, 91, 104, 168–69, 172–73, 182, 242, 333, 356
Luke (person), 37, 160, 344
Luther, Martin, 53, 168, 170–72, 191, 197–98, 256
Lutheran Church in America, 72, 185
Lycia, 97
Lyles, Jean Caffey, 186
Lystra, 92, 105

MacArthur, Douglas, 56
Machiavelli, 67
Madison, James, 177, 179–80, 182
Magnificat, the, 170
Malta, 96–97
Marian College of Fond du Lac, 226
*Marian Helpers,* 348
Marian Order of Priests, 350
Mark (book of), 24, 43, 102, 182, 221, 242, 261, 356
Mark (companion of Barnabas), 92–96
Mark (person), 35, 344
Mars, 49
Marx, Karl, 67, 69
Mary (mother of Jesus), xv, 34–42, 44–45, 54–55, 59, 150, 160–73, 190, 197, 253–54, 288, 314, 332–33, 337–39, 347, 349, 353
*Mary and Jesus,* 288, 347–48

# ABOUT THE AUTHOR

Donald Charles Lacy is a "son of Indiana." He was born in Henry County, north of New Castle. He attended elementary school in Blountsville and junior and senior high school in Delaware County at Center (now Wapahani). Ball State Teachers College in Muncie granted him a bachelor of science degree in 1954 and a master of arts in 1958. He earned his master of divinity in 1961 and his doctor of ministry in 1976 from Christian Theological Seminary in Indianapolis.

Lacy taught American history, Indiana history, and English in the public schools of Redkey and Dunkirk in Jay County. He has pastored United Methodist churches across the state of Indiana since 1958, and his appointments have taken him from rural areas such as Hagerstown to the city of Indianapolis.

Dr. Lacy has spoken and written frequently on ecumenical and inter-religious issues and has served on various committees. He has appeared twice on *Sunday Morning in Chicago*, and each of the appearances was broadcast over WGN radio. Lacy has published numerous materials dating back to 1960. His work appears in the anthologies *Contemporary Authors* volume 105 and *Contemporary Authors New Revised Series* volume 59. His works are currently housed at the Indiana Historical Society as well as DePauw, Anderson, and Ball State Universities.